D1074539

Women in Espionage

A Biographical Dictionary

G. Lacoste, Circa 1940. Poster Collection, Hoover Institution Archives, Stanford University, Palo Alto, California.

Women in Espionage
A Biographical Dictionary

M. H. Mahoney

ABC-CLIO

Santa Barbara, California
Denver, Colorado
Oxford, England

Library of Congress Cataloging-in-Publication Data

Mahoney, M.H., 1922–
    Women in espionage : a biographical dictionary / M. H. Mahoney.
      p. cm.
    Includes bibliographical references and index.
    1. Women intelligence officers—Biography—Dictionaries. 2. Women
spies—Biography—Dictionaries. I. Title.
    JF1525.I6M25   1993   327.1'2'082—dc20   [B]   93-36559

ISBN 0-87436-743-3

99 98 97 96 95 94 93   10 9 8 7 6 5 4 3 2 1

ABC-CLIO, Inc.
130 Cremona Drive, P.O. Box 1911
Santa Barbara, California 93116-1911

This book is dedicated to my wife, Marjorie Locke Mahoney, and our children, Elizabeth, Paul, Matthew, and Sarah.

Contents

Preface, ix

Introduction, xi

Women in Espionage, 3

Bibliography, 241

*List of Acronyms and
Abbreviations Used
in This Book, 245*

Index, 247

Preface

One of the major problems that I had in choosing the female spies for inclusion in this book was self-denial. If I had had my way, almost every candidate initially considered for inclusion would have made the cut. Unfortunately, constraints of space prevented including any woman without field experience and more than a dash of daring as an espionage operative.

Underlying the selection criteria has been the intention to present women with varied expertise who have engaged in espionage. This has meant including some lesser-known espionage agents because they represented a particular facet of the "game," i.e., the intelligence business, that rightfully should be represented.

Outside experts in clandestine lore were consulted. Each proposed her or his favorite spies or had some objection to an already-selected candidate. In the end, I was in charge of the selection process, and the choices are solely my responsibility.

There may be some errors because the very nature of the business requires any good spy to cloud her antecedents and live her cover. As any devotee or practitioner of the profession knows, cover should be completely deceptive. Even so, although every effort has been made to ensure accuracy in these stories, I make no apology for honest mistakes or interpretive differences that may have crept into the text.

I wish to express my appreciation to the librarians of the Wheaton Public Library and other libraries, who helped trace many elusive sources; the lovely women of OSS and the Agency who gave unstintingly of their cooperation; the many fellow intelligence officers with whom these cases were discussed and evaluated (they know who they are and how much I respected their suggestions); and my editors at ABC-CLIO, Suzanne Chance, Sallie Greenwood, and Amy Catala.

—M. H. Mahoney

BEWARE

—OF—

FEMALE SPIES

Women are being employed by the enemy to secure information from Navy men, on the theory that they are less liable to be suspected than male spies. Beware of inquisitive women as well as prying men.

SEE EVERYTHING
HEAR EVERYTHING
SAY NOTHING

Concerning any matter bearing upon the work of the Navy

SILENCE IS SAFETY

Introduction

Nature often makes a woman shrewd,
hard work makes her learned, upbringing
makes her [patriotic and] pious, and
experience makes her wise. What, therefore,
prevents her from playing a full part
in public affairs?

—John Case

Since early antiquity there have been female spies, even though, in previous eras, a career in intelligence work usually was not a culturally acceptable choice for a woman. Societal prejudices have not yet changed substantially; so far, there is no popular concept of a "Jane" Bond.

One anonymous commentator has said that the history of women in espionage shows that " women will be forgotten if they forget to think about themselves." Even in the supposedly gender-neutral world of professional intelligence work, women have been relegated almost entirely to subservient roles as report writers, analysts, radio operators, code clerks, or administrative assistants; they seldom have been case officers or operations officers, directing agents and projects. Traditionally, "women's work" in intelligence has been valued less than men's work, even though almost every male case officer can recall

situations in which the mere presence of a woman was vital to an operation. Despite these limitations, women did enter the field.

Possibilities for a career outside the home and family multiplied for women during World War I. Suffrage organizations helped to increase women's active roles by becoming wartime service organizations. What was new in World War I was the relatively widespread feeling that women's traditional support services were not enough in a struggle that demanded that men risk their lives in such horrible ways as modern warfare required. Women insisted on active participation, often over the objections of their families and men who rebuffed their efforts. Two other factors made it easier for women to enter the field of intelligence during World War I: any change of women's status gained immediate publicity and, in most cases, acclaim; and there were striking and dramatic changes in women's dress and manners that allowed them infinitely more freedom both physically and psychologically.

During World War II many women worked as equals with men in the resistance movement in Occupied France and in the China-Burma-India theater of operations. Great Britain drafted women into administrative/support jobs, and Russia drafted them into combat. In other countries where there were occupation forces, women joined the resistance. In the United States noncombatant roles for women were created in all of the armed forces. The Air Transport Ferry Service, for example, used mostly women pilots. Women constituted the majority of the couriers between the Warsaw ghetto and the "Aryan" world outside; if they were searched by the police, they could pass as Christians more easily than Jewish men, whose circumcision would almost certainly identify them as Jewish.

Even in the post–World War II era, women in espionage are subject to a stereotype of female spies. The 1963 Profumo case has become a classic in the field of espionage and is cited as an example of what most people consider to be the "woman's role in espionage." It is covered in *The Art of Espionage* (Altavilla 1965), in a chapter provocatively entitled, "There Is No Pussy Galore":

> It has been rumored that Christine Keeler was a Soviet spy. In reality her relationship with Captain Peter Ivanov of the Soviet Embassy in London was never clarified. Christine's friend, Mandy Rice-Davies, told the court that a famous politician present at a luncheon wore a mask and nothing more. The luncheon was held in the home of millionaire Horace Diblen who had married a young girl of Czech origin, Mariella Novotny, who when in New York was suspected by the FBI of running a call-girl ring with the task of seducing United Nations diplomats to wheedle secrets from them. Three suspected call girls, an Englishwoman, Janette Malcolm, a Swedish girl, Jean Fergusson, and an American of Hungarian origin, Illona Palevicz, were on the verge of being arrested when someone warned them and they crossed the Mexican border, got to Cuba, and from there reached Prague on a Czech airliner. There they were escorted to the Alcron Hotel by an American secret agent who then followed them to a castle where the Czech secret service had one of its espionage schools. In former times the three girls had been friends of Colonel Stig-Wennerstrom, the Swedish spy—a strange circle of intrigue.

It may be true that the perceived traditional woman's role in espionage cases is as a sex object. On those rare occasions when this type of role is required, it is usually only a very small part of the overall operation.

The feminist movement of the post–World War II period has been responsible for encouraging women and men to see all careers as gender neutral. The movement, however, does not seem to have been important in encouraging women to seek careers in the field of espionage. The most significant factor that determines whether a woman enters the intelligence field today seems to be simply the availability of an open position. Even when operational requirements dictate that a woman fulfill a specific type of job, landing an intelligence position is still largely a matter of opportunity and luck. Despite all the obstacles, women continue to enter the profession.

Usually, there has been nothing in the outward appearance of women who were engaged in espionage that set them apart from their contemporaries. They shared no common demeanor or speech; their mannerisms were no different than those of their classmates or neighbors. What was the *sine qua non* of these remarkable women? The answer is unwavering courage, patriotism, and a determination to see things through regardless of obstacles. Their characteristic love of country did not mean that other women were not as patriotic; but they had a faith in the ideals of their political creed that amounted to a reverence.

One female intelligence professional, whom I respect enormously and who is a dear friend as well as a candid and honest veteran of the Office of Strategic Services (OSS) and successor intelligence organizations, had this to say:

> As for reasons women are in intelligence work: I think it is a bunch of garbage that either women or men plan a career in intelligence in the way that someone would prepare for medicine or banking or a legal career. I have read some of the fiction that another woman wrote about being lured into intelligence and it just isn't true. In World War II the word *intelligence* was never used. Ninety-nine percent of the people who ended up in intelligence (both male and female) were there because it was the most interesting job "at the time" and over the years developed into something else.

I know of one person who planned from day one of private school, was fluent in three languages, graduated cum laude from an Ivy League college in history and foreign affairs, passed our [CIA] battery of written and oral tests with top marks, passed the field check and the polygraph but was not hired because she was "too eager" for a career in intelligence work. She went on and got an MBA and ended up in a corporation with a position in the elite salary class and now laughs about the naivete of those who study for a career in intelligence.

By and large those women who make careers of intelligence work are not the best or the brightest. There is the lure of the travel and adventure to the foreign assignments. I didn't sign up for OSS. I was in Coordinator of Information (an OSS predecessor). I had employment offers from three government agencies. After talking with a family friend I went to the one with the shortest line, which turned out to be Office of Emergency Management in the Executive Office of the President. OCI was our personnel parent and OSS developed out of OCI. I then transferred directly into OSS.

References

Altavilla, Enrico. *The Art of Spying*. Englewood Cliffs, NJ: Prentice-Hall, 1965.

MacLean, Ian. *The Renaissance Notion of Woman*. New York: Cambridge University Press, 1980.

Mandell, William. *Soviet Women*. New York: Doubleday, 1975.

Norden, Peter. *Madam Kitty*. London: Abelard-Schuman, 1973.

Peterson, Bonnie A., and Judith P. Zinsser. *A History of Their Own*. Volume II. New York: Harper & Row, 1988.

Robertson, Priscilla. *An Experience of Women: Patterns and Change in the Nineteenth Century*. Philadelphia: Temple University Press, 1982.

Rowan, Richard Wilmer, and Robert G. Deindorfer. *Secret Service: 33 Years of Espionage*. New York: Hawthorn Books, 1967.

Women in Espionage

A Biographical Dictionary

Sarah Aaronsohn
Jaffa
ca. 1895–ca. 1917

Sarah Aaronsohn abandoned the comforts of her wealthy family to spy for the British against the Turkish and German armies that occupied her country. Together with her brother, she created an efficient network of spies that produced valuable information for the British.

Her Jewish family lived in Jaffa's Palestine sector during World War I. There was heavy fighting in the area with mainly the British on one side and the Turkish and German troops on the other. Sarah and her brother were pro-British by family tradition and culture. They were vehemently anti-German and anti-Turkish because they observed the German troops' cruelty and barbarism on a daily basis. Both wanted to do something more for the British than sit on the sidelines as cheering spectators. Furthermore, they knew that by helping the British they would be helping their own people, because they had been promised a homeland for the Jewish people if the British prevailed in the war.

There was no one to contact who could give them guidance or who could suggest what information would be important to the British, but several German officers had forced the family to give them quarters in their home, so Sarah and her brother eavesdropped on what these German officers said, whom they met, and what they did. They collected every bit of information that they thought would be important to the British, but they had no way to pass the information across the line to the British command, where it could be used. They decided that there might be one way they could get through. Her brother would take a small boat and row out to sea as if on a fishing trip. Once out of sight from the land, he would row along the coast, past the German-Turkish trench system, until he came to a place on the shore that would be behind the British lines. He could then row ashore and try to contact the British commander.

The British greeted her brother with considerable pleasure, because they had no other source of information from behind the German-Turkish lines. The brother and Sarah continued to collect very valuable combat and strategic intelligence for the British. Sarah was particularly successful in expanding their sources to include many of their friends from different areas. This enabled the British to obtain a broader and more comprehensive picture of the German-Turkish forces.

When Jaffa fell to the British on 17 November 1917, they entered to mop up the remaining pockets of German-Turkish resistance. Before the city fell, the Turkish and German counterintelligence services had become brutally punitive and vengeful on

3

anyone they suspected may have helped the British. They arrested Sarah while her brother was away on one of his "fishing trips," but she refused to implicate her brother or the friends that had helped them collect information against the Turkish and German armies. The Turks viciously tortured her, and before they had to flee the city, they murdered her in a most cruel fashion.

When her brother learned of Sarah's horrible ordeal, he was enraged. He borrowed a submachine gun from his British friends and returned to Jaffa. When he arrived, he learned firsthand what the Turks had done to his sister. They had kept her in a filthy cell, whipped her, and burned her flesh until she had little skin left on her raw body. They then pulled out her fingernails one by one over a period of days and allowed the raw wounds to fester when she refused to name her accomplices.

Her brother and a hastily recruited small group of their friends set about murdering the Turks remaining in Jaffa until they ran out of ammunition. It was said by the Jewish elders that the revenge he took for his sister's mutilation, torture, and death could never atone for the Turks' barbarity against Sarah.

Rowan, Richard Wilmer, and Robert G. Deindorfer. *Secret Service: 33 Years of Espionage.* New York: Hawthorn Books, 1967.

Mercedes Abrego de Reyes
Colombia
ca. 1780–ca. 1810

Although Mercedes Abrego de Reyes had strong emotional ties to Spain, she chose to fight and spy for the independence of her colonial home, Colombia. Few women had her courage.

De Reyes was born in Colombia to a wealthy Castilian family and married Don Marcelo Reyes, who was also from a prominent Castilian family living in Colombia. She was a fervent advocate of Colombia's independence from Spain's imperialistic colonialism.

She was well educated for that time in colonial Spain and was also exceptionally skillful with her hands. She embroidered a uniform for General Simon Bolivar, the leader of the colonists in the War of Independence against Spain. Bolivar was known as the "Liberator" and the "Great Emancipator" of South America. De Reyes presented the uniform to Bolivar after his victory against the Royalists in the Battle of Cucuta.

De Reyes gave the patriots highly valuable information when they were being pursued by the Royalists. Eventually, she was arrested by the Spanish for espionage. The Royalist commander decided to use her as an example of what happened to spies and had her shot without a trial. He had her executed in the presence of her sons in the city of San Jose de Cucuta. A statue was erected in Cucuta to commemorate her valor.

Schmidt, Minna M. *Four Hundred Outstanding Women of the World.* Chicago: Minna Moscherosch Schmidt Publisher, 1933.

Theodora Acacius
Constantinople
ca. 503–547

Theodora Acacius was the wife of the Byzantine emperor Flavius Petrus Sabbatius Justinianus, known as Justinian I. She was a genius at court intrigue who knew the details of the lives of every notable person at court. In order to keep current on the latest gossip, she employed literally hundreds of spies to keep her informed of any treachery planned against her husband.

Justinian I was the great Byzantine emperor whose legal and architectural achievements have lasted until the present. His reign began with every promise of greatness—he erected magnificent buildings, fortified his territories, and his code of laws would become the basis for subsequent European jurisprudence—but he also had to face threats to his empire's borders and the bubonic plague during his reign.

His wife, Theodora, was known throughout the vast Byzantine Empire—which encompassed nearly all of the civilized world of that time—as the Courtesan-Empress of Justinian. She was born in either Cyprus or Constantinople in the early years of the sixth century, probably in 503. She was the daughter of Acacius, a bear feeder in Constantinople's amphitheater. Her health was delicate, and she took all possible care of it. She frequently left Constantinople for the seclusion of her villa on the Asiatic coast, which was believed to have a more healthful climate.

In her youth, many years before she assumed the throne as Justinian's consort, she had been an actress. She had appeared completely nude in pantomimes of obscene buffoonery until a law was enacted against nude performances. She accommodated the law but avoided its spirit by wearing a cloth of minuscule dimensions.

Justinian was captivated by Theodora's beauty but could not marry her because of the law that forbade senators from marrying women who had been on the stage. Justinian, still a senator himself, had the law repealed and married Theodora. They were admitted into royalty in 527, and, four months later—when Justin died—they became the sole rulers of the mighty empire.

Theodora was not just Justinian's consort; he had her elevated to his empress regnant. All Roman officials took an oath of loyalty to Theodora as well as to Justinian.

Theodora recruited legions of spies not because she was concerned with the empire's external enemies but because she wanted to be aware of her rivals in influence and anyone who might have had any capacity for revolt against her dictatorial rule. Theodora was despotic and without mercy. The victims of her displeasure usually perished in filthy, dank dungeons of starvation or torture. A few were permitted to reappear without their eyes or limbs and with broken spirits and bodies as vivid reminders of her wrath.

She was the self-proclaimed defender of the Emperor Justinian and was dedicated to eliminating every rival, male or female, to him and to her position as consort and empress regnant. There were many instances when she conspired to remove and exile Justinian's generals and political henchmen who had displeased her. Justinian knew of these intrigues but did not rebuke Theodora, because her services and worth to him were ample reason for his loyalty to her. On one occasion Theodora's courage and her reliance upon her covert spies saved Justinian's throne.

It was at the peak of the rioting and civil disobedience of the Nika turbulence (532) when Justinian and all his generals agreed that immediate flight from Constantinople was their only hope for survival. All agreed that Justinian's reign was at an end. In the face of this crisis, Theodora suggested a covert counterrevolt, using her legions of spies as the nucleus. For five days the city was abandoned to pillaging and rioting. Theodora's spies were sent out with vast sums of money to corrupt the riot leaders and to rekindle their previous, implacable animosities against each other. Finally, 2,000 savage Goths and Heruli, the most fierce barbarian mercenaries, who were still loyal to Justinian, were set free in the city to remove the last of the rioters. These savage fighters marched into the city and massacred more than 30,000 rioters. Although her power had been great before this incident, Theodora's ability to quell the riot with her spies increased her influence over Justinian.

Theodora's many spies were charged with reporting any comments made against her, even in jest. She introduced much pomp and needless ceremony at the court and demanded that petitioners approaching the throne abase themselves in a manner that was outrageous even for that time. Her spies reported any dissatisfaction with court etiquette, and the complainers were quickly brought to repentance by immediate punishment and public ridicule.

Theodora died in 547. She had a daughter by Justinian who survived her. She had had a son before she married Justinian, but he disappeared from her life and history.

Encyclopaedia Britannica 1946, vol. 22: 56.

Panati, Charles. *Extraordinary Endings of Practically Everything and Everybody.* New York: Harper & Row, 1989.

Sylvia Ageloff
United States
1909–ca. 1975

Ageloff, while not a professional spy, was an accomplice in one of the most audacious assassination operations of the twentieth century.

Ageloff was one of three daughters of a Russian-born Jew, who became a wealthy real estate operator in Brooklyn, New York. She was well educated, having attended courses at New York University and taken a master's degree at Columbia University in psychology. She was employed as a social worker in the New York Welfare Department.

Early in her adult life she had become a Communist. Her principal motivation was her conviction that only Joseph Stalin, the great leader, and communism, the theoretically invincible salvation of the downtrodden, could protect the Jews from Hitler. She was later appalled by Stalin's purges and shunned the Soviet brand of totalitarian communism in favor of the more moderate communism of Leon Trotsky.

Trotsky, together with Vladimir Lenin, had been the founder of the Communist state of the Soviet Union. Lenin had appointed Trotsky to be his heir and to succeed him as the ruler of the Soviet Union. Stalin, by connivance, cheating, and murder, had defeated Trotsky for the leadership. Stalin, in 1929, made the mistake of his life, exiling Trotsky instead of murdering him. Stalin was paranoid about Trotsky, imagining him to have a large following with the potential to overthrow Stalin by military force; in truth, Trotsky was a toothless tiger.

Stalin ordered his Soviet intelligence service, the NKVD, to find Trotsky and kill him. Trotsky settled in Mexico and the original plan to murder him was to have a commando-type raid on his house to be led by the Mexican painter, David Alfaro Siqueiros. In support of that raid the NKVD needed all of the intelligence on Trotsky's habits and defenses. In their search for someone who could penetrate Trotsky's defensive circle of advisers

and be privy to the plans of Trotsky's entourage, the NKVD came across Ageloff.

Sylvia Ageloff had two sisters, Hilda and Ruth. Hilda had met Trotsky and was a fervent adherent of Trotsky's Fourth International. Ruth had briefly done some secretarial work for the John Dewey Commission that had cleared Trotsky of the charges levied against him by Stalin's purge trials. Sylvia had met Trotsky and done some small secretarial tasks for him. In fact, the NKVD was mistaken in their initial assessment and none of the Ageloff daughters knew Trotsky well but in the end it made no difference.

The NKVD was convinced that Sylvia was a Trotskyite courier and a close confidante of Trotsky's. It was due to this mistaken belief that NKVD targeted Sylvia Ageloff for recruitment to provide the entrée into Trotsky's entourage.

Louis Budenz, a native of Indiana who looked typically American, was the editor of *The Daily Worker,* the newspaper of the CPUSA, and an agent of the NKVD. As part of his cover Budenz adhered to the slogan that, "Communism is twentieth-century Americanism." (Levine 1959, 44) Budenz's NKVD case officer was Dr. Gregory Rabinowitz, who was in the United States under cover as the representative of the Soviet Red Cross.

Rabinowitz told Budenz to find someone in the CPUSA who knew Sylvia Ageloff and could, in turn, introduce her to the person the NKVD wanted to penetrate Trotsky's inner circle. Budenz knew Ruby Weill who had been a close friend of Hilda Ageloff, Sylvia's sister. Weill, through Hilda, insinuated herself into the group surrounding the Ageloff girls and soon developed a close friendship with Sylvia Ageloff.

During her summer vacations Ageloff sometimes traveled to Europe and Mexico. A secret world conference of Trotsky's followers in the Fourth International was scheduled for Paris in the summer of 1938. The NKVD assumed that Ageloff would attend and primed Weill to go with her. Budenz gave Weill a considerable sum of money to buy new clothes, have a telephone installed at her house so she could receive his calls more rapidly and, in general, prepare herself to accompany Ageloff to Europe.

The NKVD's intention was for Weill to introduce Ageloff to a sophisticated man-about-town in Paris who could sweep her off her feet. The man chosen for this assignment was Ramon Mercader. It was assumed that once he had seduced her she would be sufficiently compliant to his demands to introduce him into Trotsky's coterie. In order to provide the link, Weill was instructed to meet Gertrude Allison, a Soviet agent, in Greenwich Village before the trip to Europe so she would know Allison when she saw her again in Europe.

Weill continued to build up Ageloff's expectations that she might meet her Prince Charming during their trip to Paris. What Ageloff didn't know was that Weill was passing daily reports to the NKVD for Mercader's study about Ageloff's likes and dislikes, her ideals, her cravings, her thoughts about romantic love, and the best ways to win her confidence.

Ageloff and Weill arrived in Paris in July 1938. Weill told Ageloff she knew a woman in Paris who knew a young student who would show them around the city. Gertrude Allison brought Ramon Mercader to their room. He was introduced under his cover name of Jacques Mornard, the son of a wealthy Belgian diplomat.

Mercader, as Mornard, wined and dined Ageloff and they became lovers. Ageloff was not a delegate to the meeting of the Fourth International in Paris but she did attend several social sessions with Mercader. He pretended no interest in politics nor the proceedings of the Fourth International but he did manage to meet several of the delegates, among them Alfred and Marguerite Rosmer.

Mercader's cover story that he was a student and a part-time sports reporter for the Argus Publishing Company had no backstopping, in other words, it was not legitimized with documentation. He never studied nor did any research. He never attended any sporting events nor hung around in the cafes where sports figures congregated. His cover story of a wealthy diplomat father in the Belgian foreign service was fraught with holes and inconsistencies. In short, his cover story was preposterous but it was good enough to convince Ageloff and, for the NKVD, that was all that counted.

The idyllic life in romantic Paris with her lover ended when Ageloff returned to her job. She left Paris in February 1939 and Mercader promised to follow her as soon as he finished some family business. In September of 1939, Mercader arrived in New York aboard the *Ile de France* documented as Frank Jacson, a Canadian.

He explained to Ageloff that he had to use the phoney documentation in order to avoid being conscripted for military service in Belgium, and she believed him.

The reunited lovers moved to an apartment in Greenwich Village in New York. Mercader went through a perfunctory job search without finding any work. The Soviets didn't want him to tarry too long in New York since his assignment was in Mexico to assist in Trotsky's assassination. Mercader suddenly announced to Ageloff that he had obtained a job in Mexico with Peter Lubeck, working for a British import/export firm. Mercader implied it was a sensitive job purchasing war supplies for Britain and France. He entered Mexico at Neuvo Laredo on 12 October 1939.

Ageloff followed Mercader to Mexico City in January 1940. She still had no inkling that he was anything but the employee of the mythical Peter Lubeck nor that his mother was in Mexico City.

Ageloff renewed her acquaintance with Trotsky and reintroduced Mercader to Alfred and Marguerite Rosmer, the French philosopher and his wife whom Mercader had met previously in Paris. The Rosmers were house guests of Trotsky and his wife Natalia. The four took long drives in Mercader's Buick sedan, which the NKVD had suggested he purchase for that very purpose of ingratiating himself with Ageloff and Trotsky's friends and guards.

Mercader told Ageloff that his office in Mexico City was in room 820 in the Ermita building. Ageloff's sister, who was in Mexico City on vacation, tried to contact Mercader there but discovered that no such room existed. When questioned about this Mercader said it was a mistake, he had intended to say room 620. (Room 620 was the office of David Alfaro Siqueiros, the Mexican artist, fervent Communist, and leader of the botched 24 May 1940 raid on Trotsky's house.) Even though this security blunder (cross-contamination of deep cover agents by using the same cover facility) occurred before Siqueiros's May 24 fiasco, once again Ageloff failed to be wary that Mercader was not who he purported to be. (Ageloff later said she assumed that her lover was really working for British intelligence and that was the reason his stories seemed so odd.)

Fortunately for the NKVD planners in their quest for a natural entrée to Trotsky, Alfred Rosmer fell ill. He had to be ferried from Trotsky's house in Coyoacan, a suburb of Mexico City, to the French Hospital, in the center of town. Mercader chauffeured Rosmer back and forth and became a familiar person with acceptable bona fides to Trotsky's guards at the house. Ageloff, who had returned to the States, received a letter from Mercader stating that he had to break his promise not to go to the Trotsky house because he had to help Rosmer. Ageloff had been concerned that if Mercader's false documentation was discovered, his regular visits to Trotsky's house would implicate Trotsky.

On 24 May 1940, David Alfaro Siqueiros had led a band of mostly Communist veterans from the Spanish Civil War on a raid of Trotsky's house. They fired 73 bullets into the bed where Trotsky and Natalia were sleeping, left several large demolition bombs that failed to detonate, and shot up the house without harming Trotsky at all. Mercader was one of the participants in the raid although in the darkness and confusion, none of Trotsky's guards recognized him. The NKVD's first plan to murder Trotsky having failed, they had to activate a fallback plan, which called for a singleton agent to murder Trotsky.

Four days after the raid Mercader met Trotsky. He went to Trotsky's house to pick up the Rosmers who were scheduled to depart from Mexico at Vera Cruz for the United States. Mercader had volunteered to drive them the 300 miles to the coast. Trotsky's wife decided to make the drive with them, which further ingratiated Mercader with the Trotsky establishment.

On June 12 Mercader was called to New York for a meeting with Gaik Ovakimian, the NKVD chief of the Western Hemisphere and in overall charge of the Trotsky assassination operation. Ovakimian was under cover as an employee of the Soviet trading company Amtorg. At the meeting Mercader was informed that he had been chosen as the singleton agent to complete the job of murdering Trotsky.

Toward the end of July 1940, Ageloff rejoined Mercader in Mexico City and they lived in room 113 of the Hotel Montejo. Mercader's behavior became very odd. He became unstable and morose, physically sick to his stomach and developed a sickly pale yellow color. Ageloff attributed his radically changed physical condition to the spicy Mexican food. On Tuesday, 20 August 1940, Mercader left Ageloff at the Montejo saying he had to go to the U.S. Embassy to take care of his visa before their planned return to New York. Instead Mercader went to Trotsky's house, murdered him with an alpenstock through the head and was captured by the Mexican police.

As the afternoon progressed Ageloff became worried about Mercader's prolonged absence. At 7:45 P.M. Ageloff arrived an hour late for a dinner appointment she and Mercader had with one of Trotsky's guards, Otto Schuessler, and his fiancée. She apologized for being late and for Mercader's failure to keep the appointment. She kept telephoning the Montejo to see if Mercader had returned. Shortly before 8:00 P.M. Schuessler called the Trotsky house and was told to return at once because "Jacson has just tried to kill the old man." (Levine 1959, 130)

Mercader admitted the killing but maintained that Ageloff was completely innocent and never had any knowledge of his intentions to murder Trotsky. When Ageloff was confronted with Mercader at the police headquarters she had to be restrained and kept shouting between sobs, "Kill him! Kill Him!" (Levine 1959, 131)

Although Ageloff was arrested on a technicality of being an accomplice to the murder solely on the basis of her common law marital relationship with Mercader, the charges were quickly dropped. Ageloff returned to the States, married, and dropped out of public view.

Mercader served 19 years and 6 months for the murder of Leon Trotsky. (There is no capital punishment in Mexico.) He was released and returned to the Soviet Union where he was given a medal by Stalin for meritorious service to the state.

(See also Gertrude Machado and Caridad Mercader.)

Brown, Anthony Cave, and Charles B. MacDonald. *On a Field of Red.* New York: G. P. Putnam's Sons, 1981.

Gitlow, Benjamin. *The Whole of Their Lives.* New York: Charles Scribner's Sons, 1948.

Levine, Isaac Don. *The Mind of an Assassin.* New York: Farrar, Straus & Cudahy, 1959.

Gertrude Allison.
See Gertrude Machado.

Inessa Elizabeth d'Herbenville Armand
(Federovna Stephanie, Petrovna, and Blonia)
France
1874–1920

Inessa Elizabeth Armand, one of the great female spies, was Lenin's mistress and an indefatigable undercover worker for the Bolshevik Revolution. In addition to being a competent professional, she was a women's rights leader and a major propagandist for the Bolshevik cause.

Armand was christened Elizabeth d'Herbenville. She learned French from her French father and English from her Scottish mother. Both parents were music hall performers. When her father died, her mother could no longer support her three young children solely by teaching music or performing, so Armand was taken to Russia by a French paternal aunt and her English maternal grandmother. Both women obtained positions tutoring the children of Evgenii Armand, an industrialist of French extraction. The Armand family was wealthy by all standards. They had extensive interests in textiles and other manufacturing and lived on an estate in Pushkino, about 30 miles from Moscow. It was there that Armand grew up.

The Armand family was considered modern for espousing liberal and progressive views on most subjects. At the age of 14, Inessa Armand and the other children were provided with a tutor who had revolutionary views based on socialist doctrines. Armand mastered Russian and German and joined the Russian Orthodox Church.

At age 18 she married Alexander Evgenevich Armand, the second son of the family. They had five children, three boys and two girls. It was her husband's older brother, Boris Evgenevich Armand, who introduced her to the emerging radical political ideas. Boris took the factory workers' position in discussions with other members of the family, who were operating the factories.

She left her husband and most of her children to live with his younger brother, Vladimir, who died of tuberculosis in Switzerland in 1908. She continued to receive generous financial support from her husband as long as he was able to provide it. Lenin's seizure of power in 1917 and the bolshevisation of the wealth resulted in the confiscation of the Armand fortune and ended her allowance. After the separation, most of the children continued to live with their father in Paris and Moscow.

Armand was a free-thinking woman. She believed that the problems that face women in everyday life could be alleviated by socialism, and the issue concerned her all of her life. She left Russia to study feminism with Ellen Key in Stockholm. It was there that she was introduced to Lenin's philosophy through her study of his writings. She read Lenin's *What Is To Be Done?* and became determined to be his disciple.

She returned to Russia on an organizing operation for Lenin's Bolshevik party but was imprisoned in July 1905 almost as soon as she landed. The Bolshevik party, even at the early stage of its development, was heavily penetrated by spies of the czar's secret police, the Okhrana. She was released, but her continued Bolshevik party organizational work and espionage operations resulted in her rearrest on 9 April 1907. Her husband furnished bail and she was released.

Undeterred, she continued her Bolshevik work and was again arrested while awaiting trial. This time she was banished for two years to the Archangel Province. She managed to escape her exile and, with the help of her husband and his money, made her way to Paris.

In Paris in December 1909, she met Lenin, Zinoviev, and Kamenev, the so-called troika of the Bolshevik party. She was joined in Paris by her two younger children, Andre, who was 11 years old, and Ina, her daughter. She soon became the star of the Paris revolutionary scene and Lenin's favorite child. She remained Lenin's favorite until her death, even with the competition of the other popular Bolshevik women such as Alexandra Kollanti and Angelica Balabanoff.

Lenin and his wife, Krupskaya, took a small house in Paris on the rue Marie-Rose #4, while Inessa and her children moved into #2 on the same street. According to Angelica Balabanoff—another leading woman in the Bolshevik movement, who knew both Armand and Lenin very well—Armand had a daughter by Lenin. The daughter, according to Balabanoff, married a German Communist named Hugo Eberlein, who was purged by Stalin. (There is another report that states that the child she refers to was really Armand's daughter, Ina Armand, by her husband. After Armand's death, Lenin and his wife did take Ina Armand to live with them, and Ina did marry the German Communist Hugo Eberlein.) There is no doubt that Lenin loved Armand, but there is conflicting evidence that theirs was a physical relationship.

In July of 1914, a meeting was held in an attempt to heal the split in the Russian Social Democratic party that had been created solely by Lenin's intransigence. The Bolsheviks were represented by three of the party's stalwarts, headed by Lenin's trusted personal friend, Armand. She read Lenin's statement to the delegates, accusing his opponents of not being good socialists, of refusing to accept discipline, of wanting to liquidate the Bolshevik underground organization, and of wanting to wreck the party program by substituting "cultural autonomy" for "national self- determination." (Wolfe 1948, 610) Her pleas were unheeded and her suggestions unaccepted.

Lenin also sent Armand to create an underground intelligence network in Russia. She was modestly successful in this endeavor. There were already so many Okhrana agents in the Bolshevik underground reporting to the czar's secret police headquarters that she was soon arrested. She contracted tuberculosis in prison and, after about a year, her husband managed to arrange her release. She immediately rejoined Lenin in Krakow, Poland.

Armand was entrusted with more special clandestine missions by Lenin than any other woman in the Bolshevik party, which was known for its conspiratorial operations. She was his principal espionage agent in some very important affairs and accompanied him on the famous German-supplied "sealed train" that took him and his principal accomplices from exile in Switzerland back to Russia. She occupied the train compartment next to that of Lenin and his wife.

Armand died on 3 October 1920 at the age of 41. Lenin's wife, Krupskaya, wrote a beautiful eulogy simply entitled, "Inessa." Armand is buried in a vault in the wall of the Kremlin, along with Lenin and Stalin.

Armand's death, following as it did so closely on the defeat of the Red Army in Poland, was a shock from which Lenin never recovered. From the day of her death Lenin began to age very rapidly.

The Okhrana, the czar's secret police, knew that Armand was Lenin's mistress. They had a large file on the relationship and were waiting for an appropriate time to use the information to denigrate Lenin. After Lenin's death, Stalin threatened his wife, Krupskaya, that unless she divorced herself from the opposition in the Kremlin, he would expose certain seamy aspects of Lenin's life. Stalin's threat doubtless referred to Lenin's relations with Inessa Armand.

Payne, Robert. *Lenin.* New York: Simon & Schuster, 1964.

Salisbury, Harrison E. *Black Night, White Snow: Russia's Revolutions 1905–1917.* New York: Doubleday, 1977.

Wolfe, Bertram. *Three Who Made a Revolution.* New York: Delta Books, 1948.

Inga Marie Arvad
Denmark
1913–1973

Inga Marie Arvad's association with prominent Nazis in Germany, including Hitler, earned her the reputation of a spy when she first came to the United States. She was famous for her affair with John F. Kennedy when he was a young naval officer, and that relationship attracted the attention of the FBI, which monitored that association and Arvad's other activities. Although there was never any proof that she was a Nazi spy, the rumor snowballed into serious charges, and she bore the label for the rest of her colorful life.

Arvad's father was a wealthy engineer-architect, and she received the best education Europe had to offer. She attended schools in Germany, France, and England. She won a beauty contest in Europe at the age of 17, when her association with people in high places began; Maurice Chevalier was the master of ceremonies who bestowed her crown. She married a member of the Egyptian foreign service and went to live in Cairo, where she found life primitive and feudal, so she divorced the Egyptian and returned to Berlin.

She was always outgoing, friendly, seemed to invite confidences, and had a curiosity to match. When she heard the rumor that Hermann Goering, the vice-chancellor of Germany, was going to marry a motion picture actress, Arvad called the actress and fibbed that she was a newspaper reporter seeking an interview. She got the story and sent it to a Copenhagen newspaper, which immediately hired her to be their Berlin correspondent.

She attended the Goering wedding and met Joseph Goebbels, the propaganda minister of Germany, who arranged a series of three interviews for her with Hitler. She accompanied Hitler to the Olympic Games held in Berlin in 1936, at which time Hitler praised her as the perfect example of Nordic beauty.

She was considered part of the Nazi entourage and thoroughly enjoyed the parties and adoration. Joachim von Ribbentrop, the Nazi foreign minister, asked her to go to Paris, all expenses paid, merely to move about in the social whirl and report what she picked up. She realized that he was asking her to be a spy and returned to Denmark. (It should be noted that this semiserious proposition by von Ribbentrop is the only morsel of evidence that she was connected in any way with Nazi espionage. Information about his overture came from Arvad herself, which further suggests that she was not a spy.)

In Denmark she made an unmemorable motion picture with the director Paul Fejos, a Hungarian World War I aviation ace. She went to the Dutch East Indies with him to capture Komodo dragons for a zoo and lived with him in a grass hut. Later they were married and met Axel Wenner-Gren, the wealthy Swedish industrialist, who agreed to finance their expedition to photograph the Inca ruins at Machu Picchu in Peru.

Arvad divorced Fejos and went to New York, where she attended the Columbia School of Journalism to pursue her desire to be a reporter. Arthur Krock of the *New York Times* befriended her and arranged for her to go to work for Frank Waldrop, editor of the *Washington Times-Herald* in Washington, D.C. The *Washington Times-Herald* was considered by the Roosevelt administration and everyone else in Washington who was pro-British to be an unpatriotic "Fascist rag" because of its vehement antiwar stance before Pearl Harbor. Arvad's background in Germany, being lionized by the Nazi party leaders, plus working for a newspaper that had a Fascist, pro-Nazi reputation, brought Arvad to the attention of the FBI.

Waldrop characterized Arvad in the early 1940s as a "Poor ignorant little girl. I'll say this: I never thought Hitler had any too great an organization around here [Washington, D.C.], but if he was depending on Inga he certainly didn't seem to know his business." (Blair 1976, 131)

Arvad was assigned to write a column entitled, "Did You Happen To See?," which highlighted second and third echelon arrivals in Washington who were helping the war effort. This column had been started by Cissy Patterson, owner of the *Washington Times-Herald.* By coincidence, Jacqueline Kennedy was a later reporter for this column.

About this time, because of the war hysteria in Washington and the rumors about Arvad's sensational past friendships with high-level Nazis, the FBI instituted a full surveillance of Arvad. (Full surveillance entails a mail cover with full identification of every correspondent and every letter examined for the use of secret inks and codes; a foot and vehicular street tail of the subject everywhere she goes with the follow-up of identification and investigation of everyone with whom she comes in contact; a discreet neighborhood check with her fellow apartment dwellers, with tradesmen who service the apartment, and with the janitors—though this may be omitted if the investigators fear it might alert her to their coverage; and, after a court order, a surreptitious entry into her apartment to search for compromising material and to conceal a well-placed listening device to be monitored 24 hours a day from an adjoining apartment.) Also at this time, Kathleen Kennedy, who was in Washington pursuing a career, introduced Arvad to her brother John, and the two became lovers. Kennedy at that time was a 26-year-old ensign working for Naval Intelligence assigned to Washington. Arvad entertained Kennedy in her apartment, where everything they did and said was overheard by the monitoring FBI agents. Frederick Ayer, Jr., who had been at Harvard University with Kennedy, was the FBI agent in charge of this investigation.

Kennedy and Arvad learned of the compromising tapes and asked J. Edgar Hoover, director of the FBI, to issue a statement absolving Arvad of any complicity with German intelligence. Hoover agreed that there was absolutely no proof that Arvad was associated in any way with Nazi intelligence but refused to give her a letter to that effect for administrative reasons. (Reeves 1991, 56)

John F. Kennedy's father, former U.S. ambassador to Great Britain, did not approve of his son's dalliance with Arvad. Arvad later was to allege that Joseph Kennedy had tried to seduce her during a visit to the family home in Hyannis Port, Massachusetts, but that she had been able to fight him off. (Arvad's son reported that his mother had told him that she "had gone to bed with both Joe Kennedy and Jack Kennedy" and that she had been Joe Kennedy's mistress before and after Jack Kennedy was her lover. [Martin 1983, 55]) Kathleen Kennedy said that Joseph disapproved of Arvad to such a degree that "he was getting ready to drag out the big guns," implying that he was prepared either to remove his son from Arvad's clutches or to smear her reputation. (Blair 1976, 134) Joseph Kennedy spoke about the matter to his Wall Street friend, James V. Forrestal, who was working in Washington as the under secretary of the Navy. As a result, his son was transferred from his post in Washington with Naval Intelligence to sea duty in the Pacific. When Kennedy was in the Pacific on sea duty, he wrote to Arvad that she had been "the brightest part of [his] extremely bright twenty-six years." (Reeves 1991, 70)

Arvad moved to Hollywood, where she took over writing the Sheilah Graham gossip column. In January 1944, she met Kennedy in San Francisco when he returned as a hero from the PT 109 incident. (The PT boat Kennedy commanded had been rammed by a Japanese destroyer, and he and his men had been in the sea for a long time before they were rescued.) Arvad said of this meeting that Kennedy looked very bad, his sense of humor was gone, and the romance had gone out of the relationship.

On 14 February 1947, Arvad married the old-time Western movie star Tim McCoy and moved to a ranch near Nogales, Arizona, where she died in 1973 of cancer. Before her death, Arvad told her son, Ronald, that he may have been the son of President Kennedy. She claimed that she had been three months pregnant when she married McCoy and honestly didn't know if McCoy or Kennedy was the father. Church and birth records support this possibility: Arvad married McCoy on 14 February 1947, and Ronald was born on 12 August 1947.

Blair, Joan, and Clay Blair, Jr. *The Search for J.F.K.* New York: Berkeley Publishing, 1976.

Martin, Ralph G. *A Hero for Our Time.* New York: Macmillan, 1983.

Reeves, Thomas C. *A Question of Character.* New York: The Free Press, 1991.

Lucie Aubrac
France
ca. 1920–

Lucie Aubrac was originally a dignified and proper schoolteacher. World War II brought out a courage never before seen by her friends. When faced with what appeared to be insurmountable obstacles, she was able to put up such a bold front that she bluffed the Nazi Gestapo into submitting to her will.

Aubrac spent most of the war in Lyon. There she worked as a teacher in public and published a clandestine anti-Nazi newspaper in private. She and her Jewish husband, Raymond Aubrac, published all the news about the Germans' occupation. News of Gestapo atrocities were gathered by her partisan reporters in every section of Lyon. Her underground newspaper was a potent weapon that sustained the morale of the French people living under Nazi oppression.

Aubrac was not content to engage only in a relatively passive protest against the Germans. She and her husband also used their printing presses and printer's know-how to forge identity cards. They made ration books and all the other documentation forced upon the French people by the German occupiers.

She managed to obtain a steady supply of arms and explosives for the French resistance through a private channel she maintained with the British SOE. She commanded a small resistance group among her reporters and trained them to use explosives to blow up the German occupiers' infrastructure, including power stations, bridges, railroad terminals, and communication lines. Her specialty was engineering brilliant escapes—or, as she preferred to call them, "rescues"—from prisons. Her most important rescue was the one that she conceived and carried out to get her husband out of Nazi hands.

In 1943, Raymond Aubrac was interned in a Nazi prison in a routine roundup of Jews. She arranged his transfer from the prison to a hospital by smuggling pills in to him that raised his temperature to seemingly dangerous levels. She then had the audacity to obtain his release by making death threats against the state prosecutor. She told the prosecutor that she, or one of her group who were bound to survive the war, would make certain that after the war he would be tried as a war criminal. Her husband was released only to be rearrested by the infamous Klaus Barbie, the "Butcher of Lyon," who would not capitulate to her death threats.

She organized the second escape for her husband by using flattery and some heavy flirtation with the guards, topped off with substantial bribes of money. Her methods may sound routine, but it was only her shrewd knowledge of German psychology and knowing just where and how to apply these techniques that made them work.

After successfully rescuing her husband, she smuggled him out of the country into neutral Spain. The Aubracs lived in Paris after the war and celebrated their fiftieth wedding anniversary there in 1985.

Life. Special Edition. Spring-Summer 1985, 36.

B

Gertrude Banda
Indonesia
ca. 1905–1950

Gertrude Banda began her career in espionage against the Japanese defending her homeland of Indonesia. After World War II she recognized the dangers that communism represented to her homeland and became a militant member of the guerrilla resistance, for whom she spied against the Communists.

Banda purportedly was the daughter of Margarete Gertrude Zelle, better known as Mata Hari. She grew into an attractive woman and had a lot of the personal charm that her alleged mother displayed. She was living with foster parents in Batavia when, at the age of 17, she learned that her mother may have been executed as a spy. There was considerable disgrace attached to spying in those days, and this revelation must have deeply shocked the young woman.

Banda was probably a Eurasian woman whose father had been Indonesian and whose mother had been white. If Mata Hari had been her mother, then Banda would have been 50 years old at the time she had her final espionage adventure. All the current accounts of her life as a spy describe her being young, beautiful, and considerably less than 50 years old. (Margarete Gertrude Zelle [Mata Hari] did have a daughter, Jeanne Louise, whom she called Non. The daughter was born in 1898 in Java, became a schoolteacher in The

Hague, and died in 1919. It is unlikely that Zelle could have had an illegitimate child in Java without her husband's knowledge. Her husband took steps to get a separation when they returned to Holland in 1902 and obtained a divorce in 1906. He made no mention of such a complaint against her at either time. He vehemently disliked Zelle, and if he could have had such an accusation to fling in her face he would have used it.)

After college, Banda became a teacher in Indonesia. Another, not inconsistent, story claims that she became the mistress of a wealthy Dutch planter when she was in her twenties and he was over 60. He kept her in luxury and treated her as his wife. He died in 1935 and left her a considerable fortune.

Banda became a social celebrity in Batavia. When the war broke out her house became a meeting place for the Japanese occupiers, much against her will. She became a spy by chance. She only had to listen to the talk of the Japanese occupiers and the gossip of their Eurasian collaborators, whom she saw every day in the normal course of her teaching duties. She passed on everything she learned to the Indonesian underground. They in turn passed it on to the British intelligence service, which was working with the guerrillas in the jungle, for relay by radio to London.

She also passed on worthless bits of information to the Japanese, which they thought were golden nuggets of intelligence because they had no other sources with which to compare her information. She was a true double agent, but her fundamental loyalty was to the Allies and the Indonesian people. She was able to collect information without resorting to any sexual tricks.

After the war, she secretly worked for Indonesian liberty with the leader of the freedom fighters, Kusnasosro Sukarno, and obtained the Dutch plans for their recolonization of Indonesia. The plans that she obtained enabled Sukarno to defeat the Dutch and achieve independence for Indonesia. Sukano subsequently was elected president of the newly freed Indonesia.

After the war she fell in love with and married an Indonesian guerrilla leader who was convinced that the only way his country could ever become independent was to be allied with the Indonesian Chinese Communist faction. Banda was able to convince him that this was the wrong approach and that they should work together against the Communists and with the British and Americans. Banda went to Washington, probably at the behest of the British, to plead for increased U.S. support for the British plan of eventually granting independence to Indonesia. While she was in Washington, her husband was murdered by Indonesian Communist agents and she was recruited by the CIA.

She continued to work jointly for British intelligence and the CIA and was sent on a mission to Communist China, where she obtained valuable information on Russian support of the Chinese Communists and the strength of the Red Chinese Army. In March 1950 she was assigned to North Korea by her joint British/American case officers. There happened to be an Indonesian who knew her from Indonesia who was working in the North Korean military headquarters. He recognized her as having been a British agent and denounced her to the North Korean command. Only a short time after she arrived in North Korea, she was arrested and executed by a firing squad.

Howe, Russell W. *Mata Hari: The True Story*. New York: Dodd, Mead, 1986.

McCormick, Donald. *The Master Book of Spies*. New York: Franklin Watts, 1976.

Ostrovsky, Erika. *Eye of Dawn: The Rise and Fall of Mata Hari*. New York: Dorset Press, 1978.

Yvonne Basedon
(Odette, Marie Bernier)
France
1922–

Yvonne Basedon was captured while on a mission in Occupied France and was tortured unmercifully by the Germans. Toward the end of the war, when other female spies were being executed, she was released. She had never confessed to being a spy despite the extreme torture that was inflicted upon her.

In 1940, Basedon joined the British WAAF at the age of 18. She qualified as proficient in wireless telegraphy, parachute jumping, and map reading. She parachuted into France in the spring of 1944 after additional rigorous training in survival techniques, sabotage practices, and commando tactics. Her code name was Odette, but there was no connection between Basedon's code name and the other SOE operatives with the same name.

Basedon's primary duty in France was that of a radio operator. In addition, she became proficient in handling night resupply drops and distributing the dropped material to the resistance groups under her team's command. This required great skill in planning to elude the German patrols in the area and still meet the other groups at a pinpoint destination on a map. Both parties would wait at the meeting site for only a few minutes so as not to be conspicuous and risk possible capture as a suspicious gathering. She adopted the cover of Mlle. Marie Bernier, a secretary looking for office work, which gave her an excuse to travel around seeking secure and mutually convenient rendezvous sites.

She was captured in a Gestapo raid when the German troops surrounded a farmhouse that she and her French underground resistance fighters were using as a headquarters. She initially thought that she had avoided capture by hiding in a woodpile for over an hour until the Gestapo had departed. She was just about to emerge from her hiding place when she was surprised by someone jerking her out of the woodpile by her hair. The Gestapo had discovered her.

She was considered dangerous and was chained with manacles when she was transported to the prison at Ravensbruck. She was cruelly mistreated at that prison both mentally and physically. Her jailers used their heavy hobnail boots to stomp on her toes and threatened her with murder by various torturous methods. She was starved and chained in a cramped, dark cell for days. She was even placed against the execution wall in the prison courtyard while her captors went through the drill of having the firing squad fire on her, but without any bullets in their guns. She bravely held out despite the inhumane methods used to try to force her confession. The final degradation that she endured was placement in a cell already overflowing with about 800 sick, pregnant, vomiting, or syphilitic women. Nothing broke her will; she never did confess.

Her terrible ordeal finally ended in April 1945, which was, coincidentally, about the same time that other female SOE agents were being shot for having taken part in similar operations against the Nazis. Yvonne Basedon was allowed to go free as a result of the intervention of the Swedish Red Cross.

Anne-Marie Bauer
France
ca. 1920–

Anne-Marie Bauer was an Alsatian woman who began her work with the French Resistance because she was a truck driver in civilian life. Her truck gave her the mobility to distribute leaflets and to case areas for good drop zones. When she was arrested, she made the mistake of exposing her Jewish identity to her German captors, who then tortured her even more. That she lived to tell

about it shows the strength of her endurance.

Bauer's brother asked her to join the resistance movement called Liberation. She immediately agreed and went to work distributing anti-Nazi leaflets and other propaganda materials in her truck. She also helped to prevent French youth from being forced to "accept" the labor draft for work in Germany. For a while she was assigned to coding and decoding messages to and from London, but she much preferred outdoors work.

Part of her task as a truck driver was to find suitable air drop fields far enough away from Nazi soldier concentrations and close enough to the resistance headquarters to enable reception teams to get the dropped infiltrators quickly into urban hiding places. Some of the sites also had to be suitable for the planes to land and take off.

She recruited a family to help her spot and recruit likely agents. The family owned a small hotel and a bus and trucking business. With their help Bauer found many suitable sites but also set up a smuggling network that was able to help used-up or blown agents and downed Allied airmen escape and to bring in supplies and fresh agents.

When the men in her unit wanted her to stay away from future air drops because, they claimed, the work was too dangerous for a woman, Bauer told them that either she went as part of the reception committee or she would not locate any more sites for them. They relented and she was, from then on, a regular part of the reception committee at all drops.

Bauer was at her best when one of the members of her resistance group was captured. For example, when one of the resistance fighters was captured and jailed in the Castres prison, she organized a rescue group that included a team of Boy Scout mountaineers who were experts in scaling cliffs and using ropes and who were to surmount the two high walls around the prison. In order to augment her plan she recruited a guard to collaborate with the resistance. He agreed to slip sleeping potions into the other guards' wine so that they would be unconscious when the rescue team arrived. The guard claimed that he cooperated because he needed the money for his sick mother, but knowing that the resistance would kill him if he didn't cooperate might also have had something to do with his cooperation.

The operation to free her friend was supposed to have been supported by an armed group from Liberation resistance headquarters, but they never showed up. Bauer decided to proceed without them, and was successful.

In August 1943, Bauer was arrested and subjected to a lengthy interrogation. She became bored and incensed. The interrogator suggested that with an Alsatian name she should be working for the Germans instead of the French. She was so exasperated with the situation that she blurted out that she was not Alsatian but Jewish and would never think of cooperating with the filthy Germans. Of course, she realized immediately that she had made a mistake in admitting that she was Jewish and refused to answer any more questions. Her interrogator tied her hands behind her and hung her from the rafters suspended from the truss made by the rope around her wrists. The Nazis then took off her shoes and stockings and held burning matches to the soles of her feet. She screamed and agreed to answer their questions. She began to tell them a fabricated story about a resistance leader named Victorine. She was so steeped in resistance lore that she could improvise a convincing but completely false story.

Bauer was sent with a female Gestapo agent to check out the locales of her concocted story. When the Nazis discovered that her story was false, the female Nazi stuck a machine pistol to Bauer's head and told her that she was about to die. When she heard the blast she thought she was dead. When she came to the Nazis were all laughing at her fright. The female Nazi had fired a blank close to Bauer's ear as a joke and to intimidate her into a confession.

The Nazis put her in solitary confinement and then moved her to Ravensbruck, the famous German death camp. She was certain that as a Jew, plus a resistance fighter, she was going to be killed in the ovens of Ravensbruck. Fortunately, she survived and was freed at the end of the war.

Schoenbrun, David. *Soldiers of the Night: The Story of the French Resistance*. New York: E. P. Dutton, 1980.

Kitty Beaurepos
England
1900–ca. 1943

Etta Shiber
United States
ca. 1910–

Kitty Beaurepos and Etta Shiber decided to become spies and resistance fighters after helping a British airman escape from Occupied France. These friends shared the work, the dangers, and the exhilaration of helping Allied soldiers escape from the Nazis in Occupied France.

Beaurepos was the daughter of a wealthy banker. She married an Italian who was much older than she and lived in Italy for several years. When her husband died—leaving her a young, wealthy widow—she moved to Paris, where she married a French wine merchant. They subsequently decided to separate but remained friends.

After the separation Beaurepos remained in Paris because she loved the city. She had an adequate income from her father's estate and managed to live well. She disliked inactivity, so she opened a small dress shop, which is where Etta Shiber met her in 1925 when she ordered dresses during her annual trip to Paris with her husband.

When Shiber came to Paris with her brother in 1933, he became sick. Beaurepos moved in with them and helped Shiber care for the brother. When Shiber's husband died in 1936, she could think of only one place she wanted to be, and that was with Beaurepos in Paris. They lived together from that time on. When World War II came they both joined the *Foyer du Soldat,* the French equivalent of the American USO. Their idyllic life in Paris came to an end when the Nazis marched in on 13 June 1940.

While they were attempting to flee Paris in the wake of the occupying Nazis, they became caught in the morass of panic-stricken refugees fleeing in the opposite direction. They decided to stop at a small inn, hoping that the chaos on the roads would subside while they had some tea. The proprietor served them in a private dining room away from the noise of the crowd. In a conspiratorial whisper he asked if they spoke English. When they assured him that they did, he begged them to translate for a British soldier he had hidden in the cellar who could not speak French.

The women spoke with the soldier and learned that he was an RAF pilot who had been unable to reach the ships at Dunkirk when they evacuated the British. He told them that all he wanted was some French civilian clothes so that he could go on alone to the Spanish border. Beaurepos and Shiber explained that this plan was foolhardy because they had seen German soldiers randomly drag young men out of cars and interrogate them. If he couldn't speak colloquial French he would be captured at the first roadblock.

The women helped him reach the Spanish border, where he could travel back to Britain to rejoin the RAF. Thus began their rat line for downed Allied airmen and escaping soldiers from France seeking freedom across the Spanish border. The number of escapees they helped is modestly underestimated, but it was well into the hundreds. They had to collect considerable intelligence to know what routes to take, what identity documents were valid or had been recalled, how to vet other members of their rat line, and how to pass along other information with their escapees for use by Allied headquarters.

They were both arrested by the Gestapo, tried, and sentenced. After a few months, Shiber was released because she was an American. She was traded for a German woman who had been arrested for espionage in the United States. She returned to the United States to wait for the war to end. She hoped that then she would be able to rejoin Beaurepos in a liberated Paris.

Unfortunately, Shiber's book, the prime source for information on Beaurepos, was written in 1943 while Beaurepos was still in

prison. There is no further information about Beaurepos. Her last known whereabouts was a German prison in 1943.

Shiber, Etta. *Paris Underground.* New York: Charles Scribner's Sons, 1943.

Aphra Behn
England
1640–1689

Aphra Behn achieved eminence as a spy but, because she was a woman, her valuable intelligence was ignored by the decision makers of her day. In an era when women were supposed to be seen and not heard, she overcame discrimination and carried out her mission. She was a vivacious woman with a ready wit and self-reliance that served her well as a spy.

Behn, one of the first famous British female spies, was born at Wye in Kent in 1640. She married a London merchant of Dutch extraction who died shortly after the wedding. Behn then had to earn a living on her own, which she did by writing books and dramas, which was a rare occupation for a woman. Her most well-known novel is *The Royal Stone.*

She had learned to speak Dutch from her husband. British intelligence made use of that knowledge when it sent her to Antwerp to collect intelligence on Dutch political intentions and military capabilities. Her coded correspondence back to London was comprehensive and well documented.

Behn was denigrated when her own British intelligence service attempted to cover up a disastrous mistake by blaming her for their negligence. She had reported that the Dutch Admiral de Ruyter planned to launch his fire ships against the British fleet, but the British fleet had not been properly informed about Behn's warning by their own secret service. In 1667, the Dutch fleet sailed up the Thames River with their fire ships ablaze and torched some of the British man-of-wars tied up in the Medway. (Deacon 1987, 86)

Contemporary commentators attempted to discredit her reports, but they were simply jealous of her accomplishments and embarrassed at not having heeded her advice.

Deacon, Richard. *Spyclopedia.* New York: Silver Arrow Books, 1987.

Johanna Koenen Beker
East Germany
ca. 1914–

If it hadn't been for a marital rift when her husband reported to the U.S. authorities that his wife was a Soviet agent, Johanna Koenen Beker might still be operating. Beker came to the United States and "slept" for many years. During that time she built an almost unassailable cover as an upright U.S. citizen who would never be suspected of being a Soviet agent.

Beker was the daughter of Wilhelm Koenen, a highly placed East German Communist official. During World War II, Beker's brother worked for Soviet intelligence in the infamous but highly efficient Roto Kapella Soviet intelligence network.

Information about Beker's activities for Soviet intelligence came initially from her former husband, Lorenz Harry Wagner. In 1949, he told an interesting story to the U.S. Army intelligence unit in West Berlin. He said that when the Nazis took over in Germany, circa 1933, he and Beker had barely escaped to Moscow to avoid persecution as Jews. While they were in Russia, amid the turmoil of rationing and battling with currency restrictions, the NKVD arrested them for illegal currency manipulation. Under NKVD interrogation, Wagner, who had been arrested during Stalin's purges of 1937, succumbed to threats of blackmail and agreed to become an NKVD agent. During the interview, the NKVD interrogator let it slip that Wagner's wife, Beker, had been working as an NKVD agent for some time.

Before being caught in World War II, Beker had obtained a visa in 1938 for the United States, where she lived throughout the war. In 1952, she was questioned by the FBI and vehemently denied that she had ever worked for the NKVD. Wagner was again questioned by the FBI regarding his assertion that his wife worked for Soviet intelligence. Wagner again swore that he was telling the truth and that the NKVD agent had told him that his wife was one of their agents. (Wagner was released from the Soviet prison and returned to Germany during the relatively halcyon days of the Nazi-Soviet Pact. Regardless of the harmony that was supposed to exist at that time between fascism and communism, the Nazis arrested Wagner. He managed to survivive in prison through the end of World War II, at which time he was released and broke with communism.)

Years later, when the members of the Soble spy ring were arrested and the case was front page news, Beker came forward to talk with the FBI. She told the FBI that during World War II she had obtained information from German refugees who were working for the OSS, information that she had passed on to the Soviet intelligence.

(See also Martha Dodd Stern and Jane Foster Zlatovski.)

Elizabeth Terrell Bentley
United States
1908–1963

Elizabeth Terrell Bentley was an American and a Communist who became a Soviet agent in part because of her love for an important Soviet spy. After his death, she became disenchanted with communism, defected, and provided valuable information to the FBI. She revealed that many U.S. government employees were actually Soviet spies. Her testimony led to increased Americans' awareness about the extent and depth of Soviet espionage in the United States.

Bentley was born on 1 January 1908 in New Milford, Connecticut. Her father was a newspaper editor and a department store manager. Her mother had been a school teacher before her marriage. In 1924, the family moved to Rochester, New York, where Bentley attended high school. She graduated from Vassar College in 1930 with a Bachelor of Arts degree in English and received her Master of Arts in French and Italian from Columbia University in 1937.

Vassar College didn't routinely teach the merits of communism, but its liberal approach to political education permitted a chapter of the League for Industrial Democracy, a Communist front, to be established on campus. Communist leaders such as Scott Nearing, a member of the CPUSA, were allowed to address the students. Bentley's studies at Vassar opened her to Communist thought and influence.

She took three trips to Italy between 1930 and 1937. In 1935, she joined the American League Against War and Fascism, a Communist front organization, because it accepted Communist beliefs of denouncing fascism, capitalism, American imperialism, the Roosevelt administration, and the League of Nations, while it supported the Soviet Union's peace policy.

In March 1935, Bentley joined the CPUSA. Three years later, in October 1938, she began working with Jacob Golos, whose real name was Jacob Rasin. Bentley claimed that she didn't know that Golos was involved with the Soviets until December 1940.

Bentley was recruited into the Communist espionage underground by Juliet Stuart Poyntz. In October 1938, she was working in the Italian Information Library of the Italian government's Propaganda Section. Her first assignment for the GRU, a Soviet military intelligence organization, was to report on the pro-Fascist activities of the library. She left this job in March 1939.

By this time Jacob Golos was Bentley's case officer for Soviet intelligence, and she did a few simple courier and cutout, or third-person intermediary, jobs for him. Golos asked her to get a job as the secretary to a right-wing businessman, Richard Waldo. She got the job and spied on Waldo, reporting his movements, contacts, and conversations to Golos until February 1940. During this time Golos trained her in tradecraft and she became his mistress. Bentley claimed that at about this time in her relationship with Golos she realized that he had some connections with the Soviet secret police.

Bentley worked for Golos for four years as a cutout, courier, and assistant agent handler. At several points in their relationship, Golos became so busy with his many operations, with maintaining his business as the principal operator of Amtorg (the Soviet trading company), and with cover business for several Soviet agents that he broke the cardinal rule of clandestinity: he failed to keep his operations compartmentalized. This meant that he allowed Bentley to know about operations that didn't directly concern her. He had Bentley operate in different espionage networks as a cutout and courier, which enabled her to know almost everything about his previously separate operations. It reached a point where Bentley was acting as an assistant case officer on some operations.

When she finally became disenchanted with communism and defected to the FBI, she knew all aspects of Golos's operation. She mentioned names of more than 100 people who, she claimed, were actively engaged in Soviet espionage against the United States. All of these people were investigated by the FBI, and 51 were prosecuted. It was discovered that 27 of these suspected Soviet agents had been employed by the U.S. government.

Bentley gave evidence for the prosecution against many of the government employees. The tentacles of the Soviet operations she testified about extended into Canada and Mexico. The testimony of Whittaker Chambers, himself a defector from Soviet espionage, corroborated much of Bentley's evidence and gave it the credence it deserved. Her contribution to increasing Americans' awareness of the threat of Soviet espionage was incalculable.

Elizabeth Bentley died in New Haven, Connecticut, on 3 December 1963 after surgery for an abdominal tumor.

(See also Juliet Stuart Poyntz.)

Bentley, Elizabeth. Obituary. *New York Times*. 3 December 1963.

Bentley, Elizabeth. *Out of Bondage*. 1951. Afterward by Hayden Peake. New York: Ivy Books, 1988.

Marguerite Bervoets
Belgium
ca. 1915–1942

Marguerite Bervoets was a professor at a prestigious university, a leader of the civilian population in peacetime, and a leader of the Belgian Resistance during World War II. She was a reserved woman with nerves of steel.

When her country was overrun with German troops, Bervoets organized a resistance group that guided downed Allied airmen out of Belgium. She also worked as a spy gathering intelligence and as a courier carrying important information from her area to a point where it could be transmitted back to the Allied command.

She was captured by the Gestapo in 1942 and taken to Germany, where she was beheaded.

Weiser, Marjorie P. K., and Jean S. Arbeiter. *Womanlist.* New York: Atheneum, 1981.

fore, because her husband had been convicted of espionage. Her information was commended as being significant to the revolutionaries in defeating the Royalists.

In April 1869, she proclaimed rights for all Cuban women at Guaimoro on the occasion of the revolutionary forces assuming power. During and after the revolution, she lobbied for women's rights and is revered to this day in Cuba as the foremost advocate of women's rights. The first president of the new Republic of Cuba, Carlos Manuel de Cespedes, commented that when history describes the decisive moments of Cuba's national life, it would be noted that Ana Betancourt, in advance of her time, had pleaded for the emancipation of Cuban women.

Rowbotham, Sheila. *Women, Resistance and Revolution.* New York: Vintage Books, 1972.

Schmidt, Minna M. *Four Hundred Outstanding Women of the World.* Chicago: Minna Moscherosch Schmidt Publisher, 1933.

Ana Betancourt
Cuba
ca. 1834–ca. 1890

When the fight for Cuban independence from the Spanish was at an impasse, Ana Betancourt provided information to the revolutionaries that helped them defeat the Royalist troops. She is revered today in Cuba as a national heroine.

Betancourt was born in Camaguey, Cuba, to a prosperous family of the Cuban upper class. In August 1854, she married Ignacio Mora y Pena. When the patriots of Cuba began working to free their homeland from Spain in the Cuban province of Camaguey in 1868, she took an active role with her husband in supplying information to the revolutionaries who were fighting the Royalist forces of the King of Spain. Her husband was executed by the Royalists on 14 October 1875, but she continued to spy for the revolutionaries despite the danger. The Royalists watched her even closer than be-

Marie Birckel
France
ca. 1894–

Marie Birckel's mother had been a spy for the French against the Germans during World War I. When she died, Marie assumed her mother's role. Trained in the arts of subterfuge and tradecraft by her mother, she became an excellent spy.

Madame Birckel, Marie's mother, was a widow and the schoolmistress of the town of Variscourt, near Château-Thierry, in Lorraine. When the German army invaded the area in August 1914, the mayor and leading men of the village went off to fight. As the ranking woman, Madame Birckel was left in de facto charge of the village. The German occupying forces frequently had to consult with her regarding problems connected with the occupation. This association enabled her to observe many things the Germans did, which she was able to pass along to the Allies.

When Madame Birckel died of dysentery, leaving her daughter, Marie, and two young nephews to care for themselves, Marie assumed the care of her two cousins and they lived together as a family. Birckel had the indomitable courage of her mother plus the will and moral stamina developed by her new familial responsibilities. She lived in a one-room garret, which was all the Germans would allocate to her. One day she returned home to find her cousins sitting on the outside stoop, shivering in the raw cold of near-zero weather. The German soldiers were playing cards in her room and had sent the children outside. Birckel stormed into her room, berated the soldiers for such callous treatment of little children, and demanded that they allow the freezing children into the room. The soldiers relented without a murmur and quietly took their card game elsewhere.

Together with the other civilians in Variscourt, Birckel was evacuated in July 1915 into other districts of France that were unoccupied by the Germans. As she had seen her mother do, Birckel carefully observed everything about the German troops, equipment, and morale before she left. She routinely reported all this to the local French military intelligence officers. They were so impressed with her reports that they arranged for her to go to their headquarters in Paris to brief the commanders on what she had observed.

Birckel offered to return to the area as a spy. She crossed the border between Holland and Belgium with the help of local smugglers who had become expert border crossers. She crossed the border on 15 May 1916 accompanied by another French agent, Emile Fauquenot, and a local guide. They split up after the crossing and went their own ways. Fauquenot was concerned about the loyalty of their guide, who had appeared too curious about their operation.

The guide had indeed turned Birckel in to the Germans, who arrested and confined her in Saint Leonard prison in Liège. Birckel was tortured and cajoled but refused to reveal anything about her fellow agents or their operations. Fauquenot was captured by the Germans two months later and was taken to the same prison where Birckel was held. They were able to communicate with each other and became friends. When they were tried before a military tribunal they sat together and conferred about the charges and the outcome of their case. They ultimately fell in love.

The Dutch authorities pleaded with the German high command for leniency in their case because of their youth. King Alfonso of Spain provided them with legal counsel. They were not executed but were sentenced to life imprisonment.

Fauquenot escaped before the war ended. Birckel was released in November 1918 after the armistice was signed. She received the Croix de Guerre and the Legion of Merit from the French government as did Fauquenot. The British government awarded both of them OBEs. They were married a few months after the armistice.

Seth, Ronald. *Encyclopedia of Espionage.* New York: Doubleday, 1972.

Edith Bonnesen
(Lotte)
Denmark
ca. 1920–

Edith Bonnesen was a member of the Danish underground during World War II. She was interrogated and tortured by the Nazis but stuck with her cover story and was released.

Bonnesen had a good job in the office of the Danish Ministry of Transport when the Germans invaded Denmark at the beginning of World War II. She immediately volunteered to work for the resistance and was assigned to help prepare an underground newspaper and other anti-Nazi propaganda. The Gestapo was quick to recognize the threat that she represented to the peaceful conduct of their occupation and made every effort to apprehend her. She was arrested three times on suspicion of counter-occupation agitation, but the Gestapo didn't realize who they had, and so they released her.

These arrests served as a clear warning to Bonnesen, who decided to leave the relative comforts of a normal life and go completely underground. She gave up her job and went to live in a series of apartments in Copenhagen, where no one knew her.

There she met the leader of the SOE network in Copenhagen, who had been ordered by his regional superiors to establish his own collection effort and radio station. This entailed building the organization from nothing and then training his agents in radio operation, organization security, and tradecraft. He turned to Bonnesen for help with this; she later also became the group's code clerk.

Once, when the team leader was waiting for a shipment from Britain of frequency crystals for his transmitter, the message announcing their arrival came when he was away, so Bonnesen went alone to pick them up. Unfortunately, the Gestapo had been tipped off about the arrival and was waiting to arrest anyone who called for the package. She was arrested and taken to the Shellhaus, the Gestapo headquarters, for interrogation. Bonnesen remained with her cover story and the Gestapo could not get a confession from her nor any admission of complicity. She managed to escape and returned to her underground activities with her team. She remained an active resistance fighter until the end of the war.

Seth, Ronald. *Encyclopedia of Espionage.* New York: Doubleday, 1972.

Mary Bowser
United States
ca. 1841–ca. 1892

Mary Bowser's cover was an illiterate slave maid for Confederate officers. She was actually an educated woman who could read and write and who remembered everything she heard about troop movements. For the Union she was a prolific source of intelligence straight from the home of Jefferson Davis, the president of the Confederacy.

In the hustle of Davis's household there was a black slave serving dinner. No one suspected that the quiet, unassuming black maid doing light household cleaning and helping in the dining room was a Union spy. Everyone assumed that she was illiterate; therefore, they weren't concerned about leaving important papers lying about. Bowser, the manumitted slave of Elizabeth Van Lew, was able to read Davis's papers because Van Lew had seen to it that she and all the other slaves on the plantation were schooled and could read and write. Bowser was better educated than most former slaves. She not only could read and write, she could also understand technical language. When she was cleaning Davis's study and dusting his desk she could read and memorize the classified documents carelessly left lying about.

Bowser also had a keen wit and uncanny perception that helped her overhear tidbits of important conversations. She listened to comments passed between Davis and members of his cabinet and army command. While she served at the dinner table for an evening's party, which was usually attended by many of the officials of the Confederacy, she could overhear their talk. The men spoke freely in front of her about troop dispositions, the state of defenses, logistics, and administration.

An established underground courier system between Davis's house and Van Lew's house transmitted the intelligence that Bowser collected to Washington, where it was considered to be some of the best they received. She was the source of much of the information about troop strengths and tactics that Van Lew transmitted to General Grant of the Union forces.

(See also Elizabeth Van Lew.)

Weiser, Marjorie P. K., and Jean S. Arbeiter. *Womanlist.* New York: Atheneum, 1981.

Belle Boyd
United States
1844–1900

Belle Boyd, who killed a Union soldier to defend her mother, became a spy for the

BELLE BOYD

William L. Clements Library, University of Michigan

Confederate Army after the humiliating consequences of her justifiable homicide. Her information led to a tremendous victory for Confederate General Stonewall Jackson.

Boyd was born in Martinsburg, Virginia, in 1844. Her father was a Union government official. When the Civil War broke out in 1861, she was only 17 years old. A Yankee sergeant attempted to raise the Union flag over her house. Her mother tried to slam the front door in the sergeant's face; he, in turn, slammed the door back open in her face. Boyd considered this an insult to her mother and killed him on the spot with her revolver. The federal troops, in reprisal, ransacked her home and arrested her. The martial law imposed at the time threw a protective arm around Boyd and found that the killing was justifiable homicide.

The fact that she was a young woman and a juvenile saved her from a prison sentence. She was so embittered by the shame and experience of being arrested by the Yankees that she vowed revenge. She decided upon a crusade to spy for the Confederacy against the Union forces. In the Shenandoah Valley the troops of the North and South surged back and forth like a tide, and it was difficult for the inhabitants to know who really controlled the area. To help gather information on the area, Boyd organized a spy ring composed entirely of teenage girls.

The correspondent from the New York *Herald Tribune* was quartered in Boyd's house. This correspondent would hold daily meetings with Union army officials for briefings on the army's intentions, failures, and successes. Boyd would only have to listen to these briefings to collect excellent intelligence.

One of her triumphs was to give the Confederacy the Union plans for operations in the Front Royal area in May 1863. This piece of intelligence enabled the Confederate General, Stonewall Jackson, to rout the Union Army. After his victory, General Jackson wrote, "Miss Belle Boyd, I thank you, for myself and for the army for the immense service you have rendered your country today. Hastily, I am your friend, T. J. Jackson, C.S.A."

Boyd used her acknowledged beauty and charm to elicit information from the federal troops in her area. They allowed her to slip through Union lines, because no federal officer cared to expose himself to unfavorable comparison with the uniformed chivalry of the South by being rude to a young woman. The gallant Union officers didn't realize that this sweet, young woman's design was to have them surprised and shot or made prisoners.

She was arrested on suspicion of spying and was lodged in the federal prison in Washington. Incarceration didn't dull her spirit. She did everything she could to keep up the spirits of the Confederate soldiers who were imprisoned with her. After she was condemned to death, Abraham Lincoln was allegedly so captivated by her that he pardoned her.

Boyd was the most famous spy of the Civil War but by no means the most effective. She apparently dealt with Union officers who were uniformly stupid, lazy, incompetent, or grossly treasonous. While she was in jail she was able to conceal $26,000 in her trunk from the supposedly watchful eyes of the warden and the guards.

In the Old Capitol Prison at the same time as Boyd was the Union spy, Kerbey was working for the Union Army in the deep South. His case officer was the secretary of war, Edwin M. Stanton. When Kerbey returned through the Union lines from his last spying mission, he was asked to sign a loyalty oath stating that he had never worked for the Confederacy. Kerbey assumed that his case officer, the highly placed secretary of war, would know that he had worked for the Confederacy in his role as a spy. Apparently, Stanton was never notified that his agent's refusal to sign the loyalty oath had resulted in his incarceration.

Boyd assumed that Kerbey, in his Confederate uniform, was a Confederate soldier, and the two conceived a plan to escape. Kerbey was to be smuggled out of prison disguised as the Negro who brought meals to the prisoners. Boyd made some clothes similar to those that the Negro wore and got some burnt cork to show Kerbey how to blacken his face and arms. She also told Kerbey the escape routes and safe houses along the exfiltration line from Washington to Richmond. (Kerbey was delighted with this information and planned to use it as positive intelligence for Stanton as soon as he was free.) Everything was arranged for Kerbey's escape when he was summoned to the warden's office, where his brother had his release, signed by Secretary of War Stanton.

When Boyd was released from prison she boarded the blockade running ship *The Greyhound* in an attempt to sail to England. The ship was captured by the U.S. Navy before it cleared the international boundary. Ensign James Hardinge was put aboard the ship to take the prize back to a U.S. port. Boyd seduced the young ensign, who became so infatuated with her that he allowed the Confederate captain of *The Greyhound* to escape. The U.S. Navy, unaffected by Boyd's charm, didn't agree with the ensign's decision and court-martialed him.

In the meantime, Boyd had reached London, where she appeared on the stage and told her story of being a daring Confederate spy. The newspapers of the English-speaking world enhanced the stories of her beauty, audacity, and competency, and exaggerated the value of her intelligence gathering far out of proportion to reality. She wrote a two-volume book that embellished her wartime exploits and personal life.

Former Ensign Hardinge followed Boyd to London, and they were married in England on 25 August 1864. When they returned to the United States, the federal government once again imprisoned Boyd. Hardinge was also imprisoned as a traitor to the Union and died in prison. Boyd was a widow at 21. The war was not yet over and the U.S. government wanted Boyd in prison, where they knew what she was doing. She was exchanged for a federal spy held in Confederate custody. Upon her release, the Richmond Blues, a crack drill team, presented arms as an honor guard for Boyd, and at night she was serenaded by the Richmond city band. After the war she again traveled to Europe, speaking about her wartime experiences as a spy.

Boyd died in 1900 of a heart attack at age 56. She is buried in the Wisconsin Dells area.

Ind, Allison, Colonel. *A Short History of Espionage.* New York: David McKay, 1963.

Amy Elizabeth Thorpe Brousse
(Cynthia)
United States
1910–1963

Amy Elizabeth Thorpe Brousse was a forthright, honest agent who realized that she would have to violate her personal ethics to complete her espionage assignments. She initiated one of the most successful espionage operations of World War II.

This legendary woman was born Amy Elizabeth Thorpe in 1910 in Minneapolis, Minnesota. In 1930, when she was 21, she married Arthur Pack, who was the commercial secretary of the British Embassy in Washington. Pack was 20 years her senior at the time. She became associated with the British establishment through her husband's work in the British Foreign Service.

In 1937, she went to Spain, where she was involved with helping some of Francisco Franco's Loyalist troops escape from Communist Republican-held areas. Her husband was unaware that his wife was a spy.

She then went to Poland, where she had a love affair with an aide to the foreign secretary of Poland. This fortuitous liaison enabled her to get information about the super-secret German cipher machine, code-named Enigma. British Prime Minister Winston Churchill said that having the secret of Enigma was a major factor in the Allies' victory over Germany during World War II.

Next she was sent to Chile but was recalled to the United States by the British liaison officer in New York, William Stephenson. This was when her formal recruitment into British intelligence took place and

Amy Elizabeth Thorpe Brousse

AMY E. BROUSSE (CYNTHIA)

From Cynthia *by H. Montgomery Hyde (New York: Farrar, Straus & Giroux, 1965)*

she was given the pseudonym Cynthia. She was then assigned to Washington, D.C., where she initiated her most famous operation. She arranged to meet and seduce the admiral/naval attaché of the Italian Embassy. Of her willingness to grant sexual favors for information she remarked, "After all, wars are not won by respectable means!" (Rowan 1967, 649) The Italian attaché quickly became so enamored with her that he gave her the Italian naval codes. The Allies' ability to read the Italian naval communications allowed the British fleet to win a decisive victory over the Italian Navy in March 1941 in the Mediterranean Sea.

The Italian admiral was a prolific source of intelligence for her. He told her of the Italian-German plan to blow up Allied ships berthed in U.S. harbors. The British passed this information to the FBI, which arranged for the State Department to declare the admiral persona non grata.

After successfully getting the Italian codes, she was asked to try to get the Vichy codes from the French Vichy Embassy in Washington. She met the public relations officer of the Vichy Embassy, Charles Brousse. Genuine love between the two soon blossomed when she learned that he had been a fighter pilot in the Free French Navy and detested the Germans who were occupying his country, despite his affiliation with Vichy. Brousse was also pro-British and agreed to help his future wife get the Vichy codes. The problem was that the codes were locked in the embassy vault and even Brousse did not have access to them.

One night they plied the embassy night watchman with champagne heavily laced with a sleeping potion. After it had taken effect, the two spies let an expert locksmith into the embassy. He quickly opened the safe that contained the codes, photographed them, and returned them to their exact spot inside the safe.

To keep the Germans from discovering that the British Government Codes and Cipher School was reading all the German radio traffic with the help of the Enigma machine, the British gave the Germans a reason to believe that some of their communications had been compromised and revealed: they leaked the fact that they had burglarized the safe at the Vichy Embassy in Washington.

In November 1945, Arthur Pack died. Brousse, keeping his part of the bargain, then divorced his wife, and the two lovers were married. They settled in France after the war. The legendary Cynthia died in 1963 of cancer at the age of 53.

Franklin, Charles. *The Great Spies*. New York: Hart Publishing, 1967.

Hyde, H. Montgomery. *Cynthia*. New York: Farrar, Straus & Giroux, 1968.

Carmen Brufau Civit
Spain
1915–ca. 1980

Carmen Brufau Civit became a spy because of what the Fascists and absentee landowners were doing to her native Spain. She believed that communism was the answer to Spain's ills and that the end justified the means. Therefore, she spied in order to get rid of the people she hated in her country. Along the way she became not only a good spy but one of the best female spies of this century.

Brufau was born in Agramonte, Catalonia, in northeast Spain. She attended local schools until she went to work for the Spanish Ministry of Education in 1937 as a schoolteacher. She worked for the Spanish Republican government teaching children orphaned by the Spanish Civil War and consoling soldiers who had been wounded in the fighting.

Barcelona was noted for its radical political movements during this time. Because she had witnessed the atrocities committed by the Royalist forces in the Civil War, she reacted against the establishment and joined the Communist party of Spain. As part of her rebellion against authority, she married a Communist from Mallorca against her family's wishes. His name was José Maria Esbert, but Brufau never used this name and never referred to him or this first marriage.

Caridad Mercader was a militant Communist leader of the Women's Battalion of the Republican Army in Barcelona, a dedicated Soviet espionage agent, and the mother of Trotsky's assassin. She was a friend of Brufau's during her work in hospitals for the Spanish Republicans. Mercader's lover was Leonid Eitingon, a leading Soviet agent in Spain and an instructor in the sabotage and assassination school under the direction of Alexander Orlov. Eitingon, abetted by Mercader, was probably Brufau's recruiter into Soviet intelligence. After her recruitment she left the hospital and worked in the Republican Military Intelligence Service (SIM for the first letters in its Spanish name, *Servicio Inteligencia Militar*). There she worked with Santiago Garces, the chief of SIM, and Enrique Castro Delgado, a leader of the Spanish Communist party and an NKVD agent.

When the Republicans were routed from the Barcelona area at the end of the Civil War, Brufau escaped to France. In a refugee camp she met an Austrian refugee by the name of Kurt Zeifurt, who had been fighting for the Republicans in Spain. About four months after she arrived in France, the Soviet government appealed to the French government to expedite the "repatriation" to the Soviet Union of Brufau and Zeifurt. They were married in Russia and, almost immediately, Brufau gave birth to a daughter. There is evidence that Brufau left the daughter with her sister, Conchita, in Moscow when she left for an assignment in Mexico. Kurt Zeifurt was killed at the siege of Leningrad fighting in the Russian infantry against the German invaders.

Brufau attended a training facility for espionage techniques and clandestine tradecraft in Moscow. She worked as a Spanish-language translator for Moscow radio and prepared Spanish-language broadcasts for Spain and Latin America. She was evacuated from Moscow to Tashkent because of German military incursions that threatened Moscow in 1943. In later years she referred to her time in Tashkent as idyllic and commented that, next to her home in Catalonia, Tashkent was her favorite area.* When the German military threat subsided, she returned to Moscow and worked on Spanish-language propaganda motion pictures. She then worked as a translator/typist in the Uruguay Embassy in Moscow.

In 1945, she left the Soviet Union for Mexico via the United States. The fact that Brufau was allowed to leave the Soviet Union indicates her special status as a Soviet agent. Reports that Brufau went to Mexico to be Mercader's radio operator in an operation to help her son, Trotsky's assassin, escape from a Mexican penitentiary are dubious. Although there is no doubt that Brufau was capable of operating an agent radio, other evidence clearly indicates that she may have initially gone to Mexico as Mercader's assistant but that she actually went for more important operations.

Brufau arrived in New York on 18 October 1945 with no passport, only an identity document from Narciso Bassols, who was the Mexican ambassador to the Soviet Union. She also had a letter from the assistant U.S. naval attaché in Odessa, Commander Johnson, claiming to authorize Brufau's transportation from Constanza, Romania, to the United States. Brufau was detained in New York for five days while her entry status was investigated. She was deported to Mexico, but she didn't have the proper documents to enter Mexico, despite Bassols's expediting identity papers, and she was detained by the Mexican authorities. She sent a telegram to a friend, a well-known Communist who was employed in the Mexican Ministry of Foreign Affairs. The friend pulled some strings, and Brufau proceeded to Mexico City from the border area to assume her duties as Mercader's assistant.

Brufau's duties as Mercader's assistant were supporting her in an operation designed to help her son, Ramon Mercader, escape from jail where he was serving a sentence of 19 years and 6 months for assassinating Leon Trotsky. Mercader was unsuccessful in her attempts and returned to the Soviet Union.

In Mexico, Brufau performed various tasks for Soviet intelligence. Her cover jobs were selected for her to give her the greatest access to information that the Soviets desired. One time she was the private secretary to one of the secretaries of the president of Mexico, Miguel Aleman. In that position she had access to all secret treaties with the United States and other information concerning Latin America ordinarily not available to the Soviet Union during the Cold War.

At this time, Mexican diplomats were well received at the White House and their liaison with all branches of the U.S. government gave them unprecedented access to much classified information that was sent back to the president of Mexico.

Brufau also served as secretary to the undersecretary who handled all government and commercial communications in and out of Mexico. This was a position of that gave her access to all traffic to and from the embassies and government departments in the Mexican capitol. The Soviets collected what little information there was from the U.S. Embassy traffic and tried their best to decode it to be sent back to Moscow.

On 12 August 1955, Brufau left Mexico by plane and arrived in Zurich, Switzerland. Three days later she went to Bern and made two unsuccessful attempts to contact someone. She was dressed exactly the same on both occasions: a white handbag, white gloves, and the same tailored black suit. The third time, after she had run the same counter-surveillance pattern of taking several taxis and checking herself for surveillance, she made her previously arranged meeting with Boris Kuznetsov of the Soviet legation in Bern. Unfortunately for all future operations that might have monitored Brufau, the Swiss police arrested her and Kuznetsov, thus alerting them to the coverage.

Brufau told the Swiss police that she had been told in Mexico that she could arrange to help her seriously ill father in Spain by contacting the Soviets in Bern. She also admitted that she had worked for the Soviet NKVD but said that she no longer worked for them. The Swiss police put Brufau on the next plane back to Mexico.

Brufau dropped out of Soviet operations after the debacle in Switzerland. She worked for a while at a gift store and remained in Mexico City for several years be-

fore moving to Merida. In the early 1970s, a friend of Brufau's told several people who inquired about her that she was destitute and slowly dying from cancer of the throat in Merida. She had always been a heavy cigarette smoker.**

(See also Caridad Mercader.)

* Personal knowledge of the author.

** Enrique Castro Delgado, former leader of the Spanish Communist party, who subsequently defected from communism, provided much of the information about Brufau. The author was acquainted with several personal friends of Brufau's and has drawn on personal recollections.

Levine, Isaac Don. *Mind of an Assassin.* New York: Farrar, Straus & Cudahy, 1959.

Anne Brusselmans
Belgium
ca. 1920–

Anne Brusselmans organized one of the most efficient exfiltration networks during World War II. She helped Allied airmen who were downed in Belgium return to Britain so that they could fly and fight against the Germans again.

Brusselmans was an Englishwoman who married a Belgian. When World War II broke out, she volunteered for the resistance forces in Belgium. Among the many women in these forces, she was notable as an extraordinarily prolific source of extremely valuable intelligence information.

She was most active in setting up and maintaining rat lines for an exfiltration operation. Before the war was over she had helped more than 180 British and U.S. downed fliers to escape from Belgium during a four-year period.

The Gestapo searched her apartment on three separate occasions but never found anything that could be used against her. At the end of the war she was the only surviving member of her original cell of underground workers.

Weiser, Marjorie P. K., and Jean S. Arbeiter. *Womanlist.* New York: Atheneum, 1981.

Grace Buchanan (Countess Buchanan)
Canada
1918–

After attending a German spy school, Grace Buchanan operated under the alias Countess Buchanan in the United States, where she attempted to obtain information about U.S. industrial production. The FBI knew about her role from the beginning of her espionage career, however, and when she was arrested and confessed, the agency persuaded her to act as a double agent. She served as one of the few women of that period in this capacity, pretending to act as a German spy while secretly working for the United States.

Grace Buchanan was born in Canada in 1918. Just before the outbreak of World War II, she was traveling in Budapest, where she met a female student from Vassar College who was acting as a spotter/recruiter for the German intelligence service. She suggested to Grace that, as a Canadian who disliked the United States, she could work against the Americans by working with the Germans. Grace then attended a rudimentary school for spies in Germany before she left Europe.

After she finished her schooling in tradecraft and communications in October 1941, she flew to the United States on the newly established Pan American Airways "Clipper" service direct to New York. She had a list of people to contact that had been given to her by her German superiors, but she didn't have any clear idea of what she was supposed to be doing in the United States for them. The Nazis had told her simply that she should send back production and industrial potential figures for heavy industry in the United States.

Buchanan was soon a part of the social scene in Detroit, passing as just another likable Canadian. She seemed to be inordinately curious about the production capabilities of the automobile factories and the Pullman Standard (railway) Car Company in Detroit, but her new American friends thought that her curiosity was merely natural and paid no attention to it.

She used the alias of Smith, but mostly she used the name Countess Buchanan. Whatever name she used didn't prevent the FBI from suspecting her of attempted espionage. Unbeknown to Buchanan, the FBI had known about her from the very beginning. They had been purposefully steering their own double agents to her to supply her with false production figures.

When she was arrested she readily confessed. She told the FBI everything about her schooling as a Nazi spy, her work for the Germans in the United States, and named her accomplices. She agreed to continue working as a Nazi spy for the FBI in order to feed the Germans false information.

Seth, Ronald. *Encyclopedia of Espionage.* New York: Doubleday, 1972.

Haidee Tamara Bunke
(Tania, Laura Gutierrez Bauer)
Argentina
1937–1967

Haidee Tamara Bunke, a dedicated Communist ideologue, worked in espionage for the East Germans and the KGB. She was recruited to monitor and report on the Cuban Communists and was later assigned to concentrate on Ernesto "Che" Guevara. She was exceptionally resourceful and aggressive and actually helped organize and participated in revolutionary guerrilla activities in the Bolivian jungle. She is rumored to have been carrying Guervera's child when she was shot and killed.

Bunke was the daughter of two veteran Communists, an East German professor, Erich Otto Bunke, and his Polish wife, Esperanza (Nadya) Bider Bunke. They emigrated to Argentina in February 1935, where Haidee Bunke was born two years later. She was 14 years old when she returned with her parents to East Germany. She spoke fluent Spanish and quickly perfected German, which she had spoken at home. She also learned her mother's Polish and quickly was fluent in Russian.

GRACE BUCHANAN

Federal Bureau of Investigation

She attended East Germany's elite, Humboldt University, where she majored in languages. She became active in Communist youth organizations and acted as interpreter at international conferences. Soviet KGB agents at these meetings began to notice her and accumulated a dossier for later use as an assessment tool for her recruitment.

In 1959, she took a job with the Cuban delegation in East Berlin as a secretary and translator. Her enlistment in the East German secret service came in January 1960. When she had learned basic tradecraft techniques, the service began using her as bait in blackmail traps. The Soviet KGB recruited her away from the East German service at this time and began using her as a spotter and recruiter of prospective agents.

The next stage of her KGB career was a thorough, advanced tradecraft training course in 1961 in preparation for a Latin American assignment for the KGB. She was trained in coding and decoding wireless transmissions, the use of firearms and explosives, the preparation and use of forged documents, various forms of clandestine communications, and all details of international courier activities.

Bunke was ideally suited for her role. It was claimed by a person in the KGB at the time that she had been picked to act as the "chaperon" for Guevara. The role was easy because Bunke had never stopped seeing her Cuban friends. She feigned a desire to get back to a Latin environment, and a Cuban official conveniently suggested that she visit Cuba to enjoy the sun and Spanish culture.

Bunke arrived in Cuba in May 1961. She didn't continue on to Argentina as she had told the Cubans she would but made herself politically active in the Cuban Communist Youth Union and especially in the militia. She also attended the University of Havana and began to develop a new cover. She became a student of folk arts and crafts and the native music. This new cover enabled her to engage in extensive correspondence with other scholars in Latin America, which would give her future operational travel in the area convincing legitimacy.

Bunke left Havana two years before Guevara. She arrived in Bolivia by way of Peru on 18 March 1964 and traveled on a forged Argentine passport, which identified her as Laura Gutierrez Bauer, language teacher. She succeeded in obtaining a position with the Bolivian government's Press and Information Office of the Presidency. She also taught German to the children of the director of the Information Office. This position gave her access to files of the Bolivian government, official letterhead that she could use to forge permits, official seals to validate forged papers, press credentials that allowed recipients access to otherwise prohibited places, and other tools of the international agent's trade.

In preparation for her assignment with Guevara, she used her interest in folk art and regional crafts to visit different areas of Bolivia. She traveled with camera and tape recorder, collecting samples of native handicraft and recording traditional songs and instrumental music. Motoring unhampered in remote areas of Bolivia enabled her to explore and map regions suitable for guerrilla centers of activity and to become familiar with terrain suitable for hit-and-run guerrilla warfare tactics. Her trips also permitted her to study Indian dialects and customs and to win the confidence of the peasantry. However, she did not have sufficient time to fully prepare either herself or her potential guerrilla Indian allies for the tasks she set for them in the coming war against the Bolivian government.

Bunke was living in a La Paz boarding house, waiting for Guevara to arrive, when she met a Bolivian student whom she made good use of for her clandestine work. She became the "older and wiser woman" for the young student and convinced him that he should marry her. After the wedding, she took out a legitimate Bolivian passport as his wife and divorced him within a year. In order to calm her jilted former husband, Bunke arranged for him to get a scholarship at an Eastern European university.

Bunke used this period, before Guevara came to Bolivia, to develop cells of sympathizers for the guerrillas' cause at the University of Bolivia, among government employees with whom she worked, and among the artists and writers she met through her folklore work. Using her legitimate Bolivian passport, she traveled to her native Argentina, as well as to Peru and Chile. She was deeply involved in setting up a detailed support structure in Bolivia for Guevara's guerrillas, which included: an intelligence network connecting La Paz with the guerrilla groups in the field, courier and wireless communications within Bolivia and to the outside world, channels of arms resupply, and food and clothing for the fighting men. All this was done without raising the suspicion of the Bolivian authorities.

In February 1967, she had become a familiar figure in the town of Camiri, which was central in the proposed guerrilla area. She frequented an Italian restaurant in the town of Marietta, where the manager recalled, after her death, that she had often come in with several men and ordered the food for the group.

Eventually, she joined Guevara after he had assembled the nucleus of his guerrilla band. Some of his men resented her, claiming that she was too commanding, loud, abrupt, and mannish. Some of this resentment may have developed because Bunke handled the money for the group and wasn't too lavish in spending it on what she considered unnecessary things such as whiskey and fast women.

She tried to integrate the Bolivian Communist party with Guevara's band of guerrilla fighters without much success. She gave lectures to the Bolivian Communist party members in clandestine operations, security, and resupply operations. By this time Guevara had established his main camp in the Bolivian jungle.

On 31 August 1967, the Bolivian army ambushed Bunke's group of guerrilla fighters as they were fording a stream. The Bolivian soldiers waited until all ten of her patrolmen were in the water and then opened fire, killing Bunke and most of the others. Among Bunke's personal effects found by the Bolivian army was a half-finished letter to her mother in East Germany: "I am a child that wants to hide, in some corner that is cozy and where no one can find me. I want to crawl away and hide. But where can I hide?"

An autopsy report stated that Bunke had been pregnant at the time of her death, and people assumed that it was Guevara's baby. The allegation that she had been sent by the KGB to spy on Guevara appears to have had legitimacy. There was another report that Bunke helped the Bolivian army locate Guevara by leaving for them to find a guerrilla jeep with sensitive maps and information leading them to Guevara, but this has not been substantiated. On 9 October 1967, Guevara was killed by the Bolivian army.

U.S. experts note that Cuba suddenly stopped eulogizing Bunke as a revolutionary heroine, apparently after learning of her espionage on Guevara for the Soviets. There has always been speculation among knowledgeable intelligence officers that Bunke was ordered by the KGB to betray Guevara because his maverick activities had become a burden for them to justify.

Ebon, Martin. *"Che": The Making of a Legend.* New York: Signet Books, 1969.

Harris, Richard. *Death of a Revolutionary.* New York: W. W. Norton, 1970.

C

Angela Calomiris
(Angela Cole)
United States
1916–

Angela Calomiris was approached by the FBI to infiltrate the Communist party in the United States. It is to her credit that she accomplished this task without any help. She started from the outside, located a member of the CPUSA, and got herself recruited. She rose through the party ranks to achieve a leadership position, which enabled her to testify against the top leaders of the CPUSA and to be instrumental in their conviction.

Calomiris was born on New York City's Lower East Side to immigrant Greek parents. Her mother was a very religious Greek Orthodox Christian, but she inherited little, if any, religious belief. Her father was a furrier by trade, but during the depression of the early 1930s, he lost his job and was reduced to accepting menial jobs to support the family. Calomiris was the smallest of her siblings, but—maybe because of her size—she was always determined not to allow anyone to get the better of her. She was determined to become an excellent photojournalist.

During her youth and young adulthood, she had never met a Communist, but she had agreed with many of their ideas and proposals. She was always skeptical, however, that anything as abstract as Communist theory could do any real good to alleviate the ills she saw around her on the Lower East Side. Also, she didn't see how the Communists could help her become a better photojournalist.

She moved to Greenwich Village and, instead of buying food, she saved money to buy a camera and practiced taking pictures of her new friends. In 1940, she took and passed a civil service examination for playground director of New York City schools and was then able to rent a larger apartment with space that she made into a darkroom.

She joined the Photo League, an informal group of people from all walks of life who were interested in photography. They rented a floor of a dilapidated building, where they installed a darkroom with space enough to hold instructional lectures by the more advanced photographers in the group. Calomiris realized that many of the members of the Photo League were Communists and that there was always Communist propaganda around. Some of the Communists tried to interest her in communism, but she didn't listen seriously to them nor did she read the literature they gave her to take home. She realized that communism was a growing, vibrant movement, but it also seemed nothing more than another minority sect and a harmless bore.

In February 1942, two FBI agents called on Calomiris and asked her if she would join the CPUSA to observe its inner workings for

ANGELA CALOMIRIS

Photograph by Fred Stein; courtesy Angela Calomiris

the FBI. She was surprised that the agents seemed to know all about her and that they almost anticipated her answers and mental responses. (The agents' ability to know "all about" Calomiris's thinking was the result of a in-depth background investigation conducted before they made their recruitment pitch.)

Calomiris told the FBI agents that she didn't understand why they wanted her to report on the Communists, because Russia was a wartime ally of the United States. The agents replied that although this might be true for the moment, Russia might change in the future. At that time the U.S. government would want to know about Russia's plans as far in advance as possible. If Russia were to change its policy, the Communists in the United States would probably be the first to know, and her access to this information would give the United States valuable advance notification.

Calomiris accepted the agents' offer even though they pointed out that there would be

no glory or payment for her work with them and that if she were found out, she would be completely on her own: the Bureau would have to disavow any knowledge of her and she couldn't expect any help from the FBI, even if she were arrested by the New York police for Communist activities. They also warned her of what could happen if the party discovered that she was an FBI plant: she would be expelled from the party, all her party friends would shun her, the party would do everything it possibly could to smear her reputation, she might be personally assaulted, and her job might be threatened by letters to her employers stating that she was guilty of every type of criminal act and of having been a Communist. Despite these warnings, or maybe because of the challenge they represented, Calomiris agreed to infiltrate the Communist party.

In anticipation of an investigation by the Communists, the agents impressed upon her that she should not change her way of living or her personality. Above all, they cautioned, she must never act conspiratorially or try to pry into party secrets or members' personal lives. What information she did obtain must come to her naturally; she was not to jeopardize her position by trying to get more information than would normally come her way. Calomiris was briefed that the Bureau wanted her to report everything, no matter how trivial she thought it was, because although there might be details that she didn't consider important, every detail might assume importance later on in completing a bigger picture.

Several weeks later, Calomiris was invited by a Photo League regular to attend a lecture where she could get the "truth" about the conduct of the war. She had expected a hall with a podium and speakers; instead, there were a few other people at a meeting in an apartment. There was a large map on the fireplace mantel, which the speaker used while talking about Russia's precarious position in the war due to lack of support from the other Allies. The lecture was artfully designed to garner sympathy for Russia.

After that evening, the Communists courted Calomiris. The Communists in the

Photo League flattered her photographic efforts and appeared to seek her confidences and respect her opinion on world affairs. She was finally invited to join the party but was told that she must take another name for security reasons, so that even her comrades in the party would not know her true name and be able to turn her in to the authorities. She was also told that she must keep her professional life and party life completely separate. The name she took for party purposes was Angela Cole.

Calomiris rose rapidly in the party. She volunteered for every menial job that no one else wanted to do; she made herself indispensable. Eventually, party leaders learned to rely upon her for jobs entailing more responsibility. As a reward for her dedication, she was given titles and assignments requiring more leadership, until she achieved the position of financial secretary of the West Midtown Branch of the CPUSA in New York City. In this position she had the real and party names of all the members of her branch, their length of service, and their assignments. Despite rigid compartmentalization, she also knew the leaders in the echelon above her, which was the highest in the U.S. party, and the leaders in the echelon beneath her. She was in a pivotal position to supply the Bureau with comprehensive information about all ranks of the party.

On 26 April 1949, the Bureau and the prosecuting officials of the Department of Justice decided to use her as a witness against the 11 top leaders of the CPUSA. A great many people who read only the headlines thought that she had been a genuine, dedicated Communist who had turned informant for the Bureau for the money they paid her. (In fact, she had received no money from the Bureau, except for expenses.)

When Calomiris took the witness stand and announced who she was and what her party position had been, there were audible gasps from the defendants. One was heard to say, "My God, she must have all the membership lists!" She identified each of the top 11 leaders and what they had told the rank and file of the party that the prosecution claimed was seditious. The next day, after the word

was out that she had been an FBI plant, her former party comrades came to court to heckle her.

Calomiris felt that her future was tied to the verdict of this trial. If the 11 defendants were found innocent, she would have spent seven years of her life in vain. If they were found guilty, she would have done a useful job for her country. On 13 October 1949, a jury found the 11 top leaders of the CPUSA guilty as charged of conspiring to advocate the overthrow of the U.S. government by force. Calomiris had been vindicated for her personal sacrifice. She returned to her profession of photojournalism and disappeared from public view.

Calomiris, Angela. *Red Masquerade: Undercover for the FBI.* New York: J. B. Lippincott, 1950.

Powers, Richard Gid. *Secrecy and Power: The Life of J. Edgar Hoover.* New York: The Free Press, 1987.

Mathilde-Lucie Belard Carré
(The Cat, Lily)
France
1908–ca. 1960

Mathilde-Lucie Belard Carré was forced under torture to confess to her participation in a spy network in Occupied France. Even though she vociferously claimed that the only reason she confessed was to save her fellow conspirators, she was ostracized after World War II and shunned as a traitor. She died in seclusion in spite of the heroic work she had accomplished before her capture.

Belard, born in 1908 into a middle-class French family, was an honor student at the Sorbonne. She married Maurice Carré, a schoolteacher, and went to Algiers with him, but the marriage was a disaster. Finally, Carré left Algiers and returned to Paris, where she joined the Army Nurse Corps.

She was recruited into the Interallie network. Her father, a military hero, had been awarded the Legion of Honor in World War I, so the idea of fighting for her country seemed a natural one. She and the team leader established their headquarters in Paris on the rue du Baubourg St. Jacques. Soon they had a network of intelligence collection agents and saboteurs that covered almost all of Occupied France. All went well with their operation until October 1941, when Sergeant Hugo Bleicher of the Gestapo arrived in Paris.

Bleicher reported that he had received information that a good-looking French woman had tried to elicit information from an employee of a Luftwaffe fuel depot. The Gestapo arrested the young woman, Christine Borue, who admitted her guilt and that she was working for British intelligence. She also claimed to be the team leader's mistress, but she turned him in to the Gestapo. Her immediate superior in Occupied France, she readily confessed, was a British agent. With this lead, the Gestapo worked rapidly, and on November 3 they identified most of the team members.

Bleicher became known as one of the most successful counterintelligence experts the Abwehr had. (The Abwehr was the German intelligence organization several steps above the Gestapo in discipline, effectiveness, and sophistication. Bleicher had been promoted from the Gestapo to the Abwehr.) His top priority was to eliminate the Interallie network.

A member of the team who had been arrested and who had confessed had agreed to help Bleicher. The network had immediately taken steps to minimize any damage that this traitor's confession could cause them, but even with damage control procedures in place, they were still vulnerable. The confession gave away so much information that changing all of their procedures and meeting places in such a short time was impossible. Changing everything meant changing the safety and danger signals and danger signs; changing meeting times and places of all the drop sites, pickup spots, and agent meeting areas; changing all codes and secret writing systems and developers; changing all aliases and street names; changing all recognition signals; getting rid of all safe houses and whatever equipment there might be in them, all accommodation addresses, rendezvous parachute drop zones, and radio call signs;

plus beginning the tedious and extremely dangerous job of vetting new safe house keepers and scouting new drop zones and dead drop sites.

Twenty-one members of the Interallie network were arrested on 17 November 1941, including the team leader. The German agents stayed at their headquarters, hoping that other members of the network would show up. Their wait was rewarded, because about three hours later, Carré walked in.

The team leader would only admit to Bleicher that he worked for the Allies; he told nothing about the Interallie network or his current operations, despite prolonged and vicious torture. Because Bleicher couldn't get anything out of the team leader, he turned his attentions to Carré.

In order to have the best possible conditions for softening Carré before interrogating her, Bleicher had her removed from the dismal prison cell she was in and established her in the luxurious Edward VII Hotel. Bleicher was a master of psychological interrogation. He promised Carré that if she would cooperate by revealing to him all of the details of the Interallie network, he would, in turn, try to save some of her captured friends in the resistance from execution by the firing squad.

Out of compassion for her fellow agents and to save herself from torture and death, Carré agreed to cooperate. She also chose to get close to Bleicher to learn about his operations. She claimed that in order to do this, she had to become his mistress. Most of the remaining members of the Interallie network were rounded up as a result of Carré's treachery.

The prize of this massive counterintelligence coup was the four transmitters that fell into Bleicher's possession. He persuaded his superiors that no leaks should be allowed about the arrests of the Interallie network that might find their way back to the British. (Usually, arrests of spies were prominently trumpeted in all the German propaganda outlets to boost morale in Germany and also as a deterrent to future resistance operations.) Bleicher wanted to "play the transmitters back" to the British headquarters in such a way as to make them believe that their network was still intact and operating free of German control. In this way Bleicher would be able to feed the British false and misleading information that they would think was coming from their own trusted operators. In return, Bleicher would learn from the British what intelligence they needed to fill the gaps in their knowledge of the Germans' intentions and capabilities. Knowing the British requirements would also reveal their weaknesses; it was almost as good as having a spy in the enemy headquarters.

Carré, still under Bleicher's control, knew all of the British codes and danger and safety transmission signals. She once again agreed to help him. When Carré had joined the team she had introduced the leader to a lawyer. After her capture, she had continued to correspond with this lawyer at Bleicher's insistence in the hope that he would lead Bleicher to other SOE operations in France. The lawyer did introduce Carré to another SOE leader. Fortunately for Bleicher, the new SOE leader had been having trouble with his radio transmitter and couldn't reach London. He asked Carré if she would help him send messages to London over her transmitter, which she did. This enabled Bleicher to monitor the operation.

When the new team leader was routinely ordered home to London, Bleicher decided to allow his return, because he thought it would increase the apparent validity of the entire operation. A Lysander bomber was sent by London to pick up the new leader and return him to Britain. Just before he took off, he had a flash of suspicion about Carré's loyalty. He asked her several questions that would have either established her loyalty beyond a doubt or proven her guilt. Carré flunked the test and, in a fit of desire for expiation, she confessed all of her traitorous activities to him. He decided to trust Carré and agreed that she could accompany him to London. As soon as they arrived in London, Carré once again broke down and confessed her traitorous activities to the SOE and told them everything she knew about Bleicher and the German Abwehr operation.

The SOE in London imprisoned Carré for the duration of the war. After the war, she was extradited to France, where, in 1949, she was tried and sentenced to death for treason. Her sentence was eventually commuted to life imprisonment. Her defense attorney offered this rationalization for Carré's treasonous conduct:

> I admit her guilt. But you must consider that this woman was faced with the choice of life or death. Do not forget that from the beginning of the resistance she was a heroine. Would you put to death those who at the beginning sowed the seed of faith and later overestimated their own strength?

She was released in September 1954 and went to live in a French rural town under a new identity. In later years she began to lose her sight and lived in seclusion until her death.

Cookridge, E. H. *Set Europe Ablaze*. London: Pan Books, 1966.

Franklin, Charles. *The Great Spies*. New York: Hart Publishing, 1967.

Edith Cavell
England
1865–1915

Edith Cavell was not a spy, but her executioners portrayed her as one. The Germans thought that they needed her execution to boost Germany's morale, but it had the opposite effect worldwide. More than any other factor in World War I, her death strengthened the will of the Belgian people to resist the Germans.

Cavell was born in England in 1865 and died in Belgium, executed unjustly by the German counterintelligence service, on 12 October 1915. She had been appointed matron of the Berkendael Medical Institute in Brussels in 1907. This facility became a Red Cross hospital at the outbreak of war in 1914. She helped to smuggle more than 200 Allied soldiers and Belgian youths of military age out of German-occupied Belgium so that they could rejoin the Allied armies. Cavell was not connected with espionage in the classic sense

EDITH CAVELL

Imperial War Museum Negative Q32930, London

but was charged with "conducting soldiers to the enemy" under Article 58 of the German military code.

After a succession of military conquests, the German army had settled down to consolidate its control over Occupied Belgium. Young men of military age were escaping in large numbers from Belgium to join King Albert's army, which was regrouping on the extreme left flank of the Allies' line of trenches. There were also many wounded Belgian soldiers and Allied stragglers to be helped out of Belgium to fight again against the Germans.

The occupying German forces had posted proclamations ordering the Belgians to report all casualties and stragglers. This only aroused the combative instincts of the Belgians. The question on every loyal Belgian's lips was, who would ever think of turning in weakened, wounded, and crippled men to the hated Boche? ("Boche" was a derogatory name for the Germans.)

A doctor who was heading the underground campaign to move wounded and draft-eligible men out of Belgium came to Brussels hoping to find a convenient way station. He needed a rest stop on the exfiltration rat line where he could rest his evacuees before they went on the last leg of their journey to the border. He knew that Cavell, the supervisor of the nurses' school on the rue de la Culture, might help. She agreed and soon had enlisted the aid of her many friends in the area.

Cavell's motives were only humanitarian; she was not interested in fighting the Germans. No one in Cavell's group was ever charged with espionage. Some of her more distant friends did engage in espionage on their own, but their activities were completely divorced from anything Cavell was doing. There were also distant friends who published underground newspapers and distributed propaganda throughout the country, but none of this touched her in any way.

Cavell became the object of suspicion when an underground worker was arrested by the Germans. She had a notebook in her possession that contained the names of her associates in the underground. Innocently listed among them was Cavell's name, but the Germans assumed that Cavell was guilty

of the same crimes as the other members of the underground.

Her execution by the Germans for "having conveyed soldiers to the enemy" caused a great outcry in Britain, but all nations executed female as well as male spies during World War I. Cavell had admitted to helping wounded soldiers escape and refused to appeal her death sentence.

The Germans were sensitive to world opinion that censured them for using uncivilized methods of warfare. Their execution of a woman—a nurse who was only doing her duty to humanity—was condemned by all Allied and nonbelligerent nations. Alfred Zimmermann, the German undersecretary of state for foreign affairs, tried to justify the execution by pointing out that Cavell had not been executed for only a single act of humanitarianism. She had, Zimmermann contended, a well-organized group handling the passage of British, French, and Belgian soldiers who had escaped from German military hospitals and were returning to their units to fight again against German soldiers.

Cavell was a disconcertingly brave woman who went to her death with incomparable equanimity. She well deserves her lofty place among the great women of history.

Franklin, Charles. *The Great Spies*. New York: Hart Publishing, 1967.

Peterson, Bonnie A., and Judith P. Zinsser. *A History of Their Own*. Volume II. New York: Harper & Row, 1988.

Janet Anne Chisholm
England
ca. 1932–

Janet Anne Chisholm was the wife of Roderick Chisholm, the MI-6 officer in the British Embassy in Moscow. She began spying out of loyalty to her husband and accepted messages from an important Russian intelligence agent who was actually working for the British and the CIA. Her actions were dangerous and courageous for a foreign citizen living in Moscow during the Cold War.

In order to properly appreciate Janet Chisholm's role as an espionage agent we must understand her role in the Penkovskiy case.

Colonel Oleg Penkovskiy, a Russian hero of World War II, a senior officer in Soviet military intelligence (the GRU), a graduate of the Soviet staff college and their rocket missile academy, was also a spy jointly controlled and directed by the British MI-6 and the CIA. Working for the Allies, Penkovskiy had single-handedly sabotaged the Soviet effort to close Berlin in 1962, and his information had been instrumental in President John F. Kennedy's successful defeat of the Soviet-Cuban missile threat in October 1962. Professional intelligence officers assessed Penkovskiy's accomplishments as some of the greatest intelligence achievements of the twentieth century.

Some people have sought to diminish Penkovskiy's status by assuming that he was a paid agent or a simple defector who stayed in his position to provide the United States with information. On the contrary, he was a determined patriotic zealot of the true Russia who despised the Stalin/Soviet regime. He also feared that Nikita Khrushchev was leading Russia into a nuclear war with the Western powers.

When Penkovskiy came out of the Soviet Union to international conferences in Europe, he was extensively debriefed by U.S. and British intelligence officers. He returned each time to the Soviet Union to collect additional, extremely valuable information. Most of his information was timely and couldn't wait until he would be allowed to make another trip out of the Soviet Union. Some secure method had to be used to collect his intelligence from inside the Soviet Union, in spite of KGB surveillance.

Penkovskiy had been introduced to Chisholm during his second trip to London, during which he had been drilled on the secure meeting procedures that would have to be used with her in Moscow. He was given a little box of Drazbe candies to use in his contacts with her; when empty, the box would

hold exactly four rolls of film. Penkovskiy also had been given a small Minox camera to use in photographing secret documents.

The head of the Second Chief Directorate of the KGB, in charge of internal security, decided (as a result of another CIA case that had been discovered in Moscow) to begin blanket coverage of the U.S. and British embassies for several weeks twice a year. These were enormous operations designed to cover diplomats' families, newspaper correspondents, resident businessmen, and employees of the embassies.

In January 1962, this routine surveillance covered Chisholm as she left the British Embassy with her three children for a walk in the park in the Arbat area of Moscow. An unidentified, well-dressed Russian man (later identified by the KGB as Penkovskiy) was observed to greet her casually (as a stranger would greet another stranger) and stop to talk with her children. The Russian man took a box of candy out of his coat pocket and gave it to the children.

The KGB watchers knew they had observed a "brush contact," where something, probably intelligence information, has been passed. (This is called a brush contact, because contact is made and information passed within the time that two agents brush against each other, allowing almost no time for surveillance to observe that anything has been passed.) The KGB followed Chisholm back to the British Embassy while another part of the surveillance team tried to follow the Russian man, but he was able to shake them.

Penkovskiy had noticed a KGB surveillance car in the vicinity of his meeting with Chisholm and suggested that future meetings be in the British or U.S. embassies, where he would normally go as a Soviet official guest at a state reception. Accordingly, on 28 March 1962, at a reception given at the British Embassy, Penkovskiy gave Chisholm a written report and six rolls of film. At the Fourth of July celebration at the U.S. Embassy, he passed a report and some film to her.

The KGB had by this time identified Penkovskiy as Chisholm's contact. They wanted to investigate him further, so they sent the family who lived in the apartment above him on a holiday to the Black Sea. They drilled a small hole from that apartment through the ceiling of Penkovskiy's apartment and inserted a "pin head" camera lens. They were able to observe Penkovskiy in his apartment using his Minox camera to photograph secret Soviet documents and using a one-time cipher pad to encode his messages.

In order to make a detailed search of Penkovskiy's apartment, they needed to get him away for several days. The KGB had a toxicologist smear a poisonous substance on Penkovskiy's favorite chair, which made him briefly but violently ill. The Soviet doctor, who had been briefed by the KGB, explained to Penkovskiy that he needed a few days' hospital treatment. During the KGB search of his apartment, they found the usual spy paraphernalia, which clinched the prosecution case against him.

Penkovskiy was arrested, sentenced, and executed for espionage and treason. Chisholm and her husband were transferred from Moscow. Her husband reportedly became a legitimate foreign service officer instead of only using the foreign service designation as their cover for intelligence work.

Andrew, Christopher, and Oleg Gordievsky. *KGB: The Inside Story.* New York: HarperCollins, 1990.

Penkovskiy, Oleg. *The Penkovskiy Papers.* New York: Doubleday, 1965.

Lona Petka Cohen
(Kroger)
United States
1920–

Lona Petka Cohen and her husband became a superb espionage team. By being at the right place at the right time, they were part of some of the most sensational espionage cases in recent history. Under a new identity, she may still be working someplace in the world.

Peter Kroger (real name Morris Cohen) met Lona Petka, his future wife, in 1940. She was born in the United States to Jewish-Polish parents. She met her husband shortly after he returned to the United States from Spain, where he had been fighting with the Abraham Lincoln Battalion on the Republican side of the Spanish Civil War. Lona Petka was working as a housemaid, and she shared Cohen's Communist belief that other people's wealth should be shared.

They were married in 1941 in Norwich, Connecticut. He joined the U.S. Army the same year, and she went to work in an aircraft production factory. After the war, he taught school for a short time until he was approached by a Soviet diplomat, who recruited him into the GRU, the Soviet military intelligence organization.

When Klaus Fuchs, the British atom scientist and spy, was arrested as a result of the Rosenberg atomic espionage investigation in the United States, he confessed that the Cohens had worked as couriers to transmit information from him to the Rosenbergs through a series of cutouts, or intermediaries. Colonel Rudolph Ivanovich Abel, the Soviet spy under deep cover in New York City, alerted the Cohens to the danger of imminent arrest by the FBI as a result of Fuchs's confession. When Abel was arrested in the Hotel Latham in New York, he had photographs of the Cohens in his briefcase. The pictures, meaningless at the time, were marked "Shirley and Morris." Five thousand dollars in cash had been attached by a rubber band to the photographs, presumably for delivery to them.

Heeding Abel's advice, the Cohens fled to California. Later, using forged Canadian passports, they went to New Zealand, where they ran agents to collect intelligence for the GRU on the underwater defenses of the Auckland Naval Base.

In 1945, the Soviets told the Cohens to prepare for a transfer to Europe. They searched the obituaries in the New Zealand newspapers and discovered a couple about their ages, named Peter and Helen Kroger, who had been killed in an automobile accident. They obtained copies of the Krogers' birth certificates and applied for passports in their names at the New Zealand Embassy in Paris.

They retained the names Helen and Peter Kroger when they moved to England, where they established themselves as proprietors of a small secondhand bookstore at 190 Strand Street in London. They advertised their specialty as being "Americana from the North to the South Pole."

They lived in a small house at 45 Cranley Street in Ruislip, where they set up espionage headquarters: the base of the cigarette lighter on the coffee table in the living room had a secret compartment filled with radio codes; attached to the phonograph in the corner was a 74-foot aerial that ran from the living room up into the attic; inside a book called *Book Auction Records* was a list of transmission procedures; behind a Bible in the bookcase was a special film for recording microdots; inside a tin of talcum powder in the medicine chest in the bathroom was a magnifying glass for reading microdots; in the hip flask in the bedroom was a cavity containing iron oxide for use in making invisible Morse code recordings on a magnetic tape; beneath the floorboards of the kitchen was a radio transmitter that could reach Moscow; and in various hiding places throughout the house were large sums of money. Nor could it be suspected that every week when Peter sent a shipment of books to the Continent there were microdots that Helen had prepared, concealed among the books; once every weekend, late at night, the radio transmitter and a tape recorder were connected to the 74-foot aerial to receive and send short bursts of high-speed messages to Moscow. The Krogers kept odd hours, and the neighbors noted that often their lights would be on at three and four o'clock in the morning, as if they had never gone to bed.

Cohen, as Helen Kroger, was an amateur photographer and sometimes blacked out the bathroom windows facing their neighbor's house. She joked that she was a lousy photographer, and those who saw her pictures agreed. Of course she was photographing classified documents in the darkroom and preparing microdots.

As the Krogers, the Cohens were part of the Gordon Lonsdale Soviet spy network. (Lonsdale's true name was Konon Trofi-

movich Molody. He was a major in the GRU. He was later arrested in London, charged with espionage, and sentenced to prison. He was subsequently exchanged for the British businessman, Greville Wynne, who was serving a sentence for espionage in the Soviet Union.)

The Cohens were that rare combination in espionage, a successful husband and wife team. They probably would not have been discovered for many years, if at all, if one of Lonsdale's subagents, an employee at a British naval base, Harry Houghton, had observed the golden rule of conspiratorial tradecraft: never spend ill-gotten gains where you are known or can be identified.

Houghton was a low-level employee with good access to highly sensitive information. The Soviets paid him well for the information he obtained from his girlfriend, Ethel Elizabeth Gee. He was probably warned by Lonsdale not to change his lifestyle by spending the money, but apparently, Houghton paid no heed to Lonsdale's admonitions and started to spend money lavishly. This brought him to the attention of the security department at the naval base. From that relatively modest beginning, Scotland Yard and MI-5 were able to uncover the entire network of Soviet spies, including the Cohens. The Cohens were arrested by MI-5 on 7 January 1960. When they were arrested, Cohen claimed that she had to stoke the boiler, because they would be gone for a long time at the police station. The police matron insisted that she must leave her purse with the police before she would be allowed to go into the basement to stoke the boiler. Cohen tried to bolt for the basement and had to be physically restrained. When her purse was searched, the police found a compromising six-page letter in Russian, a typed sheet of cipher text, and three microdots.

The Cohens were each sentenced to 20 years' imprisonment. In 1969, they were exchanged for Gerald Brooks, a British lecturer, who had been imprisoned by the Soviets for passing out what the Soviets claimed to be subversive propaganda.

The couple had made arrangements with the GRU to live in Poland and left

London on a Polish airline. Morris Cohen was given a job teaching English at a college in Lublin, Poland, and, as far as is known, Lona returned to being a housemaid and wife. They apparently were retired from the active ranks of the GRU.

Donovan, James B. *Strangers on a Bridge: The Case of Colonel Abel.* New York: Atheneum, 1964.

Liston, Robert A. *The Dangerous World of Spies and Spying.* New York: Platt & Munk, 1967.

Reader's Digest. *Great Cases of Scotland Yard.* Pleasantville, NY: The Reader's Digest Association, 1978.

Judith Coplon
United States
1921–

Judith Coplon was an American who worked at the FBI and passed classified information to the Soviets. She was aggressive and successful in obtaining secret documents and forwarding them to her Soviet contacts. Her highly publicized case embarrassed the FBI and prompted a change in agency policies.

Coplon was 27 when her case achieved international notoriety. In his book about the FBI, Don Whitehead says, "In all of the controversy involving the FBI and its operations, there were none which was worse than that which exploded in the Government's espionage case against Judith Coplon." (Whitehead 1956, 287)

In May 1948, Coplon, a graduate of Barnard College, was employed in a $3,550 per year position in the New York office of the Foreign Agents Registration section of the Department of Justice. She had been commended by the attorney general of the United States for the excellence of her work in political analysis. For her good work, she was promoted to the Washington office of the same section.

Information came to the FBI in December 1949 from a reliable source that the Soviet Embassy in Washington was regularly receiving documents with information obtained from the U.S. government. This information had to do with the activities of certain diplomats in Washington, foreign agents working against the U.S. government, and U.S. Communists. The source of this information could only tell the FBI that the person supplying these documents to the Soviets had been working in the Foreign Agents Registration office in New York, had recently been transferred to the Washington office of that same section, and might be a woman. This was a substantial lead, much more specific than many others the Bureau had received.

The FBI quickly learned that there was only one person working in the Foreign Agents Registration section who matched this profile. They immediately placed Coplon under full surveillance and informed her superior of the investigation. A full surveillance usually meant following the subject's movements 24 hours a day and checking out everyone with whom she came in contact. It also meant monitoring her mail, planting a telephone tap at her office and home telephones, and, if warranted, planting a concealed listening device in her apartment.

Her neighbors told the investigators that Coplon was a quiet intellectual type of girl who never brought men to her apartment. In contrast to what the neighbors thought, after a month's surveillance, the investigators knew that she was seeing men in her apartment. About five weeks into the investigation, Coplon asked her supervisor if she could see the top secret list of Soviet agents known to be operating in the United States. Her supervisor stalled her and notified the FBI's Washington field office. They instructed her supervisor to tell her that the report was being used by someone else and was therefore not available at that time. Merely to have denied her access would have served as a warning that could have caused her Soviet handlers to cease all operations. This would have effectively stopped the FBI from developing additional leads from the case and identifying her handlers.

The Bureau contrived a fake letter with a top secret classification. The letter purported to tell of three Soviet agents working in Amtorg, who were really working for the

JUDITH COPLON
AP / Wide World Photos

FBI, who would soon be given a loyalty check. (Amtorg was the Soviet commercial trading and travel company in the United States. It tried to arrange business ventures between U.S. and Soviet groups and arranged all the travel of tourists and businessmen between the United States and the U.S.S.R. It had served as a cover organization for Soviet intelligence agents since its inception circa 1934.) Coplon's supervisor was to give the fake letter to her as an assignment to do the necessary background research on the individuals named.

She was given the new assignment on Friday, 14 January 1949, at the beginning of the work day. Just before noon, Coplon asked her supervisor if she could have the afternoon off in order to enjoy a long weekend. The FBI had instructed her supervisor to appear friendly with Coplon, and he readily approved her afternoon's leave.

She took the one o'clock train from Washington's Union Station to Pennsylvania Station in New York. A squad of four FBI agents took the train with her in order to observe her movements and to follow anyone she contacted during the trip. They also radioed ahead to the FBI field office in New York to have a squad of fresh faces, that Coplon would not have seen before, pick up her surveillance when the train arrived.

Coplon disembarked in New York and went immediately to the ladies room, where she remained for 45 minutes. She then placed her small overnight bag in the baggage check room, casually browsed through a bookstore, and had a chicken salad sandwich at the drugstore counter in Pennsylvania Station. She then took a subway to 191st Street in Manhattan. It was dark when she ascended the stairs from the subway to the street, which made surveillance more difficult. She slowly walked down the street for about ten minutes before stopping at a jewelry store, where she stared at the display in the window for about seven minutes. She probably was checking for surveillance in the reflection of the window.

A short, well-dressed man joined her at the jewelry store window. They did not appear to recognize each other or speak, but when he left she followed him. They went into a restaurant, where they sat at the same table and engaged in a lively conversation. They constantly played the juke box, and the music drowned out their conversation so that the agents sitting around them could not overhear them. They remained in the restaurant talking and laughing for well over an hour.

They took the subway toward downtown, and as the train was pulling out of the station at 125th Street, the man abruptly squeezed through the closing doors onto the platform while Coplon continued on alone. The man's sudden departure was a routine counter-surveillance technique to test whether any agents would leave the train with him or to catch them off guard so that they would not be able to follow him. He continued using counter-surveillance measures, taking several different taxis and buses and using the same abrupt departure technique on all of them. The FBI surveillance kept up with him through most of these countering moves without revealing that they were surveilling him, but they lost him before he arrived at his destination.

The man's Slavic appearance suggested to the FBI that he might be a member of the staff of the Soviet Consulate General in New York. Early the following morning, the FBI agents who were on the surveillance the preceding night were posted where they could observe the staff of the Soviet Consulate General arrive for work. It wasn't long before they observed the same man entering the Soviet Consulate. When he came out, the FBI followed him to his apartment at 64 West 108th Street. He was then identified as Valentine Gubitchev, a Russian engineer who worked at the United Nations Architectural Department.

The FBI was almost positive that Coplon was the person passing classified information to the Soviets, so they instructed her supervisor to transfer her to another office, where access to classified material would be substantially less. When he advised her of her transfer, Coplon demanded to know why

she was being transferred. Her supervisor placated her by telling her that she was the best-qualified person in the office to handle this new assignment. She continued to visit her former office. She kept offering to assist her replacement so that she could continue to have access to classified material she could pass to the Soviets.

On 18 February 1949, Coplon again requested the afternoon off. She repeated the procedure that she had followed in her previous trips to New York. This time the FBI surveillance team had a female agent, who was able to follow Coplon into the ladies room at Pennsylvania Station, but nothing unusual or sinister was observed there.

The FBI followed her through all of her counter-surveillance moves, and she once again met with Gubitchev on a dark street just off Broadway. It was too dark for the FBI agents to see clearly, but they were fairly certain that some papers were passed between the two. Gubitchev once again used extreme counter-surveillance evasive tactics after he left the meeting.

The next known encounter was on March 3, when Coplon again asked for a half day off. This time she went to New York but spent the weekend with her parents. The following week she again asked her supervisor if she could use the top secret files on Soviet agents in the United States. He stalled by telling her that he had more information on the three FBI sources working in Amtorg and wanted her to process that information.

This latest bait for Coplon was purportedly a letter from the director of the FBI, J. Edgar Hoover, to the attorney general of the United States. The letter stated that the FBI had information that Amtorg was making inquiries about geophones, which were used in atom bomb testing. Hoover, in this phony letter, asked the attorney general if this interest of Amtorg's in classified equipment represented a violation of U.S. law.

Coplon went to New York almost immediately after receiving this letter on 6 March 1949. She went through the same procedure, but when she met Gubitchev, the FBI pounced on them. Both tried to escape but were caught at 16th Street and Third Avenue. They were handcuffed and taken to the FBI New York field office.

The FBI found nothing incriminating on Gubitchev. Coplon had nothing incriminating on her person, but inside her purse, concealed in a sealed cellophane wrapper of an advertising circular, were copies of 34 top secret documents stolen from her office in Washington. These documents included a copy of the phony memorandum concerning the three FBI sources supposedly working for Amtorg. There was also a written note in her handwriting apologizing for not having been able to make a copy of the top secret list of Soviet agents operating in the United States.

Both Gubitchev and Coplon denied everything and charged that the documents had been planted by the FBI, but the evidence to the contrary was overwhelming. Coplon was convicted of espionage, and Gubitchev was declared persona non grata and deported.

During the trial, Coplon admitted that she was in love with Gubitchev and that the only obstacle to their happy union was that Gubitchev was already married. Coplon believed Gubitchev when he professed undying love for her and promised to divorce his wife and marry her. She was convinced of this, she maintained, because she knew that Gubitchev really loved only her. Coplon was released on bond, pending appeal of her conviction. While she was waiting for her appeal to be heard, she married her lawyer.

There were two trials of Coplon, one in New York and one in Washington, D.C. The New York conviction was reversed because Coplon had been arrested without a warrant. The District of Columbia conviction was remanded and subsequently reversed because conversations between Coplon and her attorney had been unlawfully monitored.

Coplon and her husband moved to suburban New York, where, at last report, she was a housewife.

Cook, Fred J. *The FBI Nobody Knows*. New York: Macmillan, 1964.

Whitehead, Don. *The FBI Story*. New York: Random House, 1956.

Pauline Cushman
United States
ca. 1835–ca. 1890

Pauline Cushman was a southern actress who hated slavery and supported the Union Army. She used her skills as an actress to charm southern officers into revealing troop movements and reported this information to the Union Army. When she was caught and imprisoned by the Confederates, she was freed by Union sympathizers and spent the rest of her stage career recounting her exploits as a spy.

Cushman, who was one-eighth Negro, was born circa 1835 in New Orleans. She grew up in the theater and became an actress herself. She hated slavery and was very strongly pro-North in the Civil War, yet she maintained a believable facade of empathy for the southern cause. Each evening at the end of her performance, she toasted "Jeff" Davis, the president of the Confederacy.

In May 1863, while performing in Nashville, Tennessee, several Union intelligence officers were so captivated by her ability to mimic people, that they offered her a job. They wanted Cushman to impersonate a southern belle and move to a town about 50 miles southwest of Nashville, called Shelbyville. After she had established her cover as a southern lady seeking respite from the war and had a chance to enter Shelbyville society, she was to report on the plans and activities of General Braxton Bragg, a Confederate troop commander operating in the Shelbyville area.

She was captured in June 1863, en route to her assignment, by the rebel raider, John Hunt Morgan, legendary Confederate cavalry officer. She managed to escape during a heavy rainstorm by tricking her guards. She was recaptured and sentenced to death. General Braxton Bragg, who used many spies in his own operations, was not moved by any feelings of southern chivalry and signed off on the final order to have her executed.

Union sympathizers stormed the jail where she was being held and convinced the Confederate authorities to free her. (The fact that Union troops were very close to

PAULINE CUSHMAN
Library of Congress

Shelbyville probably helped convince the Confederate authorities to free her.) The Union troops who were approaching Shelbyville were using information that had been provided by Cushman.

When she was released from prison she teamed up with the Union forces on the front lines. Her encyclopedic knowledge of the back roads and small towns in Tennessee, Georgia, Mississippi, and Alabama—gleaned from hundreds of one-night stands with her performing troupe of actors—helped her guide the troops unerringly over the rough country roads. This gave the Union troops the edge over the Confederate troops every time.

Cushman frequently put on an informal uniform of a major in the Union Army. After the war was over, she played the bur-lesque and vaudeville circuits of the nation dressed in this "patriotic" outfit and told her story about being a Union spy. She appeared at P. T. Barnum's Museum in New York City and toured California with a wild west show.

Her active life eventually caught up with her. She had severe arthritis and only a few friends toward the end of her life. She was working as a cleaning woman in a San Francisco boarding house when she died of a heart attack. The Women's Relief Corps of the Grand Army of the Republic donated money for her burial.

Rowan, Richard Wilmer, and Robert G. Deindorfer. *Secret Service: 33 Years of Espionage.* New York: Hawthorn Books, 1967.

Weiser, Marjorie P. K., and Jean S. Arbeiter. *Womanlist.* New York: Atheneum, 1981.

Lilia Ginsburg Dallin
(Lola Estrine, Paulson)
Latvia
1898–

Lilia Ginsburg Dallin was a remarkable woman who never lost her composure through a series of partial compromises and accusations when working for the Soviets as a provocation agent. She was the partner of a senior OGPU agent, Mark Zborowski, while he planned and carried out the assassination of Trotsky's son in Paris. Dallin denied that she knew anything about this murder.

Dallin was born in Liepaja, Latvia, in 1898 as Lola Ginsburg. In 1914, she moved to Moscow, where she studied law. In 1923, she emigrated to Berlin, where she married a man named Estrine, a Communist party functionary. They moved to Paris in 1933, but she always maintained her Soviet citizenship and renewed her Soviet passport regularly.

Mark Zborowski was born in the Ukraine on 21 January 1908 and became a Communist after the Bolshevik Revolution. He went to the University of Grenoble and, as he later testified before a U.S. congressional committee, became an agent of the OGPU while a student there.

In 1936, Zborowski was under cover in Paris as the administrative secretary of the Union for Repatriation to Russia. This union was an OGPU sting operation to lure émigré Russians, especially former czarist officers, back to the Soviet Union. The union also served as a ready reservoir of OGPU agents who could be dispatched from Paris to trouble spots. In reality, Zborowski was in charge of the union and all its activities and reported only to the case officer in the Soviet Embassy in Paris. Zborowski's principal task, in addition to luring Russians with czarist sympathies back to their deaths, was to infiltrate Trotskyite organizations and eradicate or dissuade all followers of Trotsky.

The headquarters of the Trotsky movement, The Fourth International, was operated in Paris by Trotsky's son, Lyova Sedov. The Fourth International published a magazine called *The Bulletin of the Opposition.* Zborowski had wormed his way into Sedov's confidence and won Sedov's loyalty. Zborowski was also a frequent contributor of anti-Stalin articles to *The Bulletin,* which served the purpose of solidifying his cover as a Trotskyite.

Not everyone in Paris and the Trotskyite movement was taken in by Zborowski. The wife (and soon to be widow) of Ignace Reiss warned Trotsky and his son not to trust Zborowski. Henryk Sneevilent, a Dutch Trotskyite, told everyone who would listen that there was an OGPU agent inside the Fourth International named Eitenne. "Eitenne" was the pen name Zborowski used for his articles and the name by which he was generally known among the members of Trotsky's Fourth International.

In late 1936, Trotsky's archives (all of the valuable research papers he was using to write a scathing biography of Stalin, his arch enemy) were transferred from Sedov's office to the International Institute of Social Studies in Paris. The clerk/secretary at the institute was Lola Estrine (later Dallin), who was also a frequent adviser to Sedov and a close personal friend of Mark Zborowski. The transfer was made at the insistence of Zborowski and Dallin, who argued that the papers would be safer at the institute.

On the night of 7 November 1936, thieves broke into the institute and stole Trotsky's papers. They knew exactly where to find them and did not touch the money or other valuables lying in plain sight. Zborowski was to admit later that he had set up the burglary for the OGPU. The French police said that the burglary had to have been done by people from outside of France because of the technique used. (Blow torches had been used to cut the iron bars on the windows. The OGPU allegedly chose November 7 for the burglary in order to make a present of Trotsky's papers to Josef Stalin on the anniversary of the Bolshevik Revolution.)

Dallin had helped Zborowski pack and move Trotsky's precious papers, but she categorically asserted Zborowski's lack of complicity in the theft, just as she swore to her own innocence. Their mutual protestations of innocence were viewed with suspicion by the members of the Fourth International. Dallin referred to herself and Zborowski as the "Siamese twins," meaning that neither would do anything without the other. Later, when Sedov was murdered, they vied in praising each other and in denying that either one of them had had anything to do with his death.

While she was working for Sedov as an unpaid volunteer, she and her husband lived in a small apartment that was always crowded with her relatives. There was her brother, Ralph Ginsburg, who professed to be a medical doctor but who didn't have a practice, and his wife, Fanny Trachtenberg, who also claimed to be a doctor. Dallin was also very friendly in Paris with the Sobelevicious brothers, known OGPU agents, who were identified years later in the United States as the famous Soviet spies Jack Soble and his brother Robert Soble.

In 1937, in Paris, Sedov, Trotsky's son, was seized with severe abdominal cramps. The persistence of the pain caused Dallin, who was helping Sedov's common-law wife, Jeanne Martin, care for Sedov, to call in her sister-in-law, Dr. Fanny Trachtenberg for a consultation. Trachtenberg diagnosed the pain as mild appendicitis. She put Sedov on a mild diet and he apparently recovered.

Inexplicably, a few days later, Sedov suffered a violent abdominal seizure. The next day, Dallin's brother, Dr. Ralph Ginsburg, examined Sedov. Drs. Trachtenberg and Ginsburg jointly recommended that Sedov be placed in the Mirabeau Clinic for an operation to remove his appendix. Dallin donated the money for Sedov's admission fee into the clinic.

The staff at this clinic was composed mostly of pro-Stalin Russians, but Zborowski told Jeanne Martin, Sedov's wife, that the Mirabeau Clinic had been chosen because it was unknown to the Soviets and it would be difficult for the them to find Sedov. Furthermore, Zborowski told Martin that to ensure his safety, Sedov had been registered in the clinic as "Martin," a French civil engineer. (Zborowski later testified before a U.S. congressional committee investigating Soviet espionage that he had told the OGPU in Paris where he was taking Sedov before Sedov was actually registered at the Mirabeau Clinic.) Dr. Trachtenberg testified before a French commission of inquiry into Sedov's death that she had chosen the Mirabeau Clinic because Zborowski had told her to send Sedov there. The clinic was, in fact, a hospital used almost exclusively by Russian émigrés who had been directed there by the Union for Repatriation to Russia.

Dr. Thalheimer, a surgeon at the clinic without any pro-Stalin sympathies, removed Sedov's appendix. He said that the appendix was normal and could not have been the cause of his severe stomach cramps. Sedov was recovering well after the operation when suddenly, he died in the early hours of 14 February 1938. The circumstances of his death were highly suspicious, and the consensus was that he had been murdered. Dr. Thalheimer testified that Sedov's death had to have resulted from a beating or from poisoning, either of which could produce internal hemorrhaging. There was never any judicial finding that determined who was responsible for Sedov's death. Both Dallin and Zborowski assured Trotsky by letter that they had had absolutely nothing to do with Sedov's death, despite prevalent rumors to the contrary.

Alexander Orlov, the former chief of the OGPU in Western Europe and a defector to the United States, who was an objective commentator about ongoing OGPU operations, wrote Trotsky a letter in which he warned Trotsky against Zborowski as an OGPU spy in Sedov's entourage. Dallin was in Mexico with Trotsky when he received Orlov's letter. She defended Zborowski and warned Trotsky not to believe Orlov. At the same time as Orlov's letter arrived, Trotsky received another letter warning him that Lilia Dallin was in Mexico for the specific purpose of poisoning him. Trotsky showed this letter to Dallin and she laughed it off, saying that the "enemy" wanted to bring suspicion on Trotsky's few remaining good friends, meaning herself and Zborowski.

Trotsky was eventually assassinated at his home in Mexico. Zborowski became a professor of anthropology at the University of California and died in the 1980s as a respected faculty member. (Zborowski did spend five years in a U.S. prison for perjury. He lied to the FBI about his former espionage career for the Soviets.) Dallin went on to lead a relatively normal life as the wife of an acclaimed author, David Dallin, author of the book *Soviet Espionage,* and became Lilia Dallin. When Lilia and David Dallin were living in the United States, they both acted as immigration sponsors for Zborowski, his wife Rivka (Regina), and their son, George. Both claimed that they never knew of Zborowski's life as an admitted OGPU agent

when they vouched for his entry into the United States.

Levine, Isaac Don. *Mind of an Assassin.* New York: Farrar, Straus & Cudahy, 1959.

Iva Toguri d'Aquino
United States
1915–

Iva Toguri d'Aquino was prosecuted as "the Tokyo Rose." Most people who lived through World War II assumed that Tokyo Rose was an American of Japanese ancestry who had defected to Japan and broadcasted propaganda to the U.S. troops in the Pacific Theater. Actually, Tokyo Rose was a composite of many English-speaking women. D'Aquino was prosecuted erroneously by the U.S. government as Tokyo Rose. The U.S. government later apologized to her.

In the beginning, the name Tokyo Rose was wholly a creation of Western journalists. The specific origin of the name cannot be traced. Many people were under the impression that the female Japanese propagandist, a traitorous American, signed off and on the broadcasts using the name Tokyo Rose, but this is not true. The GIs in the Pacific Theater came to refer to the many Japanese women who broadcasted propaganda over the radio at them as Tokyo Rose or Madame Tojo. Toward the end of the war, some of these women did sign off using the name Tokyo Rose after it was discovered to have such wide currency among the GIs.

The broadcasts, directed at GIs fighting in the Pacific and the China, Burma, and India theaters of war, were filled with propoganda designed to wreck their morale and exhorted them to desert or to murder their officers. The many voices of Tokyo Rose pleaded, cajoled, threatened, entreated, and begged the GIs to consider their plight at the battlefront and how they would soon be killed or, worse, too mutilated to ever be able to have sex again. She frequently suggested that the GIs would lose their genitals in the fighting or their ability to have sex after the

IVA TOGURI D'AQUINO
AP / Wide World Photos

war if they stayed in the heat and humidity of the Pacific.

The broadcasters not only called the GIs by their names, which had been culled from U.S. hometown newspapers, they also claimed that the sweethearts they had left behind were sleeping with the 4-Fs (those exempt from military service) and the servicemen who had the easy jobs back in the States. The major theme of the broadcasts was that the GIs doing the fighting were forgotten men, that nobody appreciated them or what they were trying to do to win the war. Therefore, since their plight was essentially hopeless, and because the Japanese superiority in men and war materials would eventually win the war, they might as well surrender and save their lives. The claims were so blatantly phony that they were amusing. Contrary to the Japanese intentions, Tokyo Rose was good for laughs and consequently good for GI morale.

Even though there was no one Tokyo Rose, after the war the Occupation Forces and the war correspondents claimed that they had found "the one" Tokyo Rose in postwar Japan in the person of d' Aquino. After a show trial in which she persistently proclaimed her innocence, and in which the "proof" of her participation in any broadcasts was dubious, she was convicted and sent to prison for five years. Throughout the trial, d'Aquino never wavered in her loyalty to the United States. She claimed that she was not guilty and that she had been railroaded by the powers of the federal bureaucracy and unscrupulous reporters, which may well have been true.

In San Francisco on 5 July 1949, the last World War II treason trial opened at the Federal District Court for the Northern District of California. In the only legal forum she had, d'Aquino, known for the record as Tokyo Rose, was the defendant. The trial lasted three months, and on September 27 she was found not guilty on seven counts and guilty on one. She served six years and two months before she was released on 28 January 1956.

The U.S. government brought deportation proceedings against d'Aquino as soon as she was released from prison. She fought the action, saying that she was a loyal U.S. citizen and wanted to remain in "her country." The government finally relented and dropped deportation proceedings on 10 July 1958. On 19 January 1977, President Gerald Ford, just as he was leaving office, signed an official pardon for her.

Duss, Masayo. *Tokyo Rose: Orphan of the Pacific.* New York: Kodansha International, 1979.

Lydia Darragh
United States
ca. 1750–ca. 1810

Lydia Darragh was a revolutionary patriot who helped General George Washington win the War of Independence. The British quartered troops in her home, allowing her to hear discussions of important war plans, which she then passed on to General Washington's officers. She may be the only female Quaker who has ever been expelled from the Society of Friends because of her espionage activities.

In 1777, Darragh lived with her husband, William, at 177 South Second Street in Philadelphia. Her house was across the street from the home of Captain John Cadwalter, who at the time was out of town fighting against the British with General Washington's Continental Army. The Cadwalter house had been commandeered by British General William Howe as his headquarters for the winter of 1777. Howe had also demanded the use of the parlor at Darragh's house for his staff meetings and private councils.

Darragh was mentally astute and courageous. She had one particularly outstanding quality: she remembered everything she heard and was unobtrusively tuned in to everything within range. She was able to overhear everything that went on in Howe's staff meetings in her front parlor. She then sent the information by her youngest son, John—who was 14 and above suspicion by the British soldiers guarding the ways in and out of Philadelphia—to his older brother,

Charles, who was a lieutenant with General Washington. Darragh's husband recorded the information on small scraps of paper in his special shorthand and she sewed the scraps into the cloth buttons on John's coat. John would then walk through the British lines to where Charles was encamped with General Washington's forces. Charles knew his father's shorthand and, after piecing the bits of scrap paper together like a jigsaw puzzle, he was able to decipher the message.

On 2 December 1777, Darragh overheard General Howe brief his staff commanders that they would march on the Continental Army on the night of December 4. She decided that this information was too important to entrust to a 14-year-old boy and decided to take the information directly to General Washington herself.

On December 3 she set out, ostensibly for the flour mill at Frankford, which was outside the city limits of Philadelphia and close to General Washington's headquarters. She arrived at Frankford just before noon. Frankford was loosely under the control of Washington's troops, but there were British military elements close enough to make it a no-man's-land.

Darragh left her sack with the miller and told him that she would call for it upon her return. She made her way directly to the Rising Sun Tavern, where she knew that Colonel Elias Boudinot, General Washington's informal intelligence chief, could be contacted. Boudinot protected the source of the information he received from Darragh by saying that he had accumulated it by questioning prisoners. By using Darragh's information, General Washington and the Continental Army were able to meet General Howe and to repulse the British Army. It was a clear victory for the Continental Army, which set the stage for the final defeat of the British.

Darragh continued to supply General Washington with vital intelligence information as long as the British remained in Philadelphia. On 18 June 1778, the British left Philadelphia, and Darragh retired from Washington's espionage service.

After the Revolutionary War, when Darragh's wartime activities became known,

the Society of Friends, whose members hold pacifist beliefs, expelled her, her husband, and her oldest son for having been too militant. John, her younger son, was not expelled because of his youth at the time of his participation.

Bakeless, John, and Katherine Bakeless. *Spies of the Revolution.* New York: Scholastic Book Service, 1959.

Weiser, Marjorie P. K., and Jean S. Arbeiter. *Womanlist.* New York: Atheneum, 1981.

Lise de Baissac
France
1910–

Lise de Baissac masqueraded as a widow seeking to be reunited with friends and relatives in order to spy against the Germans in Occupied France. She wandered about the country, mentally cataloging fortifications and troop dispersals. Her information on the coastal defenses was crucial for planning the Allied invasion on D-Day.

De Baissac was a plain woman, whose ordinary features were an asset as a spy in Occupied France. As a resistance fighter, she parachuted into France in the fall of 1942, accompanied by another agent. Her cover was that of an impoverished widow, still in mourning for her deceased husband; therefore, she was dressed in plain black, which added to her ability to remain inconspicuous.

Part of her cover for moving around the area was that she was collecting rock specimens and birds' eggs. She borrowed a bicycle from a local priest to help her get around faster. This cover and her unobtrusive appearance caused the Germans to ignore her for 11 months. During this time she was able to collect considerable valuable intelligence.

She told the story in later life of how a German soldier had tried to take away her bicycle. She grabbed it out of his hands with a savage jerk and berated him severely for attempting to steal her bicycle. Her furious attitude so stunned the soldier that he not only relinquished his hold on her bicycle, he also failed to notice the parts of her radio transmitter that had fallen to the ground from her clothes during the scuffle.

After D-Day, when Normandy was under the control of the Allied troops, she could proudly say that she had helped make the landing possible. Her reports, augmented by her detailed knowledge of the area, made the success of D-Day more probable.

Hoehling, A. A. *Women Who Spied.* New York: Dodd, Mead, 1967.

Charles Geneviere Louis Auguste Andre Timothee d'Eon de Beaumont

> (Chevalier D'Eon, Mademoiselle
> Lia de Beaumont)
> France
> ca. 1734–ca. 1780

Charles Geneviere Louis Auguste Andre Timothee d'Eon de Beaumont, Chevalier D'Eon, as he is more commonly known, is included in this work because, for the majority of his life, he was known as a woman and did his best espionage work as a woman. D'Eon was an accomplished female impersonator who worked as an agent in the French and Russian courts.

D'Eon was probably one of the most gifted female impersonators who ever lived and was a very competent spy when dressed as a woman. He first achieved notoriety as an espionage agent in 1755, when he made the perilous journey from Paris to St. Petersburg, Russia. He made the journey as a clandestine courier and emissary of Louis XV of France.

Rather than make the trip as a man and be subject to attack by highwaymen, he made it as a woman, hoping that the prevailing code of chivalry would protect him. However, the principal purpose of his female disguise was to keep France's enemies from learning that he was on an official mission to solicit Czarina Elizabeth's agreement to reopen diplomatic relations with France.

Louis XV of France wanted desperately to reopen diplomatic relations with Russia. His original emissary, Chevalier de Valcroissant, had been imprisoned in Russia at the behest of the British diplomats in St. Petersburg and charged with being a French spy. He was about to be executed when he was released. Many male couriers had tried to reach the czarina, but, because the regular business of the court was accomplished through bribery and corruption, they had been unsuccessful. The agents of King George II of England had arrived at the Russian court first and had generously bribed all officials who had any access to the czarina. These bribed officials wouldn't convey any messages to the czarina except those from or approved by the British envoys.

When he was a youngster, Chevalier D'Eon's mother had dressed him in a somewhat feminine fashion until he was seven years old. Dressing as a woman came naturally to him and he comported himself as a woman without any affectation. He was a handsome man of delicate airs and sensibilities. He took a doctor of law degree and became a fencing master. It is alleged that he even fought duels dressed as a woman.

D'Eon, traveling as Mademoiselle de Beaumont and dressed in the latest Parisian fashions, left for Russia with a male companion, Chevalier Douglas, whose cover was traveling to Russia "for his health." Douglas had a doctor's order that he must live for a while in a cold climate. D'Eon was alleged to be Douglas's niece. Douglas and D'Eon had tried out their charade at several parties before they left France and had been a social success. D'Eon had a high-pitched, melodious voice, which enhanced his female disguise. In disguise, he was described as reserved, shy, coquettish, and mysterious. There was always a problem of what should be done if a man became too attracted to D'Eon and had to be deterred or repulsed without causing attention. Some men were attracted, but, fortunately, didn't press their ardor too forcibly.

During the journey, D'Eon spent most of the time reading a book that had been given to "her" as a going away present, *L'Esprit des Lois.* The book obviously enthralled her, because she read it constantly, to the exclusion of all other diversions. Concealed within the book's binding was a letter from Louis XV to Czarina Elizabeth. The letter asked the czarina to enter into secret correspondence with him with a view toward reopening diplomatic relations between the two countries. A secret code was included for her and her anti-British, pro-French vice-chancellor when writing to Louis XV. This was a tricky situation for a novice spy, because the Russian court was a viper's nest of intrigue. The czarina was alleged to be pro-French and anti-British, but her chancellor was equally violently pro-British and anti-French.

When the duo reached St. Petersburg, Douglas found his way to the czarina very effectively blocked by the British-bribed courtiers around her. His "niece" managed to contact the anti-British vice-chancellor and found him amenable to reopening diplomatic relations with the French. It was the vice-chancellor who presented the beautiful Mademoiselle de Beaumont to Czarina Elizabeth.

The czarina was an old woman who indulged herself in every kind of instant gratification. She was constantly emulating the younger people of her court and delighted in youthful pleasures. It was a stroke of good fortune that Mademoiselle de Beaumont had come from the capital of fashion, Paris, and represented all that was stylish, youthful, exuberant, and outrageously "modern." The mademoiselle also was a new face to listen to all the czarina's tired old stories. Mademoiselle de Beaumont was appointed a maid of honor at the czarina's court before returning to Paris. "Her" spy mission to St. Petersburg had been a great success.

When D'Eon returned to Paris in 1757, he allegedly brought back a valuable document that was an exact copy of the testament left by Peter the Great to his descendants and successors to the Muscovite throne. This so-called "testament of Peter the Great" paints in broad strokes an alarmist picture of Russia's constant need for expansion. It is one of the great hoaxes of history but was considered valid intelligence at the time and was a genuine coup for D'Eon.

Several times after his Russian triumph, D'Eon had to use the female disguise to carry out other intelligence missions for France. Later, when he was out of favor with the French court, agents of the King of France persuaded him to blackmail the king with a threat of exposing some of his letters written while under the influence of the Parc aux Cerfs, which was a harem established for him by Madame de Pompadour.

Even in exile in England, D'Eon exerted influence favoring France in the American Revolution. He met John Wilkes, a flamboyant member of the British Parliament, who introduced him to Arthur Lee, who represented the American colonies in London. D'Eon introduced Lee to Caron de Beaumarchais, who was another secret agent of France at the British court in London. Lee and Beaumarchais schemed together to supply French arms and munitions to the American colonists to advance their revolution against the British crown.

When D'Eon returned to France from London in 1771, Marie Antoinette demanded that he put on feminine apparel. Thereafter, he wore feminine clothing exclusively. He called himself La Chevalière D'Eon.

McCormick, Donald. *The Master Book of Spies.* New York: Franklin Watts, 1976.

Peterson, Bonnie A., and Judith P. Zinsser. *A History of Their Own.* Volume II. New York: Harper & Row, 1988.

Weiser, Marjorie P. K., and Jean S. Arbeiter. *Womanlist.* New York: Atheneum, 1981.

Louise de Bettignies
(Alice Dubois)
Belgium
ca. 1880–1917

Louise de Bettignies was a nurse who, because she was appalled at German brutality during World War I, turned to espionage to fight against the Germans. Nevertheless, to honor her oath as a nurse, she continued to treat the German sick and wounded.

On 12 October 1914, the Belgian town of Lille capitulated after a devastating bombardment by the German artillery. The number of wounded on both sides needing immediate medical care quickly swamped the local hospitals, so private homes were commandeered by the Germans to house their wounded. Doctors, hospital staffs, and nurses were soon working around the clock, but the wounded continued to arrive. De Bettignies was one of the Red Cross nurses who was pressed into service as a surgical nurse. She was the seventh child of eight children born to Henri de Bettignies and his wife, Mabille de Poncheville. They were of aristocratic lineage and lived in St. Omer, Belgium.

De Bettignies had an uneventful childhood, but she displayed an early maturity and an intellect that promised great accomplishments. When she reached young womanhood, she cajoled her mother into allowing her to attend Oxford University in England. After she graduated from Oxford, she didn't know what to do with her education, because there were few opportunities in pre–World War I Belgium for a young woman with a higher education. She finally had to take work as a governess and remained a governess for ten years. She was very selective about her employers. For example, she would not accept a position as governess for the children of Archduke Ferdinand, heir to the Austrian-Hungarian throne. She could afford to be independent, because she had a small private income from her father's estate.

Her brother had become a priest, and when she returned to Belgium she vowed to renounce worldly things and become a nun. Wise administrators of the church advised her to wait. They counseled her that she was only 34 and should reflect on life a while before taking her religious vows. This enforced period of reflection was to everyone's advantage, except possibly the Germans', because it was during this waiting period that she decided to become a Red Cross nurse.

De Bettignies's knowledge of languages prompted the occupying Germans to press her into service as a translator. Seeing maimed bodies and dying young men moved this pacifist nurse to rebel against the Germans. In keeping with her introspective manner, her rebellion was quiet and self-contained.

She left the hospital, discarded her uniform, and became a plain country woman, determined to take a more active part against the inhumanity of the Germans' methods of warfare. She wandered around Belgium in her disguise for only a short time before she began to realize that what she was seeing, Belgium's allies could not see. She began to concentrate on scraps of information about the Germans and their activities that would be of value to the Allies. Her magnificent intellect enabled her to memorize most of the things she observed.

She went to her brother's church, still undecided about what she should do with the information that she had collected. Her brother agreed to help her get the information to the Allies. He suggested that, in her disguise as a peasant woman, she should join a small group of refugees who were exfiltrating Belgium. Her group went first to Ostend, Holland, where they were able to get a ferry for Folkstone, England.

She astounded the officials of British intelligence by saying that she wanted to return to the St. Omer area of France. She modestly told the British that she thought she could be of use there. She was asked, as part of her operations in France, to assist in hiding and exfiltrating young French and Belgian men of military age and escaped prisoners of war. If she were able to gather intelligence and operational support information, she was to send it on, but this was to be a secondary task.

The British trained her as best they could in codes, field expedient concealment devices, and tradecraft. De Bettignies even developed her own ingenuous concealment devices for hiding messages. She used balls of wool, children's toys, artificial limbs, spectacle rims, bars of chocolate, half-eaten sausages, and a host of other clever devices that completely fooled the Germans. She was assigned the pseudonym Alice Dubois, and her cover was a representative of a Dutch cereal company. She returned to Lille and set up her headquarters at her family home on rue d'Isly.

She quickly recruited agents who could help her hide and transport the escapees and young Belgian men of military age seeking to go to England. Her chief assistant was a like-minded, religious woman from the town of Roubaix, which was on the Belgium border, named Marie Leonie van Houtte. Van Houtte was assigned the pseudonym Charlotte.

Sometimes de Bettignies would travel as the representative of a homemade lace organization and van Houtte would travel as the saleswoman of a homemade dairy products group. The two of them made the journey into Holland, across hostile borders bristling with guards, at least once a week. They guided groups of exfiltrators out, SOE agents in, and picked up escapees on both journeys. One place where they had to cross the border required swimming across a canal. De Bettignies was a strong swimmer and had no problem, but van Houtte couldn't swim a stroke. They solved this problem by keeping an old kneading trough, that had been used by a Belgian baker, hidden under a bush at the side of the canal. Van Houtte would sit in this "boat," and de Bettignies would push her across.

Van Houtte, a well-known and respected member of the religious welfare community, was able to enlist helpers from one end of Belgium to the other; they saturated the area offering help to escapees and young men of military age. The entire organization worked well together and earned the respect and admiration of the populace. The entire operation became well known as Alice's Service, after de Bettignies's pseudonym.

De Bettignies's principal antagonist was the chief of the German army's counterintelligence service, Colonel Walter Nicolai. His assistant in the Lille area was Captain Hermann Himmel. Unbeknownst to de Bettignies or van Houtte, Himmel knew about each operation almost from its inception. He had tight surveillance on many of their agents and planned to use devious methods to stop the operation. Alice's Service was so successful that Captain Himmel decided to take drastic measures. The northeast area of France, around Lille, had been the "cradle of the resistance," and most of this fame was due to de Bettignies. Himmel started to cordon off a square mile area of Lille every night

to thoroughly search the area by ransacking every house; his men averaged about 100 houses per night.

(Among the agents in de Bettignies's net were two Lille engineers who developed a forerunner of the microdot for transmitting written messages. They were also able to reproduce personal identification documents that passed the German checkpoints as if genuine. One of the engineers and his wife published an underground anti-German newspaper that gave the Germans added incentive to capture them. The engineers became so adept at microdot, invisible ink, and microscopic engraving that they wrote entire messages on the inside of a rosary, on labels of cans and bottles, on cigarette papers, and on almost any small object. One of their unique methods of transmitting messages was to write the message on the inside of an artificial eye. The police soon became aware of this method and would shine their flashlights into a suspect's eyes to see if both pupils contracted. If one pupil did not contract, then it was an artificial eye and the wearer would be arrested and his eye minutely gone over for messages.)

One of de Bettignies's best agents for observing troop movements was Madame Elsie-Julie Leveugle, who lived in a château that overlooked the railroad yards of Lille. She would sit by her window knitting all day and far into the night, counting the railroad cars and troop carriers. She would tap her foot on the wooden floor for each car, and her son, sitting in the room beneath her, would keep count of the taps. At the end of the day's and night's activities, the son would take the tally to de Bettignies for inclusion in her regular letter to Allied intelligence.

De Bettignies's success, unfortunately, made her complacent. On 5 August 1915, Edith Cavell, a nurse in Belgium who had been smuggling escaped prisoners across the border, was arrested at her hospital in Brussels, the Depage Clinic. Cavell was executed on 12 October 1917 at Tir National, a former Belgian army rifle range.

About a month later, the Germans renewed their wrap-up operation and arrested van Houtte at the Hotel St. Jean in Brussels.

De Bettignies was in Holland when van Houtte received a strange message asking her to go to an isolated inn. She obeyed, and outside the inn was a German posing as a Belgian, who asked her many questions about her underground activities. She denied knowing anyone named Alice Dubois and was eventually allowed to return home.

Early the next morning, shortly after midnight, the Germans searched van Houtte's home and arrested her. A message was sent by other members of the net to de Bettignies, warning her not to come back, but she had already started home. The Germans knew when she returned home, and they watched her for several days, learning most of her operational contacts and routines.

On 19 October 1915, de Bettignies was arrested in Brussels and taken to St. Giles Prison. In the cell next to her was a Belgian girl, Gabrielle Petit. Petit's fiancé had been killed by the Germans, and she had tried to forget him by immersing herself in undercover work against the Germans.

Himmel had tried many counterintelligence tricks to capture the members of de Bettignies's net, but they had failed until he resurrected an old trick. He secretly put out the word that the plans for the German fortifications were for sale. He even hired a turncoat Frenchman to pose as the ostensible seller. Petit, thinking that she could engineer a coup against the Germans, fell for this trick and was arrested.

On 19 March 1916, the valiant de Bettignies was sentenced to death. Emperor Wilhelm, in a moment of gallantry, commuted her sentence to 25 years' imprisonment and van Houtte's to 15 years.

De Bettignies became ill due to the poor living conditions at the prison and was moved to the Women's Prison at Siegburg, near Cologne. She was not a model prisoner; she would not work at the German munitions plant, and she endured the hardship of prison without giving the Germans the benefit of seeing her suffering. She continued to suffer from the cold and dampness of the prison, and her condition worsened. Finally, she was removed to a hospital, where she was operated on for what the German doctors errone-ously diagnosed as pleurisy. The German doctors botched the operation (possibly on purpose), and de Bettignies died on 17 September 1917. The Belgians took de Bettignies and her bravery to their hearts, and she became a folk hero.

De Bettignies was posthumously awarded the Croix de Guerre. Marshal Foch, the supreme commander of the French forces, awarded her the Ordre de L'Armes. Probably the most fitting tribute came from an official of the British intelligence service who said:

> Through her we learned with a precision, a regularity and rapidity that was never surpassed by any other organization all the movements of the enemy, the exact position of their batteries and 1000 details that were of great help to our headquarters. . . . we admired, almost revered this young French girl. We adored her.

(See also Edith Cavell.)

Editors of Army Times. *Heroes of the Resistance.* New York: Dodd, Mead, 1967.

Hoehling, A. A. *Women Who Spied.* New York: Dodd, Mead, 1967.

Andree de Jongh
(Postman)
Belgium
1916–

Andree de Jongh began her espionage operations by helping downed Allied airmen escape from Belgium and then enlarged her operation to collect intelligence. She was captured by the Germans but escaped execution because her records were lost by prison mismanagement.

De Jongh was born in Brussels, where her father was a schoolmaster and her mother was a housekeeper. Before World War II, she trained as a nurse. When the war came, she was working in a hospital with wounded British soldiers. She quickly gathered a group of friends who also pitied the wounded British soldiers who were in a hospital commandeered by the enemy.

She began helping downed airmen and escaping soldiers who were trying to return to England. She instituted her exfiltration operations without any assistance from Allied headquarters. Her friends helped her collect intelligence information about the movement of German troops, numbers of tanks, planes on an airfield, and their dispersion under camouflage. They reported everything else that a sharp-eyed civilian could find out about the German occupiers. She soon had an extensive network of reliable reporting agents.

In August 1941, she escorted an escaping British soldier, and two Belgian men who were trying to escape and join the Free Belgium Forces being created in England, across the Pyrenees to Bilbao, Spain. She left France and, with the help of a Basque guide, led her group over some of the roughest country in the Pyrenees.

She contacted the British consul in Bilbao, who was surprised that such a frail-looking young woman could have led the group over such rugged country. She proposed to the British consulate that, in return for some money—to be used for bribes and supplies for her intelligence network—she would continue to bring out downed Allied airmen. She told the British Consulate that her father was a partner in the operation and therefore they shouldn't be concerned that such a young woman was in charge of the operation. She told the consular officer that her headquarters was located in her home.

The British consul asked de Jongh what the cost would be to arrange the exfiltration of a downed airman from Belgium. She estimated that the cost would be 6,000 Belgian francs to bring the airman to the foot of the Pyrenees in France and another 1,400 Spanish pesetas for the Basque guide. De Jongh knew that the consul would have to submit her proposal to his superiors, so she told him that she would return with another group of escapees in three or four weeks and would expect his answer then. The consul's caution in approving her proposal was prompted by good operational security. The Gestapo were always attempting to penetrate such an escape organization.

When de Jongh appeared as promised with another group, she was debriefed by a British intelligence officer from the MI-9 section, who came from the British Embassy in Madrid. This officer agreed to pay her direct expenses for moving the escapees. De Jongh continued to successfully deliver several Allied flight crews across the mountains to the British authorities in Spain. The suspicion that she might be a Gestapo penetrator subsided, despite her insistence on being paid, as she continued to deliver escapees. She was given the code name Postman, because she delivered the goods.

In February 1942, the Gestapo became suspicious of her and arrested her sister. On April 30, her father narrowly escaped arrest but was able to flee to Paris, where he continued to direct part of the exfiltration operation. However, six days later, the remaining top three men in the organization were arrested by the Gestapo, which closed down the original operation.

De Jongh was able to join her father in Paris, where they regrouped and were able to continue their mission with phenomenal success. Unfortunately, the very success of their operation again brought them to the attention of the Gestapo. De Jongh was arrested by the Gestapo on 15 January 1943 in a concentrated roundup of more than 100 people from across Belgium and France. She was sent to a Gestapo concentration camp, where her luck returned. Her identity papers were lost in the German bureaucracy, and she survived the war. She was still alive and living in Brussels when last heard from.

Neave, Airey. *The Escape Room*. New York: Doubleday, 1970.

Baroness de Kaulla
Prussia
ca. 1850–ca. 1910

Baroness de Kaulla was recruited by the Germans to carry on an affair with the French minister of war during the Franco-Prussian War. She became the minister's confidant and easily passed on France's plans for the upcoming war against Germany. When her position was revealed, she was deported, but her Jewish heritage fueled anti-Semitic sentiment in France and led to the arrest of a high-ranking Jewish-French officer.

In the Franco-Prussian War of 1870, French General de Cissey had been taken prisoner by the Germans. Unlike ordinary soldiers, who were taken as prisoners of war and confined to a cell, the rules of war at that time required a certain amount of gentlemanly conduct toward captured officers. General de Cissey was given the use of a small villa with minimal staff but with a well-stocked larder and wine cellar. He was also given freedom to move about without restraint as long as he gave "his word as a gentleman" that he would not try to escape. He used this freedom and was a sought-after guest at balls and parties, even though he was an enemy officer. It was at one such party that he met Baroness de Kaulla. The two became immediate friends, and it wasn't long before they were lovers.

De Kaulla was young and beautiful, and the general found her irresistible. He spent the remainder of his time in this "prison" in her company. When hostilities ceased, the general was repatriated, he returned to his wife, and his friendship with the baroness became dormant. When intelligence reached the German general staff that France was contemplating rearming to seek revenge against Germany for their defeat in the war, the German chief of intelligence, Wilhelm Stieber, was aware of the baroness's previous intimacy with General de Cissey. He asked her if she would be willing to go to Paris, renew her relationship with the general (who had become France's minister of war), and send back any information she acquired about the French intentions and capabilities. Stieber put his request to the baroness on purely patriotic principles, and she readily agreed to the plan.

Stieber supplied her with a fully staffed apartment in Paris, a new wardrobe, and a generous allowance. A few days after she was comfortably installed in her new apartment, she sent a discreet message by her butler to the general, suggesting that she would be delighted to renew their old relationship. He replied with alacrity and resumed his old position in her life.

De Cissey, with all of the burdens of his position as France's minister of war, found solace, consolation, and reinvigoration with the baroness. Despite the fact that his wife and family were in Paris, he spent most of his time away from the office with the baroness. After an all-night session of the French cabinet, he would hurry to have breakfast with her. He was more to blame for the resulting scandal than she was, because he talked to her, unprovoked, about affairs of state. Such conduct didn't go unnoticed in the exclusive circles of Parisian society. The French counterintelligence service became aware of the potential problem that the baroness might pose for French security and took action.

It was common knowledge that France was rearming for war with Germany and, depending upon the state of the preparations, everyone knew that the conflict might erupt at any time. The French counterintelligence service also knew that General de Cissey was the principal planner and strategist for the war, so they acted quickly. They deported de Kaulla, over the general's strenuous objections. The damage, however, had already been done. De Kaulla had been able to supply the German general staff with most of the salient features of France's mobilization and defense plans.

De Kaulla was Jewish, and her notoriety nourished anti-Semitism in France. This extreme prejudice, fostered by the French fear of a resurgent Germany, ultimately culminated in the arrest of the Jewish-French officer, Alfred Dreyfus.

Rowan, Richard Wilmer, and Robert G. Deindorfer. *Secret Service: 33 Years of Espionage.* New York: Hawthorn Books, 1967.

Louise de Keroualle
France
1649–1734

Louise de Keroualle was a spy who worked hard for her rewards and was one of the few

LOUISE DE KEROUALLE
Portrait by P. Mignard (1682), National Gallery, London

spies who became wealthy through her work. Two kings paid this astute woman handsomely to be not only a good spy but also a mistress.

In 1681, de Keroualle worked for Louis XIV of France as an espionage agent against the King of England, Charles II. De Keroualle went to England initially not to spy but to convince Charles II to capitulate to France. She charmed Charles II into reluctantly agreeing to the odious terms of the Treaty of Dover as part of the price that he would have to pay to have her remain with him in England.

She cleverly worked for both rulers and was well paid. The King of France gave her money and jewelry and, as the mistress of the King of England, she received money, jewelry, and property. Not only was she paid an estimated equivalent of $3 million, she also was elevated by King Charles to the nobility as the Duchess of Portsmouth for her service to the British crown. The King of France saw fit to match that gift by making her the Duchess of Aubigny for her services to the French crown.

Her divided loyalty was also a battle for souls. While Charles II was trying to keep de Keroualle as his lover, Louis XIV was equally dedicated to keeping her as his companion and to winning Protestant Charles II over to Catholic France and bringing him into the "true Church." The cost of making de Keroualle happy and giving her the opportunity to spy on him was enormous for King Charles II: he had to abandon the Triple Alliance and declare war upon the Dutch. He must have realized that this brazen beauty from France owed her fundamental loyalty to France, but he did everything he could to make her happy and keep her by his side in England.

De Keroualle died impoverished, because Charles II's successors, Queen Mary and King William, stopped her pension.

Peterson, Bonnie A., and Judith P. Zinsser. *A History of Their Own*. Volume II. New York: Harper & Row, 1988.

Rowan, Richard Wilmer, and Robert G. Deindorfer. *Secret Service: 33 Years of Espionage*. New York: Hawthorn Books, 1967.

Countess Roberta de Mauduit
United States
ca. 1910–

Roberta de Mauduit was an American who married a Frenchman. During World War II she lived in a castle to which downed Allied airmen were naturally drawn. She arranged one of the most extensive rat lines out of Occupied France, enabling Allied airmen to return to Britain, from where they could fly again against the Germans.

Countess de Mauduit was born in the United States and married the Count de Mauduit before the war. She had been living in France for some time when World War II began. She and her husband lived in his ancestral home in the Côtes-du-Nord area near the English Channel. As soon as the war started, her husband left France by fishing boat for Britain, where he joined the Free French Forces of General Charles de Gaulle.

De Mauduit made her castle available to the French Resistance fighters. This gave them a safe place to store their ammunition and radio spare parts. They also used her castle as a rendezvous point, but—in the interests of good security and protecting de Mauduit—they never transmitted from her castle. De Mauduit also used her castle as a station on the rat-line out of France for downed Allied airmen and escaped POWs on their way back to Britain.

The Gestapo's suspicions of de Mauduit eventually resulted in her arrest. When she was arrested, there were five U.S. airmen hiding in the double floor of her castle's attic. They were not discovered by the Gestapo troops that arrested her, and eventually all escaped back to Britain.

De Mauduit spent two years in prison, until she was freed by the end of the war. For her actions during the war, she was highly decorated. She received the George Cross from England and the American Medal of Honor from the U.S. government.

Hoehling, A. A. *Women Who Spied.* New York: Dodd, Mead, 1967.

Nymph Roussel de Preville
France
1786–ca. 1835

Unbeknownst to her mother, who was a spy in the same espionage network, Nymph Roussel de Preville became a spy for the British, who were actively working against Napoleon in France. She dressed as a man to escape detection during her work as a messenger for the British.

When Napoleon sought to impose a blockade on Britain, there were many on both sides of the English Channel who breached it constantly and with impunity. Helping them were a number of priests in France, whose Royalist sympathies made them covert allies of the British. One of the most effective of these Royalist clerics was Abbé Leclerc, who was known as Boisualon.

From a house in the rue du Pot-de-Fer, Abbé Leclerc directed a large number of subagents. One of his most trusted agents was Madame de Preville, the widow of a captain in the Royal Navy and a well-connected member of Boulogne society. Among her children was Mademoiselle de Preville, who was 18 in 1804. Mademoiselle de Preville was, by all reports, a lovely young woman who looked the opposite of the stereotypical espionage agent; therefore, she would probably confound any secret service agent who was looking for someone who looked like a spy.

De Preville was devoted to the Royalist counterrevolutionary movement and offered her services to Abbé Leclerc without her mother knowing it. Leclerc encouraged her to choose the disguise of a young man when she was acting as a courier. She easily passed as a handsome young man, operating under the code name Dubuisson. She was fortunate and always got through with the messages she carried. Many times she took risks that made her journeys more dangerous, but she always managed to complete her assignments. She was so successful that she was promoted to paymaster for several subagents who were assigned to work for her.

When Napoleon's secret police were getting close to Abbé Leclerc and his operations, Leclerc went underground and took refuge in the home of one of his agents. De Preville went into hiding with him. The secret police raided the home where they were hiding, but Leclerc and "the boy Dubuisson" could not be found. Mademoiselle de Preville had disappeared. A year later, she was sentenced to death for espionage *in absentia* by Napoleon's military commission. In the meantime, she had traveled across Europe to Russia and eventually to England. In London, the grateful British government gave her an annual pension of 600 francs for her work against Napoleon.

Rowan, Richard Wilmer, and Robert G. Deindorfer. *Secret Service: 33 Years of Espionage.* New York: Hawthorn Books, 1967.

Edwige de Saint-Wexel
France
1923–

Edwige de Saint-Wexel is revered among the survivors of German brutality because she was tortured beyond belief, yet she defied the Germans and eventually emerged victorious. She set a standard for resistance to torture.

In 1940, when she was 17, de Saint-Wexel was arrested by the Germans. The Germans had invaded and occupied her home area of northern France, and she was determined that they should not prevail, so she joined a student protest in November 1940 at the Arc de Triomphe in Paris. Even though the demonstration was nonviolent, she was singled out by the Gestapo and arrested.

She was beaten, burned, and tortured to an abnormal degree, even by Gestapo standards. She was placed in solitary confinement for three months. Even though she had a dislocated ankle from the beatings, she was not given any medical treatment while she was in solitary. She was starved and not permitted to bathe, which increased the torment of fleas and lice on her body and in her wounds. Her treatment was barbaric, but she persevered and was at least alive when she was released.

When she was allowed her freedom, she was filthy, crippled, and dressed in rags. Her release was intended to show the populace the folly of resistance and what a terrible fate awaited anyone who opposed the Nazis.

After her release, she joined a small resistance group. She was not only courageous but was also determined not to allow the Nazis to prevent her from fighting for her homeland's freedom. In her new capacity she definitely risked recapture by the Gestapo. Throughout the remaining years of the war, she and her small group of resistance fighters worked to help Jews and Allied pilots escape from Occupied France back to England. They were able to collect considerable intelligence on German occupation troops in France, information which they sent to Allied headquarters in London.

Fortune, plus an uncanny sense of survival, allowed her to escape rearrest. After the war, she became a banking executive in Paris.

Peterson, Bonnie A., and Judith P. Zinsser. *A History of Their Own.* Volume II. New York: Harper & Row, 1988.

Maria Kretschmann de Victorica

(Miss Clark, Maria de Vussiere)
Argentina
1882–1920

Maria Kretschmann de Victorica married a Chilean and used her neutral Chilean status during World War I to move about freely in the United States. She fooled U.S. counterintelligence and established an extensive German espionage network.

De Victorica was born Maria Kretschmann in 1882 in Buenos Aires, Argentina. Her father had fought in the Franco-Prussian War, and her mother was of the German nobility. After the war, the family moved to Argentina, where her father operated a profitable import-export business. In her late teens, she left Buenos Aires for Germany to continue her education. She attended the University of Heidelberg and the universities of Berlin and Zurich.

During her school days in Germany, she became acquainted with Colonel Nicolai, one of the ranking officers of German intelligence. The colonel knew of her through her parents' connections in German governmental circles. She was an accomplished linguist who could speak several languages fluently, which also piqued the colonel's interest.

She married Jose de Victorica of Chile in November 1914 at a private ceremony at the Chilean Embassy in Berlin. The best man and most of the guests at the wedding party were members of the German intelligence service. The marriage was short-lived, because Jose disappeared immediately after the wedding and was never heard from or seen again. There was speculation that Colonel Nicolai had arranged the marriage so that Victorica would have the citizenship of a neutral country to enable her to travel freely on her espionage duties during the war that everyone knew was coming.

As a citizen of Chile, de Victorica was free to travel to the British Isles. She settled in Ireland, where she instituted a subtle campaign to have the Irish nationalists revolt against British rule. Her campaign also encouraged dissident Irish to enlist in the British armed forces, where they would carry on, with even greater intensity, their revolt against Britain by placing bombs in the holds of ships and by pouring acid into machinery.

De Victorica may have been one of the instigators of the rebellion on Easter Sunday 1916, when the Irish Republican Brotherhood staged an armed uprising against the British troops in Dublin. She may also have taken part in the sabotage of Lord Kitchener's ship when it embarked from Ireland on a secret mission to Russia. Kitchener was Britain's secretary of war, and his ship, the *HMS Hampshire,* was lost off the Orkney Islands with only 12 survivors. Sabotage was suspected because there had been no storm or other natural reason for his ship to go down.

As World War I dragged on and the entry of the United States became more of a possibility, the German general staff knew they would have to close their diplomatic outpost in Washington. It was, therefore, important to German intelligence to immediately establish a listening and reporting post in the United States. De Victorica, by now an experienced agent, and another veteran agent, Carl Rodiger, under the cover name of Lieutenant Commander Herman Wessels, allegedly of the U.S. Navy, were assigned to Washington, D.C. Their tasks were to monitor South American relations with the United States, especially U.S. relations with Mexico; sabotage U.S. war industries and ships; and report on political events in the United States that would effect Germany. They arrived in New York on 21 January 1917.

In November 1917, the U.S. government belatedly received word from London that an agent of the German government had slipped out of Madrid to deliver $10,000 to someone on Long Island. They had two addresses that might be those of the recipients of the money. When U.S. counterintelligence agents checked the two addresses, they found them abandoned and the former occupants untraceable.

On a last-ditch hope, the U.S. agents staked out the addresses. They finally intercepted two letters, which appeared to have been switched and placed in the wrong envelopes. They were able to trace the letters to a steward from a European steamship, who admitted that he had switched the letters inadvertently. He told the investigators that he had carried the letters in his shoe all the way from Europe and that when he got ready to mail them, he discovered that they were dirty and wrinkled. He put them in new envelopes to mail them and probably switched letters in the process.

U.S. authorities eventually traced the letters to de Victorica. They found that she had been staying at the Knickerbocker Hotel in New York City, where she had registered in January 1917, but she had left long before the agents got on her trail. Another lead,

from a source in London, reported that she had collected $35,000 from a German businessman in New York. On 14 February 1917, de Victorica had received $35,000 from a German exporter who had an office in New York City. German intelligence had arranged payment of de Victorica's operational expenses from several German-owned firms that had been established in the United States by German intelligence many years earlier for the explicit purpose of providing support for operations such as hers.

On 3 February 1917, diplomatic relations between Germany and the United States were terminated, as had been expected. De Victorica knew that this gave another dimension to her status as a spy. Her mission, which had been to be a listening post, had changed to active participation in espionage and sabotage. Her second concern was that, as a spy captured in enemy territory during wartime, she would be subject to execution.

She had adopted the alias of Miss Clark and changed residences in an attempt to preserve her security. German intelligence continued to send her copious messages in low-grade cipher and secret ink. They were apparently unaware of the skills and talents of Herbert O. Yardley, the foremost expert in decoding and developing secret writing in the United States. Yardley was ultimately able to unravel the secrets in the ciphers and develop the secret inks to reveal de Victorica's identity.

As time went on, de Victorica started to take greater precautions to preserve her security. She moved out of New York to the Hotel Nassau on Long Beach, Long Island. About this time, she hired an Irish woman, Margaret Sullivan, as a helper. Sullivan had lived in the United States for more than 25 years, although she still thought of herself as an Irish patriot and was ready to help de Victorica fight the British.

One of de Victorica's accomplices, Turkish-born Despina Storch, was arrested by the U.S. counterintelligence service. While she was in prison on Ellis Island, she bit the poison capsule that she had concealed inside her body and committed suicide. Before she died, she named de Victorica as her superior in the spy ring. U.S. authorities were then able to follow a young blonde, whom Storch had identified as the agent who carried the payroll for de Victorica.

The young woman was followed to St. Patrick's Cathedral, where she was observed kneeling as if in prayer. When she left, she left behind in the pew a folded newspaper. Next, a man entered the cathedral and took the same seat. He deposited his empty newspaper in the pew and took with him the newspaper that the woman had left. He took the newspaper with him when he rode by a taxi, a train, and another taxi to the Hotel Nassau. There he pretended to forget his newspaper when he left his seat in the lobby. A short time later, a plump, blonde woman collected the newspaper that he had "forgotten" and left a similarly folded newspaper in its place. The newspaper contained $20,000 that had been smuggled into the United States from the German Embassy in Mexico City for de Victorica's operational expenses.

On 27 April 1918, de Victorica was arrested. In her room, U.S. agents found the money and a silk scarf imprinted with the German's top secret "F" ink for secret writing. De Victorica and other members of her net were charged with espionage in time of war. She spent the last five months of World War I in Bellevue Hospital. Her health failed rapidly; some claimed that she was taking small amounts of poison in an attempt to foil her executioner. She was a drug addict at the time of her arrest, which would have increased the damages to her health of any poison.

After the armistice, de Victorica was released under a $5,000 bond and, having no place to go in the United States, she accepted the residence offered by the Sisters of Charity, a Catholic order of nuns. She lived with them for two years until she contracted pneumonia and was removed from the convent to Dr. Maluk's Sanitarium. She died there on 12 August 1920. Her remains were buried at the Gate of Heaven Cemetery in Hawthorne in Westchester County, New York.

A rumor sprang up after her death that she was "the beautiful blonde of Antwerp," that is, the famous Elsbeth Schragmuller. De Victorica probably did receive some training in tradecraft techniques from Schragmuller, but she was not "the beautiful blonde of Antwerp."

(See also Elsbeth Schragmuller.)

Franklin, Charles. *The Great Spies.* New York: Hart Publishing, 1967.

Ind, Allison, Colonel. *A Short History of Espionage.* New York: David McKay, 1963.

Delilah
Philistia
ca. 1150 B.C.–ca. 1100 B.C.

Delilah was a dedicated spy for the Philistines against the Israelites and is most famous for discovering the source of Samson's phenomenal strength and for destroying that strength.

Samson, an Israelite, was born to a woman who had been promised by Jehovah's angel that her son would help free the Israelites from the oppression of the Philistines. Samson did became a very strong man who performed great feats.

Even though the Philistines were the enemy, Samson married a Philistine woman. At the wedding feast, he gave the Philistines a riddle. If they arrived at the correct answer, he would give them 30 sheets and 30 changes of clothes. If they could not answer the riddle, they would have to give him 30 sheets and 30 changes of clothes. The riddle was exceedingly difficult, so the Philistines went to Samson's wife—who was, after all, one of them—and demanded that she get the answer to the riddle from Samson. They threatened reprisals against her family if she didn't get the answer.

Using all of her cajoling powers, Samson's wife succeeded in wheedling the answer out of him. When the Philistines gave their answer, Samson was astounded and realized that he had been swindled, and— what made it worse—his own wife had betrayed him. He became so angry that he killed 30 of the Philistines to get the 30 changes of clothes to settle the wager and deserted his wife.

After a while, when Samson attempted to reclaim his wife, he learned that her father had given her to be the mistress of another man. Samson took revenge by causing great damage to the Philistine's crops and possessions. The Philistines then killed the father and daughter, Samson swore revenge and killed many Philistines, and then went into hiding.

The men of Judah didn't want to have the vengeance of the Philistines brought upon them, so they captured Samson themselves. They bound him with rope and delivered him to the Philistines. When he was turned over, he broke his bonds and slew a thousand men with the jawbone of an ass.

After a while, Samson took Delilah, a woman from the valley of Sorek, as his lover. The Philistines instructed Delilah to spy upon Samson to learn the secret of his great strength. Samson realized Delilah's intention when she repeatedly asked how he might be subdued, but out of vanity or a false sense of his own ability to withstand temptation, he did not perceive her as a real threat.

After Samson gave her three false answers, she said, "How can you say, 'I love you,' when your heart is not with me? You have mocked me these three times, and you have not told me wherein your great strength lies" (Judges 16:15). Finally, Samson told her that the secret of his great strength was his long hair. Delilah then made him sleep on her knees and called a man to shave off Samson's hair. He was, indeed, weakened, and the Philistines put him in prison.

For successfully completing her mission, Delilah received 1,100 pieces of silver that the Philistines had promised her.

Azimov, Isaac. *Guide to the Bible.* New York: Avenal Books, 1981.

Blaikie, William G. *A Manual of Bible History.* New York: Ronald Press, 1940.

Rowan, Richard Wilmer, and Robert G. Deindorfer. *Secret Service: 33 Years of Espionage.* New York: Hawthorn Books, 1967.

Velvalee Malvena Blucher Dickinson
United States
1893–?

Velvalee Malvena Blucher Dickinson's affinity for Japanese culture led her to work for the

VELVALEE DICKINSON
Federal Bureau of Investigation

Japanese as a spy. Her lifelong love of dolls was used as cover for her spying activities.

Dickinson was born in Sacramento, California, in 1893 to a wealthy couple from an old southern family. Her father was from West Virginia, and her mother was originally from Kentucky. She graduated from Sacramento High School in June 1911 and from Leland Stanford University with a Bachelor of Arts degree in 1917. She went to work in a combination bank and brokerage house in California, where she handled the accounts of many Japanese produce wholesalers. Her good looks attracted many customers to the brokerage house.

The owner of the brokerage house, Lee Taylor Dickinson, was equally attracted to her. They were married shortly after she went to work for him. This was her third marriage. (The identities of her two former husbands are not known. There is also evidence that she had many lovers between and during her marriages.)

The produce business boomed, and Dickinson opened a branch brokerage office in California's Imperial Valley in the early 1930s. Most of his clients were Japanese truck farmers. Through their Japanese clients, both Dickinsons became very friendly with the Japanese consul and military attaché of the Japanese Consulate in San Francisco. To help create goodwill with their Japanese clients, they joined the Japanese-American Society. Dickinson's interest in the Japanese community prompted her U.S. occidental neighbors to call her a "Jap lover."

When the husband's brokerage firm failed in the depression of 1935, he worked for a while for the California State Emergency Relief Administration and then with the County Welfare Department as a social worker. Regardless of how hard her husband tried to find a job and how much she tried to work for both of them, things weren't working out for them in California, so they moved to New York.

There is no firm evidence that the Dickinsons moved to New York at the behest of Japanese intelligence. The move may have been orchestrated by the Japanese intelligence service to place the Dickinsons into an existing East Coast Japanese espionage network around Washington. Alternatively, they may have been the nucleus around which the Japanese intelligence service intended to build an espionage network on the eastern seaboard.

In 1937, they moved to New York and rented a room in a second-class hotel on West 11th Street near Washington Square, which was all that they could afford. In December of that year, luck started to come to them when Dickinson got an $18 a week job selling dolls at Bloomingdale's. Dickinson had had a fondness for dolls since childhood, and as she grew older, the fascination remained as a hobby. After a short time at Bloomingdale's learning the business aspects of dealing in dolls, she opened her own doll store in her apartment at 680 Madison Avenue. Her business was an instant success, and a short time later she moved into larger quarters at 718 Madison Avenue. She became a recognized expert on dolls and was consulted on matters concerning dolls and their proper attire. She had many movie stars and society women as her clients.

She reestablished her association with the official Japanese community on the East Coast and became especially friendly with Kaname Wakasugi, the Japanese consul general in New York, and Tchira Yokoyama, the naval attaché in the Japanese Embassy in Washington. She joined the Japanese Institute in New York and socialized at the Nippon Club. Dickinson often dressed in traditional Japanese attire. When she did, her diminutive figure helped create the illusion that she was, in fact, a Japanese woman.

After Pearl Harbor, in December 1941, the Japanese officials that she had been friendly with were expatriated. Many of Dickinson's other Japanese friends were either interned or under surveillance by U.S. authorities.

During the first six months of 1942, Dickinson and her husband traveled to the West Coast, back to New York, and then to Seattle and Oakland. They spent $100 bills for all of their travel expenses and seemed to have an inexhaustible supply of the bank notes. The Japanese intelligence service had funded the Dickinsons from the Japanese consulate office in New York before it was closed. Dickinson never cooperated with U.S. authorities to reveal her financial arrangements with the Japanese intelligence service nor to reveal her communications systems for transmitting reports. The only transmittal system known to have been used by her was an ill-conceived mail dead drop in Argentina that used an open code. Either the Japanese service didn't consider her information important enough to warrant a higher-grade communication system or they just didn't have the staff in the United States to instruct her in a better code and to give it the necessary support.

About this time, the FBI began receiving complaints from U.S. women that undelivered mail was being returned to them. Supposedly, they had written the letters, but actually, they had not. All of the letters had been sent to a Senora Inez Lopez de Malinali, 2563 O'Higgins Street, Buenos Aires, Argentina.

The odd thing about these letters, ostensibly sent by many different women, was that they all contained references to personal matters that were true for each woman. Furthermore, they all had reasonable facsimiles of each woman's signature. The contents of each letter dealt with personal matters, everyday events, bills to be paid, and normal household routines. The only factor common to all the women who had received these returned letters was that each had at one time been a customer of Dickinson's doll shop or had corresponded with her about dolls. All of the letters had been written on the same typewriter, using an open code to transmit military information. U.S. cryptographers were able to break this code in a matter of minutes. The FBI knew that the author of these letters was Dickinson but, rather than arrest her, they preferred to let her lead them to other members of the net.

In March 1943, her husband had a fatal heart attack. On 21 January 1944, the FBI, confident that they had identified all of Dickinson's accomplices, arrested her after she tried to resist the agents. When they finally handcuffed her, they found $15,940 in her safety deposit box in $100 bills, all of which could be traced to the Yokohama Specie Bank in New York. This was part of the more than $50,000 that the Japanese had paid her for espionage against the United States.

Dickinson was indicted for espionage and for violating censorship laws. The charge of espionage was dropped, but she was convicted of violating censorship laws. On 14 August 1944, she was sentenced to ten years in prison and given a $10,000 fine. She served her time in the Reformatory for Women in Alderson, West Virginia. She was paroled, with time off for good behavior, on 23 April 1951.

After her last mandatory report to the U.S. probation officer in New York on 13 February 1954, she disappeared. Her present whereabouts, if she is still living, are unknown.

Rowan, Richard Wilmer, and Robert G. Deindorfer. *Secret Service: 33 Years of Espionage.* New York: Hawthorn Books, 1967.

E

Amelia Earhart
United States
ca. 1908–ca. 1937

Amelia Earhart was a famous aviator who held many records for flight endurance and air performance before she tried to become the first woman to fly around the world. She captured the hearts of the American public with her daring and fortitude. She flew across the Pacific under circumstances that made the Japanese suspect that she was spying. There has never been proof that she was spying, but it was a serious charge at the time.

Earhart's case has provided the tabloids with more sensational reportage than any other aviation mystery. As late as March 1992, a "scientific" expedition alleged that it had found a piece of aluminum from Earhart's plane and one of her shoes on an atoll in the Pacific. This assertion was just as quickly debunked the following day by the manufacturers of Earhart's plane, who denied categorically that the piece of aluminum could have come from the plane that they had fabricated for her flight.

Earhart took off on the Pacific part of her round-the-world flight from Lae, New Guinea, on 2 July 1937. She planned to fly the 2,556 miles across empty ocean to Howland Island in the central Pacific. She was accompanied by her navigator, Fred Noonan. Somewhere over the Pacific, they disappeared.

The Japanese alleged that the Pacific portion of Earhart's flight was a purposeful overflight of some Japanese-held islands. The Japanese were trying to rearm those islands in secret in preparation for the war that they planned to launch against the United States. They were convinced that Earhart's flight was, in fact, a spying mission under the guise of setting an aviation record.

After World War II, residents of various Pacific islands claimed that they had seen Earhart and Noonan captured by the Japanese after they had crash landed on a Japanese-held island. The suspicion that the Japanese may have shot down her plane was supported by Japanese statements asserting that they would not permit any overflights of territory that they considered theirs. It was acknowledged that Earhart's flight plan did come close to some Japanese-controlled islands.

Some details do seem to confirm that she was on a spy flight for the United States. Her flight was supposed to have been a strictly private venture, but President Roosevelt ordered two U.S. Navy ships to patrol along her flight path in case she was forced to land in the ocean, and he had a landing strip built for her on Howland Island. On the other hand, Earhart was a very popular American, and Roosevelt's help was in keeping with routine government assistance to a person of national prominence. In addition, it was smart politics for Roosevelt to be associated in the public's mind with this charming all-American heroine. There was absolutely nothing in his assistance to Earhart that in any way proves that she was on a spy flight.

Noonan, Earhart's navigator, had once been employed by Pan American Airways on the Pacific run. The U.S. Navy was responsible for patrolling the Pacific and had a very close working relationship with Pan American Airways. It had always been assumed that Noonan, and other airline employees, would routinely provide aid and information to the Office of Naval Intelligence with the fullest encouragement of the company. This was another factor that lent weight to the assertion that the flight was really a spy flight. In reality, the fact that a U.S. company was helping the U.S. Navy is not surprising and is not grounds for conjecturing anything other than that the relationship was one of mutual support. Earhart's choice of Noonan as her navigator merely showed her desire to have the best possible assistance on her flight.

After World War II, U.S. intelligence agents spent an inordinate amount of time investigating the Japanese end of the mystery. They were unable to find any credible evidence to show either that her plane had been shot down by the Japanese or that they had captured her.

Volkman, Ernest, and Blaine Baggett. *Secret Intelligence: The Inside Story of America's Espionage Empire.* New York: Doubleday, 1989.

Sarah Emma Edmonds
(Franklin Thompson)
Canada
1841–1898

Sarah Emma Edmonds, dressed as a man, joined the Union Army, and served as a male nurse during the American Civil War. After a soldier (who may have been her lover) was killed, she infiltrated the Confederate Army disguised as a black male nurse. In that position, she took enormous risks to gather intelligence behind Confederate lines and passed it along to the Union Army.

Edmonds was born in December 1841 in New Brunswick, Canada. She ran away from home at an early age to escape a tyrannical father. Already disguised as a man, she took the name Franklin Thompson and worked selling Bibles for a Hartford, Connecticut, publisher. She moved west to Flint, Michigan, and was living there when the Civil War broke out.

A friend, William R. Morse, organized a volunteer infantry company called The Flint Union Greys. Edmonds, as Franklin Thompson, immediately enlisted in what became a part of Company F of the Second Michigan Regiment of Volunteer Infantry. There was no physical examination required, so she had no difficulty at induction. Shortly thereafter, by June 1861, she was at the front in Virginia. Part of her service was hospital duty as a nurse.

She wrote to friends when a young man from New Brunswick was killed; it was a great emotional shock to her. The young man, whose name is unknown, may have been her lover and someone who shared her secret that she was a woman in male clothing. No longer content to be a "male nurse," and wanting more direct revenge for the young man's death, she volunteered to General McClellan to be a spy.

Edmonds was an abolitionist of strong conviction. She was audacious in her espionage duties and often took personal risks that seemed foolhardy, but she always accomplished her objectives. For example, during the fierce fighting at Hanover Courthouse, she mounted a horse and operated as General Kearney's messenger. She galloped from his headquarters to the beleaguered outposts through heavy artillery bombardments and sniper fire for a total of 11 arduous and dangerous journeys in one day. She routinely carried messages through the lines and brought back intelligence about the disposition and condition of the rebel troops. On several occasions she disguised herself as a black youth and called herself "Ned." In Yorktown, Virginia, while in this disguise, she was relegated to the squalid hovels where the Negroes had to sleep, but she managed to sleep elsewhere by bribing a male Negro to take her place. During the day she worked on the fortifications of Yorktown, which provided a good intelligence report for the Union soldiers, who were preparing to attack Yorktown. She made a detailed sketch of the fortifications and concealed her notes under the inner sole of one of her shoes. While she was in the rebel camp, she overheard the Confederate commander General Joseph E. Johnston remark that he was probably going to be forced to evacuate. As she was making her way back to the Union lines, a rebel cavalry officer challenged her. Another black standing close by vouched for "Ned," and the rebel officer released her. He gave her a rifle and told her to take a position in the line and to defend it against the Yankees. She managed to reach the Union lines and gave General McClellan her report and sketch. He thanked her profusely and sent the rifle to Washington.

Edmonds was a master of disguises and dissimulation. On one occasion she stole a musket and Confederate uniform and posed as a rebel sentry to get intelligence. On another occasion she dressed the part of an immigrant Irish woman selling apples at a stand close to a military target.

She never forsook her original dedication as a nurse and spent her spare time between missions tending the wounded as a male nurse. Once, while she was on a mission behind the lines, she encountered a dying Confederate soldier. She nursed him and cared for him until he died. If she had been discovered in enemy territory, it would have meant the firing squad for her as a spy.

In the spring of 1863, the Second Michigan was transferred to Kentucky to join the Army of the Ohio to stop the rebel guerrilla attacks. In April of that year, Franklin Thompson deserted. Edmonds had severe malarial fever and was afraid that if she reported to the hospital, her gender would be revealed. On 22 April 1863, Franklin Thompson was listed on the Union rolls as a deserter.

Edmonds went to Oberlin, Ohio, where she received medical treatment for her ma-laria and changed back into female attire. In 1865, she wrote a book that sold more than 175,000 copies (a very large number for that time). She gave away most of the money she made from the sale of the book to help wounded veterans.

She returned to New Brunswick and in 1867 married a mechanic named Seelye, whom she had known since childhood. They settled in Kansas, where they had three children, all of whom died in childhood. They adopted two boys.

Edmonds communicated with her old comrades in arms and eventually received a pension of $12 per month. She suffered greatly from malaria and partial paralysis in her later years. She died in La Porte, Texas, in 1898.

She had worked as a spy for more than two years, longer than any other known female Union spy. She was the only woman admitted to the George B. McClellan Post No. 9 of the Grand Army of the Republic (GAR). On Memorial Day of 1901, her remains were removed to Washington Cemetery in Houston to a GAR plot. She is the only woman buried in a GAR cemetery.

Edmonds, Emma E. *Nurse and Spy in the Union Army.* Hartford, CT: 1865.

Holt, Patricia Lee. "Female Spy, Male Nurse." *Military History* 5 (1).

Vera Erikson
(Viola, Vera de Witte)
Russia
1912–

Vera Erikson was one of the few female spies to work as a double, and possibly even a triple, agent. Although her true loyalty was to Britain, she managed to convince the Germans that she was working for them.

In pre–World War II Britain, the Abwehr, a German intelligence organization, was trying to establish a network of spies. They propositioned an Italian countess living in London who, from her outspoken pro-Fascist philosophy, seemed to be as pro-German as she was pro-Italy. She agreed to work for the Abwehr.

She was in diplomatic society before her husband died, and her cover was chosen to take advantage of her familiarity with a segment of the London aristocracy that the Abwehr desperately needed to penetrate. She was given funds to rent a lavish flat in Mayfair, purchase a stylish wardrobe, and to entertain royally. The Abwehr told her that they would assign a younger woman to her to help out with the more physically demanding aspects of operating an espionage base in enemy territory. The woman would pose as the countess's niece. The woman they chose, Vera Erikson, spoke native French and very good English. The Abwehr did not tell the countess that Erikson had been the mistress of a senior Abwehr official who had grown tired of her.

Erikson was born in 1912 into a well-known Baltic German family that had been closely associated with the czarist court. She had been brought up in luxury amid the Russian nobility. The 1917 Russian Revolution radically changed the family's life; her father, a czarist naval officer, was murdered by the Bolsheviks, and the family was exiled to Siberia. Erikson's mother then wrote to a former lover, a Bolshevik Jew, who sent them money to escape from Siberia to Paris. They first settled in Latvia and then in Copenhagen, where Erikson's mother worked as a language teacher and interpreter.

When they got to Paris, Erikson's mother took a job in a Russian restaurant. Erikson looked considerably older than she was, and she had a lovely singing voice, so she began singing in the restaurant where her mother worked. She quickly became a success and was in demand at other nightclubs. When her mother moved to Brussels, Erikson remained in Paris to make a career as a singer and dancer. She eventually received a booking in London, where she was less than popular. She fell in love with a Frenchman who was on the same bill with her and became his dancing partner. They returned to France, where they continued their act. There, Erikson, as a former Russian prisoner, came to the attention of the OGPU and was recruited by them as an agent.

A German traveling salesman, an Abwehr agent using the name Mueller, saw her dance and became infatuated. Despite the jealousy of her French dancing partner, Erikson became Mueller's mistress. One night her jealous French dancing partner physically attacked Mueller and a fistfight ensued in the nightclub. The fight caused her to lose her job, and Mueller took her back to Germany with him.

In Germany, "Mueller" confessed that his real name was Hans Dierks and that he was a captain in the Abwehr. Dierks had been traveling with two other Abwehr agents, Robert Petter and Karl Druegge. The three had been traveling in France and the Low Countries setting up sleeper agents to be activated later, during the war that everyone knew was fast approaching.

After leaving Paris, Erikson probably didn't have any more direct contact with the OGPU. In the next few months she traveled with Dierks in France and neighboring countries while he set up agents and caching sites. In April 1940, Dierks told Erikson that he was going on an espionage mission to England and that she could not accompany him. She had no other place to go, because all of her contacts in France or with her mother had been cut off, and she was destitute. She cried and felt deserted; she attempted suicide by swallowing half a bottle of sleeping pills.

The Abwehr decided to allow her to accompany Dierks to England on his very important espionage mission. Even though she was untried and inexperienced, the Abwehr officials in Berlin assigned her to the position with the countess. She was sworn into the Abwehr and sent to spy school to learn radio transmission, microphotography, elementary sabotage, ciphers, and tradecraft in general. She completed her training three months later, in July 1940, and was told that the operation would be mounted from Norway.

She and three other spies were scheduled to leave Norway for Scotland on September 3, but the operation was called off and restarted several times before they actually departed. Finally, Erikson and two other spies, Druegge and Petter, left on September 30. Their Luftwaffe flying boat landed in choppy water in Moray Firth, near Fraserburg, Scotland. They arrived on the shore in their dinghy about six o'clock in the morning, wet, bedraggled, and exhausted.

They buried the rubber dinghy, but the bicycles that they had planned to use had been lost in their difficult landing. They had been given no alternate plan, so they had to improvise. Contrary to their case officer's admonition, they decided to take the railroad. At the Port Gordon railroad station, where Erikson and Druegge went, they first aroused the suspicion of the stationmaster because they had wet clothes; they had too much money to be refugees, as they claimed; and their accents were suspicious. The stationmaster told the porter to keep them talking while he called the police, and that was the end of Erikson and Druegge. Petter was captured soon after, because he had aroused suspicions for many of the same reasons.

The police constable asked Erikson and Druegge for their national registration cards. Erikson replied that she was Danish and Druegge said that he was Belgian. They produced the identification cards that the Abwehr had made for them. The "1" in the year "1940" on their supposedly British identification cards was written with a European flourish, unlike any English style. That was all the constable needed to convince him that the two were not what they claimed to be.

According to official records, both of the male spies were convicted and executed. As soon as Druegge had been escorted from the room, Erikson asked the inspector for a word with him in private. She showed him a slip of paper with the countess's address. She asked him to please contact the Special Branch of Scotland Yard, because they would know all about her and her current situation. The countess, who was key to the whole operation, had been working for British intelligence all the time and had only been bait for the Germans.

Erikson agreed to work for the British as a double agent and eventually was allowed to retire after the war to the Isle of Wight.

Wighton, Charles, and Gunter Peis. *Hitler's Spies and Saboteurs*. New York: Holt, Rinehart & Winston, 1958.

Elise Sabrowski Ewert
(Mrs. Szabo, Annie Bancourt,
   Mrs. Harry Berger)
Poland
ca. 1895–ca. 1939

Elise Sabrowski Ewert was part of a husband and wife team of senior Soviet spies. She operated as an inspector, checking undercover Soviet agents in the field and monitoring their performance. She was a professional's professional when it came to the basics of espionage. When the Soviets sent her on an assignment to Brazil that was fraught with problems, she was arrested, extradited to Germany, and was murdered in the Nazi ovens.

Ewert's maiden name was Sabrowski; she was known to her Comintern subordinates as Mrs. Szabo. Sometimes she worked alone as an inspector for the Comintern. In that role she terrorized those Comintern operatives who hadn't conformed to the strict edicts emanating from Moscow. Most of the time she worked with her husband as an equal or a separate agent, implementing Communist subversion in countries throughout the world. She was a full-fledged Comintern operative working with a partner who happened to be (either for cover purposes or for convenience as they traveled around) her husband.

Ewert and her husband, Arthur, were sent to Shanghai in 1931 as Comintern representatives from Moscow to assist the embryonic Chinese Communist party organize its clandestine apparatus. Together with Gerhardt Eisler, who was later to be the Comintern representative to the CPUSA, they were in charge of the Far East bureau of the Comintern. During the post–Bolshevik Revolution in Russia, the Ewerts were involved in organizing the Communist party of Russia. After that they went to Canada,

79

where they helped establish the clandestine Communist organization there. They were arrested in Toronto in 1919 by the Royal Canadian Mounted Police. The police had raided a boarding house suspected of catering to subversives and had confiscated a large amount of ammunition, some firearms, and a considerable amount of Communist literature advocating the violent overthrow of the Canadian government. The police arrested the Ewerts, who had been found living in the boarding house. She was using the alias Annie Bancourt. Both were jailed for instigating an organization designed to overthrow the government of Canada.

Her husband was released after a short jail term, but she, considered the more dangerous of the two, was kept in prison for a longer sentence. Her husband went to Detroit, Michigan, where she met him after her release from the internment camp for enemy aliens.

In Detroit they worked to establish the Communist party of Michigan. The Ewert Comintern team trained the Michigan Communists in subversive tactics. They schooled them in underground organizations and how to maintain an innocent-looking cover while engaging in subversion of the U.S. government.

When the Ewerts returned to Germany, they were involved in developing the Communist party of Germany. They then returned to Moscow, where Arthur, and to a lesser degree Elise, were considered sufficiently senior to conduct a series of lectures in subversion at the Communist University of Leningrad.

In 1927, the Ewerts, both of whom spoke good English, were sent to the United States to settle a dispute among the various factions vying for recognition as the Communist party of the United States. When they returned to Germany, her husband fell out of favor with the German Communist party hierarchy because of some ideological difference. In 1930, they were expelled from Germany and returned to Soviet Russia. There they were summoned to the Comintern headquarters and were told that they were going to Latin America to spread subversion and organize Communist parties.

On their first trip to Brazil they traveled as Mr. and Mrs. Harry Berger. Their mission was to work with the Communist nucleus to form a viable Communist party of Brazil and prepare it to lead the violent overthrow of the Brazilian government.

The Ewerts also served in China and Uruguay. In China they both worked closely with Agnes Smedley and Ursula Kuczynski. Their job was to end the revolt of the Chinese Communist party against Stalin's ally of the moment, Chiang Kai-shek.

In July 1934, the Ewerts were recalled to Moscow, where they were reunited with Luis Carlos Prestes, the Brazilian Communist. Prestes was ordered by Comintern to surreptitiously return to Brazil. The Ewerts were to help him overthrow the Brazilian government of Getulio Vargas and replace it with a Soviet government of Brazilian workers and peasants. Olga Benario, a German officer in the Soviet Red Army, was detailed to accompany Prestes, posing as his wife. In reality, she was his bodyguard and watchdog, reporting his every movement back to the Kremlin and Stalin. (Benario was a close friend of Ursula Kuczynski.) The Ewerts arrived in Rio de Janeiro with Arthur as Mr. Berger and Elise as Machla Lenczycki and Prestes and Benario as Sr. y Sra. Antonio Vilar. The Communist revolt in November 1935, which they were supposed to lead and inspire, was a fiasco, and all four were arrested.

The two women and Benario's baby daughter by Prestes, who had been born in Brazil, were deported to Germany. The baby was taken by Prestes's mother. They were incarcerated by the Gestapo in Ravensbruck concentration camp, where they were exterminated.

(See also Agnes Smedley and Ursula Ruth Kuczynski.)

Pincher, Chapman. *Too Secret Too Long*. New York: St. Martin's Press, 1984.

Hekmath Fathmy
Egypt
ca. 1920–

Hekmath Fathmy was an Egyptian exotic dancer who hated the British, who occupied her country. It was this hatred plus her love for a German spy that motivated her to spy against the British for the Germans. She had all the attributes of a femme fatale and used her talents to get top secret information out of her unsuspecting sexual partners.

During World War II, Fathmy entertained British troops in a nightclub called the Kit Kat Club in Cairo and lived in a houseboat on the banks of the Nile in the Cairo suburb of Zamalek. She was a friend and source of much information for John Eppler, a German spy living in Cairo and operating for Field Marshal Rommel, who was still in the desert fighting the British.

Eppler needed a safe house from which he could operate his clandestine radio transmitter. Fathmy suggested that he rent one of the houseboats near her and explained how convenient it would be if he were living close to her and she came home late at night with information that he should send immediately to Rommel. She knew that the British officers from the general staff that she entertained in her houseboat were talkative.

Most of the British officers whom Fathmy entertained at the Kit Kat Club and at her houseboat were convinced that she was a loyal supporter of the British Eighth Army. She was not only a lively companion when she sang for them and drank with them at the club, she also wrote to them when they were at the front, fighting in the desert. She was all things to the British officers who had information for her: sweetheart, lover, mother, and confidant. She was very clever at concealing her deep hatred for the British.

She made it clear to her German friends that she would work for them as a spy as long as it took to get the British out of Egypt. When she met Eppler, she recognized a chance to vent her anti-British feelings and exact revenge. As far as Eppler was concerned, Fathmy was an ideal agent. She had many friends in all walks of life and all areas of the city. She even had a large number of friends among her enemies, the British, and she was not averse to sleeping with them if she thought a little sex would get them to talk.

After Eppler moved into his floating apartment, Fathmy was his loyal helpmate. She ran errands for him and organized parties where he could meet good contacts for future operational exploitation. She even brought British officers to his parties who were just back from the front and who were eager to talk about their battlefield experiences. She also acted as a courier between Eppler and the anti-British Arab leaders.

Eppler and Fathmy plotted with a young Egyptian army officer, Anwar Sadat, to overthrow the British and retake Egypt for the

HEKMATH FATHMY
From The Cat and the Mice *by Leonard Mosley*
(London: Arthur Barker, Ltd., 1958)

Egyptians. Eppler cautioned them that there would be no revolt supported by the Germans in Cairo until he got the signal from Field Marshal Rommel that he had broken through the British defenses and was marching toward Cairo.

Eppler's downfall came from having too much money. One night he picked up a young "French" girl by the name of Yvette in the Dug Out Bar of the Metropolitan Hotel in Cairo, which was a favorite hangout for British officers in from the front and a gathering

place for many war correspondents. He took Yvette home to his houseboat and paid her off the next morning with £20 from a very large wad of bank notes. During the night, when Eppler thought Yvette was asleep, he had spoken German to a male friend who was also staying the night on the houseboat. Yvette, who was an operative of the Jewish Agency in Egypt, was shrewder than Eppler thought. She recognized Eppler's German as having a Saarland accent. The next morning, she reported her suspicions to the Jewish Agency (which was, essentially, the Jewish intelligence service). They did nothing about her denouncement and failed to alert the British.

One night, a British major came to see Fathmy at the Kit Kat Club. He told her that he was on his way to the front with top secret dispatches that couldn't be entrusted to ordinary courier or sent by radio. Fathmy, recognizing an opportunity that comes once in a spy's career, told the major that it wasn't fair for him to leave without giving her a chance to say good-bye in the proper way. The major eagerly agreed to what he thought would be a night of drinking and sex. Fathmy slipped the major a potion of knock-out powder and called Eppler to come to her houseboat to get the British dispatches for transmission to Rommel. The dispatches that the major carried contained information vital to the British order of battle defenses and would have been of extreme importance to Rommel.

All night, Eppler tried unsuccessfully to make radio contact with Rommel's communications unit. Fathmy went into Cairo and got Sadat, who, in addition to being an Egyptian army officer, was a radio expert. Sadat examined the transmitter and suddenly thought that he knew what was wrong. He was convinced that Eppler had himself put the transmitter out of order. Sadat thought that Eppler had found life as a German spy in Cairo—with plenty of money, women, and the good life—too enjoyable to give up. Sadat thought that Eppler was, therefore, withholding vital information from Rommel in order to prolong his life of luxury in Cairo. In this case, however, Sadat was wrong: that night the British had captured two German radio operators, who had been manning a relay station in the desert between Cairo and Rommel's headquarters.

Finally, the Jewish Agency told the British that Yvette suspected Eppler of being a German spy. The British, after conducting their own investigation, agreed. They raided Eppler's houseboat, arrested him and a fellow German spy, and took the two into custody.

On the day of Eppler's arrest, Fathmy returned from an all-night swimming date in Alexandria with a British staff officer. She saw the crowd of curious people around Eppler's houseboat. When she went over to see what had attracted the crowd, she was taken into custody by a British officer, who had been waiting for her. In her moment of triumph, or in a desire for expiation, Fathmy told the British that she had read all of the British major's top secret dispatches and that the information had not been sent to Rommel because the transmitter had broken down.

The British couldn't get Eppler to confess using the usual means of civil interrogation, so they finally decided to stage a mock trial at which Fathmy testified against him. Fathmy denied knowing that Eppler was a German spy. Eppler was convicted by this mock court martial and was sentenced to be shot, but he didn't confess even when faced with a firing squad. He was imprisoned until the end of the war. Today, Eppler has a successful business in Hamburg, Germany, and lives well—as he did in Cairo.

Fathmy served a year in prison for her part in the espionage operation and was released. She returned to Upper Egypt, where she retired from nightclub entertaining.

Mosley, Leonard. *The Cat and the Mice.* New York: Harper & Bros., 1958.

Sadat, Anwar. *Revolt on the Nile.* London: Wingate, 1957.

Nancy Lake Fiocca
(Lucienne Carlier)
New Zealand
1917–

Nancy Lake Fiocca became a spy after impulsively helping a downed airman in Paris who was seeking a way to get back to Britain. She organized an intelligence reporting and exfiltration network that proved invaluable to the Allied cause. She also became an expert at ambushing German patrols.

Fiocca was born Nancy Lake in New Zealand and grew up in Australia. She was on a world tour as an Australian journalist when she met Henri Fiocca in Marseilles, France. He was a wealthy industrialist and 14 years her senior. They were married in 1939. She was a journalist in France at the beginning of World War II.

Her husband was called to service in the French army in 1940 when the Germans invaded France. She enlisted as an ambulance driver and helped the wounded French soldiers evade the advancing German armies. When France collapsed, her services as an ambulance driver were no longer needed, and she returned to Marseilles.

When her husband was wounded, he returned home to convalesce. One day she was waiting for him at a sidewalk cafe in Paris when she noticed a sandy-haired, rosy-cheeked young man in civilian clothes seated at a nearby table, reading what appeared to be an English book. When her husband joined her, they both speculated that the young man might be a Gestapo provocation agent using the obviously English book as bait to entice French resistance fighters, who would ordinarily try to help any Englishman stranded in France.

The young man really was a downed English pilot trying to attract the attention of anyone who could help him. The Fioccas helped him escape to Spain. Soon their apartment was a virtual staging site for downed Allied flyers trying to escape from France. Fiocca guided groups of airmen along a secret rat line through France, over the Pyrenees, to freedom in Spain. She personally helped more than 2,000 men return to England.

She also delivered packages of money and radio equipment to fighting groups along the coast. The Gestapo soon realized that a new force had entered the resistance movement in France and called this new force The White Mouse.

Her husband rightly feared for her life and persuaded her to leave France until it was safer. She tried five times to get to Spain over the rat line that she had created, but something always happened to prevent her making the final leg of the journey. On the sixth attempt she made it out of France and arrived safely in England in June 1943. She joined the British SOE and, in the early morning of 29 February 1944, she parachuted back into France, using the code name Lucienne Carlier.

Fiocca dropped into a group of resistance leaders who refused to cooperate with each other. She announced that she would henceforth be in charge of and approve all parachute resupply missions. Those who were with her would get weapons from the resupply drops; those that continued to squabble could fight with their bare hands. Soon she was commanding a maquis force of some 7,000 men and women who were all loyal to her.

One of Fiocca's favorite targets was German truck convoys. She would have her men hide by the side of the road. Then, as the trucks rumbled past, the men would wreck the first and the last trucks in the convoy, forcing all the trucks to stop where they could be raked by machine gun fire. She is also famous for leading the raid that destroyed the German high command headquarters at Monthucon.

In the winter of 1944, when the Allied invasion forces were wrapping up the last German forces in France, she returned to Marseilles. She learned that her husband had been tortured and murdered by the Gestapo. He had died rather than reveal the whereabouts or the identity of The White Mouse.

Weiser, Marjorie P. K., and Jean S. Arbeiter. *Womanlist.* New York: Atheneum, 1981.

Elizabeth Gurley Flynn
United States
ca. 1890 – 1964

Elizabeth Gurley Flynn grew up in a radical socialist family. She was a civil rights advocate for the ACLU, but when her Communist party membership was revealed, she was forced to resign from her position. She then

ELIZABETH GURLEY FLYNN
Archives of Labor and Urban Affairs, Wayne State University

devoted her life to communism and subscribed to the violent overthrow of the U.S. government.

Flynn was born in Concord, New Hampshire, to Thomas Flynn, an Irish-American civil engineer and a confirmed socialist. At the age of 15 she became a street orator for the Socialist party. She was so successful and combative in her oratory that one year later they were calling her "The Socialist Joan of Arc." She played a prominent part in the activities of the Industrial Workers of the World (known as the Wobblies) campaigns at that time.

She was 30 when the country became obsessed in the early 1920s with the idea that a Communist conspiracy was being launched against the U.S. government. Although she never served a prison sentence, during most of her career she was in and out of jails for strikes, disturbing the peace, inciting to riot, and radicalism. As a Communist agent for the Soviet Comintern she openly advocated the violent overthrow of the U.S. government and its replacement with a totalitarian, Soviet-style Communist regime. She was an excellent propaganda agent for the Soviet government.

For many years she concealed her membership in the CPUSA from the ACLU, in which she was very active. In 1937, she admitted that she had been a card-carrying Communist for many years. In 1940, after a stormy battle, she was dropped from the board of the ACLU because of her membership in the CPUSA.

She was also active in the Women's International Democratic Federation, a Communist-dominated front group, which was appointed a consultant to the Economic and Social Council of the United Nations. She devoted much of her time to raising money for the defense funds of Communists who had been jailed for sedition and treason against the United States. She chaired the Workers' Defense Union and its successor, the International Labor Defense, and was particularly active in the defense of Sacco and Vanzetti.

Flynn was known as the "Rebel Girl" for her ability to organize strikes and work stoppages. She was particularly active in helping the Wobblies organize their strikes. She was also aware of inequities even among strikers. In a Communist publication she once very forcefully described the physical dangers and insults to which women on the picket line were subjected. She vividly described discrimination against women when she wrote about the textile strike in Lawrence, Massachusetts. The men in the picket line resented the women's participation so much that the women had to hold separate meetings. Flynn described the women marching in the snow with their babies bundled in blankets and with signs proclaiming, "Bread and Roses."

Once when the Communist party leaders were brought to trial, all the leaders were either on trial, hiding so that they wouldn't be brought to trial, or had already been sentenced. During this time, Flynn literally ran the CPUSA from her office on the ninth floor of the CPUSA offices at 35 East Twelfth Street in New York City.

A heart condition in the late 1920s forced her to live quietly in Portland, Oregon. She maintained throughout her long illness that the CPUSA was the only viable political party left and continued her propagandistic efforts in its support.

When she was 50, her only son died and the ACLU, an organization that she had been associated with since its beginning in World War I, expelled her. She died a short time later.

Rowbotham, Sheila. *Women, Resistance and Revolution.* New York: Vintage Books, 1972.

Sochen, June. *Movers and Shakers.* New York: The New York Times Book Company, 1973.

Spolansky, Jacob. *The Communist Trail in America.* New York: Macmillan, 1951.

Marie Madeleine Fourcade
(Hedgehog)
France
1909–ca. 1985

Most resistance fighters, especially spies, excel as independent agents. Yet, Marie Madeleine Fourcade was not only a successful spy, she also was an excellent executive. She organized the chaos of thousands of resistance fighters with difficult temperaments and their own agendas into a cohesive fighting and intelligence-producing team.

By the time she was 34, Fourcade, the former wife of a French army officer, was one of the most active leaders of resistance operations in France. She was the only woman to head any of France's resistance movements.

In 1940, when she was 31, she was the executive secretary for a publishing firm led by a World War I hero whose specialty was intelligence. Her employer asked if she would organize the underground aspects of an intelligence apparatus in France. She responded by asking the officer who would obey her and, more importantly, who would follow her and be loyal to her? She had doubts because, she told him, she was only a woman. The officer replied that the very reason he had chosen her was because, as a woman, she would be above suspicion.

Between 1940 and 1944, Fourcade successfully directed the largest and most productive resistance organization in Western

Europe. The network she commanded numbered more than 3,000. Her group was able to exfiltrate thousands of downed British and U.S. airmen out of France to Britain and to send much valuable intelligence to the Allied command. The group also assisted in infiltrating many spies and other clandestine support personnel, such as radio operators and demolition experts.

Fourcade had a spectacular career, including two arrests and two escapes. She once fled France to Spain by doubling up in a mailbag that was being delivered over the Pyrenees to the French Embassy in Madrid. She almost froze to death en route. Another time she fled France by clandestine aircraft, aboard a British Lysander that landed in the dead of night to pick her up. Her flight flew under cloud cover to Britain, hiding from German night fighters and bouncing over bursts of antiaircraft flak.

Her organization had to rebuild several times because of provocateurs sent into the group by the Gestapo and because of malcontents within the group. Early in the war, a member of her group, Jean-Paul Lien, was captured by the Nazis and forced to turn in his underground comrades. The rest of the group didn't know about his capture, so they didn't take defensive precautions when he returned. Lien had penetrated Fourcade's group and reached all the way to its apex. A gambler and spoiler by temperament, Lien had betrayed the organization for money.

Fourcade had such a good reputation for daring and exercising firm but fair command that many men who met her for the first time were surprised to learn that Hedgehog was a woman. Eventually, she was captured by the Gestapo, who placed her in a run-down local jail in the south of France. In the middle of the night, she was able to squeeze through the bars of her cell and escape. She had to take off her outer garments and carry her dress in her teeth in order to squeeze through the narrow space. She took the back roads on her way to a château where she knew her second-in-command was staying that night. She had to warn him and the other members of her network that they were in imminent danger

of arrest by the Gestapo.

The Gestapo, assisted by a large contingent of German soldiers, pursued her and literally beat the bushes for miles around in an attempt to flush her out of hiding. She could see the soldiers setting up road blocks and checking every woman's papers, so as she was crossing a field in which some old peasant women were busy gleaning, she joined them. She continued to move forward, as if she were just another gleaner, and the Germans ignored her. She avoided recapture and arrived at the resistance headquarters in plenty of time to warn her second-in-command of the dangers.

Her network was called the Alliance-Druide and was very active in reporting the existence of the German V-weapons. They identified the launching sites, the puzzling "ski jumps" whose identity had eluded Allied headquarters for so long, and pinpointed Peenemünde as the lair of the rocket scientists.

After the war, a July 1943 report on V-weapons from the Churchill top secret files was given to Fourcade as a souvenir. At the reunion of the Alliance held in September 1977, Fourcade was still a beautiful woman, but she was in considerable pain from arthritis and walked with the aid of a cane.

Ehrlich, Blake. *Resistance: France 1940–1945*. Boston: Little, Brown, 1965.

Frenay, Henri. *The Night Will End*. New York: McGraw-Hill, 1976.

Laska, Vera. *Women in the Resistance and in the Holocaust: The Voices of Eyewitnesses*. Westport, CT: Greenwood Press, 1983.

Life. Special Edition. Spring-Summer 1985. p. 36.

Schoenbrun, David. *Soldiers of the Night: The Story of the French Resistance*. New York: E. P. Dutton, 1980.

Bellitote Foures
France
ca. 1790–ca. 1845

When she masqueraded as a man, Bellitote Foures unwittingly accomplished what the

British had been trying to achieve for some time. When she was discovered as a stowaway aboard Napoleon Bonaparte's ship and discarded her male apparel, Napoleon was so smitten with her that he neglected his military campaign.

John H. Barnett was a British officer who served as a secret agent for his government against Napoleon. He was an implacable foe of Napoleon's and was willing to attempt any operation against him. Knowing of Napoleon's susceptibility to women, Barnett sent a bevy of beautiful women to cross his path but was unsuccessful in planting a female reporting source next to Napoleon. Napoleon left France on his Egyptian expedition without succumbing to any of Barnett's female provocations. Barnett left Britain determined to find some way to subvert Napoleon.

About this time, a young and very attractive wife of a Gascon officer who was attached to Napoleon's Egyptian army, named Bellitote Foures, wanted to join her husband on the French fleet. She dressed as a man and smuggled herself aboard one of the French transports bound for Egypt. When attractive Foures was discovered, she was brought before Napoleon to be interviewed. He was quickly enraptured with her, and she was soon ensconced as his companion and mistress. She easily diverted Napoleon's attention from his various military strategies. She was the one person who provided the distractions that kept Napoleon from his conquest of the Middle East, as Barnett had intended.

Napoleon still had the problem of Foures's husband. He decided that "military necessity" would keep Foures occupied. Napoleon had used the excuse of military necessity before. It was how he had permitted the massacre of British prisoners of war at Jaffa rather than attempt to find provisions to feed them. In short, military necessity gave the aura of legitimacy to an otherwise unconscionable act. Nothing so drastic as execution, however, was planned for Foures. He was told that he had been especially chosen as a courier to Paris for the most important dispatches from the field headquarters.

Through his other spies in Napoleon's camp, Barnett learned of Foures's mission and that it was designed to eliminate him. Barnett was able to capture the ship Foures was on and take him prisoner. He then persuaded Foures of the folly of his mission and convinced him that he was being cuckolded. Foures begged Barnett to let him return to the French camp to murder Napoleon and avenge his honor.

Barnett arranged for Foures's freedom and transportation back to Cairo and Foures made it back to the French field headquarters, where Napoleon and his wife were living. There he saw his wife openly displayed as Napoleon's mistress and realized that everything Barnett had told him was true. His wrath at being cuckolded turned into a simple desire to continue living. He realized that any attempt on Napoleon's life would bring him instant execution. Foures resigned his commission and returned alone to France. Napoleon eventually tired of his wife. She was quietly retired from his entourage and disappeared into obscurity.

Rowan, Richard Wilmer, and Robert G. Deindorfer. *Secret Service: 33 Years of Espionage.* New York: Hawthorn Books, 1967.

Marguerite Francillard
France
ca. 1898–1917

Marguerite Francillard proved that not all spying is glamorous. She was victimized and badly mistreated by her German case officers and eventually escaped only through death.

Francillard was a dressmaker's assistant in the town of Grenoble. She was only 18, and probably slightly feeble-minded, when she fell under the spell of a German agent pretending to be a traveling salesman for a French silk company. He seduced her, and she thought he was genuinely in love with her. She agreed to do anything he wanted.

She was to be an accommodation addressee for the German's clandestine mail. She would receive mail from the German's subagents and hold it to deliver to the principal agent when he came to town. She would readdress certain designated pieces of mail and forward them to another accommodation address, where the German agent would collect them. The German principal agent also used Francillard to act as a courier, having her carry messages that she had received in her mail to him in Switzerland.

Someone, possibly the local mailman, who would have wondered at the increase of mail to this simple seamstress, raised his suspicion with the French counterintelligence service. Francillard was watched and eventually arrested in Paris. She had in her purse a compromising letter from a German subagent that she had just picked up at a post office box in Paris.

She was imprisoned in St. Lazare Prison in cell number 12 (the same cell that Mata Hari had occupied). On 10 January 1917, she was executed at Vincennes. Her fellow prisoners remembered her as a sweet young woman who was very pious and thoughtful of others.

Seth, Ronald. *Encyclopedia of Espionage.* New York: Doubleday, 1972.

Sylvia Callen Franklin
(Sylvia Callen, Sylvia Caldwell,
Sylvia Doxie)
United States
ca. 1905–ca. 1980

Sylvia Callen Franklin was a spy for the Soviets. Her interception of Leon Trotsky's communications sent to his United States supporters was instrumental in setting up Trotsky's assassination.

Franklin was born Sylvia Callen. She also used the name Sylvia Caldwell in her espionage work for the OGPU, the Soviet intelligence service. In the late 1930s, the OGPU knew that Leon Trotsky, the recently deposed minister of foreign affairs and leader of the Red Army, would settle in exile in Mexico. They knew that Trotsky could do little in the world arena to fight Stalin from Mexico. All of Trotsky's contacts from Mexico with the rest of the world would have to go through his man in New York, James Cannon.

The OGPU wanted to plant a spy in Cannon's office to report on Trotsky's actions and intentions. The chief of the OGPU in the United States was Dr. Gregory Rabinowitz, a medical doctor who was working under cover as the Russian Red Cross representative in the United States. Rabinowitz used the name Roberts in his contacts with U.S. agents. Rabinowitz instructed Louis Budenz, at that time the editor of *The Daily Worker,* the CPUSA newspaper, to find someone who could infiltrate Cannon's office in New York. Budenz, who later defected and cooperated with the FBI by relating all of his operations for the OGPU, met Franklin in Chicago and recruited her for the job.

Roberts (Rabinowitz) gave Franklin $300 to make the trip from Chicago to New York. He arranged a preliminary job for her in New York with a doctor who was also a Soviet agent until she could get work in Cannon's office. He also arranged for Franklin's husband, Irving (Zalmond David) Franklin, who had completed an espionage assignment in Canada, to be located in an apartment in the Bronx so that she could visit him. Franklin had represented herself to Cannon as a single woman, because Roberts had information from a prior penetration of Cannon's office that the Trotskyites insisted that any female worker in their office must be single.

Franklin first volunteered for a temporary job at the Trotskyite headquarters and took on every dirty, thankless job in Cannon's office and did them all well without complaining. She made herself so indispensable to Cannon that he made her his full-time, private secretary. In this crucial position, Franklin was able to make copies of all correspondence between Trotsky and Cannon and gave the copies to Rabinowitz. Rabinowitz was replaced by a man known as "Sam," who was later identified as Jack Soble. (A decade earlier, Soble, then working under the name Senin, had infiltrated Trotsky's home on an island.) Franklin became a member of the Soble spy ring, which included Boris Morros, Martha Dodd Stern, and her husband Alfred Kaufman Stern. None of the network's members knew that Morros was an FBI penetration and was reporting everything the members said and did to the FBI.

Franklin remained Cannon's secretary until after Trotsky's assassination, when various Trotskyite members suspected her of being a Soviet agent. There was never any specific condemnation of her by the majority of the Trotskyites; and Cannon, out of loyalty to his hard-working secretary, maintained that she must be innocent of any charges of working for the OGPU/NKVD.

Franklin was called to testify before the House Committee on Un-American Activities but chose to take the Fifth Amendment on almost every question. She refused to answer questions about her Communist affiliation or about whether she had ever worked for the OGPU.

(See also Martha Dodd Stern.)

Budenz, Louis. *The Whole of Their Lives.* New York: Charles Scribner's Sons, 1948.

Phoebe Fraunces
United States
ca. 1758–ca. 1795

Phoebe Fraunces was the daughter of a famous tavern owner in New York. Living constantly with danger made her alert to the possibility of sabotage against the tavern's customers. She is credited with saving General George Washington's life.

Fraunces's Tavern was a well-known gathering place for Continental soldiers and officers. In addition to her duties around the tavern, Fraunces was also a housekeeper for General Washington's rooms and served him at the dinner table each evening.

One day in the summer of 1776, one of Fraunces's suitors warned her that the British were planning to poison General Washington. As she was serving creamed peas to Washington, Fraunces noticed their odd consistency. She stooped over and whispered something in the general's ear. He immediately got out of his chair and threw the peas out of the window into a chicken coop below in the yard. The chickens ate the peas, and in a few hours, most of them were dead. They had been poisoned by the peas from Washington's plate.

Fraunces acted as a principal agent and received information from a subagent.

Weiser, Marjorie P. K., and Jean S. Arbeiter. *Womanlist.* New York: Atheneum, 1981.

G

Joy Ann Garber
(Ann Baltch, Bertha Rosalie Jackson)
Russia
1919–

The woman known as Joy Ann Garber had several names before Garber, and her real name is still unknown. She and her husband, Alexander Sokolov, spied for the Soviets in the United States.

On 26 February 1919, Sokolov was born in Tiflis, Russia. He grew up in Paris because his parents didn't want any part of the new Bolshevik regime in Russia. In Paris he became fluent in French, English, and his parents' native Russian. His parents were conservative anti-Communists, but he acquired a leftist liberal orientation while frequenting the Bohemian bistros on the Left Bank. He was as a committed Communist before World War II. After the war, Sokolov was recruited by Soviet agents, he renounced his French citizenship, and went to spy school in Moscow. When he graduated two years later, he was sent to East Germany under cover as an officer of the Soviet army of occupation. He stayed in Germany for three years, mingling with Americans and acquiring an American accent to his English. In Germany he met and married a Polish woman, Joy Ann Garber. When he returned to Russia, he took her with him.

Garber, also known as Ann Baltch and Bertha Rosalie Jackson, was a hairdresser by trade. When she went to Russia she received training in spy tradecraft while her husband received additional espionage instruction preparatory for their assignment. The newly commissioned espionage duo operated first in Central America, Mexico, and Central Europe. They probably came by separate routes into the United States, most likely overland through Mexico. Once they were in the United States, in late 1958, they initially lived apart and pretended not to know each other. Sokolov took the name Robert Baltch and rented an apartment at 413 West 48th Street in New York; Garber rented an apartment at 105 Riverside Drive.

Garber allowed Baltch to "pick her up" after a "chance" meeting. She agreed to a date and, after a reasonable interval, Baltch proposed and Garber accepted, even though they had already been married for some time. This was done solely to backstop their cover and give a reasonable explanation of how they met. Baltch got a job at Berlitz Language Academy at Rockefeller Center, where he was to teach French; he neglected to advise the Academy that his native language was Russian. Garber, in keeping with the KBG's instructions to make everything about their life in the United States as "all-American" as it could be made, took a job as a hairdresser at Pierre's Beauty Salon.

They were married in April 1959 at a matrimonial chapel called the Spiritual

Science Mother Church, which was presided over by a female pastor known as Reverend Argoe. Although the ceremony was private, witnesses—as required by law—had to attend and could later identify the two. Baltch identified himself as Robert Keistutis Baltch, born in Dormont, Pennsylvania, on 17 February 1924. The real Robert Keistutis Baltch had been taken to Lithuania by his parents when he was very young, but in 1947, he had returned to the United States to study for the priesthood. After the real Baltch was ordained, his parish was in Amsterdam, New York, only about 150 miles away from the phony KGB Baltch in New York City.

Garber's mixed-up antecedents were worse than Baltch's. The real Joy Ann Garber had been born in Springfield, Massachusetts. Her father, a Russian by the name of Ossip Garber, had been convicted of forging passports and had served two years in prison. The details that the KGB Garber furnished to the Maryland authorities for her beautician's license were essentially the same as those of the real Garber. Of course, she didn't know that the real Garber's father had served time. The real Garber had become a schoolteacher and married a man named Robert Seskin in Norwalk, Connecticut, which was very close to where the KGB Garber lived.

For more than seven years the KGB Baltches lived in New York as a fairly typical lower-middle-class couple at 450 East 139th Street in the Bronx. These seven years, as far as can be ascertained, were an investment for the KGB in the couple's cover. They were dormant, or sleeper, agents. The KGB Garber applied for a New York beautician's license in April 1960 but had to complete the required number of practical work hours before it would be issued. The couple moved to Baltimore, Maryland, where Baltch got a job teaching languages and Garber went to work in a beauty shop. The KGB had instructed them to move so that they would be closer to Washington, D.C., to be available for operations.

In May 1961, a shipyard worker named Kaarlo Tuomi rented a furnished room in a private house at 107 Hillyer Street in East Orange, New Jersey. His landlady was puzzled about his job, because he seemed to do no work; he just hung around the U.S. Navy shipyards and the U.S. Army base on the waterfront. When he wasn't at either of these two places he could be found in the bars and lunchrooms where the shipyard workers and enlisted men from the army base congregated. Tuomi had come to the attention of the FBI as a possible Soviet agent several years before he arrived in New Jersey. He seemed to be of sufficient potential as a prospective double agent, so the Bureau called in the CIA, which recruited Tuomi to continue his work for the Soviets while reporting everything to the Bureau and the Agency.

Tuomi was cut off from other members of the Soviet network. He received his instructions and delivered his reports through dead drops and letters with secret writing. All of this changed in September 1962, when he was instructed by his Soviet case officers to meet two men at the Greyhound bus station in Yonkers, New York. The two men turned out to be Alexi Ivanovich Galkin, first secretary of the Belorussian delegation to the United Nations, and Pyotr Egorovich Maslennikov, first secretary of the Soviet mission to the United Nations. Tuomi, of course, reported all of this to the FBI.

The Bureau began a stakeout of the dead drops used by these two Soviet diplomats. After long hours of watching with no results, they eventually spotted the Baltches servicing one of the dead drops. Surveillance revealed that the Baltches, although they were of modest financial means, had incurred the expense of changing their apartments every few months and had purchased a woodsy vacation retreat in the Dulany Woods in the Maryland/Pennsylvania border area. The Bureau's surveillance noted that the Baltches visited their cabin infrequently but regularly, almost as if they had a schedule for their trips to the woods. The FBI later discovered that the Baltches had a high-powered transmitter in the cabin, which they used for scheduled messages to Moscow.

In November 1962, the Baltches moved to Washington, D.C., where they rented a comfortable apartment. Baltch got a job teaching French at George Washington University. Baltch strung a wire across the hall of the apartment as an aerial. The FBI made a surreptitious entry into the apartment and planted several microphones so that they had listening coverage of all the rooms. They continued to monitor the Baltches rather than arrest them in the hope that they would lead the FBI to more members of the network.

The Bureau continued its monitoring of the Baltches with few results until 28 April 1963, when the Baltches went to New York. Baltch and Garber went to the Long Island railroad bridge between 35th and 38th avenues, where they appeared to inspect the girders underneath the bridge. The Bureau watchers surmised that they were looking for a dead drop, but the Baltches did nothing.

The Bureau added this location to their stakeout and began the weary vigil at the bridge. On the evening of 25 May 1963, a man and a woman put a small magnetized capsule under one of the girders and quickly walked away. The couple were identified as Ivan Dmitrevich Erogov and his wife, Alexandra. He was a newly appointed personnel officer for the Soviet United Nations delegation. Two hours later the Erogovs came back and removed the capsule. A few minutes later, a man arrived and searched the girders where the capsule had been hidden. When he couldn't find anything he went away.

On 17 June 1963, Baltch made a trip from Washington to New York to pick up a message at the bridge dead drop. The Bureau later ascertained that the message warned him of impending danger and told him to be prepared to flee. He returned to Garber, and they immediately began to pack for an instant departure.

The Baltches and the Erogovs were arrested at the same time. When the Baltches' apartment was searched, the Bureau found microdot-making equipment, photographic facilities, codes, radio schedules, several passports with aliases, and about $5,000 in small-denomination bills. The Baltches and Erogovs were put on trial on 22 July 1963 in Brooklyn, New York. The Soviet Union complained that, as a member of the Soviet mission to the United Nations, the Erogovs should have diplomatic immunity and therefore should not be subject to U.S. laws. The Soviets claimed that they had never heard of the Baltches.

After much skirmishing between the United States and the Soviet Union, a trade was arranged for all four defendants. The prosecutors had been stymied in the Baltches' case because the Supreme Court recently had handed down a decision that evidence obtained by eavesdropping would no longer be admissible at trial. This meant that a large portion of the corroborating information against the Baltches could not be used. Furthermore, in secret negotiations the Soviets admitted that the Baltches were their agents and offered to exchange them for two Americans jailed for a long time in the Soviet Union.

On 15 October 1963, Baltch and Garber were put aboard an Air India flight bound for Prague, Czechoslovakia. No more has been heard of them in the West.

Cookridge, E. H. *Spy Trade.* New York: Walker & Co., 1971.

Ethel Elizabeth Gee
(Bunty)
England
1915–

Ethel Elizabeth Gee sought refuge in pubs from days spent working and nights spent caring for elderly relatives. It was in a pub that she stumbled into espionage when she met a British naval employee, Harry Houghton, who had been pressured into spying for the KGB. Her affair with Houghton and an attraction to espionage prompted her to agree to pass secrets from her job to the KGB and to become embroiled in a complex KGB operation.

Gee was the daughter of a Hampshire blacksmith, but she had received a private education. In her mid-forties, she lived with and felt responsible for the care of her aged mother and an equally elderly uncle and aunt. The press later characterized her as a love-starved spinster who was drawn into espionage only because Houghton gave her the love that she had always craved. This was not the case; she had been engaged to a carpenter who was much more attractive than Houghton. It was the shared enthusiasm for drinking and thrill of spying more than love that brought them together.

In April 1959, the CIA had a source who was a defector in place working for them in Polish intelligence. Their code name for him was Sniper. (He was code named Lavinia by MI-5 in Britain.) Sniper reported that there were two spies working for the KGB in Britain; one was in British intelligence and the other worked somewhere in the British navy. These two spies were given the code names Lambda 1 and Lambda 2. (Lambda 1 turned out to be George Blake, a British foreign service officer, who was later convicted of espionage and sentenced to 40 years' imprisonment.)

All Sniper knew about Lambda 2 was that he had served in Warsaw with the British Embassy and had been blackmailed into espionage by the Polish intelligence service. In March 1960, Sniper had further information that Lambda 2's name was something like "Hutton" and that he had been taken over by the KGB from Polish intelligence when he returned to London to work someplace in the British navy. The only man who fit that description was Houghton, who was working in the Underwater Weapons Research Establishment at Portland, Dorset. When MI-5 began their investigation of Houghton, they found that his wife, Peggy, had reported to the security officer at Portland that her husband had deserted her for a woman at the naval base; that he regularly had meetings with foreigners, whom she could not further identify; and that he had large amounts of money stored in tin cans in the garden workshed. Her report was dismissed by naval security as probably being only the malicious accusation of a deserted wife.

When Sniper's report was received, MI-5 reacted with alacrity. They mounted a discreet investigation, which revealed that Houghton visited London once every month with his girlfriend, Gee. On a July 1960 visit, they observed Houghton and Gee give a man a bag on Waterloo Road and receive an envelope in return. The man was identified as Gordon Arnold Lonsdale, a Canadian who ran a juke box rental business. Lonsdale was later followed to the home of Peter and Helen Kroger, a couple from New Zealand who ran a bookstore that specialized in books on Americana and antiques. Subsequent investigation disclosed that Lonsdale was really Konon Molody, a Soviet KGB officer masquerading under the identity of the deceased Lonsdale. The Krogers were really the Americans Morris and Lona Cohen. They were all eventually apprehended with compelling evidence of their espionage.

Houghton was a navy veteran of World War II. He had been torpedoed several times and promoted to the highest noncommissioned officer rank. He was demobilized in 1945, served as a civilian clerk in the navy, and in 1951 was assigned to the British Embassy in Warsaw. In Warsaw he was seduced by a pretty Polish woman named Christina, who worked for Polish intelligence. She induced him to get involved in illegal black market deals, which gave Polish intelligence a blackmail handle over him. His illegal operations eventually brought a mild rebuke from his superiors in the embassy and a transfer back to Britain. Incredibly, upon his return, he was promoted to Grade 1 clerical status and assigned to the Underwater Weapons Research Establishment at Portland.

In 1957, Houghton's personal affairs were in a mess: he had an expensive drinking habit and many more expenses than his income could cover; his wife was leaving him (she subsequently divorced him in 1958), and he had only his salary and a modest pension from the navy, which were inadequate. Four years after he left Warsaw, and in the midst of domestic strife and financial ruin, he received a telephone call from a man who claimed to be a friend of Christina's from Warsaw. It was actually a KGB officer, who said he wanted to see Houghton.

The KGB officer demanded that Houghton supply him with naval information, but Houghton later claimed that he refused. The KGB officer next threatened Houghton and his wife with bodily harm if he refused. The officer told Houghton how future meetings would be conducted and that the next meetings would be activated by his receiving a promotional pamphlet on Hoover vacuum cleaners. Houghton was given £8 for expenses and was dismissed.

At the next contact, Houghton hadn't produced much, and the KGB officer told him that if he didn't produce, he and his wife would be in danger. Houghton told the officer that they were in England and that nothing like that could happen to them. The officer simply suggested that Houghton remember Trotsky, who had been killed in Mexico in spite of a 20-year wait and a fortified villa that had been protected by machine guns and guards.

Houghton ignored the next two Hoover pamphlets until December 1957, when two men arrived at his trailer and beat him senseless. He claimed that he was too frightened to go to the police, and when the next Hoover pamphlet arrived, around September 1958, he made the meeting. In the meantime, Lonsdale had taken over as Houghton's Soviet case officer.

The problem was that Houghton did not have access to much classified information. The solution was to recruit his drinking companion, Gee, who worked in the records office of the Portland establishment. Gee was 46 and had a salary of £10 a week, out of which she gave her aged mother £3. In 1958, their relationship had been cemented when Houghton moved into a trailer near Portland that he had bought with £200 that he had borrowed from Gee. He was no longer living with his wife. His courtship of Gee consisted of visits to her family, Sunday dinners with her aged mother, weekend trips to Bournemouth, and trips to London for the theater and quiet afternoons at the Cumberland Hotel.

In 1959, Houghton bought a cottage near Portland for £9,000, and Gee helped him decorate it. She felt they were working on the cottage, just hoping things would straighten out so they could get married. About this time, Houghton arranged for Lonsdale to meet Gee. Lonsdale told her that he was Alex Johnson, a naval attaché at the U.S. Embassy in London. He convinced her that the Irish were withholding naval research from the Americans, which should have been pooled under NATO agreements. What convinced Gee to cooperate with Lonsdale is not precisely known, but it is certain that she was willing to work in espionage with her beloved Houghton.

Gee would bring a batch of classified documents home on a Friday evening for Houghton to photograph, and she would return them to the files on Monday morning before they would be missed. Once a month Lonsdale would drive to Weymouth to pick up the "take," or Houghton and Gee would take it to London to deliver it to Lonsdale.

On 7 January 1961, Houghton and Gee were arrested together with Lonsdale at a meeting outside the Old Vic Theatre in London. In Gee's shopping basket, beneath a few market items, was a bundle of notes on the nuclear submarine *Dreadnought,* four secret test pamphlets, and a number of photographs of classified British admiralty documents. There was also a small biscuit tin sealed with tape, which contained undeveloped film. The film contained 310 photographs of top secret documents and blueprints of classified naval projects.

In a subsequent search of Gee's home, the investigators found a matchbox with a double bottom, which contained a neatly drawn map of London with the meeting sites with Lonsdale clearly marked; many classified naval papers and charts; the summarized results of underwater tests; and other spy equipment.

At the trial Houghton and Gee were convicted of espionage and were sentenced to 15 years each. (Lonsdale was sentenced to 20 years but was later traded back to the Soviet Union. The Cohens were sentenced to 20 years each, but they too were traded back to the Soviet Union.) When they were released from prison, Houghton's divorce had been granted, and he and Gee were married.

(See also Lona Petka Cohen.)

De Gramont, Sanche. *The Secret War*. London: Andre Deutsch, 1962.

West, Rebecca. *The New Meaning of Treason*. New York: Viking, 1964.

Wright, Peter. *Spycatcher*. New York: Viking Penguin, 1987.

Stella Goldschlag
Germany
1923–

After enduring extensive torture at the hands of the Nazis, Stella Goldschlag's basic survival instincts took over, and she agreed to spy against her own people. Goldschlag used all the subterfuges and guile of a professional spy to make certain that she and her family survived. Eventually, her complete lack of scruples turned even the hardened Nazis away from her.

Goldschlag was 14 in 1937. As Hitler came into power, his pogroms against the Jews intensified, and Goldschlag was trapped in Germany with no way out. She was captured by the Nazi Gestapo because she was a Jew and was tortured until she agreed to work for them, ferreting out and denouncing other Jews. The quid-pro-quo of her agreement with the Gestapo was that they would not "deport" her parents. ("Deport" meant sending them to a concentration camp, which was tantamount to sending them to their deaths.)

She developed into an efficient "catcher," which was the street jargon for a Jew who singled out other Jews who had gone underground to avoid being captured and exterminated by the Nazis. She became the most despised of all Jews, a Nazi collaborator. Goldschlag made the rounds in Berlin and other towns of the theaters, movie houses, cafes, coffee shops, operas, railroad stations, and streets, looking in the faces of the people for telltale signs of their Jewish identity. She denounced people on the merest suspicion of their being a Jew. The simple denunciation was enough, however, for the Gestapo to arrest such people and, usually, to wring a confession from them that they had a Jewish background.

She acquired the sobriquets "the blond ghost" and "the blond poison." She was a spy with her own mission of survival. She reported on her former friends and colleagues, who were quickly arrested and "deported." There was a rumor that among themselves the Gestapo referred to her as "the blond Judas."

At the end of the war the Soviets, usually loath to prosecute anyone for persecuting a minority, arrested Goldschlag as part of their program to curry favor with the conquered German population. She was sentenced to ten years of hard labor after a show trial. When she was released from prison she converted to Christianity and became a professional anti-Semite.

Wyden, Peter. *Stella: One Woman's True Tale of Evil, Betrayal and Survival in Hitler's Germany*. New York: Simon & Schuster, 1992.

Maud Gonne
Ireland
1866–ca. 1910

Maud Gonne was a lifelong fighter for Ireland's independence from Britain. She inspired a famous Donegal legend about a woman, surrounded by birds and dogs, who would come to the aid of the Irish in times of oppression. Throughout her efforts on behalf of Irish sovereignty, Gonne always traveled with several caged birds and at least one dog. She was also the lover of the poet William Butler Yeats, a fellow Irish sympathizer, with whom she planned and executed many political campaigns on behalf of Irish independence.

Gonne was born in 1866 in Donegal to an English mother and an Irish father. She took an oath early in life to rid Ireland of the British oppressors. She had first been angered at the persecution of the Irish peasants, who were evicted from their homes during the Land League War, when Irish patriots fought against the British foreign landlords.

Gonne always had with her many birds in cages and several dogs. One time, in order to join a local land battle against the eviction of poor Irish farmers, she rode up on a large white horse, festooned with birds in cages and followed by her large Great Dane, Dagda. She dismounted and helped to erect temporary huts for the dispossessed, whose cottages had been smashed and burned by the British.

When working in the Irish rain made her ill and her lungs started to hemorrhage, her aunt took her to Royat, France, to recuperate. While she was there, she met a fellow patient, a right-wing French journalist and politician, Lucien Millevoye, who was ten years her senior. Millevoye hated the Germans for having taken Alsace-Lorraine away from France, and he especially loathed the British for having vanquished Napoleon. He aroused a similar hatred in Gonne and admonished her to free Ireland. They made a pact that he would help her free Ireland from the British and she would help him free Alsace-Lorraine from the Germans.

They entered into a conspiratorial alliance to avoid detection by British intelligence. He even bought her a small revolver for protection against the British. He sent her on a mission to St. Petersburg, Russia, with secret papers sewn inside her clothes. She was to try to arrange Russian help to free Alsace-Lorraine from the Germans. In St. Petersburg, Gonne had to evade the sinister intentions of a female British spy who was trying to impede her mission.

Gonne had an independent income from her father's estate and lived mainly in Paris but maintained rooms in Dublin above a bookstore on Nassau Street. There she aligned herself with Jack O'Leary, the fiery Irish separatist intellectual. When she heard a rumor that the British had issued a warrant for her arrest, she knew that any time spent in a damp and dirty British prison would destroy her fragile lungs, so she quietly left Ireland for Paris.

Millevoye was waiting for her in Paris. He suggested that they were going about the task of trying to free Ireland in the wrong manner. Instead, he counseled Gonne, she should join him in civilized diplomatic intrigues against the British.

In 1891, Gonne happened to be on the mail boat carrying the body of Charles Steward Parnell back to Ireland for burial. The channel boat was loaded with reporters who could not help but notice her. Standing on the dock at Kingston, waiting for the arrival of the mail boat that morning in October 1891, was the Irish poet William Butler Yeats, who was reverentially in love with Gonne.

Gonne convinced Yeats to help her launch a propaganda effort that would assist in establishing the groundwork for the forthcoming insurrection against Great Britain. She traveled around Ireland to the small towns, lecturing to literary societies. She always included in her talks subtle hints about the need for Irish independence. Yeats would follow her lectures, taking up a collection, which he would leave in each village to help start a local library.

Around 1892, Gonne returned to France because Millevoye was despondent over a friend's suicide and she feared that he might follow the friend's example. Some time later, Yeats followed her to Paris and found her deeply embroiled in the campaign to strengthen French antipathy for the British. She was publishing a news bulletin about British atrocities in Ireland called *L'Irlande Libre* (Free Ireland). She circulated this bulletin to all the French newspapers. She was also touring France, telling her audiences about the British evils in Ireland and writing articles for Millevoye's *La Patrie* (Homeland) about the barbarities inflicted on Irish prisoners by British jailers.

When Gonne noticed Millevoye's waning interest in the anti-British crusade, she returned to pure Irish nationalist politics with Yeats. One reason that Gonne favored Yeats at this time was that he was becoming more embroiled in Irish nationalism and had joined the secret nationalist society, the Irish Republican Brotherhood (IRB). Gonne also wrangled her way into the IRB, even though it did not intend to admit female members. Yeats was elected president of the IRB and toured Ireland, speaking to patriotic groups. Gonne accompanied him on these trips and is given credit for instigating anti-British riots around the country to mark Queen Victoria's Jubilee.

Around 1893, Gonne began to work closely with Arthur Griffith, a young journalist who published an often-banned nationalist newspaper, the *United Irishman.* Gonne urged Griffith, Yeats, and Jim Connolly, another Irish patriot, to form the ultranationalist separatist movement Sinn Fein (ourselves alone). Gonne then left for the United States to raise money for the organization. She lectured and collected the equivalent of more than £1,000.

Once she was back in Ireland, Gonne used the outbreak of the Boer War in South Africa as an opportunity to embarrass the British government. She formed the Daughters of Erin, which would physically attack any Irish woman who went out with a British soldier. She also organized counterdemonstrations during Queen Victoria's visit to Dublin.

She worked with Griffith to recruit a brigade of Irishmen to go to South Africa to fight with the Boers against the British. She also promoted the idea of a French force landing in Ireland to foment insurrection against the British forces in Ireland. (The French were outraged at British atrocities against the Boers in South Africa and may have considered such an idea.)

In 1902, Gonne instigated a plan to manufacture time bombs that looked like lumps of coal. The IRB planned to place these bombs in the bunkers of British warships with the hope that they would explode when the ships were far at sea. Gonne went to Brussels to see the European agent of the Boer Republic, Dr. Leyds. He told her that he could not openly fund her project but promised her a contribution of £2,000 for some unspecified revolutionary activity in Ireland.

Almost as soon as Gonne had left Dr. Leyds, an Irishman called upon him. The unknown Irishman, who obviously had heard about the offer through a leak in Gonne's organization, told the doctor that carrying such a large sum of money was too dangerous for a woman and that he would take the money for her. The doctor promptly gave the unidentified Irishman the money, and that was the last that anyone saw of him or the money. Suspicion centered on an old enemy of Yeats, F. Hugh O'Donnell. The IRB sentenced him to death but later relented and granted him a reprieve, because they didn't have any firm evidence against him.

Both Gonne and Yeats resigned from the IRB because it didn't seem to be successful in promoting Ireland's separation from Britain. Gonne's next venture was to develop an open revolutionary movement. She took a house on Coulson Avenue where she, Griffith, Yeats, and several others drew up a program for an organization that linked all of the existing nationalist groups in Ireland. Yeats wrote a stirring patriotic play for the new venture called *Cathleen ni Houlihan.* Gonne played the lead, and the effect was galvanic, sensational, and—for some—emotionally exhausting. One critic commented that plays like *Cathleen ni Houlihan* should be banned unless one was prepared for people to go out after seeing the play to riot, shoot, and be shot.

Yeats had often asked Gonne to marry him, but she always refused. Yeats knew nothing of her affair with Millevoye or, at least, chose not to believe the gossip if he heard it. Gonne bore Millevoye two children, but only a daughter, named Iseult, survived. They were never married, and Gonne would never acknowledge that Iseult was her daughter. In Catholic Ireland, where illegitimacy was frowned upon, Gonne always referred to Iseult as her niece or, as she grew older, as her "kinswoman." Even in her memoirs, Gonne referred to Iseult as a child that she had adopted.

In August 1903, Gonne married John McBride, a fiery Irish nationalist, in Paris. He was a poor husband, a good drinker, and a fair fighter. The marriage ended after two years with a legal separation, because divorce was banned in Catholic Ireland. A son was born from this marriage.

Gonne continued to live in France and to fight for Irish independence but without the vigor she had brought to the fight in her youth. Yeats visited her from time to time, but the visits grew further and further apart. Gonne died before World War I.

Barker, Dudley. *Prominent Victorians.* New York: Atheneum, 1969.

Betty Gordon
England
1927–

Betty Gordon was a dedicated woman who went under cover to work in the British Communist party (BCP) on a temporary assignment. She remained on the assignment for 33 years. She rose in the BCP to a position of leadership and trust and was a valuable information source for MI-5.

Gordon worked for several employers before she entered government service with MI-5. She had been hired as a stenographer but left that position when it was discovered that she had a unique ability to work undercover. She was assigned to penetrate the BCP.

In 1949, there had been a danger of Communist subversion in labor unions in England and the socialist government did not want to be mistakenly identified in any way with the social programs of the Communists. Clement Atlee, the Labor party candidate who had recently been elected prime minister of Great Britain, was greatly concerned about the issue of Communist encroachment. There was also a very real danger that Soviet espionage would use the increasingly potent indigenous Communist movement as a cover to infiltrate the British government. MI-5, which was principally responsible for fighting communism in Britain and for counterespionage, asked Gordon if she would try to infiltrate the BCP.

She began to associate with party members, to whom she listened and from whom she learned the jargon that they used in discussing political issues. She was able to mimic their phrases until she sounded like a doctrinaire Communist ideologue. She learned the party's position and aped its members' opinions. Eventually, the BCP or-

ganizers noticed her as a likely candidate for recruitment.

At the instruction of MI-5, she volunteered for the most menial tasks in order to ingratiate herself with party officials. She attended meetings of her cell religiously and always made herself noticed at demonstrations and mass protests called by the party. She sold more copies of *The Daily Worker,* the official Communist paper, than her fellow cell members and always paid her party dues promptly. She advanced steadily in the party hierarchy and was given additional organizational responsibility. Her reward was a job on the glossy *Soviet Weekly,* a magazine published in conjunction with the press section of the Soviet Embassy and an adjunct of the KGB's propaganda campaign. During the era of Chinese Communist rapport with the Soviet Union, she taught English to the Chinese diplomats at the Communist Chinese Embassy in London.

When she took time out to have a baby, one of the most prominent Communist women in England, Betty Reid, and her equally prominent Communist husband, John Lewis, offered her and her baby room and board in their home in return for her being a part-time nanny for their children. Living with Reid and Lewis gave Gordon access to high-level BCP discussions and plans. She was able to identify the visitors to the house and report on overheard conversations among the leaders of the BCP.

She became acquainted with other members of the Central Committee of the BCP, and in 1958 her top-level friends in the BCP arranged for her to work on an English-language magazine published in East Berlin. In this capacity she had access to the plans of the German Democratic Communist party and reported all that she learned to the MI-6 officers in West Berlin.

In 1962, when she was back in England, she told her MI-5 case officer that she wanted to resign from her undercover work and devote herself to her child. MI-5 allowed Gordon to retire without prejudice and paid her £200 severance pay.

After retirement she made no attempt to conceal her past life as a penetration of the

BCP and she lost all of her party acquaintances and all her former "close friends." She was able to find new friends and remade her life around her child. Several years later, Gordon suffered a nervous breakdown, which the doctors attributed to the strain of leading a double life for many years.

Payne, Ronald, and Christopher Dobson. *Who's Who in Espionage.* New York: St. Martin's Press, 1984.

Christine Granville
(Jacqueline Armand)
Poland
ca. 1920–1952

Christine Granville, whose proper name was Countess Krystyna Gisycka Skarbek, was born into the upper class and was able to use her contacts to the utmost advantage for spying. She was a rugged survivor who parachuted into Occupied France and organized resistance movements. After the war, she was murdered by a jealous suitor.

Granville was born in Poland as the Countess Krystyna Gisycka. At age 17 she won a beauty contest and was crowned Miss Poland. Her first marriage, while she was a young woman, was short-lived. She divorced quickly and married again, this time to Count George Skarbek, who was twice her age. Skarbek, a writer, had work that took them to Africa, where they were when World War II erupted. When it did, they immediately returned to England. She offered her services to British secret intelligence and he joined the Free Polish Forces. British intelligence accepted Granville at once. She was a resourceful woman with a keen intellect and could speak several languages fluently. It was at this time that she assumed the name Christine Granville. (Her husband was lost in combat in Poland's last stand against the German Panzer tanks; his body was never recovered.)

Granville was assigned to Budapest under journalistic cover. The real purpose for the assignment was to help refugees escape across the Polish border. On her first mission she skied across the Tatra Mountains into Poland and escorted back a small party of escaped and wounded Polish prisoners of war. She established several rat lines out of Poland to smuggle Polish patriots and Allied officers to England. Granville worked closely in this operation with a Polish cavalry officer named Andrew Kowerski, whose fundamental loyalty was with the Allies. Subsequently, Kowerski changed his name to Andrew Kennedy, became a British agent, and worked with Granville on Polish operations.

One of Granville's first missions was to get information on a new German antitank gun that was supposedly capable of penetrating heavy armor at 200 yards. She made the acquaintance of a Polish patriot who was in exile in Hungary and who had buried a prototype of this gun on his family estate in Poland. Despite the personal danger involved, the Polish patriot agreed to return to Poland, dig up the gun, and bring it back to Budapest for Granville. He succeeded, and the specifications of the new German gun enabled the Allies to manufacture a similar one, which proved decisive in combat.

Granville was apprehended on a mission inside Poland, but she managed to escape when she held two live hand grenades above her head and told the Germans that if they moved or shot her, the grenades would explode, killing them all. Shortly thereafter, while escorting four British pilots who had been shot down over Poland across the border into Yugoslavia, she was again arrested. This time she convinced her captors that she and the four airmen were merely going on a picnic. She even persuaded the border guards to help her start her stalled automobile.

Granville and Kowerski were captured together by the Germans in the fall of 1941. They were able to make their escape and traveled across Greece, Turkey, and Palestine before they reached Cairo. Granville had been recalled from Budapest for parachute training at a British base near Cairo. She easily qualified as a parachutist in preparation for a jump in 1942 into Occupied France. There she joined the "Jockey" network.

The Special Operations Executive of British intelligence dropped her into the

Vercors Plateau of southern France. She used the code name Jacqueline Armand. She and her group held out against such a large number of Germans for such a long time that the area she was defending was referred to half-jokingly as the Republic of Vercors. She helped organize the French Resistance and, across the border in Italy, she organized the Italian Partisans so that the two groups worked effectively together.

The leader of the Jockey network wrote in a commendation for Granville that she was perhaps the greatest person he had ever known. At one time a Jockey network officer and an American officer from the OSS were imprisoned by the Germans. They were about to be executed when Granville went to the prison and literally talked the Germans into releasing them. She went to the German prison commander and identified herself as a niece of General Montgomery, a British military leader. She swore that if the two Allied prisoners scheduled for execution were not released immediately, she would see to it that he and all other German officers assigned to duty at the prison would be put to death as war criminals. At the time she raised this threat, even die-hard Nazis realized that the end of the war was near and that they would have to answer for their crimes.

Unfortunately, as soon as the war was over, Granville was "demobbed" (as they say in Britain for being released from the intelligence service, or for being discharged from military service), with only two months' severance pay. It has been speculated that the degrading treatment that Granville received at the war's end was due to her assertion that she had evidence that a Polish general's death in an air crash had been the result of British sabotage.

Granville had no income and no professional talents to fall back on, so she worked first as a saleslady at Harrod's department store in London for the equivalent of $14 per week. She obtained her British citizenship in 1947. She then worked as a wardrobe attendant at the Paddington Hotel. She was forced to take whatever job she could find, including that of stewardess on an ocean liner, the *Winchester Castle*. In 1952, a steward aboard

this ship, Dennis George Muldowney, claimed that he was madly in love with Granville and that he was inconsolable without her. She rejected him. On 15 June 1952, in a fit of jealous rage, Muldowney followed Granville to a London hotel, where he stabbed her to death.

The government of Great Britain had awarded her the George Medal and the Order of the British Empire after the war. Buried with her were a medal from Poland, the French Croix de Guerre, the ribbon of the Order of the British Empire, the George Cross, and the badge of French Resistance.

Rowan, Richard Wilmer, and Robert G. Deindorfer. *Secret Service: 33 Years of Espionage.* New York: Hawthorn Books, 1967.

Rose O'Neal Greenhow
United States
1819–1864

Rose O'Neal Greenhow, a widow who lived in Washington, D.C., during the Civil War, was able to pass valuable information about Union troop movements and other Union Army activities to the Confederacy because of her social contacts. She was one of the few female spies to have her own network, which she continued to supervise even after she was caught and imprisoned.

Greenhow was born Rose O'Neal and was raised as a southern lady. She married Dr. Greenhow, a U.S. government cartographer, and received from him a liberal education in law, diplomacy, some medicine, and history. Dr. Greenhow died in California in 1854, leaving his wife wealth and a mansion in Washington, D.C.

After his death, she lived in a large house at Thirteenth and I streets, Northwest, with her four daughters. She became a prominent Washington hostess and the friend of many congressmen, senators, and other highly placed federal officials. Her niece was the granddaughter of Dolly Madison, wife of the former president, and was married to Senator Stephen A. Douglas, who had been a

ROSE GREENHOW WITH ONE OF HER DAUGHTERS
Library of Congress

candidate for the presidency. She gave and attended socially important parties and learned a lot about the conduct of the war from the Union side by listening to table talk.

At various times she was linked romantically with many of the Washington men, bachelors and married men alike, who attended these parties. Greenhow's name was linked romantically with that of Colonel E. D. Keyes, General Winfield Scott's military secretary. At one time Washington gossips rumored that they were to be married. Other romantic interests from whom Greenhow may have been extracting information were Senator Henry Wilson of Massachusetts and an officer who was in charge of the fortifications for the city of Washington.

Greenhow was a vehement secessionist and pro-Confederist and made little effort to conceal this attitude from her Washington friends. She made no excuses for her convictions.

She was inducted into espionage for the Confederacy on the impulse of a former Union officer who followed his conscience by leaving Washington for Richmond at the start of the war. Colonel Thomas Jordan was a West Pointer and had been an officer in the Union Army before he resigned his commission. Before leaving Washington to become adjutant general of the Confederate Army of Manassas, knowing Greenhow's sympathies, he hurriedly met with her. He boldly discussed the possibility of her helping the Confederacy by supplying information about conditions in the Union capitol and about their armies' intentions.

Greenhow eagerly agreed. The colonel showed her a simple cipher to use in her reports to the Confederacy. Later, when she was ready to send her reports to Richmond and the rebel troops quartered near Manassas, she enlisted the aid of a servant girl, Miss Duval, to act as her courier.

Greenhow began her career in espionage in April 1861; by November of that year, Allen E. Pinkerton, chief of the Union secret service, had become suspicious of her activities. Pinkerton instituted a surveillance of Greenhow, which soon revealed that she had a Union officer reporting information to her

and that many important Washington men were visiting her. It wasn't too long before Pinkerton was convinced that he had enough evidence on her to get a conviction, and he had her arrested.

Pinkerton hoped to use Greenhow's house as bait for other southern sympathizers who were reporting information to her. He staked out the house and waited for the subagents to report in, but none showed up. The explanation wasn't discovered until it was too late: Greenhow's eight-year-old daughter had climbed a tree that overhung the sidewalk and told every passerby that her mother had been arrested.

On the day Greenhow was arrested, Lillie MacKell, her most devoted friend and collaborator, did call at the house while Pinkerton's men were searching it for incriminating evidence. MacKell was allowed to visit with Greenhow and left unmolested. When MacKell left the house, she was carrying messages for the Confederacy wrapped around her ankle.

Greenhow's intelligence was timely, comprehensive, accurate, and allowed the Confederacy to resoundingly defeat the Union forces at Bull Run on 23 July 1861. Her espionage network consisted of more than 50 agents, of whom 48 were women. The net continued to operate on its own even after she had been arrested.

Pinkerton imprisoned Greenhow in the Old Capital Prison. Even from prison she continued to send messages filled with good intelligence to the Confederacy. One Union general commented that Greenhow often knew about his plans before he did. She was allowed to write letters from prison, and Pinkerton himself examined them for secret correspondence. Most of the letters were addressed to "Dear Aunt Sally" and were filled with inanities uncharacteristic of Greenhow's intelligence. The letters were obviously in some form of open code, but Pinkerton apparently never recognized their sinister content, because he allowed the letters to be sent. Greenhow was also allowed to have yarn for weaving in her prison cell, from which she made tapestries of considerable intricacy. Using a technique that has been used

ALINE GRIFFITH
Marcia Gerardi; courtesy of the Countess of Romanones

throughout history to transmit information, she wove codes based upon the sequence of different colored yarns.

Greenhow's many influential friends were able to bring pressure on the Union government to obtain her release. She passed through the Union lines under a flag of truce to the Confederate side. After her release, President Jefferson Davis of the Confederacy sent her to Europe to plead the Confederate cause before the crowned heads of Europe and to ask for material and financial aid. She was a social triumph in Europe and was received by Napoleon III and Queen Victoria. Her tour was such a success with the British minister to France, Lord Granville, that he wanted to marry her. In August 1864, she left for the United States, leaving Lord Granville behind.

She returned to the United States aboard the fast, specially constructed blockade-runner *Condor*. When the ship neared Wilmington, a Union gunboat gave chase. For three hours the chase continued, but the *Condor* ran aground on the New Inlet Bar when it tried to avoid a floating hulk. The Union gunboat closed in and Greenhow demanded that she be put ashore before the Yankee boarding party captured her. The captain warned her that the sea was too rough for a small boat, but she insisted.

As she was being rowed ashore, she fell into the water and drowned. Her voluminous green silk dress became waterlogged and dragged her under water. She was also weighed down by the money belt that she had concealed on her person, which was crammed with gold sovereigns.

On 20 October 1864, Greenhow was buried with full military honors in the Oakdale Cemetery at Wilmington. The coffin was draped with a Confederate flag and escorted by Confederate troops. A marble cross was erected over her grave, inscribed: "Mrs. Rose O'N. Greenhow, a bearer of dispatchs [sic] to the Confederate Government." The cross stands there to this day. Every year on Memorial Day, the Daughters of the Confederacy place a wreath of laurel on Greenhow's grave.

Ind, Allison, Colonel. *A Short History of Espionage.* New York: David McKay, 1963.

Nolan, Jeannette Covert. *Spy for the Confederacy: Rose O'Neal Greenhow.* New York: Julian Messner, 1963.

Aline Griffith
(Countess of Romanones)
United States
1923–

Aline Griffith, who worked as a model before World War II, was, according to her own account, recruited into the OSS to work in Madrid just after World War II. In her two books about her life, she claims that she was asked by the CIA to track down NATO moles. Griffith's own published accounts of her career are the primary sources of information about her espionage activities.

Griffith was born in Pearl River, New York, in 1923. Her first OSS assignment was to Madrid, where she met and married the

Count of Quintanilla, who later became the Count of Romanones. She was an OSS employee (but not an operations/case officer) in neutral Spain, performing the routine functions of any such OSS station in a neutral country.

According to Griffith, in 1966 the CIA, allegedly with no other, better-qualified agents available, called on her to track down a mole that had been stealing NATO secrets.

Supposedly, Griffith had to enlist the help of the Duchess of Windsor, Wallis Warfield Simpson, and others of a similar ilk, in order to track down her quarry.

Griffith, Aline (Countess of Romanones). *The Spy Went Dancing*. New York: G. P. Putnam's Sons, 1990.

Griffith, Aline (Countess of Romanones). *The Spy Wore Red*. New York: Charter Books, 1988.

H

Mata Hari.
See Margarete Gertrude Zelle.

Mildred Fish Harnack
United States
ca. 1902–1943

Mildred Harnack wanted to be a literature professor; instead, she reluctantly followed her German Communist husband into espionage. She was one of the most academically oriented of all female spies. While living in Germany, she helped her husband spy for the Soviets against the Nazis by seducing senior German agents and questioning them in bed. She was caught and convicted of espionage and spent her last days translating Goethe while awaiting execution.

Harnack was born into a midwestern, middle-class family as Mildred Fish. She studied hard and became a lecturer in literature at the University of Wisconsin at Madison. She wasn't a radical but was caught up in the social reform protest movement common to U.S. universities in the early 1920s. Arvid Harnack, a student from Germany, was attracted to her erudition and her extreme democratic leanings. In 1926, they were married. She followed her husband's orders, but she was basically nonpolitical; literature remained her love.

The Schulze-Boysen/Arvid Harnack espionage network operated in Germany for Soviet Russia and was known to German counterintelligence as the *Rote Kapella* (Red Orchestra), a name it was given by the German DFing, or radio directional finding, operators who listened to their radio transmissions. It had many informants and was a most prolific and accurate collector of intelligence for the Communists. Harnack was a teacher of languages in the Faculty of Foreign Scholarship at Berlin University, where she operated to recruit informants and collect intelligence.

One of the Red Orchestra's best informers was Lieutenant Herbert Gollnow, a naive young German officer who was working in Section II of the Abwehr, which dealt with sabotage operations. He became Harnack's lover and never guessed that while he was in bed with her he was being systematically elicited. Harnack was basically a reserved academic who was respected by all who knew her. There is no knowing what attracted her to Gollnow. She may have been in love with the impetuous young officer or she may simply have been obeying her husband's order to make love to Gollnow to get information from him. The latter explanation seems the most probable. During a Gestapo interrogation, when she was asked the reason for her actions, she answered, "Because I had to obey my husband." (Hohne 1971, 142)

MILDRED HARNACK

From L'orchestre rouge *by Gilles Perrault (Paris: Librairie Arthème Fayard, 1967)*

Gollnow entered Harnack's life by placing a newspaper advertisement in which he asked for language training. Harnack taught him English. Her husband attended all of the language lessons because Gollnow was an important prospective source of intelligence. Gollnow was the associate of the chief of German intelligence, Admiral Canaris. Gollnow's task was to coordinate all airborne operations in the Sabotage Section of the Abwehr. In this position he was privy to all the secret German air operations behind the Soviet front, which were of vital interest to Moscow.

Harnack's husband would begin his conversations with Gollnow with an innocuous discussion of the day's war news and lure Gollnow into citing some classified information to support a fact. He would feign disbelief of Gollnow's information, which in turn would make Gollnow more eager to cite more classified figures and incidents to prove his point. Then, to follow up on what Gollnow

had revealed, Harnack would continue probing for details later, when they were in bed.

On 7 September 1942, a Gestapo detachment searched Fischerdorf guest house in a suspected area of East Prussia and by breakfast time had found the Harnacks, who were on vacation, and arrested them. While she was in prison, the Gestapo had to use the strongest preventive measures to keep her from committing suicide.

Manfred Roeder, the German prosecutor, was angry at the Nazis' routine and flagrant circumvention of the law and was inclined to be lenient with the prisoners. In the case of women, he often found it especially hard to play his role of pitiless prosecutor. When Harnack was first sentenced to imprisonment, he said, "Let's let her go!"

Harnack was given only six years' imprisonment at hard labor, principally because the court believed that she had acted "more out of loyalty to her husband than of her own volition."(Hohne 1971, 193) Her sentence was obviously dictated by sympathy for "a highly educated woman interested in all questions of public, and particularly, social affairs." (Hohne 1971, 193) Initially, she was sentenced only as an accessory to espionage, not for complicity.

New evidence, however, was soon introduced regarding her participation. Gollnow had told Harnack about 12 planned Abwehr sabotage operations behind Soviet lines. She gave the information to her husband, who passed it on to Moscow. As a result, the Abwehr saboteurs were greeted as they landed with machine gun fire from the Soviet reception committee, and three dozen German soldiers were killed. The court considered this proof that during her intimate sessions with Gollnow, Harnack had systematically questioned him.

Harnack's husband was hanged on 22 December 1942. On 12 January 1943, Harnack was condemned to death. On 21 February 1943, Gollnow was shot by a firing squad. Four days later, on 25 February 1943, "his lover, her hair had turned grey during her captivity and she was terribly emaciated." (Hohne 1971, 203) She was executed by the guillotine on 26 February 1943. Her last words were, "And I loved Germany so much!" (Hohne 1971, 195)

Dallin, David J. *Soviet Espionage*. New Haven, CT: Yale University Press, 1955.

Hohne, Heinz. *Codeword: "Direktor."* New York: Coward, McCann & Geoghegan, 1971.

Marguerite Harrison
United States
1879–1967

Marguerite Harrison was one of the best spies in the last hundred years. She was born wealthy but supported herself and arranged her own cover as a journalist.

Her father had been the owner of a steamship company, and her brother-in-law was a governor of Maryland. Her first husband, Thomas Harrison, a stockbroker, died of a brain tumor at the beginning of World War I. He left her with a 13-year-old son, Tommy, and a debt of $70,000. She was an impoverished widow at the age of 36, but refused help from her wealthy family because she was determined to support herself.

She convinced a part-owner of *The Baltimore Sun* to give her a letter of introduction to the editor, who hired her as an assistant society editor. She also wrote a series of articles for the Committee on Public Information, to stimulate enlistment in the U.S. armed forces and to invigorate Americans' patriotism.

She didn't believe the horror stories produced by the U.S. and British propaganda mills about the German soldiers eating Belgian babies and bayoneting pregnant women for sport. She wanted to see for herself and decided, on the spur of the moment, that the way to do it was to join the Military Intelligence Department of the U.S. Army.

Her father-in-law was a friend of the chief of the Military Intelligence Department. The word was quietly passed to him and she was told, even more quietly, that she was to meet a certain gentleman in civilian clothes in the lobby of a Baltimore hotel. After this clandestine meeting, she was recruited, trained, and made ready for her first assignment.

She was given the rank of captain in military intelligence. Originally, she had been slated for an assignment in Switzerland, where she was to build her cover under a new identity, get an alias passport, and then enter Germany. Her task in Germany would have been to gather social and economic data rather than any military or political information. Before she could start, the armistice of 1918 canceled the need for that assignment.

Military intelligence still sent her to Germany but on a different mission. She received a salary of $250 per month and another $250 per month for personal expenses. Her mission was to report on economic and political matters that might be of interest to the U.S. delegation at the Paris Peace Congress. With the knowledge of Editor Frank Kent, she traveled under the cover of a correspondent for *The Baltimore Sun*.

Harrison always took good security precautions and used sophisticated tradecraft techniques to enhance her operational efficiency. The one time that she allowed herself to get sloppy, she was discovered. Fortunately, it wasn't the opposition that discovered her but a "friendly" agent of British intelligence. Mrs. Stan Harding, a British journalist married to a German, had arrived in Berlin at the same time as Harrison. When Harrison discovered that Harding was a convivial companion who needed a place to stay, she invited Harding to stay with her.

Harding pieced together scraps of an intelligence report that Harrison had been working on and had discarded in the wastebasket instead of flushing them down the toilet or burning them. Harding boldly proposed that they work together on the collection of intelligence information. Harrison decided to make the best of a bad situation and believed that she could still salvage the operation and silence Harding if she paid her as a piecework reporting source. Her G-2 case officer agreed, and they paid Harding a set rate for each piece of intelligence information that she produced.

There was a lot of Communist propaganda circulating in Germany among the

MARGUERITE HARRISON
Society of Woman Geographer   Collection, Library of Congress

U.S. troops during the war, which was being distributed by Robert Minor, an American and a former cartoonist for *The St. Louis Dispatch*. His propaganda urged the U.S. troops to revolt against their officers by shooting them if necessary, to quit the occupation of Germany as soon as possible, and to go home. Military intelligence didn't have the final piece of evidence that they needed against the cartoonist in order to successfully prosecute him and put him behind bars. Harrison was asked to collect this vital evidence. She went to Düsseldorf, posing as a socialist radical, and was able to elicit a confession from the printer of the subversive leaflets that he had done the work for the cartoonist. This was the crucial piece of evidence that G-2 needed for prosecution.

Harrison returned to the United States after this successful operation to learn that she had inherited $85,000 from her father's estate. She used the money to pay off her husband's debts and continued to work for *The Baltimore Sun* until military intelligence sent her to Russia under cover as a correspondent for that paper. She sailed in November 1919, accompanied by her son, Tommy, whom she planned to place in a school in Switzerland. She got as far as Warsaw, Poland, where she met Captain Merion C. Cooper at an American Red Cross dance. At that time Cooper was the leader of the Polish flying group known as the Kosciusko Squadron. Harrison eventually reached Moscow after a difficult journey.

In Moscow she interviewed Leon Trotsky and Alexandra Kollantai, heard Caliapin sing, and attended a speech by Lenin. She also routinely collected intelligence information wherever she could and sent it back to G-2 headquarters via the military attaché communications system. One morning, she was arrested and placed in Lubianka #2, the Cheka, or Soviet security force, headquarters. Lubianka #2 was the notorious headquarters of the Soviet secret police, famous for torture and executions. It had formerly been the headquarters of a Russian life insurance company, whose motto still hung over the entrance and seemed to give ironical advice to the prisoners of the Cheka who

passed through the doors. The sign read: "It is prudent to insure your life!"

The first night, Harrison slept on a wooden shelflike platform without blankets or a mattress. The following morning, she was taken to a well-furnished office, where she was politely interviewed by several members of the Cheka. The senior officer present, Moghiliesky, told her that they knew that she was a representative of the U.S. Secret Service. He claimed that they also knew that she had acted as a courier in Germany the year before. They had, he told her, reports from the United States and Germany to prove all of his statements. Moghiliesky then told her that he had a copy of one of the reports that she had prepared for military intelligence while she was in Germany and handed her a copy of the report as proof.

Unbeknownst to Harrison, an article had been published in the U.S. magazine *The Army and Navy Journal,* which had referred to the undercover work performed by a female U.S. agent who had been in Berlin after the armistice. Harrison later realized that Moghiliesky must have figured out who she was from that article. She pretended to accept Moghiliesky's offer to act as an informant on foreign visitors to Russia, but secretly she managed to send a message to the chief of U.S. military intelligence telling him that she had been turned and asking him to warn other agents in Russia to stay clear of her. She was able to continue filing intelligence reports to her case officer with G-2, right under Moghiliesky's nose, by sending reports out through "friendlies" to the U.S. military attachés in neighboring countries.

About this time, Harding, who was also in Russia, was arrested as a spy. In order to put pressure on Harrison, Moghiliesky made it appear to Harding that she had been arrested through Harrison's denouncing her as a spy. Of course this was a bluff, but Harding didn't know it. As a result, Harding hated Harrison for the rest of her life.

Using her limited freedom, which she had bought by agreeing to be an informant for Moghiliesky, Harrison managed to give some assistance to the other Americans who were still in prison. She was under constant surveillance and knew it, but she didn't think that helping her fellow countrymen would be considered anti-Bolshevik by Moghiliesky. She was surprised to find her old friend from Warsaw, Major (formerly Captain) Cooper in prison, charged with spying for the United States. She brought him food and clothes, which he later claimed literally saved his life.

Moghiliesky had hoped that Harrison would help him catch many spies, but, with the exception of some low-level innocuous information on a few unimportant visitors to Russia, her worth as a spy catcher had been nil. On 24 October 1920, Moghiliesky had had enough of her charade and had her arrested again. She then spent more than ten harrowing months in the Cheka's Lubianka jail as prisoner #2961. Most of the time she spent in a cramped room with an average of ten other women. Conditions were filthy, the vermin voracious, the diseases rampant, the interrogation incessant, and she came down with a sickness that could have developed into tuberculosis. The Cheka agreed, finally, to move her where conditions would help her regain her health. At the new jail, called Novinsky, there was sunshine, palatable food, beds with sheets and mattresses, baths, and clean clothes.

She had not been forgotten at home while she was in jail. Her family was well connected politically, her brother-in-law had been elected governor of Maryland, and her family had been agitating the federal government to procure her freedom. *The Baltimore Sun* sent a man to New York to plead with Ludwig C. A. K. Martens, the head of the Soviet Information Bureau in the United States, for her release. The real impetous for her release came from Herbert Hoover, whose American Relief Administration was beginning to distribute food to the millions of starving Russians. Hoover told Lenin that if he didn't release every American in captivity in Russian jails, he wouldn't get one morsel of food to feed his starving people. Senator Joseph I. France, (R) Maryland, also went to Moscow to seek Harrison's release and happened to be there when the pressure from Hoover's ultimatum took effect.

Before her departure, the Bolsheviks offered her tremendous inducements if she would become a double agent. Moghiliesky offered her a large estate and fabulous jewels (formerly property of czarist nobility), and free education for her son, Tommy, who had returned to the United States from school in Switzerland. She refused the offer.

Major Cooper met her as soon as she was released. He had been plotting a military raid to storm the prison to get her out. Fortunately, she was released before Cooper could blow up the jail. While the two of them were in Paris after her release, Harrison agreed to loan Cooper money to make a motion picture. The condition that she attached to the loan was that Cooper had to take her with him. After they completed the motion picture, Harrison returned to Baltimore, where she wrote several books about her experiences. Her thirst for adventure soon sent her to the Far East, where she wrote a series of fascinating articles about the area and her travels.

Eventually, she traveled back to Russia and was again arrested by Colonel Moghiliesky. It turned out that he had an amorous reason for pursuing her. He tried every way he could think of, short of force, to make her succumb to his advances. Harrison didn't capitulate. Once again she was arrested and this time was sent to Butykra Prison for ten weeks until the U.S. government again secured her release.

In 1925, she left with Cooper for almost a year in the wilds of Turkey, where they filmed a motion picture called "Grass." In 1926, she married Arthur Blake, an unsuccessful British actor. The couple moved to Hollywood, where Blake had a few minor parts in minor motion pictures until he died in 1949. Harrison then returned to Baltimore, where she did some writing and engaged in charity work. Toward the end of her life she lived with her son and his family. She died at the age of 88 on 16 July 1967.

(See also Alexandra Kollanti.)

Harrison, Marguerite. *There's Always Tomorrow: The Story of a Checkered Life.* New York: Farrar & Rinehart, 1935.

Olds, Elizabeth Fagg. *Women of the Four Winds.* Boston: Houghton Mifflin, 1985.

Author's Note: The author is particularly grateful to Mrs. Thomas Harrison for providing information about her mother-in-law.

Nancy Hart
United States
ca. 1836–ca. 1895

Nancy Hart was a self-taught spy who relied on her keen powers of observation. She was imprisoned by the Yankees but contrived her own escape. She took with her the details of the fort where she had been imprisoned and thus enabled the southern forces to attack it.

When the Yankees were encamped in West Virginia during the Civil War, Hart was a frequent visitor to their tent area. While using her charms on the young Yankee soldiers, she kept her eyes and ears open for any information that she thought would be of value to the Confederacy. She collected information about the Yankee troops and their plans for future battles and sent this information by slave couriers through the Yankee lines to Richmond, where it was read by Jefferson Davis himself.

Eventually, she was discovered by the Yankees, who had grown suspicious of the way she always found an excuse for hanging around the camp and for asking questions. She was arrested as a spy and was imprisoned in a Yankee jail to await trial. Her guards were the same simple Yankee soldiers that she had learned to charm so well in West Virginia. She set her sights on a particularly susceptible young Yankee and so charmed him that he allowed her to examine his rifle. With no compunction about killing the enemy, she promptly shot the young man in the head and killed him with his own rifle.

Legend has it that she then dashed from the jail without being caught. She took her time to choose the best horse in the corral, mounted the horse like a man, and rode off to freedom. She had learned the details of the Yankee encampment so well while she was in prison that she was chosen to lead a subsequent raid on it. One week after her escape, she returned, leading a Confederate cavalry of more than 200 men. She and her men easily recaptured the town that the Yankees had held.

Weiser, Marjorie P. K., and Jean S. Arbeiter. *Womanlist.* New York: Atheneum, 1981.

Gudrun Heidel
(Ute Schwarz)
Germany
1939–1968

Gudrun Heidel was the epitome of the spy who operated under such good cover that she could not be identified. Heidel was dead before the Germans exposed her and discovered her real name.

On 16 December 1968, a woman in West Berlin was struck by a taxi and was badly injured. The driver insisted that the woman had jumped in front of his cab, and his version of the accident was supported by witnesses. The woman died before regaining consciousness. Why she apparently committed suicide remains a mystery.

The name of a Frankfurt salesman was found in the dead woman's purse. He was called to West Berlin to help identify the body. He vaguely remembered the woman and a brief encounter that he had had with her. His story was that he had been in West Berlin on business, had picked her up, and had spent the night with her. She had told him that her name was Ute Schwarz and that she was a schoolteacher from Hanover. She told him that she lived at the Frühling guest house near the zoo.

An inspection of the rooms that she had occupied revealed a passport in the name of Ute Schwarz. Subsequently, the investigators in Hanover learned that the real Schwarz was alive and knew nothing about her namesake in West Berlin. Inside the lining of an old handbag in the imposter Schwarz's rooms, the inspectors found some papers covered with ciphers and an address in East Germany. It was discovered that the passport found in the imposter Schwarz's room was a forgery. West Berlin authorities assumed that the dead woman, whose identity was unknown, was one of the many low-level spies sent into West Berlin by the East German Communists.

One of the many photographs of the dead woman that were circulated throughout Germany brought a response from Heinrich Heidel of East Germany. He told the investigators that the dead woman was his daughter and asked that the West German authorities exhume the body and send it to East Germany for a proper family burial. He told the West German counterintelligence investigators that his daughter had been born on 14 August 1939 at Chemnitz, East Germany. He could offer no explanation for her presence in West Berlin.

The West German counterintelligence service was able to prove beyond any doubt that Heidel had been an agent of the East German Ministry of State Security. Recognizing that they had a tradable commodity with Heidel's body, West German authorities contacted the unofficial East German trader and dealer in spy exchanges, Wolfgang Vogel. The East German government admitted that it had two West German spies in its prisons that it would trade for Heidel's body. After some haggling over the exact conditions for the swap, Heidel's body was exchanged for two live West German spies.

Cookridge, E. H. *Spy Trade*. New York: Walker & Co., 1971.

Marie-Louise Henin
Belgium
ca. 1905–1944

Marie-Louise Henin practiced dental surgery before World War II and was known for her versatility as a spy. She recognized the need for and facilitated the coordination of clandestine propaganda with covert action and espionage. She ran an efficient organization, but her luck evaporated before D-Day, and she was arrested. The Germans beheaded her.

Before World War II Henin had been a Belgian dental surgeon. When the Germans overran Belgium, her patriotic heritage demanded that she fight the invaders. She helped establish an underground propaganda network that published anti-German newspapers, which contained the only accurate news about the war that the Belgian people got. (The Nazi-controlled propagandistic newspapers printed only information favorable to Germany. They reported German victories and inflated their importance in order to give a false sense of German strength. Allied defeats were trumpeted with much glee, and Allied victories were downplayed into insignificance.)

Henin was also active in guiding escaping soldiers, Belgian youths eager to join the Free Belgium Forces in Britain, and downed Allied airmen to safety so that they could fly again against the Germans. In addition, she organized her network to pass along intelligence concerning the German occupation forces. She made a most valuable contribution to the Allies in assessing German capabilities and intentions.

When the Gestapo captured her, they took her to Germany, where she was executed by decapitation.

Weiser, Marjorie P. K., and Jean S. Arbeiter. *Womanlist*. New York: Atheneum, 1981.

Joan Chase Hinton
(Peking Joan)
United States
ca. 1918–

Joan Chase Hinton, a brilliant American scientist, firmly believed that her country was aggressively conquering the world. She therefore dedicated her talents and all the classified information that she obtained from working on the U.S. atomic bomb project to the Chinese Communists.

Hinton was born into a progressive family that valued social reform ideas. Her mother, Carmelita Hinton, operated the Putney School, which was nonconformist and experimental. Its faculty were politically leftist and included some notorious Communists. Among her mother's friends who influenced her were Owen Lattimore, the United States' top Chinese Communist apologist, and Gregory Silvermaster and his wife, Helen, who were ranking members of Elizabeth Bentley's espionage apparatus. Some of the other notable persons who frequented the school were Alger Hiss and his wife, Priscilla, and Harry Dexter White, the assistant secretary of the treasury, who was also a Soviet agent. Hinton acquired her political beliefs from these people. She believed that Fascist reaction was rampant everywhere except in progressive Communist countries.

At an early age her interest in science absorbed her academic life. She saw beauty in the orderly world of mathematics, physics, and chemistry. She attended Bennington College in Vermont. She never dated, nor did she have any social life outside of her beloved scientific laboratories. She always received top grades in her subjects, especially nuclear physics. She went to Cornell University to do advanced work with that school's cyclotron. Hinton was a dedicated, near-genius scientist. When she transferred to the University of Wisconsin for additional advanced studies, she already had a reputation among her peers and professors for extreme competency.

Hinton decided that she wanted to work at the Manhattan Engineering District at Los Alamos. She may have made the decision on her own, but in light of her subsequent career, she may have been directed toward the project by her Communist case officer. She was already aware of the type of experimental work that was being done at Los Alamos and applied directly to the project for acceptance.

Dr. J. Robert Oppenheimer, the director of the Los Alamos project, was a close friend of Hinton's mother. They were sufficiently close that Oppenheimer had loaned the mother his ranch in Upper Pecos for her vacation in the summer of 1945. It is speculated that despite warning signs in Hinton's background that would have identified her as a possible security risk, Oppenheimer facilitated her acceptance at Los Alamos.

Hinton received a top secret clearance at Los Alamos in addition to special clearances that permitted her to go anywhere and see everything in the project. She had the title of research assistant but was sufficiently well regarded professionally to be present at the assembly and firing of the first atomic bomb. She would later recall, during one of her "Peking Joan" propaganda broadcasts from Communist China, that she had held the atomic bomb in her hands. She seemed to imply that she could have sabotaged the project and saved the world had she known how the United States was going to use the bomb against helpless people.

It is even more difficult to understand how she could have been granted a top secret clearance with full access at Los Alamos when the other members of her family are considered. Her sister, Jean, was involved in overt pro-Communist activities and married William Green, a nonpolitical and wealthy businessman who provided her with money and position before divorcing her. She became a part of the Washington scene that was immersed in Communist affairs. Gregory Silvermaster, her mother's old friend and Soviet spy master, got Jean a government job in Washington. Her house on Harvard Street became the gathering place for known Soviet agents, fellow travelers, and espionage contacts.

Although little is known of Hinton's brother, William Howard Hinton, before she went to Los Alamos, he was an active Communist in later years. William remained in Communist China throughout most of the Korean War. He had been a conscientious objector during World War II but changed his mind when he learned of the bravery of the Soviet Union at Stalingrad. He then tried to enlist, but the military rejected him. He became a propagandist for the Office of War Information. In this capacity he was closely associated with the antinationalist Chinese and pro-Chinese Communist faction of State Department and Institute of Pacific Relations members. These two groups so dominated U.S. policy toward China that no other substantive opposition was tolerated. William Hinton eventually went on the Chinese Communists' payroll as an "agricultural adviser."

When World War II ended, Joan moved in with her sister, Jean, in Washington. She claimed that she had resigned from the Manhattan Project at Los Alamos in shame when the United States dropped the bomb in Hiroshima. Hinton was told by her Communist friends that it was her duty to return to Los Alamos and to rise with the project, where she would eventually be more valuable to the cause. She asked Dr. Enrico Fermi (one of the leading scientists at the University of Chicago's Arogonne National Laboratories, where experiments in nuclear physics continued) for a job. Fermi hired her as his assistant, and the University of Chicago gave her a fellowship.

In late 1946, the security of the Manhattan Project was taken over by the FBI. The directors of Soviet espionage in Moscow recognized that the Bureau would soon be closing in on its agents. In New York, Elizabeth Bentley had begun to tell her story of Soviet espionage in the U.S. atomic program, and Harry Gold, the courier for the Soviets, had been called before a federal grand jury in New York. Moscow panicked and advised the Americans in its network to leave the country.

In early 1947, Hinton received credentials from the China Welfare Fund, cited by the attorney general of the United States as a Communist subversive organization. She asked for a passport from the Department of State to go to China as a relief worker and claimed on her passport application that she was also going to China to be married. On 12 December 1947 she left the United States for Communist China with a suitcase filled with notes and data on her work at Los Alamos and Arogonne National laboratories.

In Shanghai she married an American who was a dairy cattle expert. She was joined there by her brother, William, and his wife, Bertha, and the four of them entered Communist China. In September 1951, Hinton appeared at a Red China Peace Conference, where she delivered a fiery speech condemning the United States in Korea for using germ warfare.

She next embarked on a series of anti-American propaganda broadcasts directed at the troops in Korea. She lambasted everything that the United States was doing as wrong and Fascist and praised everything that the Chinese Communists were doing as right and enlightened. She was christened "Peking Joan" by U.S. officials for these broadcasts.

Burnham, James. *The Web of Subversion.* New York: The John Day Company, 1954.

de Toledano, Ralph. *The Greatest Plot in History.* New York: Duell, Sloan & Pearce, 1963.

Milada Horakova
Czechoslovakia
1901–1950

Milada Horakova's kind of leadership was rare. This gallant woman was not only a national leader of her country's women in peacetime but was a spy for her homeland against the Germans in World War II. She again became a spy when the Soviets invaded Czechoslovakia after the war. She became a national heroine after she was executed by the Soviets.

Horakova was born on Christmas Day 1901 in Prague, Czechoslovakia. Her father owned a small pencil factory, and her mother was a housewife. In World War I, Horakova helped tend the wounded soldiers, which led her to think that she wanted to study medicine. Before she could begin her medical studies, she switched to law. She was familiar with the many political theories that were popular as the new Republic of Czechoslovakia grew.

In 1923 she became an understudy to Senator Frantiska Plaminkova, who was the leader of the Czechoslovakian Women's Movement. In 1927 she married the editor of Prague's radio station, Bohuslav Horak. In 1933 they had a daughter, Jana.

When Germany invaded Czechoslovakia on 15 March 1939, Horakova joined the resistance movement. She sent information to the Allies throughout World War II and was a genuine heroine of the Czech Resistance.

On August 2 she was arrested and was

taken to a small cell that resembled a chimney, where she was forced to stand; if she sagged, she was refreshed with a bucket of cold water. She was transferred to the infamous "Jewish cell" in Pankrac Prison, where the Nazis beat her with switches and harassed her night and day. Her wounds became infected and remained untreated, but she did not confess. They then placed her with a group of syphilitic prostitutes who had sores that were oozing pus, but she still did not capitulate.

She was next transferred to the "death prison" at Fortress Terezin. There she decided to further confuse her captors by talking too much. She gave them a great deal of information, but most of it was false and only served to mislead the Nazis. The information that she gave them only had enough truth in it to make it believable. Her new trick kept the Nazis occupied for several months before they realized that they were being duped. As punishment, she was placed in Terezin's darkest, foulest dungeon.

She was removed to Germany for trial, where the court sentenced her to eight years and her husband, as coconspirator, to five years. She was imprisoned in the women's prison at Aichach, 27 miles northwest of Dachau. She was liberated by the American tank troups of General George Patton's force and returned to Prague on May 20, two days before her husband was released and rejoined her.

When the Soviets took over Czechoslovakia after the war, Horakova organized 78 national Czechoslovakian women's organizations into one cohesive group, the Czechoslovakian Women's Council, to combat the Communists. The group was, however, heavily infiltrated with Communist spies, who undermined the anti-Soviet stance of the organization.

Horakova and her husband tried to fight the Soviet domination of their country by passing vital intelligence to the United States. On 27 September 1949, Horakova was arrested by the KGB and was interrogated for 60 hours without interruption. Her husband managed to escape to the West.

Horakova was tried and convicted of espionage for the United States. She was hung in Pankrac Prison in June 1950.

Hoehling, A. A. *Women Who Spied.* New York: Dodd, Mead, 1967.

I

Noor Inayat Kahn[*]
(Madeleine, Jeanne Marie)
Russia
1914–1944

Noor Inayat was an almost mystical person who fought fascism by parachuting into Occupied France, where she spied against the Germans. Her stoicism in Nazi prisons was a comfort to other prisoners. She was executed and became a heroine because her courage inspired others to continue the fight.

Inayat was born 1 January 1914 in a private apartment inside the Kremlin in Moscow. (Her full first name was Noor-un-Nisa, which means "Light of Womanhood.") Her East Indian father was a descendant of the Sultan of Mysore, a musician, and a mystic. He had married her mother, Ora Ray Baker, an American, during one of his visits to New York. (It was rumored that Inayat's mother was related to the founder of the Church of Christ Scientist, Mary Baker Eddy.) Her father had been ordered by the Murshid, the leader of the Sufi sect of Indian Muslims, to make the Sufi philosophy known to the Western world. As a consequence, he had traveled through much of the world and happened to be in Russia when his daughter was born. He was a friend of the famous Russian author, Leo Tolstoy, and the Russian mystic-charlatan, Rasputin, who arranged for Inayat's mother to give birth in the Kremlin.

The family left Russia just before the October 1917 Bolshevik Revolution and moved to London. In 1920, they moved to France, where they settled in the Tremblay area north of Paris. Her father went to Geneva, Switzerland, to the International Headquarters of the Sufi movement. The following year he moved the family again, to the Wissous area, south of Paris. The next year he converted a wealthy Dutch widow to Sufism, and to show her gratitude, she offered to buy a house for his family. He chose one at Suresnes, a Paris suburb.

In 1927, her father contracted pneumonia during a visit to Delhi, India, and died. Her mother moved the family back from Holland where her father had been proselytizing to their new house in Suresnes. At this time, the family consisted of Inayat, her mother, a sister, and two brothers.

Inayat attended the College Moderne des Filles in Suresnes and the École Normale de Musique de Paris before entering the Sorbonne, where she planned to earn a degree in juvenile psychology. Carrying a heavy scholastic work load proved too much for her fragile health, however, and she had a nervous breakdown. Her mother sent her to Christian Scientist friends in the south of France and in Spain, who helped her to recover. In 1937, she entered the prestigious École de Langues Orientales at the University of Paris, where she studied for two years.

119

NOOR INAYAT KAHN
From A Man Called Intrepid *by William Stevenson*
(New York: Harcourt Brace Jovanovich, 1976)

She was in Paris when World War II started. She had been writing children's stories for broadcast over Radio Paris on "The Children's Hour." In 1939, she and a French publisher founded a children's newspaper called *Bel Age*. Thanks to her father's tutoring, she was talented in music and literature.

She had to flee to England with the rest of her family in 1940 when the German armies were getting close to Paris. They settled in Oxford. One of her brothers enlisted in the Royal Navy, and Inayat worked as a nurse's aide in a maternity house for officers' wives, but this didn't satisfy her longing for a more active participation in the war. She joined the WAAF and was given the entrance rank of aircraftsman 3C. SOE was desperately seeking experienced radio operators with linguistic ability at this time. In February 1943, she applied to SOE as a radio operator and was accepted on 8 February 1943.

Inayat first landed in France near Paris on 16 June 1943 with two other women, Diana Rowden (code named Paulette) and Cecily Lefort (code named Alice). The three women joined a larger team already in place, called Prosper, which operated from the École Nationale d'Agriculture in the suburb of Grigon, near Versailles. Unfortunately, soon after Inayat joined the group, it was broken by the Gestapo. One of the members of the reception committee was Henri Dericourt, a double agent working mainly for the Gestapo. At the time of the drop, he was already under suspicion by his comrades. Inayat was the only team member to escape the surprise raid.

When she moved to Suresnes, her girlhood home, many people in the area remembered her and helped her to hide from the Gestapo. In September, she thought that the search for her must have ended and felt safe enough to move back to Paris. There she rented an apartment on the rue de la Faisanderie. She was able to reactivate her radio link with SOE and tried to give them a damage assessment of the operation. She was told that a Lysander bomber would be coming to France to take her back to London.

She was determined not to leave until another radio operator could be dropped in to assume her duties. She waited too long, and the appropriate night landing conditions passed, forcing everyone to wait another month until the moon was in the proper phase again. Before the moon phase reappeared, Inayat was arrested in mid-October. She had been betrayed for the equivalent of $1,000 by a supposed friend who lived in her apartment building. (After the war, Renée Garry was charged with betraying Inayat to the Gestapo.)

Inayat had been sent to France without adequate training. No doubt one of the reasons that she was compromised was the lack of proper training in operational security. For example, while she was in France, in a denied area and a hostile environment, she left her code books strewn around her room unconcealed. She just wasn't attuned to the need for security.

Inayat violently resisted arrest. As soon as she was in prison, she managed to escape through a fifth floor bathroom window. She tried to escape by dodging over rooftops, but was unsuccessful. The Gestapo recaptured her and led her back to jail.

One of her fellow prisoners was a handyman named John Starr. The Gestapo used him as a general repairman around the prison. Starr always managed to keep a few tools after each day's work when he was returned to his cell. He and his fellow prisoners used the stolen tools to remove the skylights from their cells. They fashioned ropes from their sheets and blankets and managed to escape. They tried to escape over rooftops, but they, too, were captured.

The Gestapo didn't want to risk any more escapes, so they shipped Inayat off to Pforzheim Prison, where she was manacled to a wall. She and three other inmates were later transferred to Dachau, a notorious death camp near Munich. When the four women arrived at Dachau, it was too late in the evening for the Nazis to "process" them for execution, so they had a reprieve until the following morning. They didn't know that they were going to be executed, but Heinrich Himmler—chief of the death camps, the SS troops, and the Gestapo—had personally given the order for their execution.

The following morning they were given a meager breakfast and then led into the courtyard. There, on 12 September 1944, while the four women held hands, the SS shot each woman once in the nape of the neck.

Inayat's commander wrote in her commendation for the George Cross that she had behaved with the greatest bravery and defiance.

*"Kahn" is a caste designation and refers only to a lady of privilege. It is not properly a part of a person's name. Many authors have been confused about this and have indexed Noor Inayat under "Kahn."

Franklin, Charles. *The Great Spies*. New York: Hart Publishing, 1967.

Jezebel
Phoenicia
875 B.C.–843 B.C.

Queen Jezebel used her power to influence the religious beliefs in her husband's country as a means of strengthening her political influence. She employed legions of spies to seek information with which she could denounce her enemies, the Israelites.

For centuries, Samaria was the capital of Israel. It had been founded by the king, Omri, who was succeeded by his son, Ahab. Under Ahab the country was allowed to sink into idolatry, licentiousness, and almost total physical ruin. The main proponent of this change was Ahab's wife, Jezebel.

Jezebel was the daughter of a neighboring Phoenician king, who was a fanatical worshipper of the god Baal. Jezebel brought spies from her father's house with her to Samaria to covertly denigrate the Hebrew religion and persecute its followers. She converted Ahab to her religion, and the two of them worked to establish it in Israel. An altar and a temple for the worship of Baal were among the earliest structures erected in Samaria after Jezebel married Ahab. Jezebel tried to unite Israel and Phoenicia under a common religion in an attempt to politically bind her father's kingdom with her husband's land. She was unsuccessful.

Her husband and a son died, as the prophet Elijah had predicted, supposedly for having rejected the Israelites' religion. When another son became sick, the Israelite prophets anointed Jehu king over Israel, and he was sent to kill the remaining men in Ahab's family.

When Jehu came to Jezreel, where Jezebel was, she put on makeup to hide her signs of grief and to appear as a beautiful queen. From her window, she taunted Jehu with having killed a king. Jehu was unperturbed and had Jezebel thrown from the window to her death.

Azimov, Isaac. *Guide to the Bible.* New York: Avenal Books, 1981.

Blaikie, William G. *A Manual of Bible History.* New York: Ronald Press, 1940.

Jesse Jordan
Scotland
1893–ca. 1950

Jesse Jordan, a British citizen, married a German and remained loyal to her husband's country. German spies from around the world used her and her address to send information to their homeland.

Jordan operated a beauty parlor at 1 Kinlock Street in Dundee, Scotland. In 1938, the mailman noticed the large amount of mail being delivered to her house. The mail came from such exotic places as Italy, Spain, Mexico, Japan, the United States and—possibly more sinister to the postman—from Germany. It was an unusual assortment of mail to be delivering in her neighborhood. MI-5, in cooperation with the FBI, placed an intercept on Jordan's mail in Britain and on the senders' mail in the United States. They soon learned that the mailman had had reason to be apprehensive about the letters.

Jordan's beauty shop was being used by a German spy ring in the United States as an accommodation address. The investigators discovered that Jordan had been married to a German national who had been killed in World War I. After that, Jordan had spent most of her life in Germany and, although she had been born in Scotland, she spoke English with a marked German accent. Her loyalty during the war between Germany and Britain was with her husband's homeland.

In addition to being charged as an accessory to espionage for operating an accommodation address, Jordan was also charged for engaging in the collection of intelligence. She was found guilty of making sketches of places that would have been useful to the enemy and was charged with plotting the locations of Scottish Coast Guard stations and other mapping activities useful to the enemy. Jordan was sentenced to four years in prison.

Deacon, Richard. *Spyclopedia.* New York: Silver Arrow Books, 1987.

K

Edita Katona
(Marianne)
Austria
1913–

Anne Marie Edith Zukermanova, better known as Edita Katona, became an agent for French intelligence in Italy and the chief of the Italian secret service's mistress. She was able to convince the chief to defect in place and to provide the Allies with all the intelligence that his key position enabled him to collect.

Katona was born and raised in Vienna, where her father had his business. The family was originally from Czechoslovakia. Her father died before the Nazis marched into Vienna in March 1938. Katona considered the timing of her father's death to be fortunate, because it would have killed him to see the fall of his favorite city. Katona and her mother sold everything they had, including the family's antiques. They smuggled the money and their jewelry out of Austria hidden in their clothes and bodies. They managed to reach Monte Carlo, where Katona met her father's old friend, Colonel Eman Petera.

Petera, another Czechoslovakian refugee, was working against the Nazis for the Deuxième Bureau, the French intelligence organization. Katona asked him if he could get her a job with the Deuxième Bureau, because she wanted to fight the Nazis. She spoke French, Italian, and German fluently in addition to fair English and her native Czechoslovakian.

The Naval Section of the Deuxième Bureau met with Katona and, liking what they saw, recruited her for their Italian operations. She was given tutorial training in photography, memory aids, secret writing, codes, and the usual tradecraft security indoctrination. She lived with her mother, who would help her with her memory training during this period. They would sit at a sidewalk cafe and Katona would try to memorize a certain automobile going past—its license plate, the color, the number of people in it, and their descriptions. Her mother would write down the same information and quiz her later in the evening.

Katona had bragged to her recruiter that she knew high-ranking officers in the Italian intelligence service, so she was sent on a trial mission to Italy, where she was to contact and elicit information from the chief of the Italian intelligence service. He pretended that he didn't know her as well as he had known her family and, in essence, rebuffed her. She returned from that operation crestfallen and discouraged. Her new mentors in the Deuxième Bureau told her that even the best operatives fail and not to be discouraged.

She made several trips to Italy and took some photographs of ships at a naval base. In her book, Katona claims that these photographs were lauded by the Deuxième Bureau as real coups. She was able to recruit some subsources in Italy, the worth of whose reports varied from good to nominal. She had several love affairs and developed several very good sources, who were able to report on Italian military capabilities. She had a torrid, lasting love affair with the chief of the Italian secret service, one of Mussolini's top advisers. Katona claimed that the chief had tried to capture her but that she had captivated him instead. By the time she began to lose interest in the chief, Katona claimed that he was willing to trade rank and respectability for her promise of continued love. A payment of 3 million French francs probably helped persuade him to defect in place.

Katona and her mother moved to Rome, where Katona carried on her love affair with the chief of the Italian secret service. Due to some interservice rivalry, Katona's mother was arrested by the Italian counterintelligence service. She was imprisoned on very flimsy evidence. The strain proved to be too much for her, and she committed suicide, which had a devastating effect on Katona, but she completed her assignment for the French secret service.

Katona refers to herself in her book as the "most successful agent of the Deuxième Bureau" (Katona 1976), but there are few references to her in official documents of the Deuxième Bureau to support this contention.

Katona, Edita, with Patrick Macnaghten. *Code Name Marianne*. New York: David McKay, 1976.

Yoshiko Kawashima
China
1922–1945

Yoshiko Kawashima was a Japanese woman who became a spy, a covert action agent, and a national folk heroine to the entire Japanese armed forces. Morale could always be raised in a Japanese unit under siege with the cry, "Hold on a little longer; Kawashima is on her way to join us."

Kawashima was the daughter of a nationalist Chinese intelligence officer who claimed that he was of Chinese royal blood and who called himself Prince Su. Regardless of her father's alleged lineage, Kawashima claimed direct descent from a prominent Chinese Manchu family.

Her father had collaborated with the Japanese intelligence service, and its director, Naniwa Kawashima, was a personal friend. When Prince Su died, she was adopted by Kawashima. She took his name as her own and became a Japanese citizen.

In later years, Kawashima was sometimes referred to as the "Mata Hari of China" for her espionage prowess. She was also called the "Joan of Arc of Manchuria" because of her preference for male attire. In 1932, she returned to mainland China disguised as a young man and under orders from the Japanese intelligence service. Her mission was to reconnoiter the Shanghai area for a Japanese invasion. She amassed considerable intelligence about her target and developed a good reporting network of subagents.

She was only in Shanghai a short time when the Japanese ordered her to Tientsin to convince the emperor of China, Henry Pu Yi, that his best interests would be better served if he left China and settled in Japan. Pu Yi was taken aboard a Japanese navy ship and Kawashima then had the task of rescuing the empress so that she could join Pu Yi in his self-imposed exile. Calm as always, Kawashima disguised herself as a male taxi driver. There was heavy small arms fire along the route to the empress's palace, but Kawashima, oblivious to the personal danger involved, drove directly to the palace. She was stopped several times by Chinese armed guards but was able to cajole and bluff her way through each time. She calmly told the empress to get into her taxi and drove her to the wharf, where a Japanese destroyer was waiting to take her to her husband.

Kawashima was arrested in November 1945 by the Chinese counterintelligence service as a collaborator with the Japanese. The Chinese did not recognize her renunciation of her Chinese citizenship; therefore, she was tried for treason as a citizen of China and was convicted. The Chinese news agency announced that a "long sought for beauty in male costume was arrested today in Peking." (Deacon 1987, 197) Kawashima was executed immediately after her arrest.

Deacon, Richard. *Spyclopedia*. New York: Silver Arrow Books, 1987.

Christine Keeler
England
ca. 1942–

Christine Keeler strived for notoriety because she thought that any publicity was good for her call girl business. She became involved in espionage and was a willing participant in the development and exploitation of recruits and principal agents. Her fame, which triggered the fall of government leaders, lasted only a short time before she returned to anonymity.

In 1963, Dr. Stephen Ward was an ostensibly reputable osteopath who catered to upper-class Britons. Ward was also a talented portrait artist, and many famous people sat for him. Unbeknown to either his medical clientele or the people he painted, Ward was also a bisexual, who numbered among his friends and sexual partners pornographers, brothel-keepers, cheap and expensive call girls, and one notable gentleman who specialized in arranging flagellation orgies. Ward had met Keeler in a London West End nightclub and had invited her to his house to sit for a portrait. She became his mistress, and he became her pimp.

Among Ward's friends were such luminaries as Lord Astor and the British secretary of state for war, John Profumo. MI-5, the British security service, also had Ward on its payroll to provide "party girls" for subjects who were of interest to them for operational reasons. MI-5 hoped to get a picture of such a woman and a diplomat in a compromising situation, which would help them force the diplomat to defect to the British intelligence service. They then could use the diplomat to obtain information on a continuing basis.

To the surprise of his friends, Ward became a Communist in 1956. In 1961, he began cultivating the friendship of Eugene Ivanov, a GRU intelligence officer who was under cover as the naval attaché of the Soviet Embassy in London. Both Ward and Ivanov enjoyed a good party and would carouse all night with Ward's friends. Ivanov became Keeler's most frequent sex partner.

At a party attended by Lord Astor and his friends as well as Ward and his friends, Keeler slipped outside for a naked dip in the Astor swimming pool. Profumo saw her naked form from the drawing room balcony and was immediately attracted to her. The two met and became lovers.

Ivanov had been pestering Ward to find out from his influential friends if the United States planned to supply West Germany with atomic weapons. Discussions of the feasibility of obtaining the top secret information from Profumo were held between Ivanov and Ward in Keeler's presence. They asked her if she would obtain this information from Profumo.

MI-5 was monitoring the Ward-Ivanov relationship very closely but, at this point, they had no knowledge that their own secretary of war was involved with one of Ward's call girls. MI-5 did know that Profumo attended Astor's parties and had discreetly warned him of Ward's association with Ivanov. Profumo believed that MI-5's warning included his love affair with Keeler and took steps to end the relationship. Keeler then told Ward of MI-5's warning to Profumo, and Ward panicked. He went to his MI-5 control officer to offer his assistance in inducing Ivanov to defect. MI-5 politely turned Ward's offer down because he was too unstable to be trusted as the go-between. Ward was not to be rebuffed and was determined to become a famous double agent by helping Ivanov obtain information for the Soviet Union from some of his friends in the British government and then helping Ivanov defect to MI-5.

The British press had heard rumors of a cabinet minister's sexual involvement with a call girl, but they lacked details and were further restrained by Parliament's limits on

CHRISTINE KEELER
UPI/Bettmann

the British press. The ingredients for a sensational exposé only needed a catalyst.

The catalyst was supplied by Keeler, who counted a Jamaican drug dealer among her frequent sexual partners. The Jamaican attacked Ward's home, where he thought Keeler was staying, and the assault ended in his arrest and trial. On the witness stand at the Jamaican's trial, Keeler told the whole story about having a love affair with Profumo, the British minister of war, at the same time as she was having a love affair with Ivanov, the Soviet GRU spy and the Jamaican. Keeler testified that Profumo would leave her within minutes of Ivanov's arrival. She also said that she had thought that it was unwise and irresponsible for a married cabinet minister like Profumo to have an affair with some unknown girl like her.

As a part of the investigation of the Jamaican's attack on Ward's house, Keeler had given a statement to the police in which she accused Ward of being a procurer of women for men in high places and of being indiscreet himself. She also made the sensational accusation that Ward had tried to coerce her to obtain secret information from Profumo.

Scotland Yard then came into the case and instituted a crash investigation of Ward. Once the investigation began, Ward became a target for other charges in an attempt to decrease the attention on Profumo, according to some. Profumo made a statement before Parliament in which he denied involvement with any aspect of the sordid affair, but no one believed him.

On 4 June 1963, Profumo resigned his post as minister of war for Great Britain. On July 22, Ward was brought to trial and was charged with living off the immoral earnings of Keeler and her roommate, Mandy "Randy" Rice-Davis. Ward took an overdose of sleeping pills the day before the jury was to bring in the verdict and died on 3 August 1963.

Keeler wrote a book, which was not well accepted, and had a brief fling as an actress in a motion picture, which was equally unmemorable. She disappeared into obscurity. She had brought the allegations of espionage upon herself with the hope of reaping financial rewards from the notoriety, but her plan didn't work. She reaped only momentary tabloid fame.

Franklin, Charles. *The Great Spies.* New York: Hart Publishing, 1967.

Helen Keenan
Canada
1945–

Helen Keenan starting passing along classified information to the South Africans not because of any ideological sympathies but because of her relationship with a Rhodesian she had met in a bar who convinced her that he needed the data for his father's business. As a result of Keenan's actions, the British government began to review employees more thoroughly to make certain that they were remaining loyal to Britain.

Keenan was born to a typical, middle-class Canadian family. In 1967, she suddenly gave up a good job as a shorthand typist and stenographer in the British prime minister's office at 10 Downing Street. She claimed that she had left what everyone agreed was an excellent job because she was "bored." Most people who knew of her decision couldn't understand her attitude, because they thought that she had access to the inner circle of government, where important decisions were made. Her position allowed her to keep current on exciting world events, but she claimed that she was bored.

MI-5, the British internal security organization, routinely checked every employee who left a sensitive position in the government. When they investigated Keenan after her departure, they discovered that she had begun to frequent a sleazy bar called the Zambezi Club in Earl's Court, a well-known hangout for colonials from Rhodesia and South Africa. Keenan, under questioning, broke down and admitted that she had been stealing copies of top secret documents concerning Cabinet meetings from the prime minister's office for Norman Blackburn. He had told Keenan that his father was in business in Rhodesia and that it would be beneficial to his father's position if he knew what the British government had in mind for the future of Rhodesia.

After investigating Blackburn, MI-5 discovered that he was an intelligence agent of the South African government's intelligence service, the Bureau of State Security. Blackburn was interested mostly in a parochial South African matter having to do with proposals of the British government concerning Rhodesia. He admitted to receiving copies of Cabinet meeting minutes from Keenan on three separate occasions. He had passed the information on Rhodesian matters to a Rhodesian intelligence officer who was based on neutral ground in Dublin, Ireland.

Blackburn and Keenan were both sentenced on 25 July 1967. Blackburn was sentenced to five years. Keenan was sentenced to six months.

Leigh, David. *The Wilson Plot*. New York: Pantheon Books, 1988.

Kim Suim
Korea
ca. 1924–1950

Kim Suim became a spy in order to provide a better life for herself. She was well trained in tradecraft and was able to conduct many espionage coups for her Chinese Communist superiors. At first, she was successful in every assignment. She rose rapidly on those successes until she was arrested by UN forces. She was executed by a firing squad for espionage.

Kim was the daughter of a Korean peasant family and grew up amid deprivation and hardship. She was fortunate to receive an education from U.S. missionaries in Korea. In 1942, her previous ambivalence to politics changed when she attended a political rally and met the personable Communist militant, Lee King-Kook. He was an urban sophisticate, compared to naive Kim, and he quickly seduced her. He also introduced her to Communist theory and ideology and taught her some basic espionage tradecraft.

Lee got her a job at the dental clinic of a local Christian missionary college. She attended classes in Communist party work in the evenings. These classes, which included instruction in clandestine operations and advanced tradecraft techniques, were referred to by the students as "Mata Hari Red University" and "Red Charm School."

At the end of World War II, Suim received her first espionage assignment for the Chinese Communists. She went to work under cover as a U.S. missionary–educated, pro–United States woman, welcoming Allied troops (especially Americans) who were cleaning the last pockets of Japanese military resistance out of Korea. She spoke good English and only made herself sexually available to officers of field grade rank. (Her mentors at the Communist school had instructed her not to waste her time "being nice" to enlisted men or officers below field grade rank.)

Because of her ability to speak both Korean and English, she got a job as a telephone receptionist at the United States Military Headquarters in Korea. She could listen in on calls between Korea and Tokyo and Washington and was able to glean considerable worthwhile intelligence from these monitored conversations.

As her Chinese Communist case officer had hoped, a U.S. colonel fell in love with Kim. Whether his loose talk was designed to impress her or was merely negligence, it enabled Kim to obtain such intelligence nuggets as the one concerning the rift between President Truman and General MacArthur, which resulted in the general's subsequent dismissal, and the one concerning the U.S. policy not to pursue the enemy beyond the Yalu River and to establish the line of demarcation at the 38th parallel. The colonel had Kim promoted to a job in the provost marshal's office in the counterintelligence section. In this new capacity she had access to top secret documents and to reports on the U.S. government's investigations of

Chinese Communist intelligence operations in Korea.

The colonel and Kim moved into a luxury house, where they entertained lavishly as a couple. (Later, when she was arrested, it was discovered that Kim had used this house as a base for her anti-American espionage activities. She had a transmitter/receiver, with codes and getaway money, hidden in the house.) When the colonel was reassigned, he didn't take Kim back to the United States. Her Chinese Communist case officer ordered her to redirect her espionage attentions toward Syngman Rhee, the president of Korea.

Before Kim could begin this reassignment she was arrested by the South Korean counterintelligence service. They had, apparently, known of her espionage activities for some time but, in the hope of saving the U.S. colonel's reputation, they had not arrested her while she was still his mistress. She protested her innocence but was told that her espionage activities had been known for a long time, and they produced evidence of her conduct and contacts over the years.

On 8 June 1950, she was tried and convicted of espionage, treason, conspiracy, and 26 other crimes against the Republic of Korea. Kim hoped until the very last minute that the North Korean army would defeat the South Koreans and save her from execution. On 25 June 1950, North Korea invaded South Korea, and three days later, Kim was taken to Kimpo Airport, where she was executed by a firing squad.

Singer, Kurt. *Spy Stories from Asia*. New York: Wilfred Funk, 1955.

Raya Kiselnikova
Russia
1940–

A love of freedom and the luxuries of life in a capitalistic society led to Raya Kiselnikova's defection. She joined the Soviet foreign service and was assigned to the Soviet Embassy in Mexico, where she became embroiled in assisting the KGB in a plot to take over the Mexican government. She defected to Mexico because she was reluctant to give up the benefits of capitalism that she had come to appreciate.

Kiselnikova was born in Russia at the beginning of World War II and grew up in the postwar era of Stalin's authoritarian dictatorship. Her parents were able to give her a better education than most women in Russia received at the time. She grew up to be an independent woman who would come to reject all Soviet authority and Communist party conformity.

She married a Soviet physicist when she was in her twenties, but he died from radiation poisoning soon after the marriage, leaving her to fend for herself. She joined the Soviet foreign service and was assigned to the Commercial Office in the Soviet Embassy in Mexico City.

Although she probably was not a KGB officer from the beginning of her Mexican tour, Kiselnikova may have been co-opted by the KGB from her job with the Commercial Office, which she retained only for cover purposes. For all practical purposes, she was a regular KGB officer. She was a popular companion for the KGB officers in Mexico because she had a sharp mind and could discuss world events with the more sophisticated KGB officers. She had been a Western literature major in school and knew things about the West that even the KGB officers were eager to learn. She made an ideal and attractive companion for them when cover as a "husband and wife" was essential for the operation.

The chief of the KGB *residentura* (the KGB office inside the Soviet Embassy), Boris Kolomyakov, enjoyed her company on nocturnal missions and relied upon her help as much as his men did. Her closest KGB companion was Oleg Nechiporenko, the case officer on the most sensitive operation that the KGB had going in Mexico: an ambitious (but poorly conceived) plan to overthrow the Mexican government and make Mexico a Soviet satellite.

It is difficult for rational people to understand the enormity and audacity of Nechiporenko's operation. He had recruited about 20 Mexican men as the nucleus of a revolutionary army that was to wrest control from the Mexican government from its constitutionally elected officials by means of a bloody revolution. Nechiporenko had sent these 20 Mexicans to school in Russia and to North Korea for advanced guerrilla training. The Soviets planned for these revolutionaries to live, once they returned to Mexico, by robbing banks for money and raiding military outposts for weapons and explosives.

Nechiporenko expected recruits to flock to this revolutionary nucleus until they had a Soviet military revolutionary force in Mexico that could whip the regular Mexican army and throw out the existing government to make Mexico a Soviet satellite. Seldom, if ever, has there been such an extensive illegal operation visualized by any country's intelligence service against the legal government of another country with whom they enjoyed peaceful relations.

Kiselnikova was privy to almost all of the KGB secret operations that were directed out of the Soviet Embassy in Mexico City, she knew many of the KGB's clandestine Mexican agents, and she knew the KGB's operational techniques. On the morning of 7 February 1970, she was reported missing from the embassy. Whenever an officer is reported missing from a Soviet embassy, there is a hurried assessment of what may have happened to the officer and of how much knowledge he or she had that could damage operations if it were leaked.

On 10 February 1970, the Mexican government ended speculation when it announced that Kiselnikova had requested and had been granted political asylum. As soon as the Soviets were aware than she had defected and had taken with her extensive knowledge of secret operations, they began a comprehensive damage assessment. In this case, the KGB didn't know what operations had been compromised, because the officers who had bragged about their operations to Kiselnikova wouldn't admit their indiscretions.

Nechiporenko was permitted to visit Kiselnikova at the Mexican Foreign Office in an attempt to have her recant her defection. She refused and told him that she was sorry, but that he should realize that she could never go back. She gave him a sisterly kiss and disappeared into Mexico with a new identity and has not been heard of since.

Barron, John. *KGB*. New York: Reader's Digest Press, 1974.

Shula Arazi-Cohen Kishak
(Pearl)
Israel
1920–

Shula Arazi-Cohen Kishak, a Jew, was in a position to help her people by reporting what she observed and overheard in Beirut. She sent valuable intelligence to Israel that helped her people defend their homeland.

Kishak was born in Jerusalem to a middle-class Jewish family. She was her father's favorite daughter and went with him to Argentina while the rest of the family remained in Jerusalem. She went to school in Buenos Aires and learned Spanish but was happy to leave when the time came for them to return home.

Her happiness soon turned to sorrow when she learned that her father planned to "sell her" for the price of a dowry in an arranged marriage. Her fears and resentment changed when she realized that her betrothal to Joseph Kishak of Beirut was only following the Jewish custom of parents arranging their daughter's marriage. She was further mollified when she learned that her parents' marriage had been arranged in this traditional way.

She soon discovered that her husband was kind and considerate of her, and she adjusted well to life in Beirut in spite of many obstacles, not the least of which was the resentment that many Lebanese bore against the Jews. She was a good wife and mother, but she never lost her loyalty to and love for the Jewish people. She remained deeply concerned for their plight, and after World War II she vowed to do all that she could to help the emerging homeland of Israel. She became one of the leaders of the Jewish community in Beirut.

The fledgling country of Israel literally

fought for its life against the traditional resentment and deepening hostility of the Arab nations in the region. One day, while Kishak was working in her husband's shop, she overheard some itinerant merchants who had traveled in southern Lebanon talking about the military installations there that were directed against Israel. She encouraged their discussion and learned about some of Lebanon's mobilization plans that would affect any fighting with Israel. She realized how vital this information was to the defense of her homeland and found a way to get it into the correct Israeli hands, where it could be used to advantage against her adopted land. This was a difficult decision for her, but she realized that a fundamental loyalty to Israel must prevail if Israel were to flourish.

She continued to collect intelligence and found additional sources of information in her friends, many of whom were unwitting of their contributions. She was given the code name Pearl by the Jewish intelligence service for the unique beauty of her information. In the course of collecting information she moved from the highest circles of Lebanese society, where her position as the wife of a successful businessman provided her entrée, to the seamy underworld of smugglers, thieves, and double agents.

Later, when the Middle East became more violent and thousands of Jews were homeless, she established relief organizations and resettlement camps for the wanderers. She also created rat lines to smuggle hundreds of Jewish refugees from Europe and Asia to safety through Lebanon to Israel.

Golan, Aviezer, and Danny Pinkas. *Shula: Code Name "The Pearl."* New York: Delacorte Press, 1980.

Maria Knuth
Germany
1906–1955

Maria Knuth claimed that she spied against her country, West Germany, to prevent it from rearming, because she didn't want it to go to war again. She was operating an efficient espionage network for the Soviets when she lost her objectivity to a new lover, who turned out to be an agent for NATO.

Knuth married a well-known German writer, Manfred Knuth, and led an interesting life. When he tired of her, they divorced. In 1948, when Knuth was having domestic problems, Karl Kunze and his mistress, Marie-Louise Frankenberg, were developing Knuth for a recruitment pitch into Polish intelligence. They had been instructed by their Polish superiors in Warsaw to organize an intelligence-collecting network in West Berlin. (It was axiomatic that Polish intelligence in the post–World War II era was a proxy for the Soviet KGB.) Knuth, who was 42 and willing to try anything after her divorce, was an easy target for recruitment.

Kunze and Frankenberg operated their West Berlin espionage network using a combination art gallery and antique store as its business cover. They found a ready reservoir of potential recruits for their network among the disaffected, anti-Allied, but also anti-Nazi, conservatives in West Berlin. After they recruited Knuth, Kunze and Frankenberg had the West Berlin net functioning smoothly. When they had everything arranged, they moved their headquarters to Frankfurt, where they had been ordered to establish a similar espionage network. The new Frankfurt operation was to control all the West German operations. Knuth had become Kunze's second mistress, but there was no jealousy among the three team members. Knuth by this time had established herself as a dependable and hard-working member of the West German operation as a courier and an accommodation addressee.

As an accommodation addressee, Knuth was the caretaker of an address (a shop, house, apartment, or post office box), where she would receive mail containing reports or instructions that were usually written in code and possibly also in secret ink. She would then send the letters on to another address in some other city. She would probably forward most of them to Kunze or Frankenberg in Frankfurt, but she could have sent some to the intelligence network's headquarters in Warsaw. She served as mail cutout, or intermediary, between superiors and their agents.

The West Berlin and Frankfurt networks were operating efficiently and securely when Kunze committed suicide. Warsaw had liberally funded the two operations for some time without requiring an audit; their intelligence production appeared to be good, so Warsaw didn't bother to question their financial affairs. Kunze knew that he could steal with impunity and had been skimming the major portion of the money coming from Warsaw to support an extravagant lifestyle. When he learned that an audit would soon be demanded, he killed himself to avoid the shame and the severe retribution that the Polish service and the KGB would demand.

The operation of the two nets suffered from a lack of leadership until Knuth was assigned to take Kunze's place. She was a natural leader and administrator; both networks exceeded their previous high levels of performance under her guidance.

All went well until 1950, when the West German government became aligned with NATO. The security standards imposed by NATO affiliation required the West Germans to create a counterintelligence service, which they called Amt Blank. The new organization's charter required it to detect, monitor, and negate or control (by penetrations) Soviet and Soviet Bloc espionage activities in West Germany.

The Soviets were anxious to monitor and repulse the activities of this new counterintelligence service, so they ordered Knuth, through the Polish service, to launch an operation to penetrate Amt Blank. She applied for a job with them as a secretary but was rejected because she didn't have either the typing speed or the shorthand skills required for the position.

It wasn't until 1952 that Knuth succeeded in penetrating Amt Blank, even though she had persistently tried in many different ways and with a variety of agents. In 1952, one of her agents introduced her to a likely penetration agent, whose real name might have been Petersen. Petersen was already an employee of Amt Blank, and he told Knuth that he was disgruntled and wanted revenge on the organization. In addition to these very desirable qualifications for the job, Petersen soon displayed other qualifications that Knuth found irresistible. Knuth became Petersen's mistress and, along the way, lost her objectivity where he was concerned.

Regardless of Knuth's infatuation for Petersen and his obvious credentials, she was still required by organizational regulations to have any new agent vetted by her headquarters in Warsaw. Warsaw informed Knuth that, although they didn't have any firm evidence, Petersen might be a provocation. Although they authorized her to proceed with Petersen's recruitment (he was already recruited and working for her), they admonished her to handle him with maximum security.

Petersen became Knuth's best source of intelligence, supplying what appeared to be high-grade intelligence about Amt Blank's agents and operations. Warsaw, however, had been correct: Petersen was a West German counterintelligence penetration of Knuth's organization. All the intelligence that Petersen produced was fabricated by Amt Blank with just enough truth in it to make it believable.

Knuth, as Petersen's mistress, had not been emotionally equipped to handle Petersen at arm's length and to keep him on a strict need-to-know basis. Petersen had learned from Knuth everything that he needed for an airtight prosecution. Knuth and her subagents were arrested on the basis of his information.

While she was awaiting trial, Knuth was operated on twice for advanced cancer, but the surgery didn't slow the cancer. Knuth, who realized that she was dying, accepted the verdict of the court that she was guilty of espionage and treason. Her only defense was that she had done what she did in an effort to prevent West Germany from rearming. Her contention was that she would rather betray her country than see her country defend itself.

In January 1953, the judge sentenced Knuth to four years of hard labor. She never completed the sentence, because she died in prison in May 1955.

Hogen, Louis. *The Secret War for Europe.* New York: Stein & Day, 1969.

Alexandra Kollanti
Russia
1872–1952

Alexandra Kollanti was one of the great women of the Bolshevik Revolution. She never wavered in her complete devotion to Lenin and the Communist cause. She was one of the first Soviet female ambassadors and was an advocate of free sexuality and women's rights.

Kollanti was born into a liberal aristocratic family in Russia. She married at the age of 20 and became an ardent socialist three years later. In 1896, she left her husband and son to study in Zurich, where she joined the international socialist community. She organized working class women in Russia into a political force in 1905.

In 1917, after the Bolshevik Revolution, Kollanti became the only female commissar in Lenin's government. She later reported directly to Lenin by personal correspondence from her post as ambassador to Mexico. She provided him with information that she did not necessarily report through her regular diplomatic channels to the Ministry of Foreign Affairs in Moscow.

After the collapse of the Romanov regime in czarist Russia, the Bureau of the Central Committee that controlled the Bolshevik party consisted of three members. One of this triumvirate was Lenin, and Alexander Shlyapnikov, Kollanti's lover, was another. From about 1910 on, Kollanti was an active espionage agent for Lenin during this time; she sent him comprehensive reports on conditions inside Russia, without which Lenin would have been ignorant of the brewing political turmoil that caused the Russian Revolution in 1917 to be followed by the Bolshevik Revolution several months later. When Lenin returned to Russia aboard the now-famous "sealed train" on 16 April 1917, Kollanti was at the Finland Station in Petrograd to greet him.

After the October Revolution in 1917, Lenin appointed Kollanti commissar of Social Welfare and created Zhenudtel, the new Communist Women's Bureau, for her to manage. (This organization was abolished in 1930.)

In 1926, she was appointed the first Soviet female ambassador to Mexico. The Soviets had been represented in Mexico before Kollanti by Pestkovski, who had only ministerial rank. President Portes Gil commented that the friction and latent animosity that had existed between the two countries subsided considerably during Kollanti's tenure. Nevertheless, most Mexican officials and members of the diplomatic corps in Mexico City snubbed her because of her predecessor's activities. Pestkovski, an obvious spy, had always been trying to ferret out information by recruiting Mexican people to the Communist cause and demanding that they betray their own government. He created and bequeathed Kollanti considerable ill will for the Soviet cause that she had to overcome.

Regardless of the turbulence of her tenure, Kollanti sent back considerable good intelligence concerning the internal political situation in Mexico vis-à-vis the United States. She also reported on other countries in Latin America. Kollanti's advocacy of free love and sexual freedom, however, alienated her from Mexican women and made it extremely difficult for Mexican officials, who had wives, to have any business with her.

Mostly because of Pestkovski's antics, the Mexican government began to prosecute Mexican Communists, obstruct Communist diplomats, and discourage Communist sympathizers. Early in 1927, the Soviet Embassy was raided and, shortly thereafter, Kollanti left Mexico. She was recalled before the Mexican government declared her persona non grata.

She continued to crusade for the rights of women but never regained the eminence that she had enjoyed while Lenin was still alive and in power. She was one of the old Bolsheviks who served Stalin faithfully.

After her death in 1952 she remained a revered historical personage in Soviet culture, and she is still respected as one of the pioneers in the international struggle for women's rights.

(See also Inessa Elizabeth d'Herbenville Armand.)

Daniels, Robert V. *Red October: The Bolshevik Revolution of 1917.* Boston: Beacon Press, 1967.

Rowbotham, Sheila. *Women, Resistance and Revolution.* New York: Vintage Books, 1972.

Roberta Konig
Germany
1939–

Roberta Konig was a sleeper agent in West Germany, who was paid to live the life of a West German until the East German intelligence service had a job for her. She probably would never have been discovered if it hadn't been for a chance surveillance that observed her servicing a dead drop.

Konig was born in Dresden, East Germany, in 1939. When she was 28 she discovered that she was pregnant. She went to an abortionist to terminate the pregnancy. The doctor was an informant for the East German police. (Abortion was illegal in East Germany, and consenting to an abortion was punishable by a hard labor jail sentence.)

Several weeks after her abortion, Konig was approached by an officer from the East German intelligence service. He knew that he could threaten her with punishment if she refused his recruitment pitch. In an attempt to sweeten his proposal, he told her that if she accepted his proposition to become an espionage agent, she would be fighting fascism and the enemies of the East German government.

Konig agreed to the proposition because she had no choice. Her case officer told her that all she would have to do was to travel as much as she could in West Germany, buy Western-style clothes, and dress and act like a West German woman. She was to spend as much time as possible making friends with West German women, learning their habits and customs. The ultimate object of the operation was for her to be sufficiently westernized to be able to pass as a loyal, politically correct, West German who could be hired by the Ministry of Defense. Her case officer was prepared to wait two or three years for the assimilation process to take effect before exposing her to possible rejection or compromise.

She was given false documentation and sent to West Germany, where she took several low-paying, menial jobs in order to acquaint herself with Western office procedures and to obtain the letters of recommendation that would be needed for a job in the Ministry of Defense. When she finally obtained the job in the Ministry, security in maintaining contact with her was paramount to her case officer.

Her reports had to be placed in a dead drop, where they were picked up by a cutout (an intermediary) and taken to the case officer. (There may have been yet another dead drop and another cutout between the first pick-up and the ultimate drop off to the case officer.) The cutout knew when to service Konig's dead drop by a small sign that she would make on a tree in the park close to the dead drop site. The cutout would notify Konig that the dead drop had been serviced by making a sign on a different tree.

When she was ready to deliver a package, Konig would go to lunch at her favorite restaurant. Presumably, the cutout would watch for the sign on the tree every day. Konig would wrap her reports in waterproof oilcloth and put the package in the water tank above the toilet in the restaurant's women's lavatory. She would affix the packet to the inside of the tank with adhesive tape. If the cutout had any messages for Konig, she would use a series of marks on a tree that might signify warnings or a job well done. The agent and the cutout never met so that if they were arrested, they could legitimately say that they did not know each other.

The operation could have run for years except for the diligence of the West German Ministry of Defense security police, who routinely followed Konig one day and became curious about her love for trees. They observed her making a mark on one tree, having lunch, and then returning to the park later in the day to look at other trees. They eventually were able to deduce what Konig was doing when they saw her repeatedly mark a certain tree with a peculiar cross-type mark. They were able to arrest not only Konig but also her case officer. He was sentenced to five years; she was sentenced to four years.

Altavilla, Enrico. *The Art of Spying.* Englewood Cliffs, NJ: Prentice-Hall, 1967.

Ursula Ruth Kuczynski
(Sonya, Ruth Werner)
Germany
1907–

Ursula Ruth Kuczynski, better known as Ruth Werner, became a legend in her own lifetime, largely through self-aggrandizement. She used her code name, Sonya, for the title of a book about her exploits in espionage. Regardless of her conceit, she was one of the all-time great female spies.

Kuczynski was born in Berlin in 1907 to wealthy Jewish parents. Her father was a noted economist, and her mother was a housewife. Her brother and father were dedicated Communists, and Kuczynski became a Communist at an early age. At 17 she joined the Communist Youth Movement. She rose rapidly in the organization and soon led the Propaganda Section of the German Communist party in Berlin.

In the 1920s, she joined her father and brother in the United States, where they were engaged in intelligence work for the Soviet military intelligence service, the GRU, under the cover of doing academic research. Kuczynski worked for a short time in a bookstore in New York but left in 1929 to return to Germany, where she married her childhood sweetheart, Rudolf Hamburger.

In 1930, Kuczynski went to China, where her husband, also a GRU agent, had accepted a cover job as an architect with the Shanghai Municipal Council. Kuczynski was

already working for the GRU and her husband's job was contrived as cover for them both to continue their intelligence activities. They were amply supplied with GRU funds and were soon well established in the social life of the international community in Shanghai.

One of Kuczynski's closest friends in Shanghai was Agnes Smedley, a U.S. journalist and senior Comintern agent. She first met Smedley at a social gathering to celebrate the thirteenth anniversary of the Russian Revolution. Not ordinarily given to superstition, Kuczynski considered it a good omen for her future as a spy to meet Smedley and celebrate the revolution's anniversary on the same day. On this same occasion, Smedley told Kuczynski that Richard Sorge, another Soviet spy in Shanghai, had been a Comintern agent in Britain in 1928 before he had been co-opted by the GRU in 1930 for his Shanghai assignment.

During this Shanghai assignment, Kuczynski, despite her husband's presence, carried on an affair with Sorge. She worked under his tutelage as a spotter-recruiter and as an occasional source of intelligence for almost two years. She also allowed Sorge to use her apartment as a safe house in which to meet agents.

Kuczynski, with Smedley's help, developed her own cover as a successful journalist. She wrote for the leftist, pro-Communist newspapers such as *Red Flag,* signing her articles "A. Z."

In 1933, Kuczynski was ordered back to Moscow for intensive tradecraft training. About six months later, she was assigned to Mukden in Manchuria, China. Kuczynski had a cover job in Mukden with a U.S. bookseller. Her real work for the GRU was to provide a communications link between the GRU Moscow control and the Chinese Communists, who were fighting the Japanese in Manchuria. In Mukden she worked for a GRU officer whom she claimed to know only as Ernst. She wrote later that it was occasionally beneficial for a good agent to break the rules of clandestinity and compartmentalization and to consort together as sexual human beings. Kuczynski may not have known Ernst's real name, but she certainly knew him well; nine months later she had a baby daughter.

In May 1935, Kuczynski was ordered to Peking, where she continued her work with the GRU. In the latter part of that year she was ordered to leave China because Sorge's replacement as chief of the GRU base in Shanghai had been arrested, and Moscow feared that he might talk and compromise her. Kuczynski's husband was also due for home leave from his architect's post in Shanghai, so the couple left China together in order to preserve the appearance of marital bliss. They visited her parents, who were now in London, where her father was teaching economics at the London School of Economics.

The Hamburgers lived with her parents in London during their home leave. There Kuczynski was reunited with her old nursemaid, Olga "Ollo" Muth. In April, Kuczynski gave birth to Nina, her daughter by Ernst. Her husband accepted the baby as his own, and Muth became the child's nursemaid. Later, when the Hamburgers were assigned to Poland, where the husband was to be the senior GRU officer in Poland, Muth went with them as nursemaid. She didn't know, at this time, of the couple's espionage activities.

In June 1937, Kuczynski was recalled to Moscow, where she was awarded the Order of the Red Banner for her work with the GRU. In 1938, she was assigned to Switzerland to establish a new GRU network. The former GRU network in Switzerland had been effectively eliminated by Stalin's purges, which had started in 1936. Before assuming her post, she went to England to look over, and possibly recruit, agents for her new network from among the returned veterans of the Spanish Civil War. From those Republican veterans in England she recruited Alexander Foote as the net's radio operator. Kuczynski had to leave England before Foote's recruitment was complete, so she left the final details to her sister, Brigitte.

Kuczynski arrived in Montreux, Switzerland, on 23 September 1938 to activate her new network. Her husband had been posted back to China at his own request, because he preferred not to work any longer

with Kuczynski. At Caux, close to Montreux, Kuczynski established her home with Muth as nursemaid to her two young children. Caux was a health spa with many tourists, which made Kuczynski's comings and goings at all hours less noticeable.

Brigitte sent Foote to Switzerland as soon as his recruitment and training were completed. Kuczynski found Foote attractive, and the two lived together. Her Swiss network was well financed with covert funds from an account that the GRU maintained at the Irving Bank in New York City. A Communist lawyer in Switzerland regularly withdrew funds from this account in the United States and gave the laundered money to Kuczynski for salaries and expenses. (Kuczynski knew this attorney from Shanghai, where he had been a Comintern agent.)

Kuczynski liked to brag that she was solely responsible for all aspects of her network's operations in Switzerland. Actually, she was subordinate to Maria Poliakova, an administrative GRU supervisor. In December 1939, Poliakova directed Kuczynski to merge her Swiss network with the famous Lucy network that was based in Geneva, Switzerland. (The Lucy network was directed by another spy of considerable professional stature, Alexander Rado.) Shortly after this merger, another former member of the International Brigades of the Spanish Civil War and a close friend of Foote's, Leon Charles Beurton, was sent by Kuczynski's sister to join the group. Foote was replaced in Kuczynski's affections by Beurton, who lived with her as her husband from the first day that he joined her organization.

At the time of the Hitler-Stalin pact, Kuczynski started a discreet disinformation campaign among her conspiratorial colleagues. She claimed that her faith in Stalin, and therefore, in all communism, had been shattered by the Soviet alliance with Nazi fascism and that she wanted to be free of all ties with communism. She claimed that she was especially concerned about remaining in Switzerland because she anticipated that the German Nazis might overrun Switzerland, and then she and her children would be exterminated as Jews.

Actually, Kuczynski had received orders from the GRU to lay the foundation for a transfer out of Switzerland into a deep cover job. For the security of her future cover status, the GRU wanted even her closest friends to believe that she was genuinely disaffected with communism and that she had severed all connections with her espionage work. In preparation for this new assignment, Kuczynski needed British citizenship. Moscow instructed her to divorce Hamburger and marry Foote, who was a British subject. The Hamburgers were divorced at the end of 1939. Then, instead of marrying Foote, she married Beurton on 23 February 1940 (which was also the anniversary of the founding of the Soviet Red Army). Soon after her marriage to Beurton, Kuczynski was able to obtain a genuine British passport.

She prepared to leave for England but didn't intend to take the nursemaid, Muth, with her. Muth was distraught at the prospect of being separated from Kuczynski's two children, whom she had grown to love as her own. She did the only thing she could think of to prevent Kuczynski from taking the children away from her: she denounced Kuczynski and Beurton to the British consular representative in Montreux as Soviet spies. No action ever was taken by the British government on this report.

Kuczynski left Switzerland by bus with her two children on 18 December 1940. She went to Lisbon and then by ship to Liverpool, arriving there in mid-February 1941. She moved in with the Reverend and Mrs. Cox at Glympton just long enough to establish contact with her new agent at Blenheim Palace and to open her radio link with GRU headquarters in Moscow.

For greater security, she moved into a furnished bungalow in Kidlington, which was closer to the agent at Blenheim Palace whom she had been sent to service. In the fall of 1942, she moved into a larger, unfurnished house in Oxford, which had been the coach house of the mansion owned by Judge Neville Laski. Mrs. Laski was active in Jewish war relief work, and Kuczynski, playing the part of a poor Jewish refugee from Europe, was often the token "Jew from Europe" at the Laski fund-raisers. Kuczynski devised a pretext to persuade Laski to allow her to erect an aerial on his roof, which she was able to use to transmit her radio messages to Moscow. She hid the components of her transmitter and receiver inside her children's teddy bears.

Beurton finally obtained permission from Moscow to join Kuczynski in Britain. He moved in with her in July 1942 but was drafted into the British army a year later. It was about this time that Kuczynski purchased a bicycle. Kuczynski later wrote that during her innocent-looking pleasure rides, she was actually servicing dead drops that had been placed by her agent from Blenheim Palace.

Kuczynski was also ordered to establish a network of spies in Britain. Her brother introduced her to an international correspondent in London; she recruited an officer in the technical section of the RAF; she recruited a locksmith, whom she turned into an alternate radio operator; and Beurton recruited an expert in Britain's amphibious landing division and several others of equally good reporting potential. With these people, Kuczynski had wide coverage and excellent sources for getting intelligence on British capabilities and intentions. It was Kuczynski's ring of spies in Britain that first reported to Moscow in 1941 that Britain was reluctant to provide military aid to the Soviet Union because the British War Cabinet expected the German army to triumph over Russia in a matter of weeks.

Kuczynski, as Ruth Werner, wrote in her memoirs:

> None of my agents [in Britain] wanted money. The British people sympathized with the Soviet Union and the delay in opening a Second Front angered many of them. None of my British agents felt they were spies, they felt only that they were helping an Allied country that was fighting hardest and making the greatest sacrifices.

(See also Elise Sabrowski Ewert.)

Foote, Alexander. *Handbook for Spies*. New York: Doubleday, 1949.

Werner, Ruth. *Sonya's Report*. London: Chatto & Windus, 1991.

Ruth Kuehn
Germany
1917–

Ruth Kaethe Suse, known as Ruth Kuehn, had an unusual espionage career because her father, mother, and younger brother were also involved. Their family was sent to Hawaii by the Japanese to provide information about troops and ships before the bombing of Pearl Harbor. Even during the actual assault, the Kuehn family continued to provide valuable information to the Japanese. Kuehn had also been a mistress of Joseph Goebbels.

The Kuehn "family" was put together by German intelligence for cover and operational efficiency. According to the cover legend created by the German intelligence service, Ruth Kuehn was born in Germany in 1917, the daughter of Bernard Julius Otto Kuehn and his wife, Friedel Kuehn. This threesome operated one of the major Japanese espionage organizations at Pearl Harbor in 1941.

They had been a happy family in Germany until, in 1935, their eldest son, Leopold, couldn't get a date for a company dance. The company was Nazi Germany's Ministry of Propaganda, and the dance was given by his superior, the minister of propaganda himself, Dr. Joseph Goebbels. Leopold was Goebbels's private secretary, and his attendance at the dance was mandatory. He couldn't get anyone else to go with him, so he had to take his sister, Ruth.

Kuehn was an uncommonly pretty girl, who looked like the ideal Teutonic reproductive machine, as popularized by Goebbels's propaganda. Goebbels was not only the third most powerful man in Germany (after Hitler and Goering), he was also one of the most lecherous and sexually insatiable men in Germany. He and Kuehn met in 1935 and enjoyed a rapturous relationship for a time, until he tired of her. Eventually, he wanted to be rid of her forever.

Kuehn's father was a friend of Heinrich Himmler, the chief of the Nazi SS troops and the infamous Gestapo. Goebbels, therefore, had to devise some reasonably civilized method of disposing of Kuehn that wouldn't arouse Himmler's anger.

Kuehn's father, Dr. Bernard Julius Otto Kuehn, had served in World War I in the German navy. He then went into medicine but was not successful. He was an early member of the Nazi party and became a member of the German Security Service under Reinhardt Heydrich. He had hopes of becoming a police chief when he was forced to leave Germany with his family after the Goebbels incident.

Coincidentally, the Japanese intelligence service had requested the assistance of its Axis ally, Germany, in recruiting Occidentals to act as Japanese agents, because their own nationals would be instantly recognized in a Western environment. A friend of Goebbels heard about the Japanese request and suggested that it offered a way to get rid of Kuehn. Goebbels ordered the whole Kuehn family (except the older son who was still Goebbels's secretary) to accept the Japanese offer and move to Hawaii.

The family was first sent to Japan, ostensibly to learn the language of the country that would become Germany's most important ally. In Japan the Kuehns suddenly found themselves wealthy. They had just come into a large "inheritance," which enabled them to move to Hawaii as wealthy citizens.

Dr. Kuehn's scholarly background enabled him to create a cover for the entire family's move. He was ostensibly studying the history of the Hawaiian Islands and the Japanese people in the Pacific. His alleged interest was the effect of the Japanese people on the Polynesian culture. The family settled easily into the idyllic island lifestyle. They had a palatial home full of objets d'art and gave the impression that they had always been wealthy and cultured. In three years, more than $70,000 was deposited to their account. Mrs. Kuehn always returned from her vacation trips to Japan with bundles of bank notes.

The studious doctor and his lovely, academically inclined daughter were unnoticed as they made many trips to the other islands in the chain. The island-hopping trips helped them to gather information on U.S. defenses on all the islands and to pinpoint the movements of the U.S. Pacific Fleet. Their cover was so good that neighbors offered to help the family when Mrs. Kuehn left on extended "vacations," during which she was acting as a courier and having consultations in Tokyo at the headquarters of the Japanese intelligence service.

Kuehn was still beautiful and was a popular date at the local U.S. military social events. The only topic of conversation of any gathering in Hawaii at this time was the possibility of war with Japan and how the islands would be defended.

The Kuehns were reporting the intelligence they collected to both the Japanese and the Germans. (The Japanese were not aware that the Germans were sharing the intelligence take from the Kuehns.) In 1939, they were instructed by the Japanese to move from Honolulu to Pearl Harbor, where Kuehn was to open a beauty shop. This beauty shop was to cater almost exclusively to the wives of U.S. Navy officers. Operating a beauty shop was excellent cover for Kuehn and her mother, who helped out from time to time. The wives of the naval officers gossiped while they were in the beauty shop. They talked about all the things that their husbands had warned them not to talk about: official business and the movement of ships and men.

Kuehn's father continued to study the history of the islands. He regularly took his young son, Hans Joachim, age six, for walks along the fortified part of Pearl Harbor or sailing along the approaches to the harbor. Hans would be dressed in a sailor's suit, and the U.S. Navy gangplank watches thought that he was cute. The officers on duty would often invite the "cute little boy" and his father aboard the ships docked along the quay. Hans had been trained on what to look for aboard a ship and was an accomplished spy at age six.

The Kuehns bought a beach house at Kalamar on Lanakai Bay on the windward side of the island of Oahu. The house was called Kalamar, and its steeply sloping roof with its dormer windows could be seen for miles out to sea. Kuehn used to signal regular reports to Japanese submarines, using a simple but effective code devised by her father. Lights burning in certain windows at certain hours meant different things and, in the daytime, signals were made with different sizes and colors of clothing drying on the beach.

The vice-consul of Japan in Honolulu, Otojiro Okudo, told the Kuehns that Japan needed the precise details of the U.S. fleet at Pearl Harbor: the movement of ships in and out of the harbor, submarine defenses at the mouth of the bay, exact geographic coordinates for ships at anchor in the bay, the state of repair of ships in dry dock, and the turn-around time for resupplying at Pearl Harbor.

Okudo gave them a simple code to be used with an on-off flashlight signal. On 2 December 1941, he tested the line of sight between the Kuehn's home and his base to be certain that he would be able to see their flashing messages. The signaling system and code worked perfectly. Okudo had a radio at his base with which he could transmit the Kuehn's information directly to the Japanese fleet, which was lying offshore, and to the Japanese Consulate in Honolulu.

In the early morning of Sunday, 7 December 1941, the Kuehns were at their posts overlooking Pearl Harbor, reporting the effects of the Japanese bombings. They reported which ships had been sunk and what targets needed to be bombed again for maximum damage. Unfortunately for the Kuehns, two U.S. naval officers saw the suspicious flashing lights coming from the Kuehn's attic window and had them arrested.

Admiral Yamamoto, the commander of the Japanese fleet, desperately needed to know before he launched his attack planes if the U.S. fleet was using anti-aircraft captive balloons above the ships lying at anchor in harbor. The Kuehns were able to assure him that there were no captive anti-aircraft balloons that Sunday. This information immeasurably improved Yamamoto's capability to destroy much of the fleet on the first sortie without any previous reconnaissance. The destruction on such a massive scale could not have been accomplished if Yamamoto had

had to send in reconnaissance planes as a first wave. The element of surprise for his attack planes would have been completely lost, and the destructive effectiveness of the actual attack would have been impossible.

If the Kuehns had not been arrested, the entire family would have been evacuated from Oahu by Japanese submarine at 9:30 A.M. the morning of 7 December 1941. When the two U.S. intelligence officers arrived at the Kuehns' house, they found the downstairs hall filled with suitcases and luggage. The suitcases were crammed with bundles of Japanese money. One of the agents guarded Hans and Mrs. Kuehn while the other agent dashed upstairs and burst into the attic. Kuehn was still standing at the window with her binoculars, observing the carnage at Pearl Harbor, while her father was on the other side of the attic, relaying the information to the Japanese consul.

The Kuehns were charged with espionage for a foreign power in time of war. To try to save each other, the doctor, his wife, and Ruth Kuehn each claimed that they had been individually in charge of the operation. The U.S. Military Tribunal finally accepted the doctor's claim that he had been in charge and sentenced him to hang. In an effort to save his life, the doctor offered to tell all about Axis espionage in the Pacific area. As a result of this cooperation, in October 1942 his death sentence was commuted to 50 years' imprisonment. He served only four years before he was released and returned to Germany.

Kuehn and her mother were interned until the end of the war and then were repatriated to Germany.

Ind, Allison, Colonel. *A Short History of Espionage.* New York: David McKay, 1963.

Layton, Edwin T. *And I Was There.* New York: William Morrow, 1985.

Liston, Robert A. *The Dangerous World of Spies and Spying.* New York: Platt & Munk, 1967.

L

Sybil Ludington
United States
ca. 1762–ca. 1805

Sybil Ludington was one of the youngest female spies in history. When she was only a teenager, she showed great courage by making a dangerous ride over mountainous terrain to warn an American detachment that the British soldiers were coming.

During this year, probably 1775, Ludington's father, a colonel in the Connecticut state militia, received word that the British soldiers were planning to raid a supply depot in Danbury, Connecticut. He couldn't leave his post, but the small detachment of Americans guarding the depot had to be warned. His daughter rode to the depot, a distance of more than 40 miles, in the dead of night to alert them.

The ride wasn't easy. The terrain was mountainous and heavily wooded. In addition, British soldiers were patrolling the area, and a woman out alone at night would have been stopped, detained, and possibly violated. Ludington managed to overcome all these obstacles, which was a testimony to her determination and courage.

Weiser, Marjorie P. K., and Jean S. Arbeiter. *Womanlist.* New York: Atheneum, 1981.

Gertrude Machado

(Gertrude Allison)
United States
ca. 1910–

Gertrude Machado was a deep cover OGPU agent and formed a good spy team with her husband. Her contribution to the Soviet Union's intelligence and assassination operations is exemplified by her participation in Leon Trotsky's murder. She set the stage for Trotsky's assassination when she introduced the assassin to a person who would unwittingly provide access to Trotsky.

Trotsky had been the leader of the Bolshevik Revolution and the founder, together with Lenin, of the Soviet Union. When he had a major dispute with Stalin—who had achieved control of the Soviet Union through deceit and a power play—Stalin had made the mistake of condemning Trotsky to exile instead of murdering him when he had the chance inside the Soviet Union. Later, when he perceived the threat that Trotsky represented, Stalin swore to kill Trotsky and ordered the Soviet intelligence service to implement his order.

In mid-1937, Louis Budenz, editor of the CPUSA newspaper *The Daily Worker,* was ordered by his OGPU case officer, Roberts (Dr. Gregory Rabinowitz, chief of the OGPU in the United States), to begin a search for someone who could provide access to Trotsky's entourage and get the assassin

close enough to Trotsky to murder him. Budenz recalled that the Ageloff sisters— Hilda, Ruth, and Sylvia, who lived in New York City—were Trotskyites and therefore, he assumed, close to Trotsky. To get to the Ageloffs, Budenz used Ruby Weill, with whom he had worked in the Conference for Progressive Labor Action. Weill had been a close friend of Hilda Ageloff, and through Hilda, she made contact with another sister, Sylvia, who had the closest association with Trotsky.

When the OGPU planners learned that Sylvia Ageloff planned to take a vacation in Europe, they decided that Weill would accompany her and would introduce her to a "charming man," who would seduce her. After the seduction, the OGPU could use Ageloff as a conduit for introducing their assassin into Trotsky's inner circle.

Rabinowitz instructed Weill to contact Gertrude Allison (Machado), who worked in a Communist bookstore in Greenwich Village, the Jimmy Higgins Bookshop. Weill was to visit Machado so that she would recognize her in Paris, where Machado would introduce Sylvia to the man who was to seduce her. Before they sailed for Europe, Machado gave Weill detailed instructions for preparing Ageloff for the seduction. Weill was to encourage plain-featured Ageloff to expect an adventurous, exciting, and very romantic vacation in Europe.

In Paris, Machado came to the hotel where Weill and Ageloff were staying and introduced them to a young man who, she said, would show them around Paris. The man was Ramon Mercader using the name Jacques Hornard. Machado then left, and Weill found other things to keep herself busy. Ageloff was left alone with her seducer, who wined and dined her and—after only a few days—professed undying love. Ageloff was smitten and reciprocated.

Before Weill had met Machado, Machado's husband, Eduardo, had been very active in the Anti-Imperialist League in New York City, which was an OGPU front organization. He had been deported from the United States twice for subversive activity. When he was unable to return to the United States, he and his wife went to Moscow in 1932.

They stayed in Russia for several years, during which time Machado made several courier trips back to the United States for the OGPU. Later, after the Weill-Ageloff operation, Machado lived in Paris in 1938 and 1939. The Machados then moved to Mexico, where they served as support agents and safe house keepers for OGPU operations. In the 1950s, they were the center of a group of Communist exiles in Mexico City who were in Mexico at the courtesy of the Mexican government, which had a liberal policy regarding political asylum seekers. An officer of the Soviet Embassy in Mexico City was the case officer for these exiles. Among them were several Communist agents who had fled their governments, including Fidel Castro and Che Guevera.

The Machados remained in Mexico but eventually, after the fall of anti-Communist President Perez Jiménez, they returned to Venezuela, where they established the Venezuelan Communist party and where they continue to agitate for communism.

Brown, Anthony Cave, and Charles B. MacDonald. *On a Field of Red*. New York: G. P. Putnam's Sons, 1981.

Marthe Cnockaert McKenna
Belgium
1892–ca. 1960

Marthe McKenna was a patriotic Belgian agent who used her nursing profession as a cover for espionage among wounded German patients and their German doctors. She nursed the German sick and wounded even though she hated them for what they had done to the innocent civilians of Belgium.

McKenna was born Marthe Cnockaert in Roulers, in southwest Belgium, in 1892. Her father was a prosperous farmer. When World War I began, she was at home on the farm taking a vacation from her medical studies. When the Germans occupied Belgium she was forced to minister to their wounded. She joined three nuns who had come from Passchendaele and converted a large old house in the neighborhood into an emergency hospital.

Her three brothers had joined the army to fight the Germans as soon as war had been declared. McKenna and her parents were left to run the farm and to face the hardships of occupation. During the fighting, their home had been used by the French army as a firing position. The French had fortified the farmhouse and made firing slots in the sides of the thick walls. When the Germans occupied the area, they accused her father of having fortified and manned this firing position. They arbitrarily ordered the farmhouse burned to the ground; her father was to be locked in the house to be executed by burning. The farmhouse did burn to the ground, but McKenna's father escaped through a cellar window that the Germans had left unguarded.

McKenna, who was 22, knew that helping Britain and France fight the Germans was the best way to work for Belgium's eventual freedom. She became a spy for the Allies, enticing and wheedling secrets from the German doctors and patients at the hospital. It wasn't too long before spy paranoia convinced the Germans that the nuns at the hospital were signaling to the Allied forces at night with lights from the topmost windows of the attic. The nuns were ordered either to leave the village within three hours or be executed. McKenna, because she was a lay nurse, was allowed to remain and continue to work at the hospital. She was an excellent nurse, and the Germans were using her linguistic abilities (she spoke Flemish, French, German, and English) to help them communicate with the Belgians.

McKenna and her mother were the core leaders of the nursing group. Together with 11 women from the village, they were the only civilians allowed to remain in the combat zone after December 1914. The Germans were paranoid about spies being everywhere. When the 11 village women were suspected of being Allied spies, they were removed from the combat area. McKenna was allowed to remain, mostly because the Germans desperately needed her nursing and linguistic abilities.

In January 1915, the Allies made a temporary incursion into German territory, which convinced the Germans that McKenna might also be a spy. Actually, she was not guilty in this case. She was then sent to Roulers with an introduction to the German military commander. There, McKenna and her mother lived in a small cottage and were reunited with Mr. McKenna. They had thought that he had been burned to death in the fire, but he had escaped, adopted a new identity to avoid recapture by the Germans, and had been working on a remote farm on the outskirts of Roulers.

Late one evening, Lucille Deldonck, whom they thought had been lost after she disappeared from Westroosebeke, returned to recruit them into British intelligence. Deldonck told McKenna and her mother that she had been working as a British agent since she had left her family farm. McKenna and her mother eagerly accepted recruitment. Before she left, Deldonck told them that they would receive further instructions in a day or two.

When McKenna was shopping in the marketplace several days later, an old woman named Canteen Ma, apparently only selling vegetables, slipped her a message asking her to go to an outlying farm that evening. At the meeting, McKenna again met Deldonck, who instructed her to collect all the information that she could from the German doctors and patients at the military hospital. She was to give this information to another agent, known to her as No. 63. In order to alert No. 63 that she had a message to be picked up from a dead drop, she was to go to the fifth house on a certain side street and tap three times, wait a few moments, and tap two more times. Someone would then know that the dead drop was to be serviced. When there were additional instructions, Deldonck would contact her.

McKenna was told that if anyone approached her wearing two white metal safety pins in their lapel or on their bodice, she was to give them her fullest cooperation, because they would be loyal Allied agents. Above all, warned Deldonck, McKenna must remain on constant alert for the German counterintelligence officers, whom the locals had dubbed the "Berlin Vampires."

McKenna had become an expert in elicitation techniques and garnered good intelligence from her patients, the German doctors, and the hospital staff. She also established some churches in Flanders as rendezvous centers for British soldiers escaping from German detention. These church safe houses were also used by British agents who were constantly infiltrating and exfiltrating the German lines.

A fortuitous offer came to McKenna when the owner of a small cafe wanted to sell his business and move his family to safety away from the war zone. McKenna convinced her parents to buy the cafe, and in March 1915 they did. McKenna wanted to control this cafe because it would enlarge the scope of her collection efforts by allowing her to listen to the German customers discuss military information. She also looked at the cafe as a way to keep her family together.

On 22 April 1915, the Germans launched their first chlorine gas attack against the Allied forces at Passchendaele. For the preceding several weeks, McKenna had sent the Allies reports containing facts to indicate that preparations for such an attack were being made. Nevertheless, she had been told by her superiors that these reports were worthless. Her first report was that barrels of chlorine had been brought into the area and had been stored under heavy guard just outside of town. She mentioned that at the same time, two German chemists had taken up lodging at her family's cafe. The second report was that these chemists had been making weather maps of prevailing winds and had gone up in a balloon to observe the wind patterns. Both reports were dismissed by British intelligence as useless, and she was admonished to direct her collection efforts to more important matters.

McKenna continued to report on German intentions and capabilities while performing her nursing duties for the Germans. The Germans were so pleased with her work that they awarded her the Iron Cross for devotion to duty. Some of her more important espionage achievements during this time included: permanently putting out of commission a telephone link between the Germans and a priest behind Allied lines; arranging the murder of a lieutenant in the German counterintelligence service who had tried to recruit her to spy on the British; getting the German operations officer at the Roulers airfield drunk so that she could reroute his reports concerning a new type of fighter aircraft to an accomplice, who copied them; and discovering an antiquated and forgotten tunnel sewer system that ran from her hospital to a terminus underneath the German ammunition dump, into which she had dynamite placed to blow up the dump. (Unfortunately, in this sewer operation she lost a gold wristwatch engraved with her initials.)

Without any warning and without any connection to her espionage work, there was an administrative shake-up at the hospital, and she was dismissed. Her firing was due to a new female superior's vendetta against her and was no reflection on the quality of her work.

In November 1916, a notice was posted on the German commandant's office bulletin board listing property that had been stolen by a thief. The notice said that former owners could pick up their property at the local police station if they had proper identification. Among the items listed was McKenna's gold watch. At this point McKenna made the biggest mistake in her life. She couldn't remember whether she had lost her watch in the sewer tunnel or if the clasp had broken sometime when she was walking in the village. As soon as she claimed her watch, the

German security forces pounced on her. They searched her room and found two coded messages concealed behind her washstand. She was charged with espionage, but she refused to cooperate by naming her accomplices and even refused the services of the "Prisoner's Friend," who was similar to a public defender. Winston Churchill commented years later, in his introduction to McKenna's book: "By all laws of war her life was forfeit. She did not dispute the justice of her fate." She was condemned to death, but because she held the Iron Cross and the German doctors at the hospital at Roulers pleaded for clemency, her sentence was commuted to life imprisonment. Fortunately, the armistice was declared after she had served two years. She was released and returned to Belgium a liberated person.

After the war, British Field Marshal Earl Haig commended her for gallant and distinguished service in the field. She was awarded the French and Belgian Legions of Honor. The British were satisfied to let Field Marshal Haig's comments stand as their only tribute to her.

After the war she married a British officer, Jock McKenna, who had processed her field reports at the headquarters of British intelligence. She then lived in England, where she wrote an account of her espionage exploits and several novels with intriguing espionage plots.

Deacon, Richard. *Spyclopedia*. New York: Silver Arrow Books, 1987.

McKenna, Marthe. *I Was a Spy*. London: Jarrods, 1953.

La Malinche
(Doña Maria)
Mexico
ca. 1495–ca. 1540

La Malinche was an Indian woman who became a national heroine to the Mexican nation even though she helped their enemy, the Spanish conquistadors, to subjugate her countrymen. Without her, the Spanish conquest of Mexico could not have taken place.

DOÑA MARIA
From Conquest of Mexico *by William H. Prescott; illustrations by Keith Henderson*
(Garden City, NY: Doubleday, Doran, 1937)

La Malinche was born in the village of Painola, near Vera Cruz. She was probably a daughter of one of the chiefs of the area. Her father died when she was a child. Soon after her father's death, her mother married another nobleman and gave birth to his son. The new husband wanted his son to be the only heir to his lands and title and convinced her mother that La Malinche must leave. When the daughter of one of their slaves died, they pretended that La Malinche had died. They buried the dead child of the slave as if it were La Malinche and went through the elaborate rituals of mourning the death of a nobleman's daughter.

La Malinche was then secretly given to a wandering tribe of Indians in an area far from Vera Cruz who later sold her to the Tabasco Indians. As she grew up among different tribes with different customs and different languages, La Malinche was acquiring the ability to adapt to various cultures and developing a facility with languages.

On 12 March 1519, the Spanish conquistador Hernán Cortés and his flotilla of galleons arrived off the shore of the Tabasco Indian nation. The Tabasco Indians tried to repel the Spanish invaders, but they were overwhelmed by the Spaniards' firearms and their horses. The Indians made a tentative, arms-length peace with the Spanish because there was nothing else they could do.

The Spanish had brought no women with them, and they soon wanted help with washing, cleaning, cooking, and other tasks around the camp. The Tabasco Indians "gave" the Spaniards 20 women to help with the chores; among them was La Malinche. She was first given to Captain Alonzo Hernandez for his personal use. It was at this time that La Malinche was baptized into the Roman Catholic faith with the name Maria. Later, because of her stature as Cortés's mistress and companion, she was given the honorary title "Doña Maria."

It soon became apparent that La Malinche was very useful in dealing with the Indians. She quickly learned Spanish (at least enough to communicate), which enabled her to translate Indian comments and observations for the Spaniards and, more importantly, to translate Spanish dictates to the Indians.

When Captain Hernandez returned to Spain, she became Cortés's translator and mistress. She loyally accompanied him and his marauding troops into the interior of Mexico. In many instances she could convince the tribes that they encountered along the way to the capital not to fight the Spanish. These tribes then were quickly conquered by Cortés and some became his allies in conquering the Aztecs of the capital, Mexico City (called Tenochtitlán).

La Malinche was an extraordinary covert action agent. Using propaganda techniques, she convinced the non-Aztec Indian tribes that it would be in their best interest to ally themselves with Cortés against the Aztecs. She was an invaluable intelligence analyst who could tell whether the information that she translated for Cortés from Indian sources was the truth or a lie or whether a provocation were hidden in the information. She was able to edit the information coming from non-Aztec Indian sources to enable Cortés to determine the best way to use that information. She accompanied Cortés everywhere and has been given credit by historians for the relative ease of the Spanish conquest of Mexico. She influenced Cortés to be more merciful toward his Indian captives, which limited Spanish cruelty considerably.

In 1524, Cortés mounted an expedition to conquer Honduras and took Doña Maria with him. In Honduras she married one of the Spanish noblemen, Juan Jaramillo. As wedding presents, and in gratitude for her help, Cortés gave her the towns of Jalolepec, Oluta, and Tetiquipape. On 14 March 1529, he gave her a large tract of land close to Chapultepec, the lovely park area where he had his palace. Chapultepec Park is now a park area in the heart of Mexico City. On July 3, Cortés gave La Malinche a large orchard area close to what is now Alameda Park in Mexico City.

Del Castillo, Bernal Diaz. *The Discovery and Conquest of Mexico.* New York: Farrar, Straus & Cudahy, 1956.

Schmidt, Minna M. *Four Hundred Outstanding Women of the World.* Chicago: Minna Moscherosch Schmidt Publisher, 1933.

Hede Tune Eisler Massig
Austria
1899–1981

At an early age, Hede Massig married a senior Comintern representative who became a power in the Communist hierarchy. She was recruited into espionage for the Soviets by another senior Comintern representative who later broke with Stalin and was murdered. After a life of intrigue, persecution, and isolated moments of happiness, she broke with communism and became an FBI informant. She was one of the crucial witnesses against Alger Hiss.

Massig's mother was the daughter of a prominent rabbi in Poland. Her father was a circus acrobatic rider. Massig was brought to the United States by her family when she was a young girl. She was able to learn English and something of the American way of life, both of which helped her cover when she later became a Soviet espionage agent in the United States. The family lived in Fall River, Massachusetts, and later in New York. Massig's father tried to start a business as a caterer, but it failed because he began to gamble and run around with prostitutes.

The family then returned to Germany, where Massig attended a finishing school. She received a scholarship to a conservatory of fine arts, where she studied drama. She thought that she wanted to become an actress but soon recognized that she probably didn't have the talent to be a really good one. The conservatory students often gathered at the Cafe Central and the Cafe Herrenhof; it was at the Cafe Herrenhof that she met Gerhardt Eisler, who would become a top-ranking Comintern/OGPU agent. Eisler had been a lieutenant in the German army during World War I but had been demoted for spreading Communist propaganda among the troops. He later became the chief of all Soviet intelligence in the Far East and in the United States.

Eisler began to come to the cafe every night. After the first week he told Massig that he loved her, that he was a revolutionary, and life with him would not be easy or soft. Then he proposed that they live with his family until they could set up a home for themselves. Massig agreed and moved in with the Eisler family the following day. Massig and Eisler were married in Vienna and moved to Berlin when Eisler became an editor of the principal Communist newspaper in Germany, the *Rote Fahne.* Eisler taught her the principles of communism but refused to allow her to join the Communist party. Massig found a job in Berlin with the Tribune Theater playing the role of Gwendolyn in *The Importance of Being Earnest.*

In 1923, Massig became ill and had to live with friends outside of Berlin. Eisler remained in Berlin and was too busy to visit her. They gradually drifted apart. That same year, Massig met Julian Gumperz, a U.S. citizen by birth but a German by parentage and choice. Gumperz was a wealthy member of the Communist party who owned a publishing company that specialized in Communist literature. Massig left Eisler and moved into a house that Gumperz's mother bought for them in a Berlin suburb. Soon after, Massig left Eisler for good. A short time later, Eisler lost his job at the newspaper. Gumperz invited Eisler to share their house.

Massig's younger sister, Elli, was also living with them. When Eisler moved in, he and Elli paired off. Soon Elli was accepted by everyone as Eisler's common-law wife. She bore Eisler a child after they had been to China together, where Eisler was the chief of the OGPU. Elli and Eisler gradually drifted apart and officially separated.

Gumperz was placed in charge of all Communist publications in Germany. In 1926, he and Massig arrived in the United States, where Gumperz did research for a book on agrarian reform in the United States. They met many leading U.S. Communists, including Mike Gold. When their money ran out, Gold got Massig a job helping with underprivileged children. Gumperz returned to Germany to finish his doctoral thesis while Massig remained in Pleasantville, New York, in order to get her U.S. citizenship, which she obtained in 1927.

In 1928, she returned to Frankfurt, where Gumperz had been hired to teach at the Institute of Social Research. A young German named Paul Massig was a senior doctoral student at the Institute. Paul Massig was the leading Marxist theoretician at the Institute but refused to join the Communist party, because he thought it would be too dictatorial and would impinge on his freedom. Soon Hede and Paul were lovers. They moved into their own apartment, but Paul Massig and Gumperz remained friends.

When Paul Massig took a job in Moscow teaching at the International Agrarian Institute, Hede Massig stayed in Berlin, waiting for Paul to find suitable living quarters for them in Moscow. During this wait she renewed her friendship with Richard Sorge, one of the great Soviet spies. She had known Sorge and his wife when they were all students together at the Institute of Social Research in Frankfurt. Sorge wined and dined her for several weeks. One evening he took her to a small, sophisticated cafe. After a good meal he told her that he knew how she could help Moscow. Sorge said that he wanted her to meet an important comrade. He took her by taxi to another cafe, where, in the back room, a small man was waiting for them.

Massig recognized the man immediately as having been one of her customers when she worked at Malik's Book Store in Berlin. It was the fabulous "Ludwig," chief of the European OGPU. "Ludwig" was eventually identified as the leading OGPU agent in Europe, Ignance Reiss. (He was assassinated nine years later by the OGPU for defecting from the OGPU.) Ludwig began Massig's training in espionage tradecraft. As her first task, Ludwig asked for a list of her friends and a detailed biography for each one.

Despite Ludwig's pleas that she not go to Moscow, Massig went to join Paul. In Moscow she worked at the State Publishing House for two months, doing absolutely nothing. She then got a job teaching German at the foreign-language Technikum. The director of this school was Fanny Borodin, the wife of the Comintern/OGPU agent Mikhail

Borodin. The Borodins originally came from Chicago. He had been one of the founders of the Mexican Communist party and the chief of the Soviet "advisers" to China before 1926. Borodin had been demoted when Massig met him at the school and he was the editor of the English-language *Moscow Daily News*.

During 1930–1931, there was a shortage of everything in Moscow. Having more to eat than did her language students because she was a foreigner embarrassed Massig. Ludwig was a frequent visitor to Moscow during this time, and he always visited the Massigs.

In the early spring of 1931, Paul and Hede Massig returned to Berlin. They found that in the short time that they had been away, fascism had grown tremendously under Hitler. Ludwig reactivated Massig as his agent and used her as a cutout, to scout out areas for dead drops, and as a courier. She went on a mission to England as a translator with an OGPU accountant while he audited the books of the British Communist party.

On 30 January 1933, Hitler was made chancellor of Germany. The Nazi party's anti-Communist purges were already being brutally enforced. On February 27, the Reichstag burned; the Jews and Communists were blamed for the arson and were arrested. Paul Massig went underground to continue helping the Communists fight against fascism and Hede Massig moved to Czechoslovakia, using her U.S. passport. A short time later she returned to Moscow.

The man in charge of Comintern finances assigned her to carry money to the Comintern representative in Paris. While she was in Paris she received a message that the Nazis had arrested her husband, Paul Massig. Fortuitously, she met Ludwig, who told her that Paul had really been working for the OGPU all the time and that she should go back to Berlin. Ludwig promised her that whatever money was needed to help Paul would be made available to her through him. Ludwig impressed upon her that Paul must be freed before the Nazis made him reveal the details of the OGPU underground in Germany.

She managed to get to the small town near the concentration camp where Paul was imprisoned. She saw him marching in a work detail outside the compound, and their eyes met but they dared not speak. Paul managed to get a message to her that she couldn't help him and that she must get out of Germany immediately. She returned to Paris determined to lose herself in work. Ludwig arranged for her to go to the United States to work as a Soviet agent.

She sailed for the United States in October 1933 with the cover of a correspondent for the newspaper *Weltbuehne*. She moved in with Helen Black, the Soviet Photo Agency representative and an OGPU agent, in New York. She had met Black through Mike Gold during her previous visit to New York in 1926.

Earl Browder, the head of the CPUSA, visited her to extend his welcome at the request of Gerhardt Eisler, her former husband, who was on Communist work in the Midwest. She made several trips to Washington, where she found a warm reception as a Jewish German refugee and as a newspaper correspondent. Harold Ware, son of the infamous grand dame of U.S. communism, Mother Bloor, was a great help in familiarizing her with life in the capital. She was fortunate to attend one of President Roosevelt's press conferences and was impressed by the democracy of the arrangement. She raved about Roosevelt as a person; later, she could never understand those Communists who referred to him as pro-Fascist.

When she received word that Paul had been released, the OGPU made arrangements for her to make a courier run back to Paris so that she could be there when he arrived. Before she left New York she met the man who was to be her new boss in the OGPU, Valentine Markin, who used the street alias Walter. (Markin was to be the chief of all OGPU activities in the United States.)

Paul returned to the United States with her to teach economics. He wrote a book about his experiences in Hitler's concentration camp called *Fatherland*. She resumed her work as an OGPU agent, getting information from her Washington contacts and making courier runs to Paris. In 1934, Markin died from a head wound that he received while he was drunk. Massig's new OGPU case officer was Walter Grinke, who used the street alias Bill. Massig was the cutout and agent handler at times for Noel and Herta Field and Alger Hiss. She later testified for the prosecution against both Hiss and Fields.

In November 1937, Paul was recalled to Moscow, and she went with him. Her case officer at the time was a woman named Helen, who begged her not to go to Moscow but to remain in the United States working for the OGPU. Helen implied that her espionage work was more crucial to the success of the Soviet effort than joining her husband on a routine visit to Moscow. Helen was really Elizabeth Zubilin, the wife of Vasilli Zubilin, who became the head of all OGPU/NKVD operations in the United States. Massig was adamant that her place was with Paul; on the first night out they discovered in the dining salon that Helen also was aboard the ship.

In Moscow they were subjected to a series of intense interrogations about their association with Ludwig (Ignance Reiss) and were entertained in the finest manner by Helen and her husband. At this point Massig expressed a desire to leave the OGPU, and the Zubilins did everything they could to convince her that her work was too important for her to leave. It was obvious that she and Paul were being kept in Moscow against their wills as virtual prisoners. They threatened to go to the U.S. Embassy and were eventually allowed to leave Russia.

They stayed in New York for the winter of 1938. The purges that Stalin had carried out in the Soviet Union had included many of their friends, such as Ludwig, and prompted them to tell their story. In October 1939, they bought the Courtney Farm in Haycock Township of Bucks County, Pennsylvania. Paul wrote and she got a job at the Todd Shipyard that, except for weekends, kept her in Hoboken during World War II.

In the summer of 1940, Massig received a message from Helen Zubilin that she wanted a meeting. Massig met with Zubilin and was polite but firm that there was to be no more work for the OGPU/NKVD. She told Zubilin that she wanted nothing more to do with the Soviets except to be friends.

In the winter of 1947, Bob Lamphere of the FBI contacted Massig for information about Gerhardt Eisler. This was the catalyst that made the Massigs tell everything about Soviet intelligence in the United States. She became an expert witness for the FBI and testified in the Hiss-Chambers perjury trial.

(See also Renata Steiner and Elizabeth Zubilin.)

Andrew, Christopher, and Oleg Gordievsky. *KGB: The Inside Story.* New York: HarperCollins, 1990.

Dallin, David J. *Soviet Espionage.* New Haven, CT: Yale University Press, 1955.

Massig, Hede. *This Deception.* New York: Duell, Sloan & Pearce, 1951.

Anna Maximovich
Russia
ca. 1910–

Anna Maximovich was born into the Russian nobility and might have been expected to become a strong anti-Communist, because the Soviets destroyed the nobility. Instead, she became a committed Communist and spied for the Soviets from her base in Paris. She and her brother worked for the legendary Leopold Trepper's espionage network.

Maximovich's father, a Russian nobleman who owed his allegiance to the Romanovs, had fled Russia in 1922 after having fought for the White Russian forces against Bolshevism. He settled in Paris with his daughter and his son, Vasili, but their mother chose to remain in Russia. Maximovich's father died soon after they arrived in Paris. She and her brother were placed in the care of Monsignor Chapital, the Roman Catholic bishop of Paris. She grew up in a convent and became a medical doctor specializing in psychiatry and neurology. Her brother also had a Catholic upbringing and became an engineer.

At the outbreak of World War II, Maximovich financed a Communist front group, the Union of Defenders of the Soviet Union, out of profits from her medical business, which was a rehabilitation home for psychiatric patients. The French authorities thought the organization had been subsidized by the Soviets and was a cover for Soviet espionage. They arrested Maximovich. When she was able to prove the validity of her business and that she had funded the union, she was released.

Her brother was also interned at the beginning of World War II by the French authorities as a possible Soviet subversive. When the Germans overran France, he was released by the Germans to act as an interpreter. He spoke French, German, Russian, and a smattering of other languages. The German who obtained his release was a general with strong anti-Nazi feelings. Soon after his release, he was approached by Leopold Trepper, director of a Soviet espionage network in France. Trepper persuaded him to join his espionage network and to obtain papers from the German general's desk.

Maximovich's brother married a German woman who worked at the German army's Department of Military Administration, which was a logistical support base that had a communication center. His wife had unlimited access to excellent communications intelligence, which she gave to her husband. About this time he was given unlimited access to the German military headquarters in Paris because he was an aide to the general for whom he did translations. This access allowed him to collect a much broader and diverse type of intelligence, which he turned over to Trepper's net. He also established another network subordinate to Trepper's network and, insofar as possible, compartmentalized from it. He recruited his sister to work for this new network.

After the war, with Trepper's financing, Maximovich established a clinic on the line between the Occupied and Unoccupied zones of Germany. Her office at the new clinic served as a meeting place for Trepper's agents who passed through the zones. In addition, through her brother's influence with the general, a large number of German officers suffering from battle fatigue, nervous psychosis, and other psychological problems came to her clinic for treatment. Her treatment of these sick German officers provided yet another excellent source of intelligence. She gave them strong "truth serums" and adroitly questioned them on sensitive military matters without their being aware of what was happening.

Trepper's entire operation was one of the most prolific producers of important intelligence that the Soviets had against the Germans during and following World War II. Soon after the Belgian and Dutch counterintelligence services started to eliminate Trepper's operations in their countries, Trepper himself was arrested in France. On 27 November 1942, Trepper lacked the courage to protect his subordinates. As a result, Maximovich and her brother were arrested by the French counterintelligence service, and the entire espionage network collapsed.

Seth, Ronald. *Encyclopedia of Espionage*. New York: Doubleday, 1972.

Eustacio Maria Caridad del Rio Hernandez Mercader

(Caridad Mercader)
Cuba
1892–ca. 1954

Caridad Mercader was tough, thorough, and versatile. She was a secret courier for the Comintern/OGPU in Europe, the leader of the Spanish Communist women in Barcelona, mother of the assassin who committed the "crime of the century," and the mistress of a senior OGPU officer. Her life influenced many other spies and clandestine operations.

Mercader was christened Eustacio Maria Caridad del Rio Hernandez. Her family was moderately wealthy, and she received what would have been considered at that time an upper-class education. She attended a school in France run by the nuns of the Daughters of the Sacred Heart. The family moved permanently to Barcelona, Spain, on 23 October 1906. She had a girlish whim that she wanted to join a religious order and served a novitiate as a sister in the Order of the Carmelite Decalzas (the shoeless).

When Mercader was 18, she married Don Pablo Mercader, who was 26. He was a caring father to their children, but wasn't interested in parties, nightlife, and the bohemian life that attracted his wife. Mercader took up painting with a Communist artist who introduced her to a more exciting life, and she became his mistress. In 1925, Mercader left her husband and took the children with her to France. Both families attempted to reconcile the couple, but she was adamant and made the break final in 1929.

She loved life on the Left Bank of Paris and became a full-fledged member of the Communist party, an underground agent of the Comintern, and a secret courier for the Comintern/OGPU between Paris and Belgium and later to Spain. In later years, she regaled her friends in Moscow with stories of her numerous and promiscuous love affairs with the French Communist leaders.

On 17 July 1936, General Francisco Franco raised the banner of revolt against the Popular Front government of Spain. The next day, July 18, Mercader, who was back in Spain, took charge of the crowds milling about the main plaza in Barcelona. The people couldn't make up their minds whether or not to attack the still-entrenched troops of the Spanish government in Barcelona. Mercader leaped to the fore and led the disorganized people against the government troops. Afterward, she openly took charge of the Union of Communist Women and had an office in the Hotel Colon Barcelona.

On 6 November 1936, Mercader, the 44-year-old mother of Ramon Mercader, Leon Trotsky's future assassin, arrived in Vera Cruz, Mexico, on a reconnoitering mission with a group of Spanish Communists. Mercader and her group arrived in Vera Cruz using Mexican passports. It was obvious to the Mexican immigration authorities that they were not Mexicans. The group was detained but refused to give any information about their true identities. The Spanish consul was called to help resolve the situation, but they refused to talk with him. Finally, the Mexican minister of the interior was appealed to, and he ruled that the Spaniards could remain in Mexico for a short time as visitors.

Trotsky, former minister of foreign affairs of the Soviet Union and leader of the Bolshevik Red Army, was sent into exile by Soviet Premier Joseph Stalin. Stalin had erred when he allowed Trotsky to leave Russia alive, because Trotsky was an implacable foe of Stalin's. The Comintern, on Stalin's orders, monitored Trotsky's movements and friends, waiting for an opportune moment to kill him. Therefore, the Comintern knew, from their own sources in the Trotskyite movement, who was arranging Trotsky's safe haven in Mexico before Trotsky himself was certain of his final destination.

Mercader was the leader of a Spanish Republican delegation of several teachers whose ostensible purpose in Mexico was to garner financial support for the children who had been orphaned by the Spanish Civil War. Their real purpose was to reconnoiter Mexico City preparatory to a Comintern assassination of Trotsky, should he eventually come to Mexico as anticipated.

At that time, Mercader was the mistress of Leonid Eitingon (General Kotov), the notorious executioner of the Spanish Civil War. Eitingon was the master planner in the field for the Trotsky assassination. (He had been Alexander Orlov's deputy in a similar capacity for the Republicans in Spain.) When Mercader came to Mexico, her son was not intended to be Trotsky's sole assassin. The plan at that time was for David Alfaro Siqueiros, a noted Mexican artist, to lead a commando-style raid on Trotsky's house, if he came to Mexico, and to murder him by gunfire and bombs. When Mercader visited Mexico the first time, she was merely doing a preliminary survey of the operational site.

Her other objective in Mexico was to galvanize popular opposition to the idea of Mexico granting Trotsky "political exile" status. Another objective was to spot and assess potential agents who could be useful if and when Trotsky came to Mexico. She and her group returned to Spain, leaving a nucleus of operational support agents in place and carrying a detailed report on the operational ambiance in Mexico for her superiors in the Comintern/OGPU.

Ramon Mercader had seduced Sylvia Ageloff, a friend of Trotsky's, who could provide access to Trotsky's compound. This enabled Ramon to reconnoiter the inside of Trotsky's villa. Ramon's casing reports were used by Siqueiros to plan his ill-fated raid on Trotsky's villa on 24 May 1940. When the raid failed to kill Trotsky, Ramon Mercader was chosen to finish the job because he had access to Trotsky through Ageloff.

On 20 August 1940, Ramon Mercader tried to murder Trotsky with a blow to his head with the sharp point of an alpenstock. His mother and Eitingon were waiting for him in a car just around the corner from Trotsky's villa. Ramon, however, closed his eyes just as he swung the alpenstock at Trotsky's head, and the blow didn't fully penetrate the skull, so Trotsky didn't die immediately and silently as had been planned. When his mother and Eitingon deduced from the crowd, ambulances, and police that gathered in front of Trotsky's villa that Ramon had been captured, they sped away and fled the country.

When Eitingon returned to his wife, Mercader was unhappy in Moscow and eventually was given permission to return to Mexico with Carmen Brufau to try to arrange her son's escape from prison. He had been sentenced to 19 years and 6 months for Trotsky's murder. Stalin didn't want Ramon Mercader freed, because he thought that it might disturb his harmonious relationships with his postwar allies, the United States and Mexico. Stalin felt that even the notoriety of an escape attempt would bring the sordid mess of the Trotsky assassination into the open once again. As a result, the Soviet intelligence service received word that Mercader was not to succeed in freeing her son, and they placed many impediments in her way until she decided that her goal was impossible.

Mercader returned to Moscow, where she continued to pester the Soviet hierarchy to arrange her son's freedom. Her son served his full prison term and returned to the Soviet Union. He served in Prague, Czechoslovakia, and in Havana, Cuba, but was returned to the Soviet Union after death. He was buried in Moscow.

Stalin presented Mercader with the Order of Lenin, the Soviet Union's highest award for civilian endeavor, for her part in the Trotsky assassination. She eventually was allowed to leave the Soviet Union and moved to Paris, where she lived with her daughter, Montserrat, until she died in the mid-1950s.

(See also Carmen Brufau Civit and Sylvia Ageloff.)

Heijenoort, Jan. *With Trotsky in Exile: From Prinkipo to Coyoacan.* Cambridge, MA: Harvard University Press, 1978.

Levine, Isaac Don. *Mind of an Assassin.* New York: Farrar, Straus & Cudahy, 1959.

Asunta Adelaide Luigia Modotti
(Tina Modotti, Carmen Ruiz Sanchez, Maria)
Italy
1896–1942

Asunta Adelaide Luigia Modotti, best known as Tina Modotti, was a U.S. citizen, dedicated Communist, and compassionate care giver who served as an operative in Mexico and Spain. She is most often remembered as the model for the caring nurse Maria in Ernest Hemingway's *For Whom the Bell Tolls.*

Modotti came to the United States in 1913 with her father. When she was 17 she married a dilettante painter named "Robo" Richey. She appeared as a bit player in a few unmemorable movies and was "discovered" as a perfect nude model by the photographer Edward Weston. Weston taught Modotti the rudiments of photography, and she became his mistress. In later years she identified herself as a photographer.

Modotti's husband died in December 1923. Modotti and Weston, who was married, went to Mexico and were quickly accepted into the artistic community of Mexico City. They soon became friends with the Communist radicals there, such as Bertram and Ella Wolfe, Diego Rivera and his wife, Guadalupe "Lupe" Marin, Carlton Beals, Xavier Guerrero Saucedo, David Alfaro Siqueiros, and others.

In 1927, Modotti became a member of the Mexican Communist party.

The Comintern recognized Modotti's potential as a trusted member of the Communist party with a U.S. passport. The Comintern assigned one of its top Latin American agents, Carlos Contreras (real name Vittorio Vidali) to be her case officer. (Contreras had been deported from the United States as an undesirable alien in March 1927. He was known as a ruthless killer and a Comintern executioner.)

Weston returned to California, and Modotti—under Contreras's influence—rapidly became involved in various Comintern projects. She was a leading member of the Anti-Imperialist League of the Americas and the Hands Off Nicaragua Committee. She worked with Rosendo Gomez Lorenzo on the Mexican Communist party magazine, *El Machete.* One evening in June 1928, Julio Antonio Mella, a leading Cuban Communist, a Comintern agent, and a political exile in Mexico, met Modotti at the offices of *El Machete.* They were instantly attracted to each other, and Mella moved into Modotti's residence.

Late in the evening of 10 January 1929, Mella was assassinated while he was walking along the street with Modotti, close to where they lived. His assassin was a Cuban gunman named Jose Magrinat. Modotti was suspected of being part of the assassination team, and Diego Rivera, the famous Mexican muralist, appeared with her to answer the charges. The Mexican press alleged that Rivera and Modotti had been lovers (they had been) and that Rivera had shot Mella because he was jealous (not true; he was genuinely trying to help Modotti). The Mexican Judicial Police searched Modotti's apartment and found some letters that contained "pornographic" material, which made an even juicier story for the Mexican press.

Two things happened about this time that made Modotti's continued stay in Mexico problematic. There was a general desire in Mexico to get rid of everything having to do with communism. The government of Mexico had outlawed the Communist party of Mexico, the Partido Comunista Mexicano (PCM), and had declared the Soviet diplomats in Mexico personae non grata. (Modotti was known as a member of the PCM, and this fact was in every newspaper article about her.) The other difficulty was that Modotti had supposedly been involved in an assassination attempt against the newly elected Mexican president, Pascual Ortiz Rubio. The police claimed that they had proof that Modotti had been directly involved in this attempt. She had not been involved, but the evidence was rigged against her.

Modotti was given 48 hours to leave the country. She traveled by a circuitous route to Moscow via Berlin. In Moscow she "happened" to meet with Carlos Contreras, who had obviously been waiting for her. In Moscow, Modotti lived at the Hotel Soyuz, which was reserved for Comintern elite. In 1932, she and Contreras took an apartment together in Moscow. Modotti worked during this time for the Red Aid, which was similar to the Red Cross. She traveled in Russia and internationally for the Red Aid.

In 1934, she left Moscow to join Contreras in Spain. Her work there allegedly inspired Hemingway to use her as the model for Maria in *For Whom the Bell Tolls*. She originally worked for the Republican Army at the Hospital Obreros (Workers' Hospital) as a nurse. She was briefly deported from Spain for Comintern activities but was readmitted in 1935 to rejoin Contreras. Contreras organized and commanded the notorious Fifth Regiment of the International Brigade. Modotti worked with the Fifth Regiment as a nurse under the alias Maria.

When the Spanish Civil War ended, the Comintern gave Modotti a bona fide Costa Rican passport in the name of Carmen Ruiz Sanchez, with which she could enter Mexico by evading the Spanish deportees' watch list. She entered Mexico at Vera Cruz on 19 April 1939 and was reunited there with Contreras. (Contreras was involved in the Siqueiros raid on Trotsky's house on 24 May 1940.)

On the night of 5 January 1942, Modotti was at a party with Contreras at the home of the architect Hannes Mayer. Six people were at the party. Contreras had to leave early to do some work at the *El Machete* office. Modotti left the party a short time later, complaining of not feeling well. She died in a taxi on her way home or to a hospital.

There are several versions of what happened to Modotti that night. The scenario advanced by Contreras and the Comintern was that Modotti (who had no recorded history of heart trouble) suddenly suffered a massive heart attack and died in the taxi. This heart attack supposedly took place without any warning or preliminary complaints of chest pains or shortness of breath.

The other theory concerning Modotti's death speculates that Modotti was planning to leave Contreras, defect from the Comintern, and leave the many Communist causes that she had been affiliated with over the years. According to this version, she wanted to rid herself of all Communist entanglements, including Contreras, so that she could devote herself to photography. Modotti knew too much about Contreras and the Comintern's crimes to be allowed to leave their discipline. In this scenario, it is alleged that Contreras poisoned Modotti to stop her from leaving and revealing what she knew. She was desperately trying to get to a doctor or a hospital for an antidote to the poison that Contreras had given her when the poison took effect in the taxi and she died.

Regardless of which version is believed, everyone agrees that the taxi driver was terrified when he discovered that Modotti was dead in the back seat of his automobile. In a panic, he abandoned the taxi and the dead body. The police found the taxi the following morning and took Modotti's body to the hospital. Modotti was buried in the Pantheon de Dolores in Mexico City.

Rexroth, Kenneth. *An Autobiographical Novel.* Garden City, NJ: Doubleday, 1966.

Wolfe, Bertram D. *The Fabulous Life of Diego Rivera.* New York: Stein & Day, 1936.

Margaret Mowbray
(Peggy Dantin)
England
1912–ca. 1965

Margaret Mowbray was an expert in counterintelligence and was responsible for solving several of Australia's most menacing cases during World War II. She showed an amazing degree of patience in developing her cases until she had evidence that would result in a prosecution.

Mowbray was born in Surrey, England. Her father was a London timber merchant who became a world lecturer on political science. After traveling with the father on his lecture tours, the family finally settled in Australia, where Mowbray attended a convent school. She became a nurse at the age of 17 and continued to study the classics at night. Mowbray was only 19 when she met her husband, Stephen Mowbray, a New Zealand engineer, who was much older. They divorced after only two years of marriage.

Mowbray was at loose ends after the divorce. She tried modeling but wasn't successful. She tried show business and appeared in a nude musical review but found the men who hung around the show too dangerous. She then went into the legitimate theater and in 1933 played in a German operetta, *The White Horse Inn,* a ribald comedy. It was produced by a company of touring German actors, and the young cast all belonged to the Hitler Youth groups. The experience gave Mowbray friendships that, in later years, gave her access to pro-Axis groups that she penetrated for the Australian counterintelligence service.

When the tour ended, she went to Brisbane to open a German-style coffee shop, which she named The White Horse Inn as a joke. Her coffee shop became a gathering place for Germans and Australian actors, intellectuals, and Bohemian hangers-on. After the coffee house was sold, she tried selling cosmetics door-to-door, but she soon quit.

She had met an Australian intelligence officer and the two soon fell in love. They wanted to marry, except that Mowbray, a Catholic, still felt bound by her vows to her ex-husband. As fate would have it, the officer died of pneumonia about the same time that her ex-husband was accidentally killed. Through her relationship with the intelligence officer, Mowbray had met many officers in Australia's counterintelligence service. They offered her a job in counterin-

telligence as a records clerk. After she had proved herself in this capacity she was promoted to work among the immigrant community of Australia, ferreting out subversives and those who were disloyal.

Mowbray was 30 in 1942 when she was employed by the Australian counterintelligence service. Her job was to mix with all classes of Australian society and visitors in an attempt to uncover Caucasians who were spying for the Japanese. In 1942, the Japanese were moving southward toward Australia, capturing island after island.

The Australian counterintelligence service would often receive a tip that a certain individual had expressed pro-Axis sentiments or opposition to Allied objectives or Australian aspirations. They were especially concerned when someone voiced sympathy for the Japanese, indicated a willingness to live under Japanese rule, or revealed any inclination to assist a Japanese invasion. It was part of Mowbray's cover to express pro-Axis sentiments and to feign sympathy for Axis policies of annihilation and genocide. If Mowbray were available, she would be dispatched immediately to the neighborhood of such an individual with instructions to check out exactly what his loyalties were. She would pretend to meet him accidentally and then cultivate him until she was privy to his innermost thoughts.

In 1942, Mowbray was on such a case with John Swanson, a sheepherder from Queensland. Swanson obviously disliked everything and everybody. Mowbray, through a series of "chance" meetings, became his daytime companion and nighttime bed partner. She listened to him argue that the Japanese could bring more prosperity to Australian sheepherders; that the Japanese were too honorable to ever think of attacking Australia; that the Nazis really weren't such bad people, only misunderstood; that the Jews deserved everything that Hitler was doing to them; and the Nazi philosophy of Nordic superiority was well founded. Mowbray pretended to agree with his venom and encouraged him by faking admiration for his "manly" views. Mowbray sent voluminous diary reports on Swanson to her headquarters on a daily basis. She explained her frequent correspondence to Swanson by telling him that she was sending letters to her family.

Swanson was also under suspicion of providing a refueling service for the Japanese submarines that were hovering near the Australian coasts. Hundreds of barrels of oil had been found on his farm, which was adjacent to the coast. The analysts at Canberra began putting Mowbray's reports together with other information (probably intercepted Japanese radio traffic) and deduced a day when they believed that Swanson would be refueling a Japanese submarine. In a note that was supposedly from her family, they alerted Mowbray that there would be a raid on Swanson's farm. Mowbray told Swanson that she had to visit a sick member of her family in Sydney on the day scheduled for the raid. As expected, the Australian counterintelligence officers caught Swanson transporting oil drums by a small boat to a waiting Japanese submarine, and they arrested him.

Another case that Mowbray handled involved a prominent doctor. He had been a brazen pro-Mussolini advocate and was thus under suspicion of having pro-Axis sentiments. Mowbray became his patient for eight weeks and learned that the doctor admired Mussolini's administrative ability but was still a loyal Australian. (Many people at that time admired Mussolini's administrative abilities. The joke was that although everything about Mussolini's fascism was bad and although Italy was falling apart, he did make the streetcars run on time.)

Toward the end of the war, Mowbray was becoming too well known to the Japanese intelligence service to continue her work. The Japanese were briefing the agents that they sent into Australia to avoid Mowbray or anyone like her. About a year before the war was actually over, Mowbray left the Australian counterintelligence service and returned to Brisbane, where she managed a beauty shop. Although she had been well known in Australia, she managed to retire to a relatively quiet life.

Singer, Kurt. *Spy Stories from Asia.* New York: Wilfred Funk, 1955.

O

Svetlana Ogorodnikova
Russia
ca. 1942–

Svetlana Ogorodnikova was either an amateur or an apprentice-level participant in the Soviet espionage operation in the United States, whose lack of espionage experience led to her downfall. She seduced an FBI agent in order to obtain classified information from him. When he was caught, the FBI agent alleged that he had seduced Ogorodnikova in order to obtain secrets about Russian espionage operations from her.

Ogorodnikova was born in Russia circa 1942 and spent her youth under Stalin's dictatorial regime. She married Nicolai Ogorodnikov and the two emigrated to the United States, probably as junior KGB clerks, in 1973. Both were placed under routine FBI surveillance but were quickly deemed insignificant. The Bureau decided that they did not pose enough of a threat to the security of the United States to warrant saturation coverage.

Ogorodnikova often bragged that she was a major in the KGB, but she was probably on the clerk or apprentice level. Alternatively, both of them may have been merely amateur spies who happened to fall into an operation by chance, which they then took to the legitimate KGB officers in the consulate in an attempt to curry favor. Richard W.

Miller, an FBI agent with more than 20 years' of honorable, if not exemplary, service, met Ogorodnikova during a routine investigation. Miller had always been a maladjusted agent with less than high ratings on his efficiency reports. He had been ordered to lose weight because he was overweight according to agent specifications. It seems that Ogorodnikova seized the opportunity to cultivate Miller with no preconceived plan of action. In any case, she gave a sympathetic ear to Miller's complaints about his financial situation and his personal problems at home and at the office. He was grossly overweight, felt that he was not properly appreciated, and had severe personal financial problems. His salary with the Bureau was $50,000 per year, with which he was trying to support a wife and eight children and carry the mortgage on his home and several other pieces of property.

In 1984, Ogorodnikova became Miller's mistress, apparently with the acquiescence of her husband. Miller agreed to supply her request for classified information from the Bureau's files as a condition for her continuing to make herself available to him. Miller gave her classified FBI documents and a manual on U.S. counterintelligence techniques, and Ogorodnikova began to make frequent trips from her home in the same area to the Soviet Consulate in San Francisco to brief the KGB officers on her take.

The FBI had a routine surveillance on the consulate and noted the frequency of Ogorodnikova's visits. During a routine follow-up surveillance of her they discovered her association with their own Richard Miller.

In 1985, Miller, Ogorodnikova, and her husband were arrested. Miller claimed that he was not being used by her but, rather, that he was using her in an effort to infiltrate KGB operations on the West Coast. He also pleaded that he was merely having an affair with Ogorodnikova and didn't even know that she was a Soviet KGB agent. Miller was sentenced to 20 years in prison for espionage.

In July 1985, Ogorodnikova was sentenced to 18 years in prison for espionage, and her husband was sentenced to 8 years. Both had pleaded guilty to a charge of conspiracy to commit espionage.

Corson, William R., and Robert T. Crowley. *The New KGB*. New York: William Morrow, 1985.

Dorothy Pamela O'Grady
England
ca. 1900–

Dorothy Pamela O'Grady might have been an actress had she not been such an outstanding spy during World War II. When she was apprehended for spying, O'Grady claimed that she wasn't a spy. She swore that she had only pretended to be a spy for the fun of it and to vex her nosy neighbors.

O'Grady was born on the Isle of Wight, off the southern coast of England. Until 1942, she led a relatively ordinary life operating a boardinghouse in the town of Sandown. At the beginning of World War II she came to the notice of the authorities. They learned that she wandered around at all odd hours of the day but mostly at night. Her meanderings wouldn't have been too suspicious, except that she skulked about in prohibited areas, blinking her flashlight on and off as if she were signaling something or someone far out at sea.

She was placed under discreet surveillance by Scotland Yard detectives, who discovered her in the act of cutting the telephone wires that led from Sandown to Britain. They arrested her. At this time (after the fall of France) the British Isles were threatened with an invasion by German forces. Activities such as O'Grady's were highly suspicious and were considered possibly subversive. The magistrate who heard the Crown's case against her dismissed her with a small fine and an admonition not to do such things again.

O'Grady then moved to the other side of the island, to Yarmouth on the west coast. The authorities were still suspicious of her and kept a watchful eye on her. She was not seen to flash any lights or cut any telephone wires, but she stepped out of character by taking ferry trips to the mainland to visit Southampton more frequently than she had in the past. Scotland Yard surveillance revealed that she was meeting "strangers" in Southampton. After a short time observing these meetings, they arrested her and found in her possession "documents of military importance." (Hoehling 1967, 144)

Officials connected with this case never revealed what type of documents were found in O'Grady's possession. In wartime in Britain, "documents of military importance" could have been anything from a railroad timetable to the plans for the manufacture of the latest weaponry. Whatever they found on O'Grady, it was enough to have her arrested. At first, she was sentenced to be hung. (This was the only death sentence imposed in Britain for espionage during World War II.) Later, her sentence was commuted to 14 years in prison.

In 1950, she was released with time off for good behavior. She insisted that she had had absolutely no sinister intentions in doing what she did, and that it had all been intended to be a big joke. She pleaded with her neighbors, asking them to consider her case one of temporary mental derangement. She told them that when her husband went off to war she had been left to herself and couldn't stand the loneliness. She claimed that she took her dog, Bob, for nightly visits to the beach for a romp and a swim. She got so lonely that she wanted to attract attention to herself. "I longed to be arrested," she claimed, "I looked forward to the trial as a high thrill!" (Hoehling 1967, 144) Whether or not she was telling the truth, her former friends and neighbors continued to shun her, and she was left more alone than before.

Hoehling, A. A. *Women Who Spied.* New York: Dodd, Mead, 1967.

Kate Richards O'Hare
United States
ca. 1890–1939

Kate Richards O'Hare was originally an active covert action agent for the CPUSA who was convicted of sedition against the U.S. government. Her harsh experiences in prison turned her into an advocate for prison reform. She eventually gained respect when she became a government official working in penology.

O'Hare had aided and abetted the enemies of the United States by providing them with information and by actively propagandizing a position in favor of her country's enemies. She was convicted for her wartime writings and speeches against the U.S. government's position in World War I.

O'Hare was released from the Missouri State Penitentiary in May 1920 after serving 14 months of a 5-year sentence for sedition. Emma Goldman, the legendary anarchist, famous for her advocacy of birth control, was released on the same day, and the two walked out together. They had been close friends in prison.

Frank O'Hare, her husband, had been a loyal and frequent visitor to the jail during her imprisonment. He had circulated the letters that she had written him from prison, and the *St. Louis Dispatch* ran a series of articles on conditions in the prison that were based upon those letters. Her descriptions of the deplorable conditions eventually led to prison reform.

She continued her activities against the U.S. government of advocating socialist and Communist positions until the mid-1920s, when she moved to California. In 1928, she divorced O'Hare and married a San Francisco engineer.

She wrote a book about prison conditions and embarked on a lifelong crusade to improve them. In 1939, she was appointed assistant state director of penology for California. During her term in office she managed to make San Quentin Prison a model penitentiary.

She died in 1948 and is best remembered for her pre–World War I propaganda activities on behalf of women for the Socialist party. O'Hare advocated sex outside of marriage, contraception, as well as other Communist ideology such as the overthrow of democratic governments.

Foner, Philip S. and Sally M. Miller, eds. *Kate Richards O'Hare: Selected Writings and Speeches.* Baton Rouge: Louisiana State University Press.

Sochen, June. *Movers and Shakers.* New York: The New York Times Book Company, 1973.

Weiser, Marjorie P. K., and Jean S. Arbeiter. *Womanlist.* New York: Atheneum, 1981.

Josefa Ortiz de Dominguez
Mexico
1773–1829

In Mexico on every independence day, September 16, Josefa Ortiz de Dominguez is honored for the assistance she gave to the Mexican Revolution of 1810. She believed so strongly in Mexico's freedom from Spain that she defied her husband, who was a Spanish official, in order to help the revolutionaries.

Josefa was born in the largest town in Mexico and was orphaned at an early age. She was sent to an orphanage, but her sister managed to take care of her, so she wasn't raised without family. She was able to attend primary school and had some secondary education. In 1791, she married Don Dominguez, the mayor of Queretaro. As the mayor's wife, she was privy to all of the planning of the Spanish military, whose Royalist troops were trying to quell the Mexican people's independence movement.

The Mexican independence movement had its origins in and around Queretaro. In 1810, Josefa warned Captain Ignacio Allende that he was about to be arrested for sedition. Allende rode to the next town, which was Dolores, and roused the village priest, Father Miguel Hidalgo, who rang his church bells to call the parishioners to revolution with the famous *Grito de Dolores* (Shout of Dolores), which is still remembered in Mexico on every September 16.

When Josefa passed information about Spanish intentions and capabilities to the Mexican revolutionaries, she wasn't being loyal to her husband, who was an official of the Spanish government. Nevertheless, her fundamental loyalty was with the people of Mexico, so she passed all the information that she could glean from her husband's activities and his talk with his Royalist dinner guests to the leaders of the independence movement.

She tried to recruit her husband to the fight for Mexico's freedom, but he remained loyal to Spain. When he left on a mission to attack the revolutionaries' munitions storehouse, he locked her in her bedroom so that she wouldn't be able to warn them. Unbeknownst to her husband, her room was directly above a room where one of the revolutionary leaders was staying. Josefa was able to whisper the information to the rebel officer through the keyhole of her locked door. He then warned the guards around the munitions storehouse in time for them to repel the mayor and his soldiers.

Josefa was accused of spying for the rebels and was incarcerated in the Convent of Santa Clara in Queretaro before she was removed to Mexico City.

In Mexico City she was imprisoned in the Convent of Santa Catarina, where she remained for three years. While she was there, she berated Father Hidalgo, one of the great leaders of the Mexican independence movement, for the bloodshed at the battle of Granaditas. She was a fiery, high-spirited woman who refused to compromise her principles. Before the revolution, she had refused an appointment as a lady of honor to the Mexican viceroy's court. She also condemned the newly elected president of Mexico, Guadalupe Victoria. She believed that after independence he had expelled too many Spanish from Mexico whom she considered to have been loyal and patriotic Mexicans. She refused to accept any compensation from the new revolutionary government of Mexico for her services as a spy for the independence movement.

When she died in 1829, her body was taken to the Convent Santa Catarina in Mexico City, where she had been imprisoned. Later, her remains were removed to Queretaro for proper internment and honors when the Mexican government officially declared her to have been a heroine of the revolution. A statue that bears her name was erected in Mexico City.

Schmidt, Minna M. *Four Hundred Outstanding Women of the World.* Chicago: Minna Moscherosch Schmidt Publisher, 1933.

P

Martha Peterson
United States
1944–

Martha Peterson was a CIA agent in Russia who worked under diplomatic cover in the U.S. Embassy. Her case illustrates the proficiency and depth of Soviet counterespionage activities. She actually worked at a full-time job during the day in the embassy in addition to her espionage duties after hours, which was unusual. Due to her excellent cover, she underestimated the extent of Soviet surveillance and was arrested while servicing a CIA drop under a Moscow bridge.

According to *Newsweek* of 26 June 1978, Peterson was 33 in 1977 when the CIA posted her to the U.S. Embassy in Moscow under diplomatic cover as a vice-consul. Her cover was real: she diligently worked an eight-hour day in the visa section, interviewing Soviet citizens who were applying for immigration visas and assisting visiting Americans with passport problems. The fact that she spent a full day, every day, working at her cover job apparently misled KGB agents, who did not identify her as an intelligence officer at the beginning of her Moscow tour.

Part of Peterson's covert duties included servicing a dead drop. She was servicing a dead drop for an agent whose alias was Trigon. His real name was Alexsandr Dmitrevich Ogordonik. While serving in the Soviet Em-

bassy in Bogota, Colombia, as second secretary, he had been recruited as an agent in place by the CIA.

On 15 July 1977, Peterson was arrested by the KGB while she was servicing a dead drop. She was apprehended as she placed a hollow rock in a crevice in a bridge that spanned the Moscow River at Lenin Hall. In the hollow of the rock there were two poison capsules, a Minox camera, some gold, and a small concealable microphone.

The KGB had had the bridge under observation for a different purpose and had first observed the very suspicious actions of a female U.S. vice-consul placing a rock in a concealed position on the bridge. They placed her under surveillance and discovered her highly suspicious activities.

The KGB arrested Peterson and roughed her up, which wasn't typical, because its agents were miffed that they had been fooled by Peterson's full-time dedication to her cover duties and had not identified her from the start as a CIA officer. She was PNG'ed (made a *persona non grata*) and allowed to return to the United States.

About a year after her expulsion, on 12 July 1978, *Izvestia,* the newspaper of the Soviet government, published a photograph of Peterson standing in front of a table upon which was the split-open, hollowed-out rock with its contents displayed around it. The accompanying article accused Peterson of providing poison for an operation to murder some unnamed Soviet citizen. No reason was given for the delay in publishing the article and the picture. There was speculation that the KGB released the story when it did because the United States had just accused the Soviets of bugging the U.S. Embassy in Moscow and because two Soviet spies on trial in New Jersey for the theft of U.S. naval secrets were both convicted. It was thought that the KGB publicized the Peterson case in retaliation.

Richelson, Jeffery. *American Espionage and the Soviet Target.* New York: William Morrow, 1987.

Wise, David. *The Spy Who Got Away.* New York: Random House, 1988.

Eliena Petrovna
Russia
ca. 1910–ca. 1981

Eliena Petrovna believed that she could save her family by succumbing to the OGPU's pressure to entertain foreign dignitaries in Russia. She was to spy on the foreigners and report their every activity. She learned too late that OGPU promises were empty and that she had been played for a fool.

Petrovna was a graduate of the Art Institute in Kharkow, and she found work in a government planning bureau in Dniepropetovski as an architect. She was married to a man who was not well and whom she no longer loved, but she continued to live with him so that she could take care of him.

Her lover was Victor Kravchenko. Kravchenko's mother met her and approved of her, saying that she was obviously a good person of strong character. She was accepted by all of Kravchenko's family and friends. Everyone thought of her as glamorous and sophisticated because she was always dressed in the latest fashions. But Kravchenko, who was closer to her, always felt as if she were living in a permanent state of tension.

One day, at a football game, Kravchenko saw Petrovna sitting in the stadium restaurant, very elegantly dressed, in the company of two foreign-looking men. They were all laughing and enjoying themselves, and the men, according to Kravchenko, looked at Petrovna boldly and hungrily. When the football game was over, Petrovna and the two men left in a large foreign automobile. Kravchenko detected nothing unusual in Petrovna's behavior the next day, but he was concerned, because contact with foreigners could be a dangerous matter for her if the OGPU learned about it. Apparently, Petrovna was either unaware of the danger she was in or she was a fool, and Kravchenko knew that she was no fool.

He recalled that Petrovna always claimed to be occupied with her business on Thursday nights, and it had been a Thursday when he saw her at the football game. The next Thursday, when Petrovna again pleaded that she was too busy to see him, he followed her. He observed her going into a large private house. When she emerged she was accompanied by two men, one of whom was in the uniform of an OGPU official.

Kravchenko didn't know how to confront her. Neither did he want to terminate the relationship. He followed her on successive Thursdays, and the pattern was the same. Petrovna was aware of the tension between them and asked him what was wrong. He told her what he had observed about her secret life. She broke down and confessed that she had been forced to work for the OGPU.

She told him that in 1930, during a visit to her parents, the OGPU had arrested her father. She was not allowed to visit him in prison, so she went to the OGPU officer in charge of her father's case, who told her that she could help her father by becoming an escort for foreign officials. She was told that she only had to act as if she were sexually available but that she would not have to sleep with the men. She refused. Eventually, she was allowed to visit her father in jail, where he was being beaten. He died soon after her visit.

A couple of years later, when her husband was also arrested on false charges, she lost her job and friends. When she again sought help from the OGPU, they again asked her to work for them, but she again refused. When she finally saw her husband in prison, he was so aged that she didn't recognize him.

That was when she agreed to work for the OGPU to save her husband from further torture. She followed OGPU orders about how to present herself to the foreign diplomats and began meeting them as arranged by the OGPU. Her husband was soon released and given a job in the town to which she had been assigned.

After Petrovna's confession, Kravchenko understood how she had been coerced into working for the OGPU. He forgave her, but their relationship was never the same. They resumed their life together for a short time but gradually drifted apart; Kravchenko become more deeply immersed in his studies, and Petrovna was transferred to Kharkow. They met several years later when Kravchenko was visiting Kharkow on business. Petrovna was still beautiful but was showing her age, and there was a sadness in her eyes that revealed desperation. She had a modest job in an architectural firm and had very few OGPU assignments. Her husband had been rearrested, and she was living with her mother.

Kravchenko, Victor. *I Choose Freedom.* New York: Charles Scribner's Sons, 1946.

Claire Phillips
United States
ca. 1920–

When Claire Phillips's husband was sent to a Japanese prison camp in the Philippines, she sold the family jewels to finance a nightclub in Manila, which she used as a base for spying against the Japanese. She was eventually captured only after a long and successful espionage career of supplying the United States with vital information about the Japanese. She was tortured but refused to divulge any information.

In February 1942, the Japanese invaded and conquered the main islands of the Philippines. Phillips's husband, a U.S. Army infantry officer, was captured by the Japanese at Bataan and was forced to go on the notorious Bataan Death March. From the day her husband was captured, Phillips resolved to do everything in her power to fight the Japanese in her own way.

At first she fled with her daughter into the mountain wilderness around Manila. When her daughter came down with malaria, she smuggled the two of them back into Manila and found refuge in the home of an old friend to whom she was related by marriage. She pawned her diamond engagement ring and wristwatch to get enough money to open a small nightclub overlooking the beautiful Manila harbor. The nightclub was named The Tsubaki Club. "Tsubaki" means "camellia" or "precious" in Japanese. From her vantage point overlooking the harbor, she was able to see what Japanese naval traffic was moving in and out. She adopted the cover of an Italian who was married to a Filipino. Her dark complexion and jet black hair helped her pass as the Italian that she claimed to be. Using this cover, she was never questioned by the Japanese, who were military partners with Italy and Germany in the Axis coalition.

A detachment of the famous Filipino Scouts, led by a U.S. Army captain, operated as a guerrilla unit in the mountains around Manila. They had a radio transmitter and were eager to relay Phillips's information on Japanese ships and convoy movements to Allied headquarters, where it could be acted upon. Phillips was assigned the code name High Pockets and became a regular contributor to the captain's daily transmissions to Allied headquarters. She often used Filipino couriers to send messages that were hidden in a banana that had been split and then cunningly resealed.

The Japanese officers from the army detachments occupying Manila frequented her nightclub, and Phillips could often deduce useful intelligence from their conversations. She reported that the Japanese were using Red Cross ships as troop transports; that aircraft carriers were leaving and in what direction from the harbor; and that on a particular morning she saw destroyers leaving and guessed that they were bound for the Solomon Islands, which turned out to be correct. She also reported on the general activity in the harbor: when ships arrived and departed and the extent and length of repairs.

Her nightclub was a success, and the money was plentiful, but the whole time she was worried about her husband and tried to get word about him. She made friends with two Filipinos who had a way to get information out and packages in to the prisoners at Cabanatuaum. She learned through this underground service that her husband had died from malnutrition.

Her Filipino contacts begged her to help the other Americans in the prison. She then set up Group U, which bribed the Japanese guards at the prison and sent packages of food and other comforts to the prisoners. This program was Phillips's downfall. On 23 May 1944, her contact man in the prison was arrested by the Japanese and apparently implicated her in his confession. Four tough Japanese military policemen descended on her and charged her with being a spy.

They knew her by her secret code name, High Pockets, and tormented her by referring to her by that name. They also had a letter that she had written to the prison chaplain and implied that they knew all about her operations. The Japanese interrogators demanded to know what the code word "cal" meant. She happily told them the truth: It was merely a shortened form for the Filipino word "calamans," meaning "oranges." The Japanese also demanded to know what the word "demijohn" meant. She knew that she would never be able to explain that a demijohn was simply a large container for liquids that she used for sending fruit juices to the prisoners.

The Japanese refused to believe her explanations and thought that she was deliberately holding back information. They tied her hands and pinned her arms to the side of her body, forced a garden hose down her throat, covered her nose with adhesive tape, and turned the hose on full blast. She begged them to stop and to look up the words in a dictionary. The Japanese refused to listen to her pleas and continued the torture until she fainted.

When she came to, the Japanese had apparently checked in a dictionary. They sent her to detention in a small cell, which she shared with 11 other prisoners. The Japanese woke her at odd hours throughout the night for interrogations. She was led out and forced to kneel with her head on the block for execution. At the last minute, the officer with the raised sword above her head pretended to change his mind and decided to let her live. He told her that she was a brave woman and that because she hadn't flinched when she was faced with execution, she must have been telling the truth.

Her reprieve lasted only three days before she was again brought before a military tribunal. She again refused to plead guilty. The court remonstrated with her, and she was punched in the face so hard that several of her teeth were broken off. Finally, unable to withstand any more physical torture, she reluctantly pleaded guilty. The court accepted her plea and on 22 November 1944 found her guilty of espionage and sentenced her to death.

She was thrown into a cramped, filthy cell and expected to be executed. Surprisingly, she was taken before another military court and this time was found guilty of actions harmful to the Imperial Japanese Government. She was sentenced to 20 years' hard labor and sent to a local prison, where she was assigned to garden duty by a kindly Filipino who had known her before the war. He made certain that she didn't have to work too hard and helped her to regain her health.

Fortunately, the war was almost over, and she didn't have to wait long for deliverance. On 10 February 1945, the Americans took command of the prison camp and released her. She quickly located her daughter and they resumed their life together.

Rowan, Richard Wilmer, and Robert G. Deindorfer. *Secret Service: 33 Years of Espionage.* New York: Hawthorn Books, 1967.

Singer, Kurt. *Spy Stories from Asia.* New York: Wilfred Funk, 1955.

Emmeline Piggott
United States
ca. 1843–ca. 1895

Emmeline Piggott was a southern woman who would have preferred not to have been involved in the Civil War, but when her property was ransacked by the Yankees, she felt compelled to fight against them in the only way she knew—by becoming a very proficient spy for the Confederate Army.

When Union troops overran her home and ransacked the area, Piggott felt that the only way to seek revenge was to spy on them. Spying was easy because the Union troops were quartered nearby and made no effort to conceal their state of readiness or their plans for future actions. Piggott was welcome in their camp and, after a while, when they became accustomed to having her with them, they spoke freely. Even the officers, just returning from high-level briefings, discussed future campaigns without worrying that Piggott was listening.

Although soldiers in the Civil War knew that spies posed a great danger, they were not sophisticated enough to believe that a simple country woman could be a spy. That attitude was Piggott's chief strength; the soldiers didn't take simple security precautions.

Piggott routinely gathered all the information that she could about the Yankees and regularly made her way through the Union lines to the Confederate troops, who were encamped nearby. She always looked the epitome of fashion in hoop skirts and bonnets. Underneath her fashionable exterior she had stolen reports and documents pinned to her voluminous petticoats.

On several occasions she was detained by Union troops. While she was in custody, before she was taken before the provost marshal for questioning, she disposed of the papers she was carrying by eating them. She was always released by the Union troops because of lack of evidence. She spied for the Confederacy until the end of the rebellion.

Weiser, Marjorie P. K., and Jean S. Arbeiter. *Womanlist.* New York: Atheneum, 1981.

Nadezhda Plevitzkaya
(Mrs. Nikolai Skoblin)
Russia
ca. 1895–1938

Between 1914 and 1917, Nadezhda Plevitzkaya was a renowned folk singer in Russia.

She entertained soldiers at the front and became a near legend. Although her voice had lost some of its quality after World War I, Plevitzkaya and her husband/agent moved to Paris and attempted to continue her musical career. Whether the move was part of an OGPU cover operation is not known. In Paris, she and her husband acted as OGPU agents, enticing Russian emigrants back to the homeland, often for execution. She helped kidnap several emigrant Russian generals.

Plevitzkaya was of peasant origins, and when she was still a child, she ran away and joined a traveling circus. Ten years later she had become Russia's foremost folk singer, a soloist for the czar, and one of the most popular and best-paid artists in the country. The Russian Revolution interrupted her career only briefly. In 1918, she followed her husband (who had volunteered for the Red Army) to the front to entertain the troops with her songs. When she was captured by a patrol of the notorious Kornilov Division of the White Army, she was soon as popular with the Whites as she had been earlier with the opposition. Eventually, she became the mistress of Colonel Nikolai Vasilyevich Skoblin, and in 1921 they were married.

In 1920, there were rumors that Plevitzkaya had urged her husband to defect from the White Army and return to Bolshevik Russia. In 1923, Plevitzkaya was in the United States, where she sang to a pro-Soviet audience. The Skoblin couple then settled in Nice, France, from where they went on concert tours with Skoblin acting as Plevitzkaya's manager. She was a worldwide success, but after a while she began to show her age and her voice began to deteriorate. The couple spent lavishly, and by 1928 there were rumors that they were broke.

In the fall of 1928, they were suddenly affluent, as if they had inherited a large sum of money. It was probably at this time that the Skoblins were recruited by the OGPU, which subsidized their lifestyle in order to provide them with continuing access to the wealthier White Russian émigrés. They moved to Paris and bought a large house in a fashionable suburb. They also purchased an automobile and hired a chauffeur, because neither of them could drive. They became frequent visitors to the nightclubs of Paris, where they spent money freely.

After the Skoblins moved to Paris, General Alexander Kutyepov, the leader of the White Russian Army émigrés in Paris, was kidnapped. There is little doubt that Skoblin had kept the general under observation and had participated in his abduction. Plevitzkaya, in a great mock show of commiseration, spent considerable time with the general's bereaved wife, consoling her over her husband's disappearance.

By the early 1930s, it was assumed by the White Russian émigrés in Paris that Skoblin and his wife were Soviet agents. A Russian-language newspaper *The Latest News* published a highly incriminating article that plainly referred to Skoblin as a Soviet agent even though the spy's identity was disguised to avoid a libel suit. The situation got so terrible that General Yevgeni Karlovich Miller, who had assumed command of the White Russian émigré organization in Paris after Kutyepov's disappearance, told his friends that someone would betray him.

Skoblin and Plevitzkaya claimed that they were tired of the insinuations against them and demanded a "trial" before their White Russian contemporaries. They were given a trial of sorts, which was presided over by White Russian General Erdeli and were exonerated of all charges of being Soviet agents. (Years later it was proved that General Erdeli had been a Soviet agent when he presided over the Skoblins' trial.)

By 1936, Skoblin was the leader of the pro-Hitler faction of the Paris White Russian émigrés and was probably the first maverick White Russian to be recruited by the Nazis as an agent.

On 22 September 1937, General Miller left his office to meet some people. He left a note with his aide, Pavel A. Kussonsky, asking him to open the note if he failed to return. Obviously, the general felt some qualms about his safety with the people he was going to meet. General Miller failed to return and Kussonsky opened the note. Miller's note specifically said that he had an appointment with Skoblin and two officers of the German military. Skoblin was immediately called to the White Russian émigré headquarters for an explanation, but despite repeated questioning, and contrary to the evidence of Miller's note, Skoblin brazenly denied the note's veracity and denied that he had had a meeting with Miller. During the interrogation, Skoblin requested permission to go to the lavatory, which was granted. This lapse of nominal security was a mistake; Skoblin went to the men's room and kept on going through an open window. He was not seen or heard of again.

When Skoblin's wife, Plevitzkaya, was arrested as an accomplice in General Miller's disappearance, she was carrying a considerable amount of money, as if she had been prepared to flee. She broke under interrogation and admitted her complicity in Miller's disappearance. When the police searched the couple's house, they found all types of spy paraphernalia: three kinds of ciphers, four Yugoslavian passports, and 400 kilograms of files.

Plevitzkaya's trial ran for eight days in December 1938. She was convicted and sentenced to 20 years of hard labor—one of the harshest peacetime sentences ever handed down against a woman by the French justice system. She died in prison in October 1944 after serving only six years of her sentence.

Many asked why the Soviet Union didn't assist Plevitzkaya. She was not a Soviet citizen, so the Soviet government was indifferent to her fate.

Bailey, Geoffrey. *The Conspirators.* New York: Harper, 1960.

Blackstock, Paul W. *Secret Road to World War II.* Chicago: Quadrangle Books, 1969.

Anne Henderson Pollard
United States
1960–

Anne Henderson Pollard's love of an ardent U.S. Zionist led to her downfall. When her husband decided to pass along U.S. intelligence secrets to the Israelis, she, out of loyalty to him, assisted and later attempted to help cover up his operation. When she was arrested and charged, she admitted that her only motive had been to support her beloved husband.

In August 1981, she was working as a secretary at the American Institute of Architects in Washington, D.C., and attending night courses at the University of Maryland. One of her roommates introduced her to Jonathan Jay Pollard, an American who was an ardent Zionist. She immediately fell in love with him and adopted his views. He was an Intelligence Research Specialist employed by the U.S. Navy in Suitland, Maryland. He had tried to get into the CIA but had been rejected. In his job with the navy, he noticed what he thought was prejudiced treatment of Israel insofar as the U.S. government was not sharing intelligence information with Israel that he thought they should.

After they were married, Pollard took a job with the National Rifle Association in the public relations department. Despite health problems, she was more concerned about her husband. She already was aware that he had decided to steal U.S. classified material for the Israelis. He was also beginning to show signs of mental instability. He told fantastic stories about having lived in South Africa and of his father having been the CIA station chief there. His credentials for access to the Naval Intelligence Department were revoked. In June 1984, he was transferred to the newly created Anti-Terrorist Alert Center of the Naval Investigation Service Threat Analysis Division. He saw this new assignment as a reward, instead of the demotion that it was intended to be, because it would give him greater access to information that he could pass to the Israelis.

With the active connivance and complete cooperation of the Israeli intelligence service, he passed them suitcases full of highly classified U.S. government secrets. His wife was a knowledgeable partner in this treachery. He told her that if he ever suspected that his thefts had been discovered, he would call her and use the word "cactus." This was to be the signal for her to take whatever classified documents there were in their apartment and get rid of them.

On Monday, 18 November 1985, Jonathan Pollard was picked up by a naval intelligence officer and questioned about taking classified documents out of a restricted area. He received permission to call his wife and told her "to get rid of the cactus." She later told the investigators that when she received that message she gathered up all the documents that she could find in their apartment, put them in a suitcase, and took them to a friend's house for safekeeping. When she returned to the apartment, her husband was there with agents from the FBI and the Naval Intelligence Service, who were searching the apartment. The agents found 57 top secret documents in a box under some women's clothing that she had overlooked. These documents described U.S. agencies' analyses of foreign weapons systems and the military capabilities of the Soviet Union and several Arab countries.

When he had a moment alone, Jonathan Pollard called his Israeli case officer and explained the rapidly deteriorating situation and the prospect of his imminent arrest. He was told to stall for time and not to worry because the Israeli government would take care of him. He interpreted this to mean that the Israeli government would somehow extricate him from the perilous situation of disclosure and arrest. He also took this to mean that the Israelis would help him and his wife leave the United States to escape prosecution.

The next day, 19 November 1985, he instructed his wife to walk casually around the neighborhood because someone (an agent from the Israeli Embassy, he hoped) would "accidentally" bump into her and quietly tell her how they could escape. When there was no notification, they became concerned and decided to seek asylum in the Israeli Embassy. On November 21, he called the Israeli Embassy and told the security officer who answered the telephone that he and his wife were "coming in." He later claimed that he had been specifically instructed by the Israelis to first shake off the FBI surveillance and then drive straight into the embassy compound. They packed their overnight bags and took their family photograph album and their cat in preparation for leaving the United States forever. They drove into the Israeli Embassy compound only to be turned away with the explanation that it had all been a terrible mistake.

Jonathan Pollard was arrested and charged with espionage. Anne Pollard was arrested a few days later, on Friday, 22 November 1985. She was convicted. At her pre-sentencing hearing she said:

> Your honor, I am speaking from the heart. What I want to tell you is of the deep love and respect and admiration that I have for my husband, that my husband is by far the most important thing that has ever come into my life and will forever be that; that I would never, and I must be candid with you, I would never do anything to hurt him and I would always try to help him in any way I thought was correct.
>
> I cannot lie and say I was unaware that my husband was assisting Israel at the time.
>
> I love Jay very, very much and when he called me in his eleventh hour, I responded because I felt that was what a wife should do. I felt that I was, while assisting my husband, not causing any harm to the United States.
>
> I just pray every day that I will be reunited with Jonathan Pollard. He is everything in the world to me. He is so special. I need him so much right now. He is my soul, my best friend ever, my intellectual conversationalist, I mean he is my greatest love. He is everything in the world to me wrapped up in one.

Jonathan Pollard was sentenced to life in prison at hard labor. Anne Pollard was sentenced to five years.

Blitzer, Wolf. *Territory of Lies.* New York: Harper & Row, 1989.

Raviv, Dan, and Yossi Melman. *Every Spy a Prince.* Boston: Houghton Mifflin, 1990.

Juliet Stuart Poyntz
United States
ca. 1910–1937

Juliet Stuart Poyntz was a highly educated and eloquent speaker, a cultured hostess, an executive organizer, an able administrator, and an effective spy. There were few women in Soviet espionage who could even begin to match her all-around potential. When she indicated a dissatisfaction with communism and a desire to leave espionage, the Soviets murdered her.

Poyntz was educated at Barnard College and spent a year at the London School of Economics. She was later a professor of history at Hunter College. She was one of the few true intellectuals in the CPUSA. She was genuinely interested in helping the downtrodden and underprivileged of the world, which led her to accept the promises empty of communism. She joined the CPUSA in the mid-1920s, seeking answers to the world's ills.

She was a fierce political activist, a dedicated Comintern functionary, and a militant labor leader working for the New York Waist and Needleworkers' Union. Probably her greatest contribution to the party was that she was the national organizer for the Women's Division of the CPUSA. She also ran for the United States Congress on the CPUSA ticket on three occasions but lost every time.

She was a teacher by profession until she was persuaded to go underground to work for Soviet military intelligence, the GRU. According to the editor of the New York *Volkszeitung,* Ludwig Lore (a former leader of the CPUSA and defector to the FBI), she was in charge of the illegal section of the entire CPUSA. She was also a close professional associate of Jacob Golos, chief of the Control Commission of the CPUSA, and an acknowledged spy master working under Amtorg cover. (Amtorg was the Soviet commercial/trucking company in the United States but provided cover for Soviet deep cover agents.)

When she was ordered into illegal work, she was required to ostensibly renounce her affiliation with communism. Accordingly, she went through the obligatory denunciation of her former association with the CPUSA. She was sent to Moscow in 1936 for training in clandestine activity, tradecraft, and how to exist in an undercover environment. She was seen in Moscow at Comintern meetings on many occasions with George Mink, a Comintern agent and GRU executioner. It was widely intimated that they were in love and deeply committed to each other.

When she returned to New York, the GRU established her in an apartment and provided her with ample operational funds. She was a top professional intelligence operative and recruiter after her return from Moscow. When the Stalinist purges became blatant in 1936–1937, her loyalty began to waver. The so-called Trial of the Seventeen, when Stalin eliminated his remaining opponents, caused her to finally lose her reverence for communism. She had also been disgusted by the ruthless purges she had seen in Moscow. She had told friends there that she planned to cease all party work and become a Trotskyite. She resolved to resign from the GRU. The problem was that no one could resign from the GRU except by death. Poyntz exacerbated the matter when she told friends that she planned to tell all about the GRU clandestine activities in a book.

On 3 June 1937, Poyntz received a telephone call in her room at the American Women's Association Club on West 57th Street in New York. She put on her coat, took her handbag and nothing else, left the building alone, and was never seen again. She didn't take a suitcase or the materials that she had been working on, or any clothes; she left everything in her room just as if she fully expected to return.

The police did not release news of her case until the New York Herald-Tribune published an article about her disappearance on 17 December 1937. When the case broke in the newspapers, the Communists hastened to do everything they could to disassociate themselves from Poyntz. The editor of the CPUSA newspaper, The Daily Worker, announced that Poyntz had ended her relationship with the CPUSA amicably in 1934. The director of public relations for the New York Branch of the CPUSA commented that they had no record of her as a member of the CPUSA and no knowledge of her whereabouts for the past ten years.

Then, in early February 1938, Carlo Tresca, one of the United States' foremost anarchists and a friend of Poyntz, reported that he had evidence that she had been kidnapped by her former lover, Schachno Epstein, and murdered. Tresca took his information to the assistant U.S. attorney, who reluctantly refused to prosecute because he didn't believe that Tresca's evidence would support a conviction. Tresca himself was murdered on the streets of New York on 11 January 1943, but before he died, he gave his evidence on the Poyntz murder to Benjamin Gitlow. (Most of this information comes from Benjamin Gitlow, who had been a leader of the CPUSA and editor of The Daily Worker before he defected to the FBI. According to Ludwig Lore, a former leader of the CPUSA and an FBI consultant, Gitlow was later murdered because he knew who Poyntz's killers were and was ready to reveal their identities.)

Epstein was the editor of the Jewish newspaper Freiheit and a Comintern agent. George Mink, one of Poyntz's killers, claimed that he used Epstein as a decoy. Mink claimed that Epstein was afraid of him and knew that Mink would kill him if he disobeyed; therefore, he did everything that Mink ordered. Under orders from Mink, Epstein telephoned Poyntz to ask her out so that they might determine if they should resume their love affair. She met him at Columbus Circle, and they walked through Central Park. There, a large black limousine pulled alongside them, two men jumped out, pulled Poyntz into the car, and sped away. Epstein was left at the curb to make his way home alone and to try to live with his conscience.

The two men took Poyntz to Duchess County, New York, close to the Roosevelt estate, and murdered her. The best information is that her two murderers were George Mink and Vittorio Vidali, alias Carlos Contreras. Both of these Comintern agents were well-known executioners. One of the killers, probably Mink, reported to a meeting of the CPUSA Control Commission that Poyntz had pleaded for her life and had promised not to write about the GRU if she were allowed to live. The killers buried her in a grave on the bluffs overlooking the Hudson River. They covered her body with lime and dirt. Over the top they placed dead leaves and branches so that hikers or dogs wouldn't inadvertently discover it.

(See also Elizabeth Terrell Bentley.)

Brown, Anthony Cave, and Charles B. MacDonald. *On a Field of Red*. New York: G. P. Putnam's Sons, 1981.

Gitlow, Benjamin. *The Whole of Their Lives*. New York: Charles Scribner's Sons, 1948.

R

Sylvia Rafael
Israel
ca. 1960–1985

Sylvia Rafael was a Jewish intelligence agent who was a member of the Israeli hit team that was formed to kill the leader of the Black September gang, which claimed responsibility for killing Israel's athletes at the Munich Olympics in 1972. Even though the Israeli team murdered an innocent man, Rafael gained notoriety while she was in prison and later when she returned to Israel. Ironically, she was finally killed in a shoot-out with members of the Black September group.

When the Israeli athletes were killed, the Mossad (Israel's intelligence and counterterrorism organization) vowed revenge against Black September, which bragged about the hit and took credit for the atrocity. Rafael was one of the hardest-working members of the Israeli hit team that went to Norway in July 1973 to avenge the murders. The Mossad had information that the perpetrator of the massacre, Ali Hassan Salameh, would be in Norway. When they arrived in Norway, the Israeli hit team killed the wrong man. They murdered an innocent Moroccan waiter named Ahmed Bouchki, who was working in Norway and had nothing to do with the Black September gang, organized and directed by the Palestine Liberation Organization.

The Norwegian intelligence service had assisted the Israeli team in identifying the target, so after the hit, even though it had been the wrong hit, the regular Norwegian intelligence service helped the hit team escape. In the aftermath of the murder, the Norwegian police arrested two suspicious people who were trying to leave the country with Canadian passports in the name of Leslie and Patricia Roxburger. During a routine search of the Roxburgers' personal effects, the Norwegian police found the telephone number of the Mossad man in Oslo, who was well known to them. Upon further inquiry, the Roxburgers were discovered to be Sylvia Rafael and Abraham Gehmer from Israel, masquerading as husband and wife.

This startling discovery exposed the entire case and the cooperation of the Norwegian intelligence service with the Mossad. Both Mossad agents were tried and convicted of complicity in the murder. They were sentenced to five and a half years of hard labor.

While she was in prison, Rafael sent a facetious get-well card to the prosecutor and signed it, "OO5 1/2—The Spy Who Came in from the Cold." She kept busy in prison writing a diary, which was later published in the newspapers. Unlike most spies, who prefer anonymity, Rafael sought publicity. Rafael was released after serving only 22 months of her sentence. She returned to Israel, where she was commended for her work in the Norwegian operation, even though she had helped to murder the wrong man.

In 1985, the Mossad sent Rafael on another operation, this time in Cyprus. Unfortunately for Rafael, this was another botched operation, and she was one of three Mossad agents killed by the PLO.

Payne, Ronald, and Christopher Dobson. *Who's Who in Espionage.* New York: St. Martin's Press, 1984.

Rahab
Jericho
ca. 5000 B.C.

Rahab was a famous biblical spy and may be the only woman in espionage canonized as a saint by the Catholic Church. Rahab was known as a prostitute in the city of Jericho when she hid two of Joshua's agents in her house to protect them from the King of Jericho's soldiers.

Jehovah had promised Palestine—the Promised Land—to the Israelites, and when Moses died, Jehovah instructed Joshua, the Israelites' leader, to lead his forces against Jericho. The city was well fortified, so before attacking, Joshua sent two men to gather intelligence about the area. After they had completed their mission but before they had a chance to leave the city, the King of Jericho heard a rumor that Israelite spies were in the city, and he commanded his soldiers to find them. Joshua's spies chose the house of Rahab as a safe hiding place.

There was a rumor that the spies had taken refuge in Rahab's house, so the soldiers went to Rahab and commanded her to produce the spies. Rahab knew that she must give the soldiers a reasonable explanation for the rumors that they had heard, so she told them that two men had come to her house as clients but had left and had gone out of the city just before the gates were closed for the night. She put the soldiers further off the trail by saying that she didn't know which way the men had gone after they had passed through the gate. She told the soldiers that if they hurried they might still be able to catch the men on the road beyond the gate. The soldiers thanked Rahab and left to chase the phantom men.

As soon as the soldiers had gone, Rahab went to the attic, where she had hidden the spies under stalks of flax. She then struck a bargain with the spies: in return for having saved their lives, they had to promise not to harm her or her family when the Israelites captured the city. The spies were so elated that they had not been arrested for execution and that Rahab was giving them a way out of the city that they agreed.

Rahab's house was built into the city wall. The city gates were closed for the night, and the only way the spies could leave was to drop over the city wall directly from Rahab's house. Rahab lowered the spies through a window and down over the city wall, and they escaped into the desert. Before they left, they told Rahab that when the Israelite armies came into the city, she should put a piece of scarlet cord in her window so that Joshua's soldiers would know that it was her house and that they must not molest it.

The spies hid in the wilderness for three days before finding a safe route back to Joshua's camp. They told Joshua of the bargain that they had made with Rahab. Joshua assigned them to enter Jericho with the first troops in order to find Rahab's house and to remove her and her family before he burned the city to the ground.

Although she had been a prostitute, Rahab was canonized as a saint by the Catholic Church as a hero of faith because she had believed that the Lord had given the Israelites the land and she swore her faith in Jehovah when Joshua's spies sought refuge with her. Her feast day is celebrated every year on September 1.

Azimov, Isaac. *Guide to the Bible.* New York: Avenal Books, 1981.

Blaikie, William G. *A Manual of Bible History.* New York: Ronald Press, 1940.

Joshua 2:1–24; 6:22–25.

Marthe Betenfeld Richer
(L'Aloutte/The Lark)
France
1889–1982

Marthe Richer was an accomplished professional spy and linguist and was in competition with Mata Hari (Margarete Gertrude Zelle) for a permanent position as mistress of the German naval attaché in Madrid. Because of the publicity surrounding her relations with the German naval attaché, she had to wait 50 years to be given the accolades that she deserved.

Richer was born in Blamont, France, as Marthe Betenfeld. She learned to fly at an early age, which—in that era—was considered a phenomenal achievement for a young woman. She was an accomplished linguist, which also made her a good candidate for the French intelligence service in World War I.

The chief of the French military counterintelligence service, the Fifth Bureau, knew that Richer would be ideal as an agent. He wanted her to penetrate the German colony at San Sebastian, Spain, because she spoke German, Spanish, English, and French. The only impediment was Richer's husband, but he died in May 1916. In order to help bury her grief, Richer accepted the offer and left for Spain within three weeks of her husband's death.

She became active in the German social circle as soon as she arrived in San Sebastian and met the acting chief of the Abwehr, the German military intelligence organization. He suggested that Richer should become a spy for the Abwehr and go back into France. Richer, acting on French instructions to find out who the real chief of the Abwehr was in France, told the acting chief that she would accept that offer only from the chief of the Abwehr himself.

The Germans desperately needed agents in France, so the Abwehr chief for France, who was the German naval attaché in Madrid, agreed to Richer's request. It was a fortuitous meeting for the attaché and Abwehr chief; as soon as he saw Richer, he fell madly in love with her, and she became his mistress.

The supreme chief of the Abwehr in Berlin insisted that Richer fulfill her assignment in France. He complained that she had tarried too long in Madrid, regardless of the excuses that the German naval attaché made for her stay. The analysts at Abwehr headquarters badly needed the production figures of an armament factory located outside of Paris, and they hoped that Richer could get them. The Germans were nothing if not thorough. They didn't want to take any chances that Richer wouldn't be able to securely send the information to the German naval attaché. They gave her some very small capsules, about the size of a grain of rice. Each capsule, when dissolved in water, produced Germany's newest secret ink, which she was to use in her reports.

As soon as Richer arrived in Paris, her superiors in the French service wouldn't believe that she had become the mistress of the German naval attaché. When she was able to identify a picture of him, they were convinced that she was telling the truth. She was commended for bringing the new German secret ink back to France. The French service had been able to intercept many messages that they knew contained secret writing but had been unable to develop the writing. They were able to use the reagents for this ink to develop some messages from other German agents operating inside France.

It was agreed that Richer should return to Madrid to monitor Abwehr activities there and their operations into France. She took back with her some information on the armament factory that had been specially prepared for her by the French service to give to the attaché in Madrid.

In Madrid she resumed her place as the German naval attaché's mistress. When the French newspapers reported the trial of Mata Hari and that she had been the mistress of the same attaché in Madrid, Richer stormed into his office and demanded an explanation. (Richer was Mata Hari's espionage contemporary in Madrid in 1916. They both stayed at the Palace Hotel.) She screamed at him that he shouldn't deny it and that it would get him nowhere. She said she knew who Mata Hari was—the dancer who was staying at the Palace at the same time she was there. The attaché, who didn't want to lose Richer, took her more and more into his confidence. As a result, her intelligence take for the French increased, and it was all well-evaluated intelligence. Richer was able to send the French information on Germany's latest submarine, the U-52. Ironically, she was sending her information to Paris using the German's own secret ink.

The attaché's wife was jealous of Richer, so she laid traps for her, but Richer was too clever to fall for any of them. The wife also had doubts about Richer's loyalties to Germany and suspected that Richer's motives in the relationship with her husband were insincere.

Richer's utility to the Germans was acknowledged when they asked her to take a message and some supplies to a German agent in Buenos Aires, Argentina. She was to take several phials of a poisonous substance that, according to her lover, could destroy all of the Allies' wheat reserves in Latin America. Richer destroyed all of the phials during the voyage to Buenos Aires. She reasoned, correctly, that communications between Buenos Aires and Madrid were so poor that the agent would never be able to inform her lover that she had never delivered the phials.

When she returned to Paris, she recommended that the French intelligence service kidnap her lover in Madrid and hold him as a prisoner of war. Richer wanted the French government to send a plane to Madrid, where she would entice her lover aboard the plane and then fly him back to France herself. At this time she and the German naval attaché were living together in Barcelona as Sr. y Sra. Wilson. French intelligence couldn't countenance the plan, because it felt that Richer was too valuable working as the attaché's mistress in Madrid. Richer, therefore, continued to send intelligence on Abwehr intentions and capabilities in France and Spain.

Richer finally tired of her duplicitous life and yearned to return to Paris and her family. She returned and went into immediate retirement. Before she left her lover, she made a full confession of all her espionage activity while she had been with him. Official French government sources later revealed that Richer had turned over to the French government all of the money that the Germans had paid her for her services during the war.

After World War I the French government refused to give Richer the credit that she was due. It seems that if she had only had a brief fling with the attaché, as Mata Hari

had with most of her sources, she would have retained, in their eyes, some of her virtue. The French government's viewpoint changed in 1933, when it belatedly awarded Richer the Legion of Honor. This award was made despite the shrill protests of outraged moralists.

Richer was also a member of the French Resistance during the Second World War, when she was in her 50s. She died in 1982.

(See also Margarete Gertrude Zelle.)

Franklin, Charles. *The Great Spies.* New York: Hart Publishing, 1967.

Peterson, Bonnie A., and Judith P. Zinsser. *A History of Their Own.* Volume II. New York: Harper & Row, 1988.

Steffi Richter
(Mary Reihert)
Austria
ca. 1897–

Due to money and personality, Steffi Richter was in a position to negotiate agreements between high-level government and business officials in the 1930s. She tried to represent German interests in the United States and was apprehended by the FBI for spying. After World War II she was released from prison and returned to Europe, where she disappeared.

In 1914, Richter, the daughter of a Viennese lawyer, married a Hungarian, Prince Friedrich Francois Augustine Marie Hoenlohe-Waldenburg, an officer in the Austrian army, in London. Six years later Richter divorced the prince, claiming that there was another woman in his life, but she retained the title of Her Serene Highness Princess Stefanie [sic].

The divorce settlement was munificent, and Richter became a familiar figure in all the capitals of Europe, although she retained London as her home. She associated with the cream of London society in the 1930s, including Lord and Lady Astor, who held definite pro-Nazi sympathies. In Germany she was a favorite of Adolph Hitler and an intimate friend of Hitler's personal aide, Captain Fritz Wiedemann. During World War I, Wiedemann had been Hitler's commanding officer.

In 1939, Richter achieved a degree of notoriety when she sued a wealthy British publisher, Lord Rothermere, for breach of contract. She claimed that he had agreed to pay her $20,000 a year for life to act as his personal ambassador to European heads of government and especially to Hitler. Richter had been negotiating secret alliances and compromises between heads of state without the approval of the governments involved. She undertook these covert missions for money and the intrigue involved at the behest of the countries' industrial and moneyed leaders. She claimed that Rothermere had sought the restoration of the Hungarian monarchy and admitted that she had reneged on the deal when Rothermere wanted to put a relative on Hungary's throne. Rothermere admitted that he had paid Richter a total of $250,000 between 1932 and 1938 (which was considerably more than the $20,000 per year that she claimed), but he denied that he had agreed to a life contract with her. The court decided in favor of Rothermere.

Richter was a covert action agent and power broker of extraordinary ability and persuasion. According to German intelligence, she made the Munich agreement between Germany and Britain possible. She met with Hitler's number two man, Hermann Goering, at his castle, Karin Hall, in June 1938 to discuss arranging a meeting between a representative of the Third Reich and Lord Halifax of Britain in the interests of preserving peace. It was agreed that the arrangements would have to be made without the knowledge of von Ribbentrop, the German foreign minister. This illustrated Richter's level of negotiation, which was above the very highest levels of the nation's appointed representatives. Goering and Richter agreed between themselves that Wiedemann would be an ideal German representative to meet with Lord Halifax.

Richter returned to London and had no difficulty in obtaining Halifax's agreement to the proposed peace meeting. The meeting never took place, but it was the precursor to a later meeting of a similar purpose at Munich between British Prime Minister Neville Chamberlain and Hitler that resulted in the famous "false peace."

Richter modestly claimed that she was nothing but a "glorified messenger." (Whitehead 1956, 233) Hitler, in a show of his appreciation for her undercover work, presented her with a golden swastika, which represented the Order of the German Red Cross. Hitler wrote to her, "I should like to express to you, highly esteemed princess, my sincere thanks for the great understanding you have always shown for our people generally and for my work especially." (Whitehead 1956, 233)

After the fiasco in Munich, the FBI was alerted that Hitler was sending Captain Wiedemann to be the German consul general in San Francisco. He arrived in New York en route to San Francisco aboard the *S. S. Hamburg* on 4 March 1939. The Bureau received information that Wiedemann's real assignment in the United States was to organize pro-German and anti-Jewish propaganda throughout the United States, encourage fascism in Mexico to the exclusion of pro-American sentiment, and convert the German Consulate in San Francisco into a headquarters for German-Japanese espionage operations. Richter, they were told, would be joining him to assist him in these operations.

Richter arrived in New York in December 1939. She parried the questions from reporters about her past and claimed that she only wanted to find a quiet place in the United States where she could write her memoirs. She deprecated her past activities by saying, "I have as much to do with politics as a rope dancer. I don't even read half the news in the daily papers." (Whitehead 1956, 234) Richter traveled to San Francisco, where she became the house guest of Captain and Mrs. Wiedemann.

The Bureau had a source placed very close to Wiedemann, who claimed that Wiedemann was losing faith in Hitler's strength. Wiedemann wanted to discuss with some highly placed British official exactly how harshly Germany would be treated by Britain if the war should end. Britain, ready to grasp at any straw that might end the war, quickly dispatched a high-level diplomat to discuss the matter with Wiedemann. When he arrived for the talks, the diplomat was initially met by Richter for a two-hour preliminary meeting.

There is every evidence that Wiedemann wouldn't have undertaken this sensitive operation on behalf of the German government unless he had been given direct orders by Hitler. His pose of having lost confidence in Hitler was apparently all a ruse to fool the British officials. Apparently, Richter had carried orders for Wiedemann's actions with her, because Wiedemann did not make any peace overtures until after her arrival in San Francisco.

The evening following Richter's meeting with the British official, they were joined by Wiedemann. It was apparent to those involved that Richter was the guiding force in the negotiations. The British official agreed that Richter's visit to Berlin to discuss the peace proposals be given unofficial approval by the British government. Richter suggested that Britain make a deal with Hitler and then "fool him," but her idea to double-cross Hitler was rejected by the British official and Wiedemann.

Nothing came of the proposed meeting, and Richter never went to Berlin. Three weeks after this meeting, the U.S. government rejected Richter's request to remain in the United States. She fought deportation with every wile she could. Her attorney told the hearing board that she had applied for a visa in 42 countries and had been rejected by all 42.

Richter became hysterical when she was taken into custody on 8 March 1941. The Immigration and Naturalization Service (INS) put her in a hospital room at their headquarters instead of in the jail cell that was waiting for her. The head of the INS, apparently succumbing to Richter's charm, released her. She went to Philadelphia under the name of Mary Reihert. There she was accepted by the social leaders, who were

eager to be seen with a princess. The Bureau arrested her the day after Pearl Harbor as an undesirable alien.

Reports reached President Roosevelt that this "enemy alien" was receiving preferential treatment in the local prison. He wrote a note to the attorney general that her situation "was getting to be the kind of scandal that calls for very drastic and immediate action." (Whitehead 1956, 236) The attorney general ordered Richter interned on 13 February 1942 at the interment camp in Seagoville, Texas. Richter was paroled from Seagoville after the war in Europe ended and made the rounds of parties in New York and Philadelphia.

It is believed that she returned to Europe, where she was lost. She was supposedly living in London and Berlin.

Whitehead, Don. *The FBI Story*. New York: Random House, 1956.

Rhona Janet Ritchie
Scotland
ca. 1954–

Rhona Janet Ritchie was a schoolteacher before she joined the British Foreign Service. Her lack of worldly experience led to her involvement with an Egyptian agent who convinced her to provide him with classified information from embassy files. The naive Ritchie relished the social whirl of embassy life in a foreign city and had no idea that her lover was a married man whose assignment had been to trap her in a compromising affair.

Ritchie left a successful academic position to join the British Foreign Office in August 1979. When she took the Foreign Office entrance examination it was noted that she had the ability to speak several languages fluently.

After the usual foreign service training in London, she was posted to Tel Aviv in July 1981 as first secretary and press attaché. As press attaché it was her job to keep current on the local press: which newspaper and columnists were pro- or anti-British, which newspapers and radio stations were considered official mouthpieces for the host government, and which were in opposition. She also had to cultivate members of the local press and electronic media to try to ensure a favorable ear for the embassy's news releases. Any press attaché must also cultivate the correspondents in the foreign country who represent the major newspaper chains in the home country. Being a press attaché is a very active job that requires an outgoing personality and a lot of socializing. Ritchie was well suited to her job.

Ritchie was very popular with the embassy staff from the beginning of her tour. She organized a Kosher cookout party on a weekly basis and was the person who always offered to help plan a social event. About three weeks after her arrival in Tel Aviv, Ritchie attended a routine diplomatic function at the Egyptian Embassy, which had opened in Tel Aviv only after the 1979 peace treaty with Israel. Ritchie received a lot of attention as the newest member of the diplomatic community. At this party she met Rifaat al-Ansari, the second secretary of the Egyptian Embassy. He proceeded to sweep her off her feet with the courtly manners of a roué. He showered her with gifts and apparent genuine affection and swore his undying devotion to her. Unfortunately, Ritchie believed him, and the two became lovers.

The lovers did nothing to hide their intimate relationship. The Israeli intelligence service knew of it almost from the start. They had no intention of trying to use the situation for their own operational purposes but continued to monitor it to see where it might lead. The MI-6 officer in the British Embassy and the security officer also must have known something about the relationship either from their own observation or from their liaison with the Israeli service.

Soon al-Ansari began to ask Ritchie for old background reports from the embassy files. She supplied them because he led her to believe that they were outdated and therefore no longer significant. He then began asking for more current information, which she supplied reluctantly at first until doing

so became commonplace. He finally demanded and was given top secret, urgent telex messages, which she took out of the embassy as soon as they were received.

Ritchie gave her lover a top secret telex at the end of November 1979 that included the itinerary of the British foreign secretary's visit to the Middle East. This was the kind of information that terrorists and assassins would want. Another telex that she gave her lover concerned the formation of a multinational force to police the Sinai withdrawal of the existing combat troops.

The Israelis learned of these dangerous leaks and felt that they had to notify the British Embassy. Ritchie was recalled to London on a pretext and was arrested as soon as she arrived. She admitted her guilt and pleaded for mercy. Ritchie's memory of an idyllic romance was shattered when she learned that her Egyptian lover had a wife and children in Cairo. She learned that the Israelis, who had known her lover's record, referred to him as the "Don Juan of the Nile." He was noted as a diplomat who had built his career on espionage through sex.

She cooperated with the prosecution at her trial at Old Bailey and was given a suspended sentence. The prosecutor, when recommending leniency, said, "Her behavior was more foolish than evil." (Raviv and Melman 1990, 231)

Raviv, Dan, and Yossi Melman. *Every Spy a Prince.* Boston: Houghton Mifflin, 1990.

Ethel Greenglass Rosenberg
United States
1915–1953

Ethel Rosenberg was convicted and executed for helping to sell secrets about the U.S. atomic bomb to the Soviets. Many, including her own mother, urged her to confess to save herself. She refused, evidently agreeing with her Communist party supporters that her life was worth more as a martyr to the Communist cause than as a mother to her two small children.

ETHEL AND JULIUS ROSENBERG
UPI / Bettmann

Ethel and her husband, Julius Rosenberg, were children of Jewish immigrants who became members of the Communist party almost as soon as they were politically aware. They had become embittered due to the privation that they had to endure during the depression of the early 1930s. They failed to understand that everyone in the country was undergoing similar privations and believed that the doctrines of the CPUSA offered panaceas for the country's ills. They were recruited into the NKVD by Anatoli Yakovlev, a Soviet intelligence officer.

In 1950, the British atomic scientist Klaus Fuchs confessed that, while he was working at Los Alamos on the Manhattan Project, he had stolen processing and fabricating secrets related to the development of the atomic bomb. The FBI took up the trail to find his accomplices and coconspirators in the United States. The entire Fuchs espionage operation had been well planned to maintain compartmentalization. It was arranged in echelons, with a series of cutouts between echelons to protect the highest levels and the ultimate recipients of the intelligence from being discovered by Fuchs. He did know, however, the person who contacted him, and that is where the compartmentalization broke down.

The trail led the FBI to Harry Gold, a Philadelphia chemist who had met Fuchs in Santa Fe and had picked up material from him. The FBI arrested Gold, who confessed that he had been a Soviet agent for 14 years. (Elizabeth Bentley had previously identified Gold as having been a member of the CPUSA.) In addition to servicing Fuchs in Santa Fe, Gold confessed that he had also picked up material from David Greenglass in Albuquerque, New Mexico. Greenglass was a sergeant in the U.S. Army working at Los Alamos on the atomic bomb. He was also Ethel Rosenberg's brother. Greenglass admitted after his arrest that he had joined the Young Communist League at the urging of his sister. He idolized his sister's husband and often said that he would do anything for

Julius. Greenglass's wife, Ruth, had visited him while he was stationed at Los Alamos with a message from Julius and Ethel that they wanted him to supply them with information about the atomic bomb that he was working on.

The Rosenbergs made it clear to Greenglass that they intended the information to be passed to the Soviets. They claimed that, as an ally of the United States, the Soviet Union was being denied this vital information about the atomic bomb that could be used by them to defeat Hitler and fascism. Greenglass accepted their rationale and supplied them with the secrets of how to construct an atomic bomb.

When Greenglass was next on leave, Julius cut identical notches in two sides of a Jello carton. This was to serve as a positive identification between Greenglass and the person who would contact him. One half of the Jello carton was given to Greenglass with the admonition that whoever had the matching half would be a bona fide courier from them. Julius passed the other half of the Jello carton to his superior in the Soviet Embassy, the Soviet vice-consul, Anatoli Yakovlev, who in turn gave it to Harry Gold. Yakovlev instructed Gold that, in addition to picking up material from Fuchs in Santa Fe, he was also to pick up material from Greenglass in Albuquerque. When Gold arrived in Albuquerque he presented his half of the Jello carton to Greenglass, who found that it matched his half. When Greenglass was on leave in September 1945, he gave Julius an oral report on the type of bomb that had been dropped on Hiroshima and Nagasaki. Ethel typed her brother's narrative report for transmission to Yakovlev.

When Fuchs was arrested on 3 February 1950, Julius Rosenberg told Greenglass that Fuchs was also a contact of Harry Gold, the man who had met him in Albuquerque. Julius was concerned that Gold might be arrested from Fuchs's description, which in turn would lead to Greenglass. As if on cue, Gold was arrested, and Julius Rosenberg told Greenglass that he would have to flee to avoid arrest. Julius had an escape plan for Greenglass that had been worked out by the

Soviets. He was to go first to Mexico, then Prague, and eventually to Moscow. Julius gave Greenglass $5,000 for expenses, but Greenglass chose not to flee.

When Greenglass was arrested, he turned state's witness and told the FBI everything about the Rosenberg's complicity in the spy ring. Julius Rosenberg was arrested on 17 July 1950; Ethel Rosenberg was arrested on 11 August 1950. Julius and Ethel Rosenberg and David Greenglass were indicated for espionage. The Rosenbergs pleaded not guilty; Greenglass pleaded guilty.

Moscow had issued specific instructions to its espionage agents all over the world that if they were caught in England they were to plead guilty, but those apprehended in the United States were to deny everything. The reason was that a not guilty plea would probably fail in England, but in the United States—where trials were prolonged and often confusing—the lengthy proceedings could have the effect of suppressing justice and obscuring the truth. In the Rosenbergs' case, the Soviet plan didn't work. The jury found them guilty, and Judge Irving Kaufman sentenced them to death in the electric chair. For his cooperation, Greenglass was sentenced to only 15 years in prison at hard labor. The Rosenbergs' sentence was reviewed no fewer than 16 times, but the trial judge's sentence was upheld. Most of these appeals went to the Supreme Court; two appeals went to President Eisenhower for executive clemency. All were rejected.

There were allegations that the Rosenbergs' attorney, Emanuel H. Bloch, was inept. Supposedly, he passed up many opportunities to discredit the government's two star witnesses, Greenglass and Gold. This allegation has been discounted by eminent jurists who have reviewed the trial transcript.

The CPUSA, and its front groups, had been silent during the trial. As soon as the verdict was pronounced, they launched a nationwide propaganda campaign against the fairness of the trial, the judge, the prosecutors, and the verdict. They charged that the entire trial had been instigated without any foundation in fact except that the

Rosenbergs were Jewish; the whole plot was a campaign of anti-Semitism on the part of the U.S. government, they claimed. The CPUSA apparently ignored the fact that Judge Kaufman was Jewish, as were two of the prosecutors.

It was largely because Ethel and Julius were such inept spies that they were apprehended by the FBI. The Rosenbergs were also apprehended because of one of the best U.S. intercept operations of the time, code named VERONA and known as BRIDE among U.S. law enforcement officers. The intercepts and decryptions of Soviet transmissions from their embassy in Washington revealed that the greatest U.S. secret of all time, the Manhattan Project and the building of the atomic bomb, was being sold to the Soviets by a husband and wife team.

When the Rosenbergs were sentenced to death, Communist parties around the world protested vociferously. The Rosenbergs' sons, who were only children at the time of their parents' execution, took up the fight when they reached maturity. Judge Kaufman, the presiding justice at the Rosenbergs' trial, saw their execution as a way to signal that the legal system was enlisted in the battle against communism. He commented that what the Rosenbergs had done in giving the Soviets the secrets of the atomic bomb "was worse than murder." He said that by "putting into the hands of the Russians the A-bomb, years before our best scientists predicted Russia would perfect the bomb," the Rosenbergs had caused, in his opinion, "the communist aggression in Korea, with the resultant casualties exceeding 50,000." He concluded: "Who knows but that millions more innocent people may pay the price for your treason." (Whitehead 1956, 317)

Some commentators of the day suggested that the indictment of Ethel Rosenberg was a prosecution ploy designed to force her husband to confess. It was thought that when Julius realized that his wife was in jeopardy, he would confess and strike a bargain with the prosecutors in order to save her life. Allegedly, when the charade failed to force Julius's confession, J. Edgar Hoover had pangs of remorse that the woman whom he

had arranged to have indicted was going to be executed. Supposedly, his conscience was salved when he heard that Ethel's mother had pleaded with her to confess in order to save herself for her children's sake. Ethel was supposed to have quipped: "Children are born every day of the week!"(Powers 1987, 304) This hard-hearted attitude turned whatever sympathy Hoover may have had for her into a determination to see justice done.

The Rosenbergs were probably responsible for the elimination of the ten-year statute of limitations in espionage cases. Their trial alerted Americans to the dangers of Soviet peacetime espionage.

The United States and other Western nations blamed the Rosenbergs for the Soviet Union's swift emergence as an atomic power. Anglo-American relations were strained as a result of Fuchs's proven disloyalty. They were strained again when Bruno Pontecorvo, an Italian-Jewish scientist, was found to have been disloyal. Both men had been cleared by the British security services to work in the United States on the atomic bomb project.

Ethel and Julius Rosenberg were executed for espionage on 19 June 1953.

(See also Elizabeth Terrell Bentley.)

Cook, Fred J. *The FBI Nobody Knows.* New York: Macmillan, 1964.

Hoover, J. Edgar. *Masters of Deceit.* New York: Henry Holt, 1958.

Powers, Richard G. *The Life of J. Edgar Hoover: Secrecy and Power.* New York: Macmillan, 1987.

Whitehead, Don. *The FBI Story.* New York: Random House, 1956.

Brunhilda Rothstein
Germany
ca. 1915–?

All that is known about Brunhilda Rothstein is that she played the role of "fiancé" for a senior Soviet agent who tried to enter the United States in 1941. She was merely part of his cover.

On 13 June 1941, the *S. S. Evangeline* docked in New York harbor and a couple disembarked. They were greeted immediately by inspectors from the INS. The woman said that she was Brunhilda Rothstein and that she was the fiancé of the gentleman who accompanied her. The man told the INS inspectors that he and his fiancé were only passing through the United States on their way to their permanent home, which was at 31 Avenida del Rio de la Piedad in Mexico City.

The man was Gerhardt Eisler, a Soviet agent who had been assigned to be the senior representative of the Comintern for the United States and Latin America, including Mexico. The INS was concerned about Eisler; they were only interested in Rothstein because she was with him. The INS had learned that both of their passages had been paid for by the United States Spanish Aid Committee of 156 Fifth Avenue, New York City. This organization was well known as a Comintern front. (Later, its name was changed to the Joint Anti-Fascist Refugee Committee.)

Eisler and Rothstein both denied that they were Communists. Eisler also denied that he had ever been to the United States before, but he was easily recognized as a Comintern agent named Edwards, who had been in the United States in 1933. At that time he had been a senior Comintern agent writing under the name Hans Berger and had instructed CPUSA members in the party's ideology.

Eisler was released on bail by the INS pending the disposition of the case after his deportation hearing. One night before his hearing, however, Eisler slipped aboard a Polish ship, the *S. S. Batory,* which was at anchor in New York harbor, and the ship smuggled him back to Moscow.

The fate of Brunhilda Rothstein remains unknown.

Spolansky, Jacob. *The Communist Trail in America.* New York: Macmillan, 1951.

S

Policarpa Salavarrieta
Colombia
1795–1817

Policarpa Salavarrieta was a young Colombian woman when she was executed in the town square of Bogata by Spanish troops. She had been spying for the colonials against the Royalist troops. As she went to her death, she made an impassioned plea to the crowd, which inspired the people with revolutionary fervor. She made a great contribution to the eventual victory of the colonials over the Spanish.

Salavarrieta was born in Guaduas, Colombia. Her parents were Don Jose Joaquin Salavarrieta and Dona Mariana Rios. It was said that with parents like those, she had to be the very purest of Spanish descent. She and all of her brothers, however, were enthusiastic revolutionaries who advocated the freedom of Colombia from Spanish domination. During the Reign of Terror (as the Spanish attempt to reconquer Colombia was called) she was a valuable and prolific source of information for the Colombian patriots.

When the Royalist troops discovered that she was giving information to the revolutionaries, they imprisoned her. She and eight of her accomplices were shot in the main plaza of Bogota on 14 November 1817. Salavarrieta walked with dignity and courage from the Chapel of the Colegio de Rosario to the main plaza. As she walked to her death, she shouted condemnation of the Spanish and asked the people to revenge her death.

Schmidt, Minna M. *Four Hundred Outstanding Women of the World.* Chicago: Minna Moscherosch Schmidt Publisher, 1933.

Odette Marie Sansom
(Odette Matayer, Celine, Lise)
France
1912–

Odette Marie Sansom was a World War II guerrilla leader of a resistance group in her native France. After a life of hazardous duty as an enemy agent in Occupied France, she married her British team leader and settled in England. She was later honored in her adopted homeland, Great Britain, as a highly decorated national hero.

She was born Marie Celine Brailly in France on 28 April 1912. At the age of 19 she married an Englishman, Ray Sansom, and they had three children, who were all still very young when World War II erupted. She left her family at their home in Somerset, England, to join the SOE.

After the British evacuated Dunkirk, the British War Office asked for pictures of the French coast. Sansom told them that she had a few snapshots of the Boulogne area. SOE was monitoring the people who brought in photographs, because they hoped that some of those people with a background or experience in France might be qualified to become agents in France. Sansom was qualified. When she was 30, in October 1942, she landed by raft on a strip of beach in Occupied France, where she joined Captain Peter Morland Churchill, code named Raoul, who was already in place directing a team of saboteurs and information gatherers. The unit was called Spindle, and Sansom was given the code name Odette Matayer.

The team was covering the area around Cannes. Churchill had Sansom operate as a courier between his headquarters, which was almost constantly on the move, and the sub-agents, who were deployed at strategic locations. Their job was to gather information on the Germans' military capabilities. Sansom's ability to speak French was invaluable to her team as it planned and executed night parachute resupply drops and conducted aerial exfiltrations of agents.

When Churchill, the team leader, was recalled to London for consultations, Sansom was in left in charge of the group. While she was in charge, she efficiently organized and brought about the largest resupply drops ever made to the maquis (the French underground guerrillas), who were hiding in the mountainous area above the Côte d'Azur in France.

In April 1943, the German SS troops arrested Sansom and Churchill in an inn near the town of Annecy. Part of their cover story was that they were married to each other. Sansom maintained this fiction even under vicious torture. The Gestapo tore out all ten of her toenails and seared her back with hot irons and a blow torch, but they could not get her to talk. Despite such barbarous treatment, she did not reveal the names of the other members of the group nor the location of the radio transmitter. When she was informed that she was about to be executed and when her many crimes against the Third Reich were enumerated to her, she told her interrogators that they could take their pick of the crimes they were going to

execute her for, because they could kill her only once.

Sansom was moved from the Gestapo's Paris prison to Ravensbruck. The Nazis couldn't decide whether or not to execute her, because they were afraid that her "husband," Peter Churchill, might be related to Britain's Prime Minister Winston Churchill, who would be directing prosecutions for war crimes after the war. She was fortunate. She was not executed at Ravensbruck, because the warden wanted to curry favor with her to save his own life after Germany was defeated. In May 1945, the warden of Ravensbruck drove Sansom in his Mercedes to the U.S. lines and surrendered himself and turned her over to the Americans. At this point, Sansom demanded his pistol as part of the surrender. She kept it as a war memento.

The warden's act of human kindness was considered in mitigation of the many crimes against humanity that were pending against him but was summarily rejected. He was executed by order of the War Crimes Tribunal at Nuremberg for the multitude of crimes that he had committed against helpless prisoners while he had been the warden at Ravensbruck.

Sansom's citation accompanying the award of the MBE and the George Medal probably sums up her heroism best:

> She drew Gestapo attention away from her commanding officer onto herself, saying that he had only come to France at her insistence. She took full responsibility and agreed that it should be herself and not her commanding officer that should be shot. By this action she caused the Gestapo to cease paying attention to her commanding officer after only two interrogations. . . .
>
> During the period of two years in which she was in enemy hands, she displayed courage, endurance and self-sacrifice of the highest possible order.

Sansom married Churchill after they were both demobbed (the English equivalent of being separated from the intelligence service) and divorced from their respective spouses. Their marriage was as stormy as their wartime experiences, and they divorced.

Sansom finally found true happiness when she married Geoffrey Hallowes of London.

Tickell, Jerrard. *Odette: The Story of a British Agent.* London: Chapman & Hall, 1949.

Irmgard Schmidt
Germany
ca. 1968–

Irmgard Schmidt was a Soviet spy who confounded U.S. counterintelligence agents by telling them the truth about being a Soviet spy. The gullible Americans assumed that she had reformed and dropped their guard: they allowed her to take a job with the U.S. government, where she had access to classified information.

Schmidt was born in Halle, in what was then East Germany. She was recruited in Germany by Soviet counterintelligence agents and was sent to spy school in Gorki to learn tradecraft and report writing.

She was assigned to West Berlin to infiltrate the U.S. government's massive headquarters. She had a unique way of initially ingratiating herself with the Americans: she basically told them (the U.S. counterintelligence agents) the truth. She told the first U.S. officer whom she encountered that she had just defected from East Berlin and wanted to get away from her Soviet handlers. She told the eagerly listening U.S. counterintelligence officers that she had been to spy school in Gorki and had been assigned to West Germany to infiltrate U.S. headquarters. She willingly gave the Americans details about the spy school in Gorki. Her best prize for the Americans was the considerable detail of the information that the Soviets had given her to dangle as bait before the Americans.

She was well received by the Americans, who regarded her recantation as almost spiritual and gave her a job in the U.S. counterintelligence headquarters in gratitude for her forthrightness and candor.

Her first two sexual conquests were U.S. counterintelligence officers. They either gave her information of a classified nature or she was able to pick out bits and pieces of information that she could put together for the Soviets. Schmidt had no trouble keeping the two Americans happy while she scouted around for more challenges to conquer. She worked her way up in the counterintelligence section by hard work and by sleeping with the right officers. Eventually, she became the secretary/translator to the chief of the U.S. counterintelligence section in Berlin. She soon was helping him around his house as well as at the office. She managed to get most of the Allies' secret plans for defending Berlin and West Germany in case of a Soviet attack.

Schmidt's downfall came during an affair with a German who worked for the CIA. The CIA agent recognized Schmidt as a provocateur and turned her in to the U.S. counterintelligence section on a charge of espionage. This was the same section that had hired her.

Altavilla, Enrico. *The Art of Spying.* Englewood Cliffs, NJ: Prentice-Hall, 1965.

Elsbeth Schragmuller
Germany
1892–1940

Elsbeth Schragmuller was an experienced field agent who had an exceptional ability to teach, in an understandable manner, the expertise of being a good agent. She was probably one of the most educated spies encountered in the annals of female intelligence agents.

Schragmuller took her doctorate in philosophy at Freiburg University in Germany in 1913 before the advent of World War I. When World War I broke out, she asked her lover, Lieutenant Colonel Walter Nicolai, chief of intelligence of the German army, to find her some patriotic work that she could perform for the good of Germany. In order to placate her, Colonel Nicolai relented and assigned her to a censorship office.

She excelled at the work in the censorship office and was able to extract worthwhile intelligence from the letters that she processed. Her intelligence reports routinely were forwarded to General von Beseler, who commanded the German Army of Occupation in Belgium. General von Beseler was impressed with the reports and asked to see the hardworking officer who had compiled them.

To reward her dedicated work, the general appointed her to a training school for German intelligence agents at Baden-Baden. The regimen at this school was exceedingly rigorous, with classes in secret ink, map reading, enemy military unit designations, memorization aids, elicitation techniques, tradecraft, wireless telegraphy, codes, and operational security.

In addition to the other sobriquets that were used by her enemies, her students referred to her as "The Beautiful Blond of Antwerp" and "The Terrible Doctor Elsbeth." For all of the admiration that the students had for her, she would never permit anyone to photograph her. Her pupils also called her the "Tiger Eye" because of her meticulous attention to discipline and her insistence that they conform to her exacting instructions. One particularly onerous requirement was that the students had to wear masks throughout their tenure at the school. This was to preserve their identities and to keep their identities from being compromised by each other. The consensus of her pupils was that she was a sadistic martinet.

At the end of the day the students had to leave the school at three-minute intervals so that none of them would know in which part of the city the others lived. She hired a group of locals to watch the students, to make certain that none violated her rules of strict nonfraternization. She was convinced that only the strictest compartmentalization could preserve the security of her fledgling spies. In the event that one was captured and talked, he or she would not be able to reveal the identities of the other students.

Her iron discipline apparently didn't make for competent spies of any great notoriety; none of her graduates achieved any popular success in the field of intelligence collection or counterintelligence. On the other hand, this may have been the hallmark of her greatness. The undiscovered accomplishments of her students may point to their success at secrecy. It is possible that none of the students' targets ever discovered that they had been spied upon and their secrets copied.

One of Schragmuller's more noteworthy achievements was promoting the idea that espionage could only be successfully developed in a totalitarian nation. She fostered the idea of "The Deliberate Sacrifice," which entailed the literal sacrifice of one agent to the enemy to detract attention away from another agent, who was on a more important assignment. It was later speculated that Mata Hari, who wasn't very astute about espionage, may have been sacrificed in this manner to preserve some other unknown spy that the Germans considered of greater importance.

Schragmuller's superiors decorated her for her accomplishments. Apparently, she had not done the exemplary job that her superiors gave her credit for: she trained two spies sent to England, who were then captured. Admittedly, this breach was something she could not have prevented.

After Baden-Baden, Schragmuller was sent to a new agent training school in Antwerp, where the graduates were being schooled expressly for penetrating the French and British channel ports. The neighbors took pictures of her students entering and leaving the school. The Belgium underground sent these photographs to the Allies so that they could alert their counterintelligence services. As a result of the underground's surveillance, many of her students were identified when they arrived in an Allied country and were arrested or their activities monitored before they could do any real harm.

It is significant that "Fraulein Doktor's" opponents were her principal imitators. The French spy school located at Dijon developed a thorough and elaborate training program that was modeled after hers. In London, an Anglo-French spy training school was organized on the principles and curriculum of her school. This imitation was particularly strong in the British Naval Intelligence school of Admiral Reginald "Blinker" Hall and in the famous British Secret Service school under the genius of Captain Mansfield Cummings.

After the war, Schragmuller returned to Germany and faded into complete and impenetrable obscurity. All attempts to locate her ended in failure. Until the early 1930s she preserved her anonymity. At that time, a still-beautiful German woman, tentatively identified as Schragmuller, was admitted to a Swiss sanatorium suffering from drug addiction. The woman was cured of the addiction. During her therapy she admitted that she had been teaching under another name at the University of Munich. She returned to her precious self-imposed obscurity after her treatment. She died at the beginning of World War II.

(See also Maria Kretschmann de Victorica.)

Rowan, Richard Wilmer, and Robert G. Deindorfer. *Secret Service: 33 Years of Espionage.* New York: Hawthorn Books, 1967.

Libertas Haas-Heye Schulze-Boysen
Germany
ca. 1918–1942

Libertas Haas-Heye Schulze-Boysen was a German citizen who was related to German nobility and who was a fervent supporter of Nazism. When she fell in love with a Communist spy, she became a Communist and spied for the Soviet NKVD. She had to pay with her life for her treason.

She was born Libertas ("Lib") Haas-Heye and was the granddaughter of Prince Philipp of Eulenburg and Hertefeld, who had been a favorite of the German Emperor Wilhelm II. Her father, Professor Wilhelm Haas-Heye, was the director of an art academy in Berlin, and her mother (divorced from her father) was Thora Countess of Eulenburg. Her mother lived on the family estate at Liebenburg, where she was a neighbor of Hermann Goering, the number two Nazi in Germany. Goering used to visit the countess to listen to her play the piano.

Libertas met Harro ("Choro") Schulze-Boysen while sailing on the Wannsee in the summer of 1935. At that time she was a Nazi enthusiast and very much opposed to Schulze-Boysen's radical communism. Harro looked upon his conquest of Libertas as adding another source to his Soviet spy ring, because she had access to high-level Nazi party leaders. He was also physically attracted to her and, despite their differences, she fell in love with him.

They were married on 26 July 1936. Hermann Goering, who was a witness at their wedding, gave the bridegroom a job in the Reich Ministry of Aviation. The Haas-Heye connection enabled Harro to penetrate the Nazi regime's centers of power and gather information for his espionage reports to Moscow.

Harro Schulze-Boysen was one of the leaders of the Leopold Trepper Soviet spy ring, the *Rote Kapelle* (Red Orchestra), which was a very efficient prewar Communist espionage network that had reporting sources in almost every important echelon of Nazi Germany. Harro was a spotter, recruiter, agent handler, and one of Trepper's principal assistants. Libertas became Harro's assistant and coworker in all aspects of managing this elaborate and very efficient spy network.

She made good use of her connections with the Reich Ministry of Propaganda, and as a member of the Nazi Cultural Film Center, she had access to the ministry's secret archives. She assiduously collected all information bearing on the possibilities of war with the Soviet Union, Hitler's suppression of Communist activity in Germany, and the proposed actions of Hitler's intelligence service in the Soviet Union.

On 3 September 1942, the Gestapo arrested her at the railroad station as she was preparing to leave for a vacation on the Moselle River. The remainder of the group's members were rounded up, and the network's operations ceased.

Libertas was the first to break down under Gestapo "inducements" (interrogations). Being faced with imprisonment changed her outlook and destroyed the make-believe world that she had been living in. She confession from her. They met 25 times for long talks; each time Libertas would blurt out some compromising piece of information against her friends and herself that betrayed the espionage net. The guard would jot down the admissions in her notebook for use later at the trial.

At the trial, the prosecutor seemed to believe that the evidence of promiscuity would strengthen his case. He introduced pornographic pictures of Libertas, but they seemed to have little effect on the court's decision. When she heard that she had been condemned to death, she broke down. In her cell, awaiting death, she wrote to her mother:

> I drink the bitter cup of finding that I had been betrayed by a person in whom I had placed complete confidence [the female guard]. But now it is a case of "eat the fruits of your labors; anyone guilty of treachery will themselves be betrayed." Out of egoism I have betrayed my friends; I wanted to be free and come back to you. But, believe me, I would have suffered terribly for the wrong I had done. Now they have all forgiven me and we go to our end with a sense of fellowship only possible when facing death.(Hohne 1971, 202)

On 22 December 1942, Schulze-Boysen was executed by the guillotine. She screamed just before the blade fell, "Let me keep my young life!"

Hohne, Heinz. *Codeword: "Direktor."* New York: Coward, McCann and Geoghegan, 1971.

LIBERTAS SCHULZE-BOYSEN
From L'orchestre rouge *by Gilles Perrault (Paris: Librairie Artheme Fayard, 1967)*

had never thought that her husband's conspiratorial activities were anything but play acting. She didn't realize that espionage, however it was portrayed as a fun, daring game, was a deadly serious business. She came to realize only in the final months before her arrest how serious her husband's work was. By then, however, the two had become so estranged that they could no longer live together as man and wife. Libertas had wanted a divorce, but her husband had pleaded with her to wait. It was his numerous entreaties that had kept her at his side until the very end.

Libertas convinced herself that, even in prison, everything would eventually turn out alright. She clung to the belief that, as the granddaughter of a crown prince, not even the Gestapo would dare to hold her for long. Her confidence was buttressed with the conviction that when she turned king's evidence against her friends, the Gestapo would be grateful enough to free her.

The Gestapo assigned a female guard to her to cultivate her friendship and to seek a

Hannah Senesh
Hungary
1921–1944

Hannah Senesh had a firm commitment to fighting anti-Semitism. She was captured, tortured, and executed but died bravely without revealing any information about her operations or companions.

Senesh was born in Budapest, Hungary, to Jewish parents who did not feel that it was important to observe the formalities of their religion, so Senesh was raised without the deep religious convictions of orthodox

Judaism. She attended an upper-class Protestant girls' school, where she experienced some anti-Semitism, which made her aware of—and keenly resentful of—the rise in anti-Semitism throughout Europe.

At the time of the Munich crisis in 1938, Senesh had seen enough blatant anti-Semitism to make her want to fight back. Despite her lack of a religious upbringing, she felt that she should defend all Jews. She wrote in her diary in 1938 that she had become a Zionist.

In September 1939, at the outbreak of World War II, Senesh left Hungary for Palestine. From that time until 1943 she learned Hebrew, worked in an agricultural commune, and generally reclaimed her Jewish heritage. When rumors about the mass executions of Jews came from Europe, the specter of racial extermination obscured her happiness in Palestine.

Senesh instinctively felt that, with her knowledge of the area and culture, she could help save some of the Hungarian Jews. She was already a member of Palmach, the underground Jewish organization, and believed that she could use this association in her rescue attempts. She contacted the British secret service and offered to work in conjunction with them if they would arrange to drop her and her small contingent of resistance fighters into Hungary.

In March 1944, she and her group parachuted into Yugoslavia. They were able to assist many Jews to escape and sent considerable intelligence back that was of great value to the Allies. In June of that year, as she and her group were crossing the border into Hungary, they were arrested by the Nazis.

Senesh was beaten and tortured but would not reveal the details of her operation nor the radio code that linked her group with the British net. Frustrated, the Nazis tried another tactic. They returned her to Budapest, where they confronted her with her imprisoned mother. They threatened both women with torture if Senesh didn't explain her code to them.

From her cell, Senesh could communicate with other prisoners in the jail. She also devised a means of communicating with people outside the prison. She cut out paper letters in her cell. Then, piling furniture on her bed, she climbed to the window and flashed individual letters into messages for anyone outside of the prison who could see them.

In November 1944, she was executed in a German prison by a Nazi firing squad. She had steadfastly refused to reveal any information.

Weiser, Marjorie P. K., and Jean S. Arbeiter. *Womanlist.* New York: Atheneum, 1981.

Etta Shiber
See Kitty Beaurepos.

Belle Siddons
(Lurline Monte Verde, Madame Vestal)
United States
ca. 1830–ca. 1892

Belle Siddons was a daring Confederate spy who passed valuable intelligence information to the Confederate Army. Her skill in developing relationships with Union soldiers allowed her access to their secrets. After the war, she turned her wits and charm to gambling and also ran a house of prostitution.

Siddons served as a courier, carrying classified messages through the Union lines to the Confederate commanders. She was also a frequent "companion" of lonely Yankee soldiers, from whom she learned much about their state of readiness and planned operations.

Siddons had several careers. During the Civil War, a Confederate surgeon, who was one of her lovers, introduced her to gambling. She became so enamored of the daring betting and the risks involved in games of chance that gambling became her second career. About this time she changed her name to Lurline Monte Verde.

After the war, she gambled in New Orleans and then moved westward. She won most of the time but was never accused of cheating. During this period she acquired the name Madame Vestal. She never married but had many lovers. The name "Madame" Vestal may have been derived from her other career, operating houses of prostitution in many of the towns she lived in on her westward trek.

After losing several lovers, she turned to drugs and alcohol. She was arrested in an opium den in 1881. She died soon after she was released from jail. Unfortunately, there were no mourners at her death, and no one remembered her contributions to the Confederate cause during the Civil War.

Weiser, Marjorie P. K., and Jean S. Arbeiter. *Womanlist.* New York: Atheneum, 1981.

Helen Witte Silvermaster
Russia
ca. 1900–

Helen Silvermaster's case raised Americans' awareness about the extent of Soviet infiltration into the U.S. government because she was the wife of Nathan Gregory Silvermaster. Nathan was the principal agent for a network of Soviet spies and was responsible for placing them in responsible government positions. Helen helped her husband gather, organize, and pass along important information from his network of government workers.

Helen was born in Russia circa 1900 to the Russian Baltic Baron Witte. Her father was known as the Red Baron during czarist days because of his Communist sympathies. She helped her father distribute Communist literature and hide Bolshevik leaders in their home to help them escape the Okhrana, the czar's secret police. She married a White Russian nobleman by the name of Volkov. With him she had a son named Anatole. She divorced Volkov soon after the birth of their son and came to the United States and settled on the West Coast. She married her second husband, Silvermaster, in the United States.

Nathan Gregory Silvermaster had been born in Odessa, Russia, in 1898. According to Jacob Golos, the director of the Soviet espionage network, he had grown up in China, where his family had gone after a vicious pogrom against the Jews in Russia. Silvermaster returned to the Communist movement, and Golos claimed that he had known him to be a secret member of the CPUSA in the early 1930s. Nathan had never been an open member of the Communist party.

Nathan came to the United States in 1915 and spent about 15 years on the West Coast. At one time he had hidden Earl Browder, one of the leaders of the CPUSA who was a fugitive, in his apartment. He became a naturalized U.S. citizen in 1927 and received a doctorate in economics at the University of California, where he met Helen. They moved to Washington, D.C., in 1935, and Nathan went to work for President Franklin Roosevelt's New Deal program. He had a series of rapid promotions with increasing responsibilities. He was also reported to be a secret member of the CPUSA and an agent of the OGPU. Once, his clearance was revoked because of these allegations, but he asked Lauchlin Currie, administrative assistant to President Franklin Roosevelt, and Harry Dexter White, assistant secretary of the treasury and an alleged Soviet agent, to have his clearance reinstated, and it was.

Nathan was the principal agent for a group of Soviet spies working in various federal government agencies in Washington. He was instrumental in placing other Communist agents of this spy ring in responsible government positions. Elizabeth Terrell Bentley was the network's courier, and—after her superior, Jacob Golos, died—she became its director in Washington. In 1948, Bentley testified that one of the Soviet espionage groups that she had handled was headed by Nathan Silvermaster and his wife, Helen.

When Helen first met Bentley, she distrusted her and told Golos that Bentley was an FBI penetration. At that time nothing could have been further from the truth; Bentley was a dedicated Communist and Golos's mistress. It wasn't until after her lover died and she became disaffected with communism that Bentley even thought of becoming an FBI agent. Helen's intuition was correct but premature.

Bentley traveled from her home in New York to Washington, D.C., to collect the intelligence from the Silvermaster espionage group about every two weeks from early 1941 to 1944. During each visit Bentley would give the Silvermasters literature from the CPUSA written by such leaders as Earl Browder and P. Green and Soviet publications such as *Pravda* and *Bolshevik*.

The intelligence that Bentley collected consisted of U.S. military intentions and capabilities, air force plans, details of aircraft production and deliveries of aircraft to various theaters of war, details of new types of airplanes being tested and designed, information on when D-Day was being planned, and virtually every other type of secret U.S. government information. Helen helped to collect and store the material if it could be retained until Bentley arrived on her regular courier run. Otherwise, Helen photographed the material in their basement darkroom so that the originals could be returned before they were discovered missing. Bentley would pick up the negatives of the copied material from Helen and deliver them to Golos for shipment to Moscow.

After Bentley and others revealed Helen's Communist espionage activities, she denied the allegations. It was noted that, for some unknown reason, she was never called to testify under oath. Her denials of the charges, therefore, have never been tested. As a result of Bentley's testimony, Helen and Nathan Silvermaster left Washington for the little village of Harvey Cedars, New Jersey.

Bentley, Elizabeth. *Out of Bondage.* 1951. Afterward by Hayden Peake. New York: Ivy Books, 1988.

Burnham, James. *The Web of Subversion.* New York: The John Day Company, 1954.

De Toledano, Ralph. *The Greatest Plot in History.* New York: Duell, Sloan & Pearce, 1963.

Countess Krystyna Gisycka Skarbek
See Christine Granville.

Agnes Smedley
(Mrs. Petroikas, Alice Bird)
United States
1894–1953

Agnes Smedley became one of the all-time great female espionage agents despite handicaps of a limited education and unpromising beginnings. She was trained by Richard Sorge, her lover and one of the greatest male spies.

Smedley was born in 1894 in northern Missouri, the oldest of five children. The family moved to Colorado when she was very young. In Colorado her father worked as an unskilled laborer, and her mother ran a boardinghouse to help support the family. Smedley didn't finished grade school and didn't attend high school. In 1911, she became a part-time student at the Normal School in Tempe, Arizona. She worked part time as a waitress to pay her tuition.

On 23 August 1912, Smedley married an engineer, Ernest George Brundin. The marriage wasn't a success and soon ended in divorce. In New York, where she moved next, Smedley attended evening lectures at New York University, where she seemed to gravitate toward the cliques of East Indian nationalists. She joined the Friends of Freedom for India, which was among the groups being monitored by the U.S. government. One of the nationalist groups' main objectives was keeping their secrets from the U.S. government. Smedley agreed to hide their codes, foreign accommodation addresses, and correspondence in her room so that this material wouldn't compromise the East Indians if they were arrested.

She moved to California in 1915 and became a part-time student at the University of California. On 18 March 1918, Smedley was arrested with Salindranath Ghose, an Indian political agitator, on charges of aiding and abetting espionage. She was indicted for fraud for helping several East Indians to represent themselves as being an accredited government-in-exile mission in the United States for the Nationalist Party of India. She was never brought to trial on this charge.

Smedley returned to New York and— probably on instructions from the Communist

AGNES SMEDLEY
From China Fights Back *by Agnes Smedley (New York: Vanguard Press, 1938)*

elements of the Indian nationalist movement— shipped out of New York on a Polish-American freighter as a stewardess. She jumped ship in Danzig (Gdansk), Poland, and went directly to Berlin. There she teamed up with Virendranath Chattopadhyaya, an Indian nationalist and international Communist agitator. They lived together as husband and wife for eight years.

In June 1921, she visited Moscow to attend a meeting of Indian revolutionaries at the Hotel Lux. In October of that year she was in Geneva, Switzerland, where she received 5,000 marks from the Soviet legation for travel expenses. At this time she was probably already a member of the international Communist organization, Comintern. She was using the alias Mrs. Petroikas and sometimes used the name Alice Bird.

In 1923, she had to leave Chattopadhyaya several times to take treatment in a Bavarian Alps health spa. Later, she became very ill and feared that she was losing her mind. She began psychoanalytic treatments and continued with therapy for more than two years, during which time she taught English at the University of Berlin and lectured part time in Indian history. She tried to get her Ph.D. at the University of Berlin but was refused because she lacked the scholastic background. Smedley also formed the first birth control clinic in Berlin.

Smedley moved to Denmark and in 1927 wrote her first book, *Daughter of Earth*. In 1928, she broke completely with Chattopadhyaya and was hired as a correspondent for the *Frankfurter Zeitung*.

She then went to China, stopping in Moscow on the way for last-minute operational briefings before traveling across Siberia. In 1929, she arrived at Harbin. She visited several cities in China before settling in Shanghai, where she quickly became a leader of leftist and Communist causes. She was criticized by the Chinese for her advocacy of "free love" and sexual freedom.

Smedley's pro-Soviet articles written in China attracted sympathy for the Chinese Communists in some U.S. homes. The articles also brought raves from leftists and Communists in the late 1920s and early 1930s. Smedley held that the Chinese Communists were not really Communists but only local agrarian revolutionaries, who were innocent of any Soviet connection. She likened the Chinese Communists to the American revolutionaries of 1776.

Smedley lived most of her life in China and the Far East. She was a dedicated, hardworking Comintern and GRU agent and worked for Sorge in Shanghai as a Soviet/Comintern agent from at least 1930 until Sorge left Shanghai for Japan. She often allowed Sorge to use her apartment as a safe house. They were also lovers.

She introduced Ruth Kuczynski (Ruth Werner, Sonya) into the leftist social circles when she and her husband, Rudolf Hamburger, arrived in Shanghai. It was Smedley, with her knowledge of Asian life, who got Ozaki Hotsumi to work for Sorge. Hotsumi was Sorge's best-connected and most prolific source of high-grade intelligence about Japanese intentions and capabilities. When Sorge needed a radio operator to complete his spy ring, Smedley allegedly introduced him to Max Klausen, a German-born Comintern agent, whom she had co-opted from another GRU operation. Klausen, like Hotsumi, became a key functionary of Sorge's network. In his memoirs—written in 1944 as he was awaiting execution for espionage in a Tokyo prison—Sorge acknowledged that he could never have been so successful in his espionage operations without Smedley's help.

In World War II, Smedley was appointed an adviser to the United States general, Joseph Stilwell, who was the military adviser to Chiang Kai-shek, the leader of non-Communist China. She used her position to convince Stilwell that the United States should send military supplies to the Chinese Communists. Stilwell approved this plan because, even though it armed the Chinese Communists, which was a danger to the stability of the Far East, it made military sense to have them help fight the Japanese at the time.

Smedley advocated Indian nationalism and detested the British for their colonial hold on India. She also detested the British-trained and British-directed Shanghai

Municipal Police. From time to time they harassed her with an arrest, because she was suspected of being a Communist agent. Even if she hadn't been a Comintern agent, the Shanghai Municipal Police still would have harassed her, because she was an obvious liberal, a radical writer, and an agitator who was continuously causing them trouble with her subversive exhortations in the press. One of Smedley's closest friends was Chinese Communist General Chu-teh, who was commander in chief of the Red Army. (He was notorious a few years later when he led the Chinese troops across the Yalu River against the U.S. soldiers in Korea.)

After World War II, Smedley didn't like living in the United States, because the FBI was keeping a close eye on her. When the report on the Sorge case from the Far Eastern Command was published, Smedley was characterized as a Soviet agent. Some politicians in Washington decried the report and apologized to Smedley. She threatened to sue General Douglas MacArthur for libel. General Willoughby, MacArthur's G-2, went on the radio and publicly stated that she was a Soviet agent. He specifically divested himself of any immunity and challenged Smedley to sue him for libel. He said that he had proof that she was a Soviet agent and would welcome the opportunity to display the evidence in open court. Willoughby and MacArthur were on solid ground; they had Sorge's own statement regarding Smedley's activities. Sorge had written that the only person in China who he knew he could depend on was Smedley. He solicited her aid in establishing his group in Shanghai and particularly in selecting Chinese coworkers. He used her in Shanghai as a key member of his group. Smedley didn't threaten to sue again.

Eventually, she decided to leave the United States after a campaign launched by the American China lobby again identified her as a Soviet agent and offered evidence to that effect. In 1950, she left for England, just before she was subpoenaed by the House Un-American Activities Committee. She died suddenly in 1953 in a London nursing home. She bequeathed her ashes and her estate to Chu-teh, the Chinese Communist commander-in-chief. She was cremated, and her ashes were ceremoniously installed in Peking in what was then described as the new cemetery for revolutionaries.

Smedley will probably be remembered most not for her writing but for the fact that she was a double agent; her primary loyalty was with the Soviets, but she had an almost equal loyalty to the Chinese Communists. In many respects she was the link between the Soviet government and the Chinese Communists.

(See also Elise Sabrowski Ewert and Ursula Ruth Kuczynski.)

MacKinnon, Janice R., and Stephen R. MacKinnon. *Agnes Smedley: The Life and Times of an American Radical.* London: Virago, 1988.

Prange, Gordon W., with Donald M. Goldstein, and Katherine V. Dillon. *Target Tokyo: The Story of the Sorge Spy Ring.* New York: McGraw-Hill, 1984.

Willoughby, Major General Charles A. *Shanghai Conspiracy.* New York: E. P. Dutton, 1952.

Frances Spawr
United States
1940–

Frances Spawr and her husband owned a high-tech business that had government contracts. Greed led them to use that business in espionage against their own country.

Walter and Frances Spawr operated a small business polishing high-tech mirrors in their garage in the small town of Corona, California, about 45 miles from Los Angeles. Walter had learned to polish glass when he was 14, when he designed and built his own telescope. When he dropped out of college after one year, his father got him a job in the electro-optical laboratory of an aviation company close to Los Angeles. In 1963, Walter joined the U.S. Air Force but quit after four years to return to his civilian job at the aviation company. He set out to master every aspect of aerospace technology as it applied to electro-optical procedures.

In 1973, the Spawrs organized their own company, Spawr Optical Research, Incorporated. The new venture wasn't doing too well until a routine evaluation of their work by the Air Force tested their proficiency. The Air Force evaluator tested their competence in processing metal by leaving a piece of molybdenum with them for polishing. Molybdenum was the metal that the Air Force had decided to use for the mirrors in its laser research. The Air Force rated the Spawrs' polishing as the best they had ever seen. Soon, Spawr Optical Research was granted a security clearance, which brought work from some of the largest U.S. aerospace companies. The clearance also gave the Spawrs access to scientific discoveries of other high-tech companies that they could use in their own business.

They were soon immersed in a top secret project referred to as "Alpha-2," which was similar in concept to President Ronald Reagan's Star Wars project. This project's goal was to explode a mixture of hydrogen and fluorine gas by light beams that were magnified through a long, mirrored chamber. The highly polished metal mirrors were absolutely crucial to the project's success. The effectiveness of a Star Wars laser capable of cutting through heavy metal in an instant is dependent on the highly polished surfaces of mirrors. The most minute particle or irregularity on the mirror's surface could diffuse the concentrated light rays and render them useless.

Within a few years the Spawrs' business had evolved into a major defense contractor. When the Air Force proposed a large research project to develop its own capability for a mirror polishing facility, the Spawrs had to reassess their position.

A German promoter, with extensive contacts with businesses in Eastern Europe and Russia, approached the Spawrs with an attractive offer to sell their product in Italy. This was a bonanza for the Spawrs, and after two very lucrative years of foreign sales, the German promoter suggested that they also sell to companies in Eastern Europe.

About this time, the KGB was seeking to acquire western aerospace secrets from western sources under the cover of sponsoring a trade fair called "Physics 75." The KGB sent the Spawrs an invitation to the trade fair. The Spawrs' German promoter urged them to accept the invitation.

The Soviets subsequently ordered mirrors from the Spawrs. Both of them knew, without a doubt—from the dimensions and design of the mirrors ordered by the Soviets—that they were intended for military purposes. The mirrors that they shipped to the Soviets measured 25–40 centimeters in diameter and had a unique cooling system of water jets that prevented bending of the mirror surface even when it was exposed to the extreme heat of a high-energy laser beam. Intelligence reports indicated that the Soviets were having great difficulty with their domestically produced mirrors because of overheating.

The Soviets immediately incorporated the Spawrs' mirrors into their weapons systems. The intricate cooling system, which had been revealed to the Spawrs only because of their top secret security clearance, was clearly an illegal sale of a highly secret United States technology to the Soviets. The Air Force estimated that the mirrors exported to the Soviets had not only advanced the U.S.S.R.'s "pointing technology" but had also saved the Soviets millions of dollars in research and nearly 100 worker years in research and development time.

On 4 May 1976, in an effort to cover their trade with the U.S.S.R., the Spawrs applied for an export license from the United States Department of Commerce. They conveniently "forgot" to list a large number of mirrors that they had already exported to the Soviets and 25 that were smuggled out of the country three months later. Two orders had been already shipped secretly to the Soviets without the permission of the U.S. government. The third shipment was in the production cycle but was blocked by the Department of Commerce. Walter Spawr than wrote his congressman, asking for his intercession with the Department of Commerce to permit the shipment. The congressman checked and was told that the Department of Commerce had information (probably from two former employees of the Spawrs' company) that the Spawrs had been trading illegally with the Soviets.

Unaware that they were being investigated, it was alleged that the Spawrs intended to disguise the third shipment by sending it through a series of middlemen consignees. They planned to send the shipment first to a Swiss forwarding company, which would send it to a company in Berlin, which would send it on its final leg to Moscow. They hoped to sufficiently cloud the shipment's ultimate destination to mislead U.S. authorities.

In the summer of 1977, the Spawrs' German agent offered them a contract, from a cover company of the Soviet KGB, to sell the entire production process of their company for $1.5 million dollars. The Spawrs were still considering the offer to sell their company to the Soviets—with all the top secret processes that they had acquired through their top secret clearance—when they were arrested on 9 March 1978. They were indicted on charges of conspiring to sell, and of knowingly selling, strategic U.S. high technology that would be used for the benefit of a Communist-controlled nation.

On 12 December 1980, the Spawrs were convicted on six counts of falsifying export documents and four counts of selling high-power laser mirrors to the Soviet Union. Walter Spawr was sentenced to ten years in prison. His sentence was suspended except for six months, which he served. Frances received a five-year suspended sentence. They were both ordered to perform 500 hours of community service, and the company was fined $100,000.

Tuck, Jan. *High Tech Espionage.* New York: St. Martin's Press, 1986.

Lydia Chkalov Stahl

Russia
ca. 1898–

Lydia Stahl became a Communist in Paris in the 1920s and agreed to become a deep cover sleeper agent for the Soviets. She was activated to become the tutor in espionage techniques for two Americans, whose confessions later led to her arrest.

Stahl was born in Russia as Lydia Chkalov. She emigrated to the United States during the Russian Revolution of 1917. When her only baby son died in 1919, she returned to Europe and took up residence in Paris. In the early 1920s, the new political philosophy of communism was a popular subject of discussion in Paris. Stahl was attracted to communism and joined the cause.

In those days the names and curriculum vitae of all new recruits to communism were passed upward. The hierarchy would review the names and pass them on to Soviet intelligence and the Comintern for possible recruitment. Stahl was recognized immediately as a potential espionage asset against communism's principal capitalist enemy, the United States, because she already had the cover of U.S. citizenship and was basically loyal to Russia: an ideal combination for a Soviet spy.

In 1928, she went to the United States with every reason to think that she would become a well-entrenched, deep cover, long-term agent. At about this time, before Stahl was settled into her U.S. assignment, American Robert Switz, whose family had considerable wealth, became a Communist. Switz foolishly was flattered when Soviet intelligence offered him the opportunity to spy on his own country. Stahl served as an able coworker with Switz, and the two of them provided the Soviets with a large amount of good intelligence.

The Soviets, aided by Switz, were able to convince his wife, Marjorie, to join Robert in spying on the United States. Marjorie was an adept pupil and was soon doing everything for the Soviet spy net that Stahl had formerly done. When the Switzes were thoroughly familiar with all of Stahl's tasks, she returned to Paris in 1933. Paris at that time was the hub of all Soviet espionage in Europe. Hitler's rise to power in Germany required that the Soviets reassess and realign their clandestine assets in Germany. This required a tremendous amount of work for

Stahl and the Paris Soviet espionage center. Stahl needed help, so the Soviets assigned the Switzes to Paris to help her.

When one of Stahl's close friends, a fellow Soviet agent, was caught engaging in espionage by the Finnish counterintelligence service, she was arrested and broke under the Finns' interrogation. She told everything that she knew about Soviet operations, including compromising information about Stahl. The Finnish counterintelligence service passed this information about Stahl to the French counterintelligence service, which began an investigation of Stahl. Through this investigation the French service discovered most of Stahl's clandestine contacts, including the Switzes. The French service observed the Switzes' meeting with the resident director of the Soviet intelligence apparatus in Paris.

When the French counterintelligence service arrested the Switzes, Stahl and most of the other members of the Soviet net managed to escape. The French service did not have enough firm evidence to sustain a successful prosecution, and the Switzes were allowed to go free temporarily . The investigation dragged on for three months, until two packages of films were unexpectedly deposited at the French Consulate in Geneva. These films, of an unknown origin, were of a highly compromising nature concerning espionage and the Switzes' fingerprints were found on the film.

When he was confronted with this new evidence, Robert Switz confessed. Five other former members of the Soviet net also confessed when they were arrested. All of their confessions implicated Stahl. The Soviet networks in France and, to a lesser extent, in all of Europe, were effectively negated. The Switzes' cooperation with the authorities helped them receive suspended sentences; they were allowed to return to the United States.

As a matter of expediency, for her cooperation, Stahl received the minimum allowable sentence for espionage of only a few months. When she was released she made every effort to disappear in order to live a life free from notoriety.

Seth, Ronald. *Encyclopedia of Espionage.* New York: Doubleday, 1972.

Renata Steiner
Switzerland
ca. 1908–

Renata Steiner specialized in surveillance for the OGPU. The pinnacle of her professional career was tracking down and assassinating Ignance Reiss, a former senior OGPU official who had broken with Stalin.

Reiss served as an agent for the OGPU for many years. He blindly followed Stalin's orders. He was the chief Comintern/OGPU agent in Vienna. His dedication and loyalty began to waver after Stalin expelled Leon Trotsky, whom Reiss greatly admired, from Russia and the Communist party. When Stalin executed several old-line Bolshevik leaders—who Reiss knew were innocent of the crimes that Stalin had used to justify their deaths—he became more disillusioned with the Soviet regime.

Reiss secretly visited his fellow OGPU/Comintern chief in Western Europe, Alexander Krivitsky, in The Hague. Reiss knew that he could confide in Krivitsky without Krivitsky reporting the conversation to Moscow. Reiss told Krivitsky that he was disillusioned with Stalin and needed to leave the OGPU and forget all about it. Krivitsky prudently cautioned Reiss to be careful, because he knew that the OGPU would demand his life in retribution if he defected.

Reiss didn't heed Krivitsky's advice. He wrote a letter to Stalin. He said that he should have written long ago, when the Bolshevik leaders had been murdered. He had kept silent then, Reiss wrote, but would try to make up for it to ease his conscience. He announced that he would no longer follow Stalin because to do so would be betraying the working class and socialism. Reiss had been awarded the Order of the Red Banner by Stalin for meritorious service as an espionage agent, and he included this medal in his letter to Stalin, saying that he could no longer wear it with honor.

When Stalin received the letter, he ordered Reiss's old friend, Krivitsky, to find Reiss and murder him. This wantonly callous dictate galvanized Krivitsky himself into defecting to the United States.

The OGPU then turned to someone experienced in finding and destroying enemies. Renata Steiner had been an OGPU agent since 1935. She was an experienced operative who was particularly adept at surveillance. She had participated in the elaborate surveillance operation of Leon (Lyova) Sedov, Trotsky's son, in Paris. In the Sedov case, the surveillance team had taken a house next door to Sedov and his common-law wife, Jeanne Martin. Steiner's team had conducted a watch on all visitors to Sedov's house. Her surveillance group was identified by the French and Swiss police as being connected with the Society for the Repatriation of Russian Emigrés, which was sponsored by the OGPU in Paris.

When she was sent to find Reiss, Steiner was 29 and lived in Paris. She was ostensibly a student at the Sorbonne for cover purposes. She had managed to follow Reiss's trail through Holland and France, until she finally located him in Switzerland. She reported this information by telephone to the OGPU headquarters in Paris, and they sent Gertrude Schildbach to help Steiner keep Reiss in one place until the hit team could get him. Schildbach was an old friend of Reiss. She had been a guest in his house and had frequently played with and cared for his children. She was also a seasoned OGPU operative and, despite her overtures to Reiss, he should have known better than to trust her.

Schildbach, it was rumored, had been wavering politically since the beginnings of Stalin's purges. She could therefore plausibly play the part of a potential defector ready to join Reiss in breaking with Moscow. Reiss knew of her waverings and trusted her. When she arrived in Lausanne, Reiss took her to dinner at a restaurant near Chamblandes to discuss her possible defection.

The hit team was made up of Roland Abbiate (aliases François Rossi and Py), a native of Monaco and an executioner for the Paris OGPU station; Schildbach, a German Communist who lived in Rome and was an agent for the OGPU in Italy; Etienne Martignat, a French Communist agent of the OGPU station in Paris; Vladimir Kondratieff, a White Russian working for the OGPU as an executioner; and Steiner.

Much to Reiss's surprise, Steiner and Kondratieff joined Schildbach and Reiss at the restaurant where they were having dinner. The new arrivals suggested a relaxing drive after dinner in a car that Steiner had rented. Reiss sat beside her in the front seat, and Kondratieff and Schildbach sat in the back seat. During the drive in the country, Kondratieff killed Reiss, and the body was dumped on the side of the road. Two days later, a car containing a blood-soaked overcoat was found in front of the Geneva-Cornavin railroad station. Police traced the rented car to Steiner, who quickly confessed to her part in the assassination and helped the authorities to solve the murder.

Reiss's body was found on the night of September 4. The body had been riddled by machine gun bullets; there were 15 bullets still embedded in the body. A strand of gray hair was clutched in the right hand. In the pocket of the suit on the body was a passport in the name of Hans Eberhart. The passport had been issued to a man born on 1 March 1899 in Komoau, Czechoslovakia, and contained a French visa. The man was registered at the Hotel Continental as a businessman on a trip from Paris. The entire passport was a forgery. Upon further checking, the police found that the body was that of Ignance Reiss, a 39-year-old, Polish-born, former OGPU agent, who had been attached to the OGPU stations in Holland, Switzerland, Great Britain, and France.

Checking further on an abandoned U.S.–made automobile in Geneva led to a woman and a man registered on September 4 at the Hotel de la Paix in Lausanne. They had fled without their luggage and without paying their hotel bill. They were Schildbach and Abbiate. Among the effects abandoned by Schildbach was a box of candy heavily laced with strychnine poison. Schildbach was to have given the poisoned candy to Mrs. Reiss and the Reiss children, but she couldn't bring herself to murder them.

The Reiss/Steiner surveillance case is a classic that is studied by student KGB officers. (See also Lilia Ginsburg Dallin.)

Andrew, Christopher, and Oleg Gordievsky. *KGB: The Inside Story.* New York: HarperCollins, 1990.

Dzhirkvelov, Ilya. *Secret Service: My Life in the KGB and the Soviet Elite.* New York: Harper & Row, 1987.

Massig, Hede. *This Deception.* New York: Duell, Sloan & Pearce, 1951.

Rositzke, Harry. *The KGB: The Eyes of Russia.* New York: Doubleday, 1981.

Martha Dodd Stern
Chicago
1908–ca. 1985

Martha Dodd Stern began her espionage career by spying on her father and stealing classified papers from his office for her Soviet case officer. She found safety only behind the Iron Curtain when she was indicted for espionage against the United States.

Stern was the daughter of William Dodd, a former professor of history at the University of Chicago and a U.S. ambassador to Germany from 1933 to 1937. She attended private schools and the University of Chicago and spent a year at the Sorbonne in Paris. When she accompanied her father to Germany, she had a love affair with a Soviet intelligence officer and stole classified national security documents from her father's safe in the U.S. Embassy to give to her Soviet lover.

Martha and her husband, Alfred Kaufman Stern, were probably the most socially prominent couple ever to be indicted for espionage against the United States. Alfred was 11 years older than Martha. He was wealthy in his own right because of an inheritance, but he received considerably more money in a settlement when he divorced his first wife, Marian Rosenwald, the daughter of the chief executive of Sears Roebuck and Company. Alfred attended meetings of the Communist party in the 1940s and was always willing to raise money for the party when called upon. He was often the only contributor to the Communist party coffers. His Soviet superiors and the CPUSA leaders joked about the many times that they played him for a sucker without his knowing it.

It was Vasilly Zubilin, the chief Soviet intelligence officer in the United States at that time, who recruited the Sterns into Soviet espionage. Zubilin also recruited Boris Morros, a small-time Hollywood producer and music publisher.

After solidifying a recruitment, Zubilin would turn the agent over to his principal agent, Jack Soble. Morros worked for Soble, and Soble worked for Zubilin. The Sterns didn't have any cover except the business of managing their money, so Zubilin decided that they needed additional cover. He arranged for Alfred to be the vice-president of the Boris Morros Music Company. (What neither Zubilin, Soble, nor the Sterns knew was that Morros had been working for the FBI as a penetration of the Soviet espionage apparatus from the time of his recruitment by the Soviets.)

Morros briefed Soble, at Zubilin's request, on how the music business had to be operated in order to leave sufficient time for him and the Sterns to handle their espionage assignments. Morros told Soble that when Zubilin had created the company, Alfred had put up $130,000 of his own money. In order to make Stern feel more important and make him feel as if he were getting something for his money, Morros and Zubilin had made Stern the figurehead vice-president in charge of the New York office.

Differences arose constantly between Morros and the Sterns, and Soble spent an inordinate amount of time in the Sterns' luxurious apartment on Central Park West, mediating disputes between them. The Boris Morros Music Company was finally dissolved because Morros and Alfred couldn't reconcile their differences. Morros remained in Soble's Soviet espionage network as a trusted agent. The Sterns repeatedly warned Soble that there was something suspicious about Morros and that he couldn't be trusted. Soble, however, dismissed these accusations as simple vindictiveness.

MARTHA DODD STERN
From Through Embassy Eyes *by Martha Dodd (New York: Garden City Publishing Co., 1939)*

One of Martha's contributions to the Soble spy operation was bringing Jane Foster Zlatovski into the net. Jane and her husband, George Zlatovski, became productive members of the espionage network.

In 1953, when the Sterns received word through an informant that the U.S. federal grand jury in New York investigating Soviet espionage in the United States was going to call them as witnesses, they fled to Mexico to avoid testifying. They arrived at Nuevo Laredo, Mexico, on 17 December 1953, but because they did not have the proper documentation, the Mexican authorities would not allow them to enter. They bribed the Mexican officials and promised that they would regularize their papers within 30 days, but they never did. They were in Mexico illegally the entire time. They paid regular, substantial bribes to fixers to avoid being sent back to the United States for lack of proper Mexican documentation.

The Sterns established two businesses in Mexico. One was the Compania Mercantil Latino Americano, S. A., and the other was Negociadores, S. A. Alfred was the president of Mercantil and Martha was the general manager of Negociadores. The office for both these companies was on the fifth floor of Reforma 104 in Mexico City. It was fairly well substantiated that the Sterns sold securities (mostly stocks in U.S. companies) valued at $15 million and transferred the money in some nefarious manner to Mexico (or at least where they could control it from Mexico), despite attempts by the U.S. government to block all of their assets and any such transfers.

In January 1957, the grand jury for the Federal District of New York again called the Sterns to testify. On 12 February 1957, the U.S. Embassy in Mexico City tried to serve subpoenas on the Sterns at their home in Polanco, a suburb of Mexico City. The Sterns immediately engaged the services of the former United States ambassador to Mexico and former mayor of New York City, William O'Dwyer. They failed to appear before the grand jury and were fined $25,000 each for contempt of court.

While the Sterns refused to acknowledge the subpoenas, the Mexican police agents of Gobernacion, who were standing by ready to enforce the extradition order, were getting impatient over the delay. They decided that the proper remedy would be to kidnap the Sterns and "push" them quietly across the bridge over the Rio Bravo (Rio Grande) between Nuevo Laredo, Mexico, and Laredo, Texas, into the waiting arms of the FBI. This would not have been, in the legal sense, an extradition but rather an "informal deportation." There was precedent for this informal procedure, which had been used to return Gus Hall (leader of the CPUSA), who had been hiding in Mexico, to the United States.

Martha and Alfred, with their adopted son Robert, arranged with Boris Kolomyakov, the KGB chief of station in the Soviet Embassy in Mexico, to get spurious Paraguayan passports. Then Kolomyakov sneaked them aboard a KLM flight that left Mexico City at 1:00 A.M. on 12 July 1957. Their Mexican attorney, O'Dwyer, may have known that his clients were planning to flee; he left Mexico for a vacation in Ireland two days before the Sterns fled.

At a news conference after they arrived behind the Iron Curtain in Prague, Czechoslovakia, the Sterns admitted that they had obtained phony Paraguayan passports. They claimed that the FBI had been persecuting them and that they had to flee.

The Sterns settled in Czechoslovakia, but they spent 1963 to 1970 in Cuba helping Fidel Castro's revolution and most of 1957 in Russia. While they were in Czechoslovakia, Martha corresponded with her ACGM (American Communist Group in Mexico) friends in Mexico. She wrote sexually explicit letters to a former lover, but her letters to other friends in the ACGM extolled the glories of the Peoples' Republic of Czechoslovakia and raved about how wonderful and plentiful everything was in Czechoslovakia. She always managed to sneak in somewhere else in these letters—after this obligatory compliment, intended to appease the censors—that she desperately needed a few things that, unfortunately, were not available in the Peoples' Republic. In each letter she begged her friends in Mexico to send her such things as soap, toilet paper, bobby pins, toothpaste,

Spam, any canned goods, writing paper, and razor blades.

On 9 September 1957, the Sterns were indicted for espionage against the United States while working for Soviet intelligence. On 30 June 1977, President Jimmy Carter was petitioned to dismiss the indictments against the Sterns. On 23 March 1979, *The Washington Post* reported that the indictments for espionage against the Sterns had been dropped. The rationale was that, after so many years, they would be impossible to prosecute effectively.

In 1986, Alfred died in Prague. In the late 1980s, Martha died in Prague. Robert, their adopted son, went to live with the Sterns' former butler/gardener in Mexico. Martha had written several books. One, about her life with her father in Germany, didn't mention stealing her father's papers for the Soviets. Her books also didn't mention that she had been recruited into Soviet intelligence.

Most of the information about the Sterns' espionage activities comes from the indictments filed by the U.S. government in the Federal District of New York.

(See also Johanna Koenen Beker and Jane Foster Zlatovski.)

Morris, Boris. *My Ten Years as a Counterspy.* New York: Viking Press, 1959.

Rose Pastor Stokes
(Sascha)
England
1879–1933

Rose Pastor Stokes was a Communist who was indicted for espionage against the United States. She blatantly supported Communist doctrine advocating the violent overthrow of the U.S. government. She cooperated with the Soviets by sending information to them.

She was born Rose Pastor in London in 1879 and came to the United States at the age of 11. She immediately went to work in a Cleveland cigar factory, where she learned about what the older workers called the "class struggle."

In 1918, when she moved to New York, she joined the burgeoning Socialist party. In 1919, the Socialists were too bland for her and she, as well as some other extremists, deserted socialism to found the CPUSA. (The use of "CPUSA" is an over-simplification. The communist movement in the United States went through a series of splits and amalgamations before it finally evolved into the CPUSA. Even then, there were still many factions, such as Trotskyism, that could not properly be included in this designation. "CPUSA" is used only as a matter of convenience.) On 26 June 1922, she attended one of the first organizational meetings of the future CPUSA, which was held in the home of Benjamin Gitlow. She used the pseudonym "Sascha" at this meeting to conceal her true identity. She was one of the leading members at the infamous Bridgemen Convention, where the illegal section of the CPUSA was formed.

Stokes was one of the real pioneers of the CPUSA. During her lifetime, she occupied an even more eminent position in the party than "Mother" Bloor. ("Mother" Reeves Bloor was a legendary figure in the early Communist party movement in the United States.) She was known nationally as the ablest agitator in the American radical movement.

During the Palmer Raids of the 1920s, Stokes was arrested by the New York police and extradited to Chicago, where she was charged with violating the syndicalist laws. The Palmer Raids were a series of arrests across the United States, coordinated and orchestrated by Attorney General A. Mitchell Palmer. After she was released on bond, she secretly shipped out of the United States to Russia, where she attended an international meeting of top Soviet and Communist strategists from other countries.

Stokes became a well-known Communist agitator in scores of strikes in the eastern United States. Her tactics for bringing about crippling economic crises became legendary. For example, she was a leader in organizing the telephone operators strike; the work-stopping strike of hotel and restaurant workers; the famous silk workers strike in Paterson, New Jersey; and the needle workers union in New York's garment industry.

She was sentenced to jail for ten years under the Espionage Act for wartime writing and speeches that gave aid and comfort to the enemy. During World War I, she had campaigned vigorously as an antiwar Marxist and was convinced that traditional political parties in the United States could never adequately support the socioeconomic revolution that she hoped to inspire.

In 1925, her millionaire husband J. G. Phelps Stokes divorced her. He, too, was committed to the cause of feminism and had originally encouraged her political action. He thought that her fervor was only a manifestation of her feminism and didn't suspect its Communist connections. He cited another man as co-respondent and charged her with adultery. She later wrote about her divorce with a very candid, pro–free love attitude, in *Colliers* magazine. The magazine printed her article with the warning to readers that the article espoused radical ideas.

Stokes remained a loyal member of the CPUSA until she died still working for her ideals at a German hospital of cancer at the age of 54 in June 1933.

Gitlow, Benjamin. *The Whole of Their Lives.* New York: Charles Scribner's Sons, 1948.

Sochen, June. *Movers and Shakers.* New York: The New York Times Book Company, 1973.

Spolansky, Jacob. *The Communist Trail in America.* New York: Macmillan, 1951.

Violette Bushnell Szabo
(Louise)
France
1921–1945

Violette Bushnell Szabo became a spy to avenge her husband's death. After he was killed by the Germans, she aggressively sought an agent's position—rather than a more typical woman's desk job—with the SOE. Szabo parachuted into Occupied France, where she was eventually captured by the Nazis, imprisoned, and tortured.

She was born in Paris, where her father, an Englishman, operated a fleet of tourist taxis. Her father had returned to France to marry the French girl with whom he had fallen in love during World War I. She was raised in the Brixton section of London and spoke French with her mother and English with her father and schoolmates. She always excelled at "boys" games and feats of muscular skill. She learned to shoot with her father at carnival shooting galleries.

In the spring of 1940, when the remnants of the French army escaped to Britain after the fall of France, she met a French soldier, Eitenne Szabo. It was love at first sight and, after a week or so, they were married. They had a daughter named Tania. Her husband was sent to North Africa, where he was killed in October 1942, fighting the German forces of General Rommel. Since the start of the war, Szabo's mother had been doing her part to fight the Nazis as an ambulance driver in the Women's Transport Service of the First Aid Nursing Yeomanry (FANYs). She wanted Szabo to join this group, but Szabo wanted a more direct role in the war.

She applied to SOE but was initially offered nothing but a routine desk job. She held out for an agent's assignment and was eventually accepted. She was put directly into training courses in sabotage and parachute jumping. Her natural athletic abilities and her rugged physical constitution were advantages during this rigorous training.

Her first assignment into Occupied France in April 1944 was a parachute jump into the Rouen-Channel coast area. She was accompanied by a veteran of several previous missions. Their task was to reconnoiter the area in preparation for the coming invasion on D-Day. An ancillary objective was to locate other SOE teams. Szabo and her partner spent three weeks in France, with a short vacation trip to Paris, before they were exfiltrated by a Lysander bomber plane back to Britain.

Szabo returned to France after a visit with her mother and daughter and a brief rest. In August 1944, she was working in France with another SOE agent in a small house in the vicinity of Salon La Tour, when they were surrounded by the Gestapo, who were backed up by a division of Panzer tanks. Szabo returned the Germans' fire and, even after she was wounded in her arm, kept up enough fire to keep the Gestapo pinned down. She begged her partner to escape, because the information that he had would be more valuable to the Allies than her continued freedom. She kept the Gestapo at bay with her rapid-firing Sten gun and, moving from window to window, covered her partner's escape. Her partner did escape and lived to recount Szabo's heroic actions.

Eventually, Szabo (known by her code name, Louise) was taken prisoner. She was placed under heavy guard in the Gestapo's Paris jail, where she was interrogated and tortured from the time of her capture in August until she was moved in September 1944. She was taken to another prison, where again she was interrogated under torture. In April 1945, she was taken to the most feared women's concentration camp at Ravensbruck, about 40 miles north of Berlin. On an unknown date in April 1945, Szabo was shot in the nape of the neck with two other female SOE agents (Denise Block, code named Ambrosia, and Lillian Rolfe, code named Nadine).

Szabo was posthumously awarded the George Cross, Britain's highest civilian award. The French government awarded her its highest honor, the Croix de Guerre.

Weiser, Marjorie P. K., and Jean S. Arbeiter. *Womanlist.* New York: Atheneum, 1981.

T

Niuta Teitelbaum
(Wanda)
Poland
1917–1943

Niuta Teitelbaum had an innocent, almost angelic look that belied her deadly composure and her determination to exterminate Nazis everywhere she found them. She was an expert executioner but was eventually captured and tortured. She refused to confess or to implicate her companions. She died while undergoing torture.

Teitelbaum was the daughter of a deeply religious Jewish mother and father. She had been born in Poland in 1917, just before World War I ended. Her family belonged to the Hassidim sect of extra-orthodox Jews, and she grew up in a household where perseverance and dedication were considered prime virtues.

She was 22 when the Nazis invaded Poland at the beginning of World War II. She lived in an area dominated by the Nazi Germans, which aroused her resentment and anger at her inability to do anything about the brutalities that she witnessed every day.

She reported to the head of the Polish underground and asked for an assignment in which she could fight against the enemy. She literally begged to work with the Polish freedom fighters. She told him her place was in the struggle for the honor of her people, for an independent Poland, and for the freedom of humanity. She became instrumental in carrying the fight to the Germans; earlier, the Poland underground had been content to engage in sniping attacks and sabotage. She became a one-woman assassination team. She was an expert killer with a gun or explosives, but she preferred the pistol.

There were many stories about her prowess. On one occasion, she walked past the guards of the Gestapo headquarters in order to murder an officer. She bestowed on each guard a beatific smile that reinforced their impression that this young woman represented no danger. (The Gestapo later gave her the nickname "Little Wanda with the Braids" because of her angelic appearance.) She feigned embarrassment when she asked to see a certain Gestapo officer on a "personal matter." The guards, led by her demure demeanor to believe that she wanted to see the officer on an affair of the heart, gave her a pass, told her the officer's room number, and waved her through the building checkpoint. She entered the senior Gestapo officer's room and found him alone. He was surprised and tried to stand when she drew her pistol and shot him dead. The silencer on her gun prevented the shot from being heard, and she walked out of Gestapo headquarters without being stopped.

On another occasion she entered a Gestapo officer's house in the dead of night and made her way to his bedroom. He awoke to stare into the muzzle of a pistol and tried to hide under the covers. Teitelbaum shot him several times through the covers until he was dead.

There was a nightclub near the Gestapo headquarters that was popular with the officers. On several occasions, Teitelbaum and her friends tossed fragmentation hand grenades into the crowded nightclub, killing and maiming the Germans.

When the Nazi high command offered a 150,000 zloty reward for her capture, the Gestapo instituted a dragnet-type search for her. Her friends urged her to quit her resistance activities, at least until the search for her stopped or abated. She refused, and in July 1943 she was captured by the Gestapo. The soldiers arrested her before she could bite down on her suicide pill. She was taken to Gestapo headquarters, where she was brutally tortured, but she refused to give any information about the other members of her organization. She died under torture.

Marrin, Albert. *The Secret Armies.* New York: Atheneum, 1985.

Beatrix Terwindt
Holland
ca. 1922–

Beatrix Terwindt was a Dutch resistance fighter and spy. She parachuted into enemy territory to deliver supplies to a British radio operation, was injured in that attempt, was captured and later interrogated, but refused to reveal anything to her captors. It is still unclear whether anyone in British intelligence knew, before she was sent on her mission, that the entire Dutch resistance movement was being controlled by the Germans.

Operation *England Spiel* (England Play) was a German operation that played captured British agent radios back to England as if they were still being operated by the original British agents. The Germans tried to make certain that the British believed that the radios were being operated

free of German control. In fact, the operators were forced through torture and other means of persuasion to continue radio contact with London just as though they were carrying out their original mission.

Usually, warning and danger signals are built into the transmission procedure, which are designed to alert headquarters that an operation has been compromised. At the stroke of midnight on the moonless night of 14 February 1943 when Terwindt dropped into Occupied Holland, *England Spiel* was about a year old and, apparently, the British service had not yet become suspicious that the entire resistance in Holland had been compromised. The Germans had been operating the clandestine radio network to order supplies and to request that new agents be dropped in to them. This not only gave the Germans supplies that they could use and more agents to interrogate, but it also denied the supplies and replacement bodies to the legitimate resistance fighters.

Terwindt had been a stewardess before World War II with KLM airlines. She volunteered for SOE to help liberate her country from the Nazis. She had a bad exit from the Halifax bomber that she jumped from that night and had a terrible landing. The wind took her chute and dragged her across the rocky drop zone, causing severe injuries to her head. She blacked out and came to in a German field hospital.

Her mission was to have been the organizing of escape routes for downed Allied flight crews and draft-age Dutch youths who wanted to fight against the Germans with the Free Dutch Forces that were organizing in England. The British had been supplying the resistance movement in Holland on a regular basis, almost so routinely that they had become oblivious to the changes in the radio transmissions from Holland; or, so it seemed. On the other hand, if the British were aware that the resistance movement had been compromised and the radio transmissions were bogus, what could possibly be gained by allowing the operation to continue?

The German Gestapo interrogated Terwindt as soon as her wounds had been dressed. She refused to give them any information. She recalled to herself the arduous training that she had undergone and how she had doubted that she would be able to withstand the Germans' interrogation. Her case officer in Britain had reassured her by telling her that the best intelligence agents had always been women. During her interrogation, the German officer told her that all the other agents had been captured, but she was the first woman to be captured. The officer commented that the English must have been getting shorthanded to send a woman. Throughout the interrogation, Terwindt refused to divulge any information to the Germans.

Terwindt had been drugged by her captors. She couldn't tell if it was to ease the pain of her head wound or a drug used as truth serum to aid them in their interrogation. Gradually, as she emerged from the drug's effects, she remembered the interrogator's statement that all 39 agents had been captured and realized that the Germans were operating a gigantic deception on British intelligence. One question kept nagging at her: Had the Germans completely fooled the English into believing that the resistance network was secure? It was unthinkable that the British would have allowed her to parachute into a trap if they had had even an intimation that the operations were not completely secure.

As her head cleared, she vaguely recalled that amid the confusion of her farewell at the airport just before she took off from England, someone had said something to her. Just as she climbed up the metal steps into the airplane, an SOE officer, who had been standing on the sidelines, had grasped her right hand, as if to shake hands farewell, and said that she should be careful and not get caught like others had. His statement suggested that at least one member of the British intelligence knew that the resistance network had been compromised and was being operated by the Germans as a deception operation.

Terwindt didn't mention this memory until much later, and then only to close friends. She was interviewed in November 1965 and stated that she did not accept that the British had been culpable in the North Pole affair by sending agents to their deaths after they knew that the Germans were controlling the operation. There must have been a higher purpose to be served.

Terwindt was kept in prison by the Germans in Holland until July 1944. She was then shipped to the death camp at Ravensbruck. Fortunately, she was still alive when the British liberated the camp in May 1945. In Holland she is a national hero. She married in 1958 and lives in Utrecht with her husband.

Gainer-Raymond, Phillippe. *The Tangled Web*. New York: Pantheon, 1968.

Three-Fifty-Five
Colonial America
ca. 1756–ca. 1800

Three-Fifty-Five was one of the true daughters of the American Revolution. She was a professional spy who so zealously safeguarded her name that her true identity has been lost forever.

One of General George Washington's most productive intelligence organizations was the Culpepper Ring, which was operated by Washington's chief of intelligence, Colonel Benjamin Tallmadge. The objective of this organization was to gather intelligence about the British military headquarters in New York. Several merchants and residents of New York were sources for this spy network. Many of them had to consort and be friendly with the British businessmen in New York and with the representatives of the British government on a daily basis.

The spy ring's most prolific source of high-grade intelligence was Robert Townsend, who used the name Samuel Culpepper, Junior, in his reports. Most of his intelligence information came from the woman who has come to us through history only as "355." She was also Townsend's mistress. Despite a thorough search of Townsend's letters, diaries, and other papers, and despite the fact that Three-Fifty-Five was his mistress, no identifiable trace of her can be found.

In 1775, when British intelligence discovered that the Americans were using a secret "sympathetic stain" as invisible ink in their secret correspondence, Washington feared that the identity of his spies would be compromised because the British could develop the secret ink. If they were able to intercept future correspondence and developed the secret writing, his spies would be revealed. To prevent this from happening, Washington ordered Colonel Tallmadge to prepare a code for members of the spy network to use. The code was a simple substitution code with three-digit numbers representing words. For example, New York was 727, Long Island was 728, and General Washington was 711. On the master document, number 355 was cited as the code name for "lady." No other identification or elaboration was given. In the ensuing months, number Three-Fifty-Five became one of the most important sources for Washington's intelligence service.

We do know that number Three-Fifty-Five was Robert Townsend's mistress and that she bore him a son. She was first described in Townsend's early dispatches as an "acquaintance" living in New York City who could "outwit them all" (this presumably meant the British). This may indicate that Three-Fifty-Five was already involved in espionage before Townsend met her. Sometime in 1780, probably close to the time when Townsend left the service, she became his common-law wife, and their son was christened Robert Townsend, Junior.

When Benedict Arnold defected to the British, Three-Fifty-Five was the only member of the Culpepper spy ring arrested. We know that she was arrested on or shortly before 20 October 1780 because one of Townsend's deputies wrote to Washington on that date of the imprisonment of a person who always had been of service to them.

The identity of number Three-Fifty-Five is forever lost to us. On all records Townsend is listed merely as a "bachelor." If his very proper Quaker family knew the identity of their son's common-law wife, they preferred to ignore her existence.

One guess about her identity is that she may have been one of the women who were close personal friends of Major Andre of the British army. Andre was known to be indiscreet with classified information. He was quartered in New York, where Three-Fifty-Five is believed to have lived. Three-Fifty-Five was a most prolific source, and all of her information was accurate and reliable, therefore her source must have been a highly placed British officer.

Dulles, Allen. *Great True Spy Stories.* New York: Random House, 1968.

Tokyo Rose.
See d'Aquino, Iva Toguri.

Luba Trepper
(Luba Brojde, Anna Mikler,
   Sara Orschizer)
Poland
ca. 1906–ca. 1970

Luba Trepper was an accomplished spy who ran agents and directed intelligence operations. She was also the assistant to her husband, Leopold Trepper, who ran one of the most extensive spy networks of the time.

Luba met her future husband in Tel Aviv in 1926. For Leopold, it was love at first sight. He discovered that Luba had come from Poland, where she had worked in a factory and engaged in militant Communist youth activities. An agent provocateur had been discovered in her group, so they decided to kill him. Luba was part of the execution team and hid the murder weapon in her house. She had had to leave Poland because of this crime and had fled to Palestine. In Palestine she first worked on a kibbutz, then as a housepainter, and then with an organization that aided political prisoners. The two became lovers and pledged to marry as soon as they could.

Leopold, a Jew, was born in Poland. When he became a Communist, he fought first in Palestine and then in France for the ideals of social justice. In 1926, he rented a room in Tel Aviv, where he could devote more time to managing the affairs of the Ichud. The Ichud—Hebrew for "unity" ("Itachat" in Arabic)—was a Communist front designed to foster closer harmony between Jews and Arabs. It had a two-point program: to open the Jewish labor union to Arabs in order to create a joint international labor union and to provide opportunities for Jews and Arabs to mix socially, particularly through cultural work.

Next, Leopold went to France to work for a Jewish Communist labor organization. In 1930, Luba joined him there and worked for the same group. She had been wanted by the British police in Palestine for Communist subversion and had had to borrow her sister Sarah's identity card to escape. She found a cover job in Paris doing piecework for a furrier while she continued her militant organizational work for the Communists. She was chosen to represent the Jewish section of the First Anti-Fascist Congress.

Leopold was sent to Moscow by the Comintern for further study, and she joined him in 1933 with their 18-month-old son, Michael. In Moscow she studied Communist party organization methods at the Marchlevski University until 1936 and worked for a while as a political commissar in the district presided over by Nikita Khruschev.

In 1938, Leopold was well established as the director of a large espionage network with headquarters in Belgium. The cover for him and some of his operatives was a raincoat company that had branches throughout Europe. Luba joined him in the summer of 1938 with their second son, Edgar, who was then a year and a half old. Michael, their older son, was kept in Russia by the Soviet secret police as a hostage.

When she finished with her household chores at the end of the day, it was part of Luba's duties in the espionage network to conduct the special liaison with their Soviet case officer, who was under cover as a member of the Soviet Commercial Office in Brussels. In addition to the large task of managing all of the detailed housekeeping jobs necessary to operating a spy network, she also handled several field agents as a case officer.

In the spring of 1940, France and Britain were at war with Germany. On 10 May 1940, the Belgian police came to the apartment on rue Richard Neuberg where the Treppers were living as Adam and Anna Mikler. The Belgian police told Luba that she must pack her things because she was being taken to a concentration camp. (All German nationals were "confined" by the Belgian authorities as enemy aliens during the war.) The police told her that even though she and Leopold were documented as naturalized Canadian citizens, the Belgian police knew that they were of German descent.

Luba convinced the police that they were really of Polish descent, and the police left to consult a higher authority. Leopold arrived home shortly after the police had left. He immediately arranged for Luba and Edgar to be smuggled into the Soviet Embassy, where they would be safe. The embassy was surrounded by Belgian police, but Luba and her son were smuggled into the embassy, hidden in the trunk of a diplomatic car.

It was a Soviet police order that the families of persons working in intelligence for the Soviets during World War II should be separated from the agent and live in Russia. The purpose was to facilitate control over the intelligence agent by having the family literally held hostage. As a consequence, Luba and her second son, Edgar, joined Michael in Russia until the end of the war.

Leopold rejected Stalin and his purges, but his hatred of Nazism led him to work with Soviet intelligence against the Germans despite Stalin's brutality. Before World War II, when Trepper had been in Brussels, he had begun to supply Moscow with information through a network of spies and radio operators (called "pianists"). As the Germans rolled across Europe, Leopold and his agents moved ahead of them to Paris, Marseilles, and back to Berlin. His network was able, through a combination of skill and luck, to conduct some of the boldest espionage operations of the war—even in the German general staff's own offices. He became the leader of the legendary Soviet intelligence network reverentially referred to by the German Gestapo during World War II as the *Rote Kapelle* (the Red Orchestra).

After the war, Stalin, for unjustified reasons, had Leopold sentenced to prison for ten years in the gulags of Siberia, five years of which he served in solitary confinement. He was released before completing his sentence when Stalin died.

Luba had received a letter from Soviet military intelligence informing her that Leopold was "missing" and had disappeared during the war. She had bought a little shack in a slum on the edge of Moscow, which was all that she could afford. She and the children tried to live a normal life after the privations suffered during the war. She was making a living as a photographer. Leopold had become a "non-person," so there was no apparent reason to doubt the original report that he had "disappeared."

As soon after Stalin's death as possible, on 23 May 1954, Leopold was released from prison. He found Luba and was reunited with his family, some of whom didn't even recognize him. The reunited family eventually moved to Poland. Luba was allowed to leave Poland and move to Britain. Michael lived in Copenhagen, and Edgar lived in Jerusalem. On 2 November 1973, Leopold became ill and was allowed to join Luba in London. He died in Jerusalem at the age of 77 in 1983.

Trepper, Leopold. *The Great Game.* New York: McGraw-Hill, 1977.

V

Elizabeth Van Lew
United States
1818–1900

Elizabeth Van Lew was a Union agent whose conscience was her greatest strength as a spy collecting intelligence information and in her direct action to free the slaves during the Civil War. She was a dedicated abolitionist who set her own slaves free. This was an unusual display of what her fellow southerners in Richmond, Virginia, must have considered a strictly "northern sentiment."

Van Lew was born into an aristocratic family of the antebellum South. Chief Justice John Marshall was an intimate friend of the family, and Jenny Lind, the famous "Swedish Nightingale," gave a concert in their mansion. Van Lew was tutored at home and completed her education at a finishing school in Philadelphia. She was in her early forties when the Civil War began.

Before and during the war, her neighbors in Richmond assumed that her loyalty and sentiments would be in consonance with those of the Confederacy. In her heart, Van Lew had opposite loyalties and very strong convictions that slavery was wrong and inhumane. She maintained her cover as a loyal daughter of the Confederacy while secretly fighting to free the slaves. Many times she put her life at risk to further the Union cause, spending much of her considerable fortune to

increase the efficiency of her espionage network and to free her own slaves. She also purchased the freedom of her slaves' family members so that they could be together.

Her case officer was a highly placed Union soldier, General George H. Sharpe, chief of the Federal Bureau of Military Information. (This organization was as close as the U.S. government got to a centralized intelligence service during the Civil War. The Union collection activities were hampered by rival bureaucratic infighting and the almost dominant position of the Secret Service.) General Sharpe was a good field case officer and assisted Van Lew with money and timely guidance. She established five secret safe houses along the rat line between her home in Richmond and his headquarters in Washington, D.C.

Her home in Richmond, on a beautiful promontory called Church Hill, overlooked the James River, and routinely was used as a way station for Union soldiers who had become separated from their units and were lost in the Virginia countryside. Her home also was used by Yankee prisoners of the Confederacy who had escaped and wanted to reach Union lines before they were recaptured and by runaway slaves who were trying to reach the freedom offered by the Union. In order to house this steady stream of illegal visitors, she constructed a secret room in her home, where she could safely hide her guests.

ELIZABETH VAN LEW
The Valentine Museum, Richmond, Virginia

She was adept at hiding messages for General Sharpe in her knitting, in baskets of eggs, and in fruit decorations. Her secretive way of life and the nocturnal meanderings observed by her Richmond neighbors earned her the title of "Loonie Betty." She encouraged this cover by acting crazy on the street, jerking her head to and fro, mumbling unintelligible grunts, sighing to herself, and staring blankly when questioned.

There were two large brass lions on either side of the fireplace in her living room. After she came under scrutiny by the Confederate counterintelligence service, she would place her messages for General Sharpe inside one of the lions. The cleaning woman would remove the papers and send them to Van Lew's farm outside of Richmond. From there, the messages were sent up the rat line to Washington.

She was a most prolific source of intelligence on Confederate military capabilities and intentions. A large part of the reliable intelligence received at Union headquarters in Washington came from her. She was commended in several dispatches from the Union War Department. In 1883, Allan Pinkerton, the head of the Union's Secret Service, published a book entitled *Spy of the Rebellion,* a roman à clef, in which a "fictitious" Miss Dix (who strongly resembled Van Lew) warned the Secret Service of the conspirators' plan to prevent the inauguration of President Lincoln.

She used her influence as a Confederate woman to obtain passes through the lines for her slaves, whom she sent out of the Richmond war zone to her family farm several miles away. She placed a young female slave by the name of Mary Elizabeth Bowser in the home of Jefferson Davis, the president of the Confederacy. She educated and trained Bowser to remember and report everything she heard at the president's dinner table and to collect and save the paper from the president's wastebasket in his study.

Much of Van Lew's information came from Yankee soldiers escaping to the North. These soldiers would tell her what they had seen along their routes through the South. They described the conditions of the economy and of the southern military. Van Lew visited the injured Yankee prisoners in southern hospitals. She loaned them books from her library. Many of these wounded Yankees had information that they would give her by underlining words in the books, which—when read together—would reveal a hidden message.

When it was apparent that Richmond was doomed, Van Lew wrote to General Ben Butler requesting a large Union flag. He sent her a 9-by-18–foot Stars and Stripes, which she concealed in her house until the armistice. Just before Richmond fell, a mob of unruly southerners tried to storm the Van Lew house. Their anger was allegedly in retaliation for all of the things that they had heard rumored about her "treasonous" activities during the four years of the war. She confronted them and, calling each by name, told them that General Grant was only hours away from Richmond and that if they torched her house, Grant would burn their houses to the ground. When the first Union Army scouts cautiously entered Richmond, Van Lew unfurled the large Union flag and flew it proudly over her house. For her, this announced to all of the people of Richmond that slavery was gone forever; she was not gloating that the Confederacy had lost.

Van Lew maintained a diary of her exploits during the Civil War but kept it buried for fear of compromising those named in it who had helped her, even though she referred to them only in a complicated code. After the war the diary was discovered, but many of the pages had been torn out, apparently by Van Lew herself, who had been concerned lest some retaliation be made against those southeners who had helped her.

Despite her valiant record on behalf of the Union, she was ignored and poorly treated by the federal government after the war. She made a claim for $15,000 to the federal government for some of her expenses that she had incurred for them during the war. General Grant, remembering the value of her work, approved the claim, but the Washington bureaucracy refused to honor her request. General Grant said: "From her I received the most valuable intelligence that ever came from Richmond throughout the entire conflict."

Later, when Grant became president, he appointed her postmistress of Richmond at an annual salary of $4,000. The postbellum society of Richmond, still smarting from the knowledge of her wartime deception and traitorous conduct, refused to socially acknowledge her. When Grant's term as president ended, these bitter, defeated southerners conspired to have Van Lew's job at the post office reduced to that of a lowly paid clerk and snubbed her socially. Her solace in this time of loneliness was that the slaves whom she had freed remained loyal and stayed with her without pay.

Friends and relatives of Colonel Paul Revere, whose life she had saved during the war, arranged to pay her a small monthly sum until the end of her life. She spent her last years in poverty. She died virtually penniless in 1900 at the age of 82.

Rowan, Richard Wilmer, and Robert G. Deindorfer. *Secret Service: 33 Years of Espionage.* New York: Hawthorn Books, 1967.

Stern, Philip Van Doren. *Secret Missions of the Civil War.* New York: Bonanza Books, 1959.

Leona Viscario Roo
Mexico
ca. 1790– 1842

Leona Viscario Roo was a valiant woman who remained in Mexico City during the Mexican Revolution, despite the danger, to observe the Spanish and to collect information about their armaments and troops. She passed the intelligence to her husband, who was one of the most famous revolutionary leaders. She is revered today as a hero of the Mexican Revolution.

Her distinguished family was living in Mexico City when she was born. She was orphaned at an early age, and her uncle, an attorney, raised her. She was well educated for a woman of that time. Andreas Quintana Roo also practiced law in her uncle's office. When the War for Independence started, Roo

joined the revolutionary movement and became one of its leaders. He maintained daily contact with Leona Viscario so that she could pass him valuable information that she had obtained from the Spanish officers who were her daily visitors.

She was privy to the decisions and correspondence of the viceroy and his staff and sent all of the information that she obtained to Roo. Her information was timely, vital, comprehensive, and of considerable value to the revolutionaries. When some of her letters were compromised by interception, she was forced to flee Mexico City to avoid arrest. Her relatives insisted that she had overreacted and that it was perfectly safe for her to return to Mexico City. They assured her that she would be fully protected from arrest.

When she arrived in Mexico City, the viceroy's police arrested her and incarcerated her in a convent. She managed to escape from the convent and hid in a small town, where Roo was waiting for her. She married him and followed him on his campaigns as a trusted adviser. Her extensive properties were seized and her wealth was confiscated by the viceroy's troops.

When independence was won, the new Mexican government made her a gift of a farm in an effort to compensate her for the losses that she had suffered and to show their gratitude for her work as a spy.

When she died, she was rendered national homage. Her tomb was inscribed:

To Sra. Leona Viscario, the respected wife of Andres Quintana Roo, illustrious Magistrate of the Supreme Court of Justice, in remembrance of her public and private ventures and very distinguished service which she rendered for the cause of independence and the general welfare of the nation. Her fame belongs now to immortality, in the history of Mexican heroines. She died on 24 August 1842. To this meritorious woman and mother of our country, the Mexican citizens, with tears in their eye, dedicate the monument.

Schmidt, Minna M. *Four Hundred Outstanding Women of the World.* Chicago: Minna Moscherosch Schmidt Publisher, 1933.

Baroness Barbara Juliana von Krudener
Germany
1764 –1824

Baroness Barbara Juliana von Krudener, born Barbara Juliana von Vietinghoff, was an unconventional and probably inadvertent spy. She learned much about the czar of Russia and exercised a high degree of control over him through the use of the "occult sciences."

Von Vietinghoff was born on 11 November 1764 in Germany. Her father was a wealthy merchant who became a senator, and her mother was the daughter of a famous German general, von Munnich. Her family arranged a marriage for her when she was 18 to the Baron Burekhard von Krudener, who was 18 years her senior. At the time of their marriage, the baron was the Russian ambassador to Germany.

The baroness was restless, ambitious, and not always faithful to her husband. For some inexplicable reason, she felt compelled to explain her extramarital affairs to the baron. He apparently didn't care if she continued the affairs, because he did absolutely nothing to stop her.

At an early age, she had started to dabble in the occult "sciences," a favorite drawing room entertainment of the time, which she made into a pseudoreligion. She returned to Russia when her husband's tour as ambassador was over and entertained the czar's court with her demonstrations of occult powers. She found an opportunity to appeal directly to Czar Alexander I when she happened to find him one day in the Imperial Palace. He was sitting alone with a Bible open on his knees. When the baroness began to chant in her singsong spiritualistic voice, the czar began to cry, so compelling was the message of salvation that she conveyed to him. He wept for more than three hours on this first occasion with her.

The czar found her services salubrious, not only for cleansing his soul but for relieving his overwrought nerves. He claimed that the baroness "brought him peace" (Rowan 1967, 230). He wanted her and her coterie of fellow occult practitioners to accompany him on his European tour in 1815. When the tour arrived in Paris, the czar insisted that the baroness be given lodging at the Hotel Montcheno, where a private walkway connected his quarters in the Élysée Palace with her rooms. He visited her rooms every night, ostensibly for occult ritual performances.

To the consternation of his advisers, the czar began taking the baroness's advice on affairs of state. For example, she advised him to approve the draft treaty of the Holy Alliance. Unfortunately, her desire for notoriety overcame the need for discretion, and she began to brag in public about the power that she exercised over the czar. Her indiscretions were brought to the czar's attention. He warned her that she should return to her religious occult devotions and not get involved in intrigues and affairs of state.

Agents of the European governments keenly followed the relationship between the baroness and the czar. Although there is no evidence that she knowingly helped any foreign government, her influence over the czar could be evaluated and gauged by foreign governments' agents. In this way, her involvement with the czar aided these agents in determining how they should advise their governments. In addition, subtle persuasion gently applied to her would in turn have an effect on the czar.

The baroness eventually fell out of favor with the czar in 1816, but some six years later she again approached him with a plea to wage a holy war against the Moslems threatening Europe from the east. He rejected her suggestion, but she was undeterred. She became involved in a covert action scheme to colonize the Crimea, which she hoped would have the effect of stopping Moslem encroachments in the long term.

Although she didn't have a sponsoring government and wasn't technically a spy, her influence with the Russian czar could be interpreted by other countries' agents to their advantage. She could subtly be influenced to direct the czar in whatever direction other countries wanted.

Rowan, Richard Wilmer, and Robert G. Deindorfer. *Secret Service: 33 Years of Espionage.* New York: Hawthorn Books, 1967.

Wang Pa Mei
China
1909–

When Wang Pa Mei's family was killed by the Chinese Communists, she sought revenge for their murders. This demure grandmother never was suspected of being a spy. She was known as Grandma Wang.

When Wang landed in Taipei, Taiwan, on 11 February 1955, she was 46 years old. She had just arrived with several hundred other women aboard the ships of the United States Seventh Fleet after having been evacuated from the Tachen Islands. At the end of World War II she had led some 7,000 guerrillas in Chekiang province against the Chinese Communist insurgents. In one battle, roughly 2,000 of her male and female fighters were lost. The rest escaped to the offshore islands of Matsu and Quemoy.

Wang claimed that her spying was motivated by her hatred of the Chinese Communists because they had murdered her husband, five of her children, and three of her grandchildren. The Communists had forced her to watch her loved ones die, which made her doubly bitter. She claimed that she was fighting a very personal war against the Chinese Communists so that her remaining children and grandchildren would know a free China.

Her husband had been a schoolteacher, and Wang was a well-educated woman. After the massacre of her family, she became the leader of a secret intelligence and sabotage service organized by the Chinese Women's Anti-Aggression League. Chinese women saw her as a symbol of freedom and of the old Chinese way of life.

Typical of the operations that she commanded was one in which she was able to help a friend. The most hated Communist of Hopei province was a fanatical martinet. He had fallen in love with a married schoolteacher who was a friend of Wang's. The Communist insisted that the schoolteacher get a divorce and marry him. If she didn't divorce the husband she loved, the Communist insisted that she become his mistress. The schoolteacher was afraid that if she didn't comply, he would murder her husband, arrest and torture her parents, and kidnap her.

She went to Wang, who consoled her and assured her that everything would be fine if she followed her advice. The schoolteacher returned to the Communist and told him that she would divorce her current husband and marry him if he met three conditions: (1) he was to arrange her husband's release from detention and ensure that he was never again taken into custody; (2) he was to pay a dowry of 20 million in the local currency to her parents; and (3) he was to guarantee that her husband's household would be protected at all costs. She received the 20 million dowry and sent her husband

and both of their families with the money to Formosa.

The schoolteacher and the Communist were married shortly thereafter. At the wedding feast, the schoolteacher urged her new husband to drink a lot to celebrate their happy event and implied that treasures awaited him in their bridal chamber later that evening. As soon as they entered the bedroom, her new husband fell flat across the bed, dead drunk and unconscious for the rest of the night. She opened the window to permit an assassin, arranged for by Wang, to enter and stab the Communist to death. The schoolteacher then quickly escaped and joined the guerrilla band that was operating in the province until she could join her husband and their families in Formosa.

Before World War II, Formosa was under Japanese control. Mao Tse-tung, the Chinese Communist leader, sent his aide as a spy to Formosa to overthrow the Japanese. The spy became well established on Formosa by creating a front group called The Communist Working Committee on Formosa. In April 1947, with the Chinese mainland in the turmoil of a civil war, the spy left Formosa for Shanghai to recruit more men for his group on Formosa and to obtain armaments for overthrowing the Japanese.

When he returned to Formosa he was under cover and was using another name. His mission was to organize an underground guerrilla force that would overthrow the Japanese and create a provisional Communist government in Formosa. In order to do this, he obtained the cooperation of an outstanding female patriot of Formosan independence, whose code name was Shan. The spy and Shan agreed to work together to overthrow the Japanese government in Formosa. The spy would be working for a Formosa dominated by the Chinese Communists, but Shan would be working toward a truly independent Formosa.

Before they could begin their cooperative operation, they received word that Chiang Kai-shek was on his way with two armies to liberate Formosa for the Nationalist Chinese government. Wang, fighting a guerrilla war on Formosa to help Chiang Kai-shek, was

able to thwart both Mao Tse-tung's spy and Shan and thereby helped Chiang Kai-shek win the battle over Formosa. Wang caught Mao Tse-tung's spy, who was disguised as a newspaperman, and executed him on the spot. Shan remained with the Chinese Communist forces on the mainland without realizing her dream of a "free" Formosa under communism.

Singer, Kurt. *Spy Stories from Asia.* New York: Wilfred Funk, 1955.

Helen Webb
Germany
ca. 1908–ca. 1947

Helen Webb was a dance hall hostess and prostitute before she became a spy for her German lover. She was assigned to spy on Americans at Pearl Harbor but fell in love with an American sailor and refused to continue spying. When the romance with the American ended, she returned to Germany, where she was accused by the KGB of being a spy for the Americans.

Webb was a beautiful Eurasian woman who was, according to one rumor, born of a liaison between a German diplomat and an aristocratic mother. In 1938, she was about 30 years old and worked as a dancer in Shanghai nightclubs, where she was very popular with the men.

In her life as a prostitute she worked in various cities. When she began working in Hankow, she made less than she had in Shanghai, but business was still good. When World War II broke out in China, the Japanese captured Nanking. The Chinese government waited in Hankow for supplies and for regrouping before attempting a counterattack. As a result, Hankow teemed with black marketeers, soldiers in uniform, soldiers of fortune, foreign observers, deposed generals, and journalists. They all went to the International Dance Hall for relaxation, where Webb worked. The dance hall was really a house of prostitution, and Webb was one of the star attractions.

The International Dance Hall was also a center of espionage. It was common knowledge in Hankow that the owner was a Japanese spy. In fact, he was a mercenary operative who worked for whoever paid him the most money. It was in this dance hall that Webb met Hans Wolf, allegedly a correspondent in Hankow for a German newspaper. Wolf was actually a German intelligence officer.

For all of her worldly sophistication, Webb fell madly in love with Wolf. He became her lover in February 1938. He was working at the time for the director of German intelligence, Admiral Wilhelm Canaris. Wolf was a courtly gentleman who lived well, with the best creature comforts and female companionship available, on a lavish expense account from Admiral Canaris. When Wolf met Webb, he recognized her as a potential spy and knew that she would work for him cheaply as long as he held her love; he thoroughly exploited Webb's love for him.

It is not known if Wolf was a farsighted planner or if he had orders from Canaris to plan ahead. In any event, from the time that he met Webb in 1939, he planned and schemed for her to go to the Philippines and to be well entrenched there in the event of a future war between Germany and the United States. Webb took up residence in Manila and started to work at the Moonbeam Club, which was where sailors from the U.S. naval bases near Manila went for relaxation. The Moonbeam Club was a combination bar and house of prostitution.

Webb filed several reports from her new position, using the open mail and writing with secret inks and in code. When war was declared after the Japanese attack on Pearl Harbor, all postal communications between the Philippines and Germany stopped. For some reason, Webb either could not or did not want to use the shortwave transmitter/receiver that Wolf had given her for radio communications between Berlin and Manila.

As soon as the Japanese captured Manila, a representative from Admiral Canaris arrived. He first wanted to know why she hadn't contacted Wolf by radio as she had been instructed to do. Webb told the German that she had fallen in love with an American submariner who had shipped out just before Manila had fallen to the Japanese. She was certain that Wolf would understand that she couldn't spy on her future husband's country. She told the German that she was finished with spying. If they wanted her to, she would find another female spy from among the women who worked at the Moonbeam Club to take her place (which she did).

Webb next turned up in Europe with a new husband, who was a German citizen and who worked as an engineer. He was allegedly very pro-Russian but staunchly anti-Communist. When World War II was over, Webb and her husband returned to Germany. She later claimed that she returned because she wanted to be near her mother in Hesse. Engineers were badly needed in postwar Germany, and it seemed that Webb and her husband had settled down to enjoy their life.

Shortly after they returned to Germany, they were both kidnapped and taken to the Soviet KGB headquarters, where Webb was accused of being a U.S. agent. The KGB officer made them a very tempting offer to change sides and work for the KGB. Webb was roughed up by the KGB but refused to accept their offer. Her husband couldn't take the pressure and caved in. He told the KGB everything they wanted to know about his and Webb's Allied contacts in the Philippines, India, and Hong Kong. The two were released with the warning that the KGB would contact them again soon.

A week later, the KGB visited Webb's mother's cottage and learned that Webb had poisoned her husband because he had turned traitor. The KGB, assuming that Webb now represented a threat to them and to the security of their operations, allegedly made her drink the remainder of the poison and murdered her.

There is no evidence that Webb was a U.S. spy, as charged by the KGB. There also is no evidence that the KGB made her drink poison.

Singer, Kurt. *Spy Stories from Asia.* New York: Wilfred Funk, 1955.

Lizzie Wertheim
Germany
1895–ca. 1965

Lizzie Wertheim and her partner ignored basic tradecraft and security principles when they spied for Germany during World War I. As a result, she was easily discovered by Britain's internal security organization.

Wertheim was born in Berlin and acquired British citizenship by marrying a German who was a naturalized British citizen. The marriage ended in a few months, mostly because of Wertheim's extravagant lifestyle and numerous affairs. German intelligence recruited her because she could speak English and had British citizenship. Furthermore, she wasn't above using her body to gain information from an informant.

She made her way to England just before the start of World War I. In 1915, she was living the good life in London's West End with another German spy, Georg (sic) T. Breeckow, who used the street alias Reginald Rowland. Rowland spoke English with an American accent and could easily have passed as an American. Rowland's role in the spy operation was to act as a courier and a communications assistant to Wertheim. She was the one who was expected to collect the high-level intelligence that the team would pass on to Berlin.

Wertheim traveled around England in a limousine with a maid, visiting areas where British naval facilities were located. She would establish herself in a luxury hotel close to the naval base and would soon have a coterie of British naval officers in attendance, vying with one another to share her favors. Once she had snared a likely subject who had both access to secret information and a weakness for her, Wertheim would pump him dry of information. Rowland would then turn the information into a coded message, often in secret writing, and transmit the information to Germany.

Wertheim lacked discretion and didn't know when to stop pushing her clients for more information. Some of the topics that she wished to discuss with her clients in bed didn't seem appropriate, and some of her partners became suspicious. Several naval officers reported Wertheim's zealousness to MI-5. MI-5 investigated Wertheim's operation and arrested her and Rowland.

Rowland admitted to having been trained in espionage techniques by the famous Elsbeth Schragmuller at her Antwerp espionage academy. He was sentenced to be shot. Just before the British soldiers were to take him out of his cell to face the firing squad, he collapsed. He never did have to face the firing squad, because his collapse had been caused by a heart attack. Wertheim was sentenced to ten years.

(See also Elsbeth Schragmuller.)

Franklin, Charles. *The Great Spies*. New York: Hart Publishing, 1967.

Barbara Wheeler
England
1920–

Barbara Wheeler was a superb technician who effectively used her talent to aid the Allies' war effort. Her meticulous plotting of aerial photographs allowed the Allies to locate the sites from which the Germans were launching the "buzz bomb" rockets that terrorized England. In terms of technical ability, she was one of the finest spies of World War II.

Wheeler was raised in Maidenhead, England, in a middle-class English family. She took a business course in preparation for a career as a stenographer and also studied commercial art and painting. These latter two courses taught her an appreciation of line and proportion, which were useful in her wartime work.

When World War II came, Wheeler wanted to do her part, so she joined the WAAF. The WAAF made no use of Wheeler's many talents; instead, it assigned her to be a mess attendant at Harwell Airfield near Berkshire Downs. Her hours at the mess hall, during one of the coldest winters on record, were from 6:00 A.M. to 10:00 P.M. each day, with only a short break after lunch. It wasn't the arduous work schedule that dismayed Wheeler but the thought that she could be more productive using her other skills.

In 1940, she was transferred to plotting navigational courses for air flights. These duties used more of her talents. She was assigned to take an advanced course in photo interpretation. The other students included university professors, artists, mathematicians, and physicists. When she graduated, Wheeler was issued a large wooden kit containing the specialized tools of a photo interpreter's trade. She was admonished that if she lost any of the instruments, the cost would be deducted from her pay, which, at the time, was the equivalent of $10 per week. Wheeler reported for work to the RAF base at Medmenham in September 1941.

There had been rumors circulating in intelligence circles about a terrible new weapon that the Germans were developing at their experimental center at Peenemünde, in Mecklenburg in eastern Germany. The overflight photography of Peenemünde was poor, making it difficult to discern solid objects from shadows, and the light conditions of the original exposure may have been such that the graininess of the developed film contributed to the blurring of definite lines. Original evaluation of the photographs indicated that the conformation of objects on the ground suggested that they could be launchers of some kind. This tentative analysis was supported by what appeared to be bulkheads or earth mounds, which could be used to contain the back blast. The continued bad weather over Peenemünde made interpretable photographs difficult to obtain.

In late October 1942, a break in the weather allowed some better photographs of Peenemünde to be taken, and they were sent to Wheeler's supervisor for analysis. The supervisor thought that she detected a plume of smoke of an odd character and form, apparently just starting up after an ignition or combustion of some kind. Wheeler and her supervisor couldn't figure out what this strange smoke column might be, so they put the photograph aside temporarily.

The resistance forces in France then sent some unconfirmed and unevaluated intelligence reports to England in February 1943 that claimed that the Germans were developing some form of long-range, self-propelled bomb that could reach England from France. As a result of this report, Wheeler and her group were ordered to reexamine all aerial photographs that covered ground within a reasonable striking distance (130 miles) of London. They were to pay special attention to factory areas.

In June 1943, the aerial photographs clearly revealed the rockets at Pennemünde. The rocket sites' features were peculiarly unique: wingless rockets either on the launching tracks or on dollies beside the tracks; earth scorch marks from the engine blasts and earth mounds to the rear of the launching tracks; railroad tracks leading into the site; blockhouses as quarters for the guard troops; and houses nearby in the compound for the scientists.

Wheeler became an expert in distinguishing these telltale features from mock or camouflage sites nearby, even when the photographic quality was poor. She developed an almost uncanny ability to spot the sites when the first signs of construction appeared in other areas, from Cherbourg to Calais. She and her group had identified 64 of these sites by November 1943, and the launching tracks were all pointed directly at England. Wheeler was able to target these sites for the air force navigators, who planned to bomb the sites before the rockets could be fired on England. She was thoroughly familiar with the sites as they were being constructed; therefore, she was called upon to do bomb damage interpretation assessments. This required her to study the photographs taken of the target areas as soon after the sorties as possible.

Toward the end of 1943 and during the spring of 1944, over 20,000 tons of bombs were dropped on these rocket sites. The Germans were ingenious and determined to repair the damage. In addition to repairing the bombed sites, they started to build modified launch sites that required less construction. As part of this diversion campaign, the Germans also began constructing dummy launching sites in the hope of luring the bombers away from the real sites.

From her monitoring of aerial photographs taken on successive days, Wheeler was able to establish that it took the Germans 120 days to construct a launching site from beginning to end. At this time she was scanning thousands of aerial photographs each night.

Many people believed that the rocket sites were a ruse on the part of the Germans in order to gain some psychological advantage over the Allies. Despite all of the construction activity at the various rocket sites, there still had not been a single operational firing. On the night of 12 June 1944, Wheeler was examining the latest batch of aerial photographs. Around 3:00 A.M. she spotted a fully operational site and shouted "Diver," which was her group's code name signal for the first site that was ready to fire. Shortly after Wheeler's sighting, other technicians found other equally ready operational launching sites in France; all were aimed at England.

Coincidentally, the next day, the first V-1 rocket landed in Kent, England. This initial firing was followed by a series of more than 144 "buzz bombs," so called because of the peculiar buzzing noise that they made in flight. The launch sites were changed frequently by the Germans to avoid retaliatory raids by British and U.S. bombers that Wheeler planned by pinpointing the targets on navigational charts. Wheeler and her fellow photo interpreters were commended for their exceptional work.

Wheeler retired from the WAAF at the end of World War II. She married an RAF wing commander and went to live in Berkshire, England, in a picturesque cottage named Whistling Bridge Field, near Twyford.

Hoehling, A. A. *Women Who Spied.* New York: Dodd, Mead, 1967.

May Wilson
United States
1886–ca. 1945

May Wilson was denounced as a spy by a former lover, presumably because she left him. Like any good spy, she was able to dodge the charges, which was prudent in Bolshevik Russia.

If an American in Russia in 1917 were charged with espionage by the Bolsheviks, it did not necessarily mean that the person was guilty. Many were charged but few were proven to be U.S. espionage agents. The evidence often was flimsy and uncorroborated at best and nonexistent at worst, but the Cheka never were deterred by a lack of substantiation. The unfounded charges against Americans in Russia might have been intended merely to embarrass the United States, to provide fodder for a propaganda barrage against the Allies in general, or to create a cache of hostages in case a Bolshevik spy were detained in the United States. For whatever reason, existing records that might support or refute espionage charges in these cases are now few or absent.

One case in which the charges cannot be proved or refuted was that of May Wilson. She was born in San Francisco on 12 April 1886, which would have made her 31 in 1917, when she was arrested. She cited her permanent residence as New York City and claimed that she was an actress and an artist.

It is evident from the various papers filed in the United States Consulate in Petrograd that Wilson had at least two male American friends in that city who, from time to time, vouched for her identity when she had her passport renewed. Nothing suspicious is known about these two men or about Wilson. All available information indicates that Wilson led an exemplary life; there was no reason for the Cheka to investigate her, much less to charge her with espionage for the U.S. government.

On 10 April 1917, Wilson was charged by the Bolshevik government in Petrograd with espionage for the United States and was arrested. The Cheka alleged that after her arrival in Russia in November 1914, she initiated correspondence with a French army officer who was stationed at the front in France. The French officer reported to the French general staff that he had received a letter from Wilson that he considered improper. The French officer claimed that Wilson was not May Wilson from San Francisco but a woman named Weifling, who had been born in Salzburg, Austria. Apparently, the Cheka had had Wilson under surveillance since this complaint in 1914. They noted in their communication to U.S. Ambassador David Francis that Wilson had been communicating with suspicious people. The Bolshevik authorities promised Ambassador Francis additional information. In the politically chaotic times of April 1917, "suspicious people" could have been anyone just a little too far to the right of the Bolsheviks.

Wilson, in an attempt to verify her status, gave as a reference the American Express office in New York City. Unfortunately, the final disposition of Wilson's case is not known.

The French officer's charge was probably false, given the multiple documentary evidence that Wilson's birthplace was San Francisco and given the testimony of witnesses who verified her birthplace. The Cheka never bothered to ask the U.S. Consulate if it had any evidence to refute the French officer's allegations.

Passport application of May Wilson from the American Consulate in Petrograd, 28 March 1914. National Archives.

Francis (Ambassador David R.). Telegram #1170 to Secretary of State (Robert Lansing). Petrograd to Washington, D.C., 10 April 1917. National Archives.

Pearl Witherington
(Marie)
England
1920–

Pearl Witherington parachuted into Occupied France without the proper reception having been prepared for her. She was almost executed before her credentials could be verified. Despite this near-deadly beginning, she took eventual command of her resistance group and managed to assist in exfiltrating hundreds of downed Allied airmen.

Witherington was born in Britain but was fluent in French. In September 1943, she parachuted into Occupied France without proper contact instructions. The French underground forces interrogated her and almost killed her because they thought that she was a Gestapo spy. Once she was properly identified, she became one of the group's greatest assets.

Shortly after Witherington joined the group, the team leader was captured and incarcerated in the infamous Colditz Prison. Witherington then assumed command of the group and increased its efficiency; the number of resupply drops increased and the overall quality of the membership improved.

Witherington concentrated on sabotaging the railroads in her sector with explosives and with other more subtle means, such as iron filings in the bearings and sand in the gear boxes. She caused reroutings, monumental confusion in scheduling, and delays of vital shipments to factories that were engaged in war production.

On 11 June 1944, five days after the Allied landings in Normandy, Witherington and about 150 of her guerrillas were surrounded by more than 2,000 German Gestapo troops. The ensuing battle lasted more than 12 hours, until the resistance fighters had expended all their ammunition. Witherington managed to escape the subsequent roundup by hiding in a cornfield, where she remained hidden until the Gestapo troops gave up the search.

A tremendous number of recently dedicated "patriots" wanted to join the French Resistance after D-Day in order to share in the glory of being resistance fighters. They all wanted to join up when the danger of imminent capture and execution was remote. Witherington took advantage of this newly created reservoir of recruits and organized about 2,000 of them into a well-trained group that fought well against the remaining German troops in France.

One of the new pupils, Henri Cornioley, and Witherington were attracted to each other and, after the war, they were married. Witherington remained in France with her new husband after the war.

Hoehling, A. A. *Women Who Spied.* New York: Dodd, Mead, 1967.

Anna Wolkoff

(Baroness Wolkoff)
Russia
1904–ca. 1975

Anna Wolkoff found a perfect espionage companion in a young code clerk who shared her bigotry and who worked in the U.S. Embassy in London. She so captivated him with her superior knowledge of Jewish "crimes" that he willingly committed treason for her.

Wolkoff, who sometimes called herself Baroness Wolkoff, was 36 years old when she met Tyler Gatewood Kent. Kent, about ten years younger than Wolkoff, fell in love with the older, more experienced, woman. Although he was equally culpable, Kent succumbed to her demands that he steal diplomatic, classified papers from the U.S. Embassy.

Kent was the pampered son of wealthy Americans. His father had been an ambassador to the czarist court of the Romanovs. Kent had taken an undergraduate degree at Princeton and finished his education at the Sorbonne in Paris. He spoke four languages fluently and was considered intelligent but unworldly. Most of all, he was thought of by all who knew him as a pampered, spoiled brat. One thing that everyone noticed about Kent was his outspoken hatred of Jews. He made no attempt to conceal this hatred, which may have accounted for his lack of professional advancement within the foreign service.

Wolkoff claimed noble lineage because her father had been an admiral in the czarist navy. Even though she had become a naturalized British citizen, she made a tacit agreement with the Germans at the start of World War II. She agreed that she would send them any intelligence information that she could get regarding the United States intentions to enter the war in Europe.

Wolkoff had a small dress shop, which was her ostensible source of income. She also painted watercolors but gave most of them away to friends as gifts. She and Kent met at a gathering of like-minded bigots in London at a party of anti-neo-Fascist Semites. When Kent discovered that Wolkoff was a like-minded anti-Semite, he agreed to do anything she asked that he thought would hurt the Jews. All Wolkoff wanted, she glibly convinced Kent, was to shorten the war. To do that, they had to take the profit away from the war-mongering Jews. Kent could help "save the world" from the Jews by giving her all the documents from the U.S. Embassy that had to do with British–U.S. relations.

Kent passed about 1,500 top secret, sensitive documents to Wolkoff. These documents included the Roosevelt-Churchill conversations. The greatest danger of his actions was that when he gave the clear text of these messages to Wolkoff, he also unwittingly compromised the super-secret U.S. diplomatic codes that had been used to transmit the messages.

The photographer who microfilmed the documents eventually revealed the duo's operation to Scotland Yard. Kent and Wolkoff were arrested in 1940. Wolkoff was given a ten-year sentence, and Kent was given a seven-year sentence. U.S. Ambassador Joseph P. Kennedy commented on the case that if America had been at war, he would have recommended that Kent be sent home to America and shot as a traitor.

Kent was paroled in December 1945 and returned to the United States. Wolkoff was paroled in 1946. She had lost her British citizenship and was a woman without a country.

Hoehling, A. A. *Women Who Spied.* New York: Dodd, Mead, 1967.

Wu Chao

China
625–705

Wu Chao established spies among the Chinese emperor's concubines and was able to wield total power over the nation when she became empress. She was a ruthless monarch who ruled through sheer terror.

At the age of 12, Wu came from obscurity to the Imperial Palace of the emperor of China to become one of his concubines. Without naming any particular woman, astrologers predicted that a female would soon be all-powerful in China.

Wu made full use of her concubinage to learn the arts of diplomacy and intrigue. It was apparent that the emperor did not have many years to live, so Wu turned her full attention to the crown prince. In keeping with her guise of humility and forbearance, when the old emperor died, Wu made the gesture of entering a cloistered sanctuary but allowed herself to be dissuaded by the former crown prince, who was the new emperor.

The new emperor quickly brought Wu back to the court and installed her as his concubine. He eventually divorced his wife and placed Wu on the throne as empress. (Wu had gotten rid of the emperor's first wife by implicating her in a bogus plot to poison the emperor. It was rumored that she had poisoned one of her own sons and had murdered several other princes to assure her succession to the throne.) Once she was given access to power, she began to assume more and more of the emperor's duties. She used her influence to eliminate all possible successors to her position. When her husband died, she became empress of China.

She was the first ruler of China to institute her own secret service, which, within the scope of its jurisdiction, was practically omnipotent. She eliminated other police agencies not under her control and established spies among the women in the concubinage. These sources were to report every bit of gossip that was derogatory to her or that could be dangerous to her position. The main task of her personal secret police—long before she became empress—was to keep her well informed about her rivals. In order to control her secret police, she purged their ranks from time to time.

By the time she became empress, she knew who her enemies were and exactly how to control them through the secret police. To ensure that her husband's family could not revolt against her power, she had the secret police eliminate the late emperor's brothers, cousins, nephews, and uncles one by one.

Wu realized that as long as her courtiers lived in terror of her secret police she was not likely to receive honest and unbiased advice or counsel from them. She genuinely wanted to have an independent source of intelligence that she could depend upon, so she created the Bronze Information Urn, which was placed outside of the Imperial Palace. Any citizen, peasant or noble, could put any note or petition or accusation in the urn.

Later, Wu set up a chief of intelligence to coordinate the intelligence that she was receiving from many sources. This chief was able to create a highly professional intelligence service for her, which served her well with accurate, reliable, and timely intelligence until her death.

Deacon, Richard. *The Chinese Secret Service.* New York: Taplinger, 1974.

Eva Wu
China
ca. 1934–

Eva Wu became a spy for the Nationalist Chinese against the Communist Chinese, who controlled mainland China. When the Communist Chinese arrested her, she avoided being discovered with any compromising information on her body, so the Communists had to let her go. She used excellent technical tradecraft aids and always got through with the information.

Her father had been a doctor in Canton, China. Wu had been one of 15 children, but her father had ensured that each child who desired a university education received one, including the girls. When the Communist Chinese came into power in 1949, before the Communists could confiscate his wealth, the father dispersed his family and gave each child a small inheritance of gold. Wu then made her way to Hong Kong, where she became an exotic dancer.

In 1954, she was approached by a representative of the Chinese Nationalists (who were based in Taiwan) with a request that she carry a letter from Hong Kong to Kowloon, in Communist China, and to note anything of significance along the way that she deemed worthy of interest. A Chinese Nationalist representative would visit Wu's nightclub on the nights that she made these trips and watch her dance. If she had any information of value for him, she would wear a white flower in her hair, but if she had no information, she would wear a red flower.

The information that Wu carried into Communist China was concealed in a microdot on an innocuous piece of paper. She never knew the content of the information that she carried. On one occasion she carried the small parts of a radio transmitter into Kowloon to a drop point at a retail silk store.

Her intelligence work progressed well, and she became a valuable member of the Chinese Nationalist intelligence service. The relationship was mutually beneficial, because her case officer was able to bring her information about some of her family members who were still inside Communist China. He also brought her information about two of her brothers, who were officers in Chiang Kai-shek's Nationalist Chinese army on Formosa. During this time, her dancing became a stellar attraction for the cosmopolitan international social set in Hong Kong,

and she and her case officer became close friends. They were often seen together on social occasions, and it was rumored that they were lovers.

In February 1955, when Wu went into Kowloon on one of her routine intelligence missions, she was stopped by two Chinese Communist policemen. They insisted upon searching her and all her possessions. She was taken to a police station, where a matron strip-searched her. They found nothing incriminating on her or in her possessions. The microdot that she was carrying was concealed on a strip of transparent cellophane about .25 millimeters wide, which was glued to the side of her hair pin. They eventually released Wu and allowed her to return to Hong Kong.

Wu continued to be a courier and observer for several years. When Chinese Nationalists' intelligence requirements changed, Wu was honorably retired. New, technical spy techniques had made her type of intelligence collection obsolete. She also retired from the stage and joined her family on Formosa.

Singer, Kurt. *Spy Stories from Asia.* New York: Wilfred Funk, 1955.

Edna Ramsaier Yardley
United States
1902–

Edna Ramsaier Yardley was married to the legendary Herbert O. Yardley, the originator of the famous "Black Chamber" for decoding and decrypting. Edna worked in the Black Chamber and was a great cryptographer in her own right.

She was born in New Jersey in 1902. In the fall of 1919 she entered a four-story brownstone at 3 East 38th Street in New York City, seeking her first job. She was 17 and had been sent by an employment agency for a job interview. She was interviewed by the boss, Herbert O. Yardley, the country's chief cryptographer. He told her that the job would be very secret, that she would be paid $20 per week, and that she was not to say anything about her work, not even to her own family.

Herbert had organized the Black Chamber for the U.S. government during World War I. This organization decoded messages sent by the German government, and by other governments, to their embassies, other outposts, and agents. It also had provided codes and ciphers for use by U.S. diplomats and the U.S. military that were very difficult to break. At the end of the war, mainly because of a quirk in the State Department budget that allowed it to finance activities only outside of the District of Columbia, Herbert had to move the Black Chamber to New York. In the brownstone on 38th Street, the Black Chamber operated under cover as a commercial code company. In those days almost all businesses that had operations overseas corresponded by telegraph (either by cable or radio telegraphy) in code. Every foreign representative had a code book that was always closely guarded from compromise by rival companies. There was a handsome profit to be made by a company that could create simple yet secure commercial codes, and the Black Chamber did just that as a cover for its government work.

Edna's first task was to type code groups on 3-by-5–inch cards. Her speed increased to about 1,500 cards a day. The code groups came from Japanese diplomatic messages, which were studied for repetitions that would ultimately solve the puzzle of the code. Part of her job was to maintain a clipping file of everything in the *New York Times* and the *Christian Science Monitor* about Japan and especially about Japanese foreign relations, military operations, and government politics. Such information, particularly the texts of diplomatic notes, might provide clues to the meaning of encoded Japanese communications. Once one learned the basic pattern of a code, subsequent messages were not too difficult to solve.

It took the Black Chamber team about five months to break the Japanese top secret diplomatic code. This breakthrough was hailed as the most remarkable accomplishment in the history of code and cipher work in the United States. The organization concentrated on the Japanese code, but also broke the diplomatic codes of Mexico and other Latin American countries.

They often obtained copies of encoded messages from U.S. and foreign telegraph companies. The drop copies from U.S. companies could usually be obtained for the asking, but obtaining copies from foreign-owned telegraph companies usually required a clandestine acquisition operation. U.S. intelligence would either obtain the copies through the other country's intelligence service or would establish a paid agent relationship with a source inside the telegraph company. Otherwise, if neither of these options were available, the United States Signal Corps would copy the messages "out of the air" during transmission.

One of the Yardleys' greatest successes (before they were married) came during the Washington disarmament conference of 1921 and 1922. The conference goal was to limit the naval tonnage of warships in an effort to forestall an armament race that might lead to another world war. Edna was instrumental in reading the secret instructions from foreign governments to their delegates. Of particular value to the U.S. delegates were the secret instructions from Tokyo to the Japanese delegation. The United States wanted to limit Japan to a ratio of six ship tonnage for every ten of the U.S. Navy. The Japanese delegation was adamantly holding out for a seven to ten ratio. The U.S. delegates were kept informed by the secret intercepts of Japan's willingness to accept a naval tonnage of 40 percent less than the tonnage allocated to the United States and Britain, but only if it were forced to accept this percentage. Edna and her future husband worked nights and weekends in order to have the latest exchange of secret messages at the State Department each morning in time for the U.S. delegates to rebut the Japanese arguments. The U.S. delegates knew, from the intercepted messages, that the Japanese would accept a six to ten ratio. The State Department negotiators held out and finally obtained a six to ten ratio.

Many commendations were given to the Black Chamber, and Edna deserved her share. Yet, despite the project's obvious value, the organization was disbanded in 1929. There is a popular myth that the project was stopped when President Hoover took office and appointed Henry L. Stimson to be secretary of state. Allegedly, when Stimson discovered what the Black Chamber was doing and that it was part of his domain in the State Department, he erupted. Supposedly, he exclaimed that, "Gentlemen don't read other peoples' mail!" This wasn't the case. The truth is that Stimson cut the Black Chamber because he didn't think that the budget justified its existence.

When the operation ceased, Edna returned to New Jersey, and Herbert Yardley returned to Indiana to write books about his experiences as a cryptographer. His books were controversial, because no one had previously dared to acknowledge that governments were trying to read each others' secret correspondence.

In July 1940, Herbert was in China, code breaking Japanese and other traffic for the Chiang Kai-shek government. The U.S. military attaché was able to locate him and asked him to return immediately to Washington because war with Japan was imminent. He was able to leave on one of the last planes out of China.

Edna and Herbert Yardley had kept in touch. In 1941, Edna returned to cryptograph work in Washington with Herbert. They were married in 1944. Edna continued her work for many years, even after Herbert died.

Yardley, Herbert O. *The American Black Chamber.* Indianapolis: Bobbs-Merrill, 1931.

Yardley, Herbert O. *The Chinese Black Chamber.* Boston: Houghton Mifflin, 1983.

Margarete Gertrude Zelle
(Mata Hari)
Holland
1876–1917

Margarete Gertrude Zelle, better known by her stage name of Mata Hari, had an undeserved, but self-generated, reputation as a great spy. She was basically an incompetent agent who bought her prized reputation with her life.

Zelle was born in Leeuwarden, Holland, in 1876. Her father, Adam Zelle, was a hatter who specialized in men's hats, and her mother was Antje van der Meulen. Zelle, who wasn't satisfied with the relatively prosaic prospect of a life spent working in her father's hat shop, longed for a more exciting future. She answered an advertisement that appeared in the "lonely hearts" section of the newspaper, which was a very daring thing for a proper young lady to do in that era. The advertisement had been inserted by John MacLeod, whom she married in 1895.

Her husband was an officer with the colonial force in the Dutch East Indies. After their marriage, Zelle lived in Java with him for six years. She was promiscuous and had so many love affairs that she scandalized even the already licentious members of the colonial Javanese society.

MacLeod and Zelle had a son and a daughter. The son died in infancy. Some claimed that he had been poisoned by a native servant who had been badly mistreated by the master. There was a rumor that Zelle herself had killed the servant in retribution for killing her son. Unfortunately, the marriage wasn't blessed by happiness. Her husband was a drunk, a brute, and an adulterer.

Zelle filled her time in Java by studying the erotic Javanese temple dances. She spent many hours with the native girls, practicing and perfecting her own performances of their wild and sensuous dances. This avocation became a passion and ultimately became her vocation.

In 1901, Zelle returned home to Holland with her daughter, Marie Louise, and her husband. (There are other reports that her daughter's name was Jeanne.) In 1902, the unhappy couple were divorced. MacLeod returned to Java, where he felt that he was beyond the law. At first his alimony payments didn't arrive on time; finally they stopped completely. In 1904, he failed to pay Zelle any money, and she was forced to find work.

In 1905, she left her daughter with relatives and disappeared forever as Margarete Gertrude Zelle. She first tried work in a circus but soon graduated to being an exotic dancer (a "hoochie-koochie" dancer, as they were called in those days). She worked her knowledge of Javanese dancing into the gyrations of her dancing. She became a sexy

MARGARETE GERTRUDE ZELLE (MATA HARI)
Bettmann Archive

sensation at the Musée Guimet in Paris. At first she broke in her new act at private stag parties. She was popular at parties held by the famous American lesbian, Natalie Barney. Part of Zelle's act at that time consisted of riding around the hall, absolutely naked, on a large white horse.

It was in 1905 that Zelle changed her identity and became "Mata Hari" (eye of dawn). She claimed that she had been born in Java, which added to the exoticism of her act. She professed that her mother had been a full-blooded Javanese temple dancer who had died giving birth to her. The temple priests had raised her, so went her new biography, and had trained her in the erotic dances of the god Siva, to whom she had been dedicated.

Her husband was attractive in the legend that she created. He became a handsome young Scots officer of the British Indian Army who found her concealed in the temple as a virtual prisoner, helped her to escape, and married her. He had cherished her lovingly until his sudden death from fever required her to escape again—from a meager widowhood—by dancing nude at the most fashionable salons in France.

Her act became popular, and she became the darling of café society. Her act exuded the promise of sex, which became synonymous with her act. Men adored her and women envied her. Her dances were performed without any clothes except for two rounded metal breast cones.

She became a well-kept courtesan, using men of high social standing as stepping stones to advance her career. She was nearly 40 years old and far from what most men would consider beautiful, yet she charged and received enormous sums for her sexual favors. Her clients, who paid outrageous prices, were the high-ranking aristocrats, military, and government officials of Paris, Rome, Berlin, London, and Madrid. Zelle sold her sexual favors to prime ministers, dukes, princes, ambassadors, and generals.

She was in Germany performing her act when World War I broke out. Berlin's chief of police was one of her lovers. He thought that she would be able to elicit information from her French clients, which she would then pass back to him. The chief believed that he had been able to recruit her because she believed his ideology. This may not have been the case. In the chaos of Berlin at the start of the war, all of her trunks had been lost. She claimed that she agreed to become a German agent only to get even with the Germans for the loss of her personal effects that were in her missing luggage. This was why she accepted money from them, she said.

Zelle apparently felt no fundamental loyalty to Germany and considered herself a free agent. She was, she always maintained, a citizen of neutral Holland and therefore could travel freely any place in Europe. She had a dalliance with an officer of German intelligence in Madrid but, to prove at least to herself that she wasn't committed to any intelligence service, she also had an affair with an officer of the French secret service.

Zelle showed no preference for or loyalty to either side. She was impressed with her own cleverness and thought that she was out-foxing both sides. Most historians don't think that she realized the seriousness of the game she was trying to play.

Word got around that Zelle was playing both sides, and as a result neither the Germans nor the French trusted her. She didn't produce any worthwhile intelligence for either side. In fact, there is almost unanimous agreement that she was not a competent spy for anyone. She produced little information and the quality was exasperatingly poor; mostly, she repeated rumors that anyone could have picked up on the streets.

According to a German code that the French had broken, a message of 4 August 1914 referred to Zelle's numbered designation in the German intelligence service as H-21. Despite her pleas that she had been working for the Germans for only a short time, the French service maintained that the "H" designation was used by the Germans only for their prewar recruitments. As if to buttress the French contention, in late 1915 the Italian intelligence service sent the French service a message describing Mata Hari as a Hindu dancer who had renounced her citizenship and become German.

About this time, one of Zelle's former lovers, a Russian cossack who had been permanently blinded by a bullet during a campaign in the war, reentered her life. He was in a military hospital and she went there to nurse him. Of the many men Zelle had been intimate with, this cossack was the only man she ever really loved.

The French couldn't obtain enough evidence to convict Mata Hari, but they wanted her out of their jurisdiction. They called her in and told her that she would be deported. She protested that she had never spied for the Germans. She added that if the French wanted her to spy for them she knew many high-ranking Germans from whom she could elicit information.

In order to test her, the French sent her to Brussels, where one of her former lovers was the German governor general of Belgium. They had given her the names of six French agents working in Belgium who could send her reports out of Belgium back to Paris. Unfortunately for Zelle, almost as soon as she arrived in Belgium, one of the six French agents was arrested by the Germans. This made it appear as if she had exposed him. She realized how this looked for her and quietly left Belgium for Spain.

Her ship put in at Falmouth in England. The chief of the British Special Branch called her into his office and gave her some advice. He told her that he knew that she was playing both sides off against each other, and he warned her that her situation was extremely dangerous. During his interrogation of her, Zelle claimed that she had come to Britain to spy for the French, not for the Germans.

She finally arrived in Madrid, where she had an affair with the German military attaché. This tryst soon became common gossip, which didn't do her reputation with the French any good. This liaison only reinforced the French contention that she was working for the Germans. The German military attaché, who believed that she was still working for the Germans, did give her some instructions about her next assignment. By this time, the Germans realized that she had become hopelessly compromised, which made

her virtually useless to them. In addition, she was becoming a demanding, conceited prima donna and very expensive in a time of declining budgets for intelligence services.

In 1917, the French secret service arrested her for espionage. The Germans basically told the French counterintelligence service that Zelle was returning to France. The Germans confirmed the issuance of instructions to her by their Berlin headquarters in a simple code that they knew the French service could break and read.

Zelle, when she arrived in Paris, checked into the swank Hotel Plaza Athénée. Fifteen thousand pesetas were waiting for her at a neutral legation in Paris as payment for "services" rendered to the Germans. She picked up the check but hadn't cashed it when she was arrested by the French. The main evidence for her prosecution was a list of payments that she had received from the German military attaché in Madrid. She countered with the defense that these payments had been for sexual services rendered as the officer's mistress.

In July 1917, her trial opened before a French military court. Her attorney was the brilliant French barrister, Maître Clunet. He honestly believed that the evidence against Zelle was insufficient to convict her and expected her to be released.

Zelle was put on the defensive as soon as the trial started when the presiding judge asked her about 30,000 marks that she had received from the chief of the Berlin police. She replied without hesitation that the chief had been her lover and had happily paid that amount for her favors. She continued to give the same explanation for all the money she had received over the years. The court was reluctant to let the matter drop and cited some of her German lovers, such as General von Bissing, the Duke of Brunswick, the crown prince of Germany, and a multitude of German naval and military attachés in European capitals. All of the military and naval attachés in that era were automatically considered to be intelligence officers.

Zelle responded to the presiding judge by calling as defense witnesses some of her highly placed French lovers, such as the former French minister of war and permanent secretary of the Foreign Office of France. She eloquently stated, "I am not French so what is to prevent my having friends of any nationality I choose? If I wrote to high ranking Germans it was only because they wrote to me and I returned their endearments, but nothing more. My letters that were sent in diplomatic bags were letters to my daughter in Holland." She noted that she had given French authorities the names of many places in Morocco where German U-boats called to refuel, and that she had been told the information was very useful.

Her trial lasted two full days, and she was found guilty. Her lawyers desperately sought clemency from President Raymond Poincaré of France, who refused to even consider their plea. Prime Minister Mijnheer van der Linden of the Netherlands (who had also been one of Zelle's lovers) asked Queen Wilhelmina to intercede with the president of France for a reprieve for Zelle. The queen refused to consider such a request.

Zelle was sentenced on 25 July 1917, but the sentence was not carried out until October 15, when she was executed by a firing squad at Vincennes, France. The irony of her execution is that she had probably never given the Germans any secret information about the French. The French government needed the publicity of a spy's execution to boost its people's sagging morale. The French national will was faltering from a series of mutinies at the front and the executions of soldiers that had been necessary to suppress these mutinies.

There was another reason for her quick execution. There was a reference in Zelle's diary to a French politician who was one of her lovers. She referred to him simply as "M," but from other references in the diaries he was quickly identified as the French minister of the interior, M. Malvy.

Zelle was courageous to the end and never gave the French government the satisfaction of having her recant her innocence, admit her guilt in any degree, or beg for mercy. On the morning of her execution, Zelle dressed herself and had the glass of brandy offered her by the prison doctor. She was calm and more composed than Sister Leonide, the nun who was attending her.

The French government finally admitted in 1932, when the head of the Conseil de Guerre examined Zelle's entire case, that it contained "*no* tangible, palpable, absolute, irrefutable evidence" of her guilt (Howe 1986, 285). In January 1929, the German intelligence service reported that, "Zelle did not achieve anything for the German intelligence service. Her case was enormously exploited" (Howe 1986, 285).

(See also Gertrude Banda.)

Howe, Russell W. *Mata Hari: The True Story.* New York: Dodd, Mead, 1986.

Ostrovsky, Erika. *Eye of Dawn: The Rise and Fall of Mata Hari.* New York: Dorset Press, 1978.

Jane Foster Zlatovski
(Slang)
United States
1912–1979

Jane Foster Zlatovski could not resist the opportunity to become a Soviet agent when a friend asked her. She and her husband, a Communist and a U.S. intelligence officer, penetrated U.S. intelligence agencies for the Soviets.

Zlatovski was born in California and attended college there. In 1942, shortly after the United States entered World War II, she went to work for the U.S. Federal Board of Economic Warfare as a junior analyst. She learned languages easily; she could speak some Spanish and spoke German, Dutch, Malay, and French fluently. Her linguistic abilities made her attractive as a candidate for the U.S. intelligence service, and on 27 December 1943, she transferred to the OSS. She was first assigned to the United States Armed Forces at Salzburg, Austria.

Zlatovski had joined the Communist party while she was living in the Dutch East Indies (from 1936 to the spring of 1940). There was a rumor that she had been married to a Dutch diplomat. OSS records indicate that she was assigned to the OSS detachment in Kandy, Ceylon, on 13 July 1944. She traveled extensively in the Far East during this assignment and was transferred to Washington on 11 December 1945.

Zlatovski was recruited into Soviet espionage by Martha Dodd Stern. According to her Soviet case officer, Jack Soble, Zlatovski produced some of the best intelligence of any American working for him. When Zlatovski was first recruited into Soviet intelligence, she provided a report on Indonesia that she had compiled from OSS files and her own extensive knowledge of the area. At the time, the Soviets were engaged in very sensitive negotiations with the Indonesian government, and they found her report—with information on the United States position and its confidential urgings to the Indonesian government—very valuable. This knowledge made the Soviets' bargaining position much stronger.

Zlatovski also provided the Soviets with valuable information about U.S. intelligence agents. In a report intercepted by Boris Morros, Jane Zlatovski claimed that, while employed by the U.S. Army in Austria in 1947 to 1948, she obtained names, photographs, and biographies of agents of the Counter-Intelligence Corps and of the Central Intelligence Agency as well as similar information concerning their "native" agents and practically every scheme they hatched. Only disruption of contact with her superiors prevented the successful delivery of this information to the Soviet Intelligence Service. This information appeared in a 1960 FBI report.

In contrast to Jane, George Zlatovski, her husband, was not too smart. George had been born in Russia in 1913 and came to the United States with his parents in 1922. He entered the U.S. Army in November 1942 as a private. In 1946, he attended the U.S. Army Intelligence School. He was then assigned to the Military Intelligence Section of the United States Forces in Austria as an interrogation expert. He had attained the rank of first lieutenant when he left active service in February 1948. George had been identified as having conducted Communist party meetings in Duluth, Minnesota, in the early

1930s. He also claimed that he had been a member of the Abraham Lincoln Brigade, a Communist-dominated unit of the Spanish Republican forces during the Spanish Civil War.

On 8 July 1957, when the indictments of the Zlatovskis were handed down by the U.S. Federal Court, both the Zlatovskis were beyond the reach of U.S. justice. They were living in France, which had no extradition treaty with the United States that included "political crimes." The U.S. government contended that espionage and treason were not "political crimes" but were heinous criminal offenses subject to U.S. domestic jurisdiction. France refused to extradite the Zlatovskis, maintaining that their preference for and loyalty to communism was basically political.

A telegram from the U.S. Embassy in Paris to the secretary of state, dated 29 January 1957, subsequently revealed that the real reason that France refused to extradite the Zlatovskis was that the French counterintelligence service was using them to obtain information about Communist espionage in France—information that they found "invaluable."

(See also Martha Dodd Stern and Johanna Koenen Beker.)

FBI report submitted to the United States Senate in 1960. U.S. Federal District Court, New York, Office of the Clerk.

Morros, Boris. *My Ten Years as a Counterspy*. New York: Viking Press, 1959.

U.S. Embassy, Paris. Telegram to the Secretary of State, 29 January 1957.

Zlatovski, Jane Foster. *An Unamerican Lady*. London: Sidgwick & Jackson, 1980.

Elizabeth Zubilin

(Liza Gorskaya, Liza Rosenberg,
    Sara Herbert, Helen)
Russia
ca. 1905–?

Elizabeth Zubilin's husband, Vasili Mikhailovich Zubilin, was the senior Soviet spy in the United States from the mid 1930s to the late 1940s. Elizabeth had a profficiency equal to her husband's in all the arcane espionage arts. At any time, she could substitute for her husband with all the agents in his network. She also ran agents of her own and was considered a capable case officer.

In 1929, she was using the name of her late husband and called herself Lisa Gorskaya. Her lover at the time was Jacob Blumkin, who had been a Soviet intelligence officer in Turkey. Blumkin had been one of the Bolshevik zealots who had assassinated the German ambassador to Moscow immediately after the Bolshevik Revolution of 1917. Blumkin confided to Elizabeth that he had arranged a communications channel between Trotsky, who was in exile, to use with his friends in Russia, who were still working for the OGPU. This was the kind of subversive Trotskyite operation that Stalin feared more than anything. Elizabeth reported Blumkin's "crime" to M. A. Trilisser, the chief of the OGPU's Foreign Department. That night, Blumkin was arrested.

Her husband, Vasili, was born in Moscow on 20 January 1900. He served for a short time as an intelligence officer in the Soviet Embassy in China. In 1941, he officially was assigned to the United States. When the Soviets requested that the U.S. State Department accredit him as a diplomat in the Soviet Embassy in Washington, they neglected to inform the Department that Zubilin and his wife had operated in the United States under commercial cover as "illegals" in the mid-1930s. They also neglected to inform the State Department that his true name was Zarubin.

The Zubilins arrived with their nine-year-old son, Peter, in San Francisco on 25 December 1941. Once they got a look at Mrs. Zubilin, the FBI was able to identify her as Liza Rosenberg. She had previously been the wife of a Soviet intelligence officer who had mysteriously died in the 1920s. When Elizabeth had worked with Vasili in the United States prior to 1941, she had applied for a U.S. passport under the name Sara Herbert. When she worked with Vasili in the United States the second time, she used the code name Helen, but to some of the agents in the net she was known as Liza.

Vasili was the senior case officer for the Boris Morros/Martha Dodd Stern espionage ring. What many people do not know is that Elizabeth, in many respects, exerted considerable professional influence over his handling of that case and his other espionage cases. In discussions concerning the network's operation, Vasili appeared to defer to his wife's opinion. Boris Morros was convinced that she was the brains behind her husband. She often displayed an imperial manner but never seemed to be condescending to her subordinates. One reason that she could afford to be so authoritarian was that she had done many favors for Stalin.

Hede Massig, who was Gerhardt Eisler's wife at one time and who later defected to the United States, met Elizabeth in 1937. (Eisler was the principal Comintern agent in the United States for many years.) Massig was becoming disillusioned with the Soviet government and Stalin's purges, so her OGPU case officer told her that he was going to introduce her to a woman who was a staunch Stalinist who would bring her to her senses and renew her faith in communism. He brought "Helen" to see Massig, and Helen tried to convince her that she should remain faithful to communism. In 1940, Massig wavered again, and again Helen came to convince her to continue working for Soviet intelligence. Nevertheless, Massig and her husband, Paul Massig, had already made up their minds to leave the Soviet net.

Elizabeth and Vasili and their son, Peter, left the United States on 27 August 1944 for the Soviet Union. Vasili resumed his true identity as Vasili Mikhailovich Zarubin and was made deputy chief of the NKVD with the rank of general. He was in charge of all illegal Soviet intelligence officers assigned to posts outside of the Soviet Union. Elizabeth, as far as is known, became a housewife and has not been heard of again in the west.

Morros, Boris. *My Ten Years as a Counterspy.* New York: Viking Press, 1959.

Bibliography

Altavilla, Enrico. *The Art of Spying*. Englewood Cliffs, NJ: Prentice-Hall, 1965.

Andrew, Christopher, and Oleg Gordievsky. *KGB: The Inside Story*. New York: Harper Collins, 1990.

Army Times Editors. *Heroes of the Resistance*. New York: Dodd, Mead & Co., 1967.

Azimov, Isaac. *Guide to the Bible*. New York: Avenal Books, 1981.

Bailey, Geoffrey. *The Conspirators*. New York: Harper, 1960.

Bakeless, John, and Katherine Bakeless. *Spies of the Revolution*. New York: Scholastic, 1959.

Banta, Martha. *Imaging American Women*. New York: Columbia University Press, 1987.

Barker, Dudley. *Prominent Victorians*. New York: Atheneum, 1969.

Barron, John. *KGB*. New York: Reader's Digest Press, 1974.

Bentley, Elizabeth. Obituary. *New York Times*. 3 December 1963.

———. *Out of Bondage*. Afterword by Hayden Peake. New York: Ivy Books, [1951], 1988.

Blackstock, *Agents of Deceit*. Chicago: Quadrangle Books, 1966.

———. Paul W. *The Secret Road to World War II*. Chicago: Quadrangle Books, 1969.

Blaikie, William G. *A Manual of Bible History*. New York: The Ronald Press Co., 1940.

Blair, Joan, and Clay Blair, Jr. *The Search for J. F. K.* New York: Berkeley Publishing Corp., 1976.

Blitzer, Wolf. *Territory of Lies*. New York: Harper & Row, 1989.

Boulding, Elise. *The Underside of History*. Boulder, CO: Westview Press, 1976.

Brook-Shepard, Gordon, *The Storm Birds*. New York: Henry Holt, 1989.

Brown, Anthony Cave, and Charles B. MacDonald. *On a Field of Red*. New York: G. P. Putnam's Sons, 1981.

Budenz, Louis. *The Whole of Their Lives*. New York: Charles Scribner's Sons, 1948.

Burnham, James. *The Web of Subversion*. New York: The John Day Company, 1954.

Calomiris, Angela. *Red Masquerade: Undercover for the FBI*. New York: J. B. Lippincott, 1950. p. 267.

Collins, Larry. *Is Paris Burning?* New York: Simon & Schuster, 1965.

Cook, Fred J. *The FBI Nobody Knows*. New York: Macmillan, 1964.

Cookridge, E. H. *Set Europe Ablaze*. London: Pan Books, 1966.

———. *Spy Trade*. New York: Walker & Co., 1971.

Corson, William R., and Robert T. Crowley. *The New KGB*. New York: William Morrow, 1985.

Crown, Duncan. *The Victorian Woman*. New York: Stein & Day, 1972.

Currey, Cecil B. *Code Number 72, Ben Franklin: Patriot or Spy?* Englewood Cliffs, NJ: Prentice-Hall, 1972.

Dallin, David J. *Soviet Espionage*. New Haven, CT: Yale University Press, 1955.

Daniels, Robert V. *Red October: The Bolshevik Revolution of 1917*. Boston: Beacon Press, 1967.

De Gramont, Sanche. *The Secret War*. London: Andre Deutsch, 1962.

De Toledano, Ralph. *The Greatest Plot in History*. New York: Duell, Sloan & Pearce, 1963.

Deacon, Richard. *The Chinese Secret Service*. New York: Taplinger, 1974.

Deacon, Richard. *Spyclopedia*. New York: Silver Arrow Books, 1987.

Delarue, Jacques. *The Gestapo: A History of Horror*. New York: Macdonald & Co., 1964.

Díaz del Castillo, Bernal. *The Discovery and Conquest of Mexico*. New York: Farrar, Straus & Cudahy, 1956.

Dijkstra, Bram. *Idols of Perversity*. New York: Oxford University Press, 1986.

Donovan, James B. *Strangers on a Bridge: The Case of Colonel Abel*. New York: Atheneum, 1964.

Dreux, William B. *No Bridges Blown*. Notre Dame, IN: Notre Dame University Press, 1971.

Duboscq, Genevieve. *My Longest Night*. New York: Seaver Books, 1978.

Dulles, Allen. *Great True Spy Stories*. New York: Random House, 1968.

Duss, Masayo. *Tokyo Rose: Orphan of the Pacific*. New York: Kodansha International, 1979.

Dzhirkvelov, Ilya. *Secret Service: My Life in the KGB and the Soviet Elite*. New York: Harper & Row, 1987.

Dziak, John J., *Chekisty: A History of the KGB*. Lexington, MA: Lexington Books, 1988.

Ebon, Martin. *"Che": The Making of a Legend*. New York: Signet Books, 1969.

Edmonds, Emma E. *Nurse and Spy in the Union Army*. Hartford, CT, 1865.

Ehrlich, Blake. *Resistance: France 1940–1945*. Boston: Little, Brown & Co., 1965.

Encyclopaedia Britannica. Volume 22. 1946.

Foote, Alexander. *Handbook for Spies*. New York: Doubleday, 1949.

Francis, Ambassador. Telegram #1170 to Secretary of State. Petrograd to Washington, DC. 10 April 1917.

Franklin, Charles. *The Great Spies*. New York: Hart Publishing Co., 1967.

Frenay, Henri. *The Night Will End*. New York: McGraw-Hill, 1976.

Gainer-Raymond, Phillippe. *The Tangled Web*. New York: Pantheon, 1968.

Gitlow, Benjamin. *The Whole of Their Lives*. New York: Charles Scribner's Sons, 1948.

Glotzer, Albert. *Trotsky: Memoir and Critique*. New York: Prometheus Books, 1989.

Golan, Aviezer, and Danny Pinkas. *Shula: Code Name "The Pearl."* New York: Delacorte Press, 1980.

Griffith, Aline (Countess of Romanones). *The Spy Went Dancing*. New York: G. P. Putnam's Sons, 1990.

———. *The Spy Wore Red*. New York: Charter Books, 1988.

Harris, Richard. *Death of a Revolutionary*. New York: W. W. Norton, 1970.

Harrison, Marguerite. *There's Always Tomorrow: The Story of a Checkered Life*. New York: Farrar & Rinehart, 1935.

Heijenoort, Jan. *With Trotsky in Exile: From Prinkipo to Coyoacan*. Cambridge, MA: Harvard University Press, 1978.

Hoehling, A. A. *Women Who Spied*. New York: Dodd, Mead & Co., 1967.

Hogen, Louis. *The Secret War for Europe*. New York: Stein & Day, 1969.

Hohne, Heinz. *Codeword: "Direktor."* New York: Coward, McCann & Geoghegan, 1971.

Holt, Patricia Lee. "Female Spy, Male Nurse." *Military History* 5, no. 1. p. 65.

Hoover, J. Edgar. *Masters of Deceit*. New York: Henry Holt, 1958.

Howe, Russell W. *Mata Hari: The True Story*. New York: Dodd, Mead & Co., 1986.

Hyde, H. Montgomery. *Cynthia*. New York: Farrar, Straus & Giroux, 1968.

Ind, Allison. *A Short History of Espionage*. New York: David McKay Co., 1963.

Katona, Edita, with Patrick Macnaghten. *Code Name Marianne*. New York: David McKay Co., 1976.

Knightley, Phillip. *The Second Oldest Profession*. New York: W. W. Norton, 1986.

Kravchenko, Victor. *I Choose Freedom*. New York: Charles Scribner's Sons, 1946.

Laska, Vera. *Women in the Resistance and in the Holocaust: The Voices of Eyewitnesses*. Westport, CT: Greenwood Press, 1983.

Layton, Edwin T. *And I Was There*. New York: William Morrow, 1985.

Leigh, David. *The Wilson Plot*. New York: Pantheon Books, 1988.

Levine, Isaac Don. *Mind of an Assassin*. New York: Farrar, Straus & Cudahy, 1959.

Life. Special Edition. Spring-Summer 1985. p. 36.

Liston, Robert A. *The Dangerous World of Spies and Spying*. New York: Platt & Munk, 1967.

McCormick, Donald. *The Master Book of Spies*. New York: Franklin Watts, 1976.

McKenna, Marthe. *I Was a Spy*. London: Jarrods, 1953.

MacKinnon, Janice R., and Stephen R. MacKinnon. *Agnes Smedley: The Life and Times of an American Radical*. London: Virago, 1988.

MacLean, Ian. *Renaissance Notion of Woman*. New York: Cambridge University Press, 1980.

Mandell, William. *Soviet Women*. New York: Doubleday, 1975.

Marrin, Albert. *The Secret Armies*. New York: Atheneum, 1985.

Martin, Ralph G. *A Hero for Our Time*. New York: Macmillan, 1983.

Massig, Hede. *This Deception*. New York: Duell, Sloan & Pearce, 1951.

Morros, Boris. *My Ten Years as a Counterspy*. New York: The Viking Press, 1959.

Mosley, Leonard. *The Cat and the Mice*. New York: Harper & Bros., 1958.

Neave, Airey. *The Escape Room*. New York: Doubleday, 1970.

Nolan, Jeannette Covert. *Spy for the Confederacy: Rose O'Neal Greenhow*. New York: Julian Messner, 1963.

Norden, Peter. *Madam Kitty*. London: Abelard-Schuman, 1973.

Olds, Elizabeth Fagg. *Women of the Four Winds*. Boston: Houghton Mifflin, 1985.

Ostrovsky, Erika. *Eye of Dawn: The Rise and Fall of Mata Hari*. New York: Dorset Press, 1978.

Panati, Charles. *Extraordinary Endings of Practically Everything and Everybody*. New York: Harper & Row, 1989.

Payne, Robert. *Lenin*. New York: Simon & Schuster, 1964.

Payne, Ronald, and Christopher Dobson. *Who's Who in Espionage*. New York: St. Martin's Press, 1984.

Penkovskiy, Oleg. *The Penkovskiy Papers*. New York: Doubleday, 1965.

Peterson, Bonnie A., and Judith P. Zinsser. *A History of Their Own*. Volume II. New York: Harper & Row, 1988.

Pincher, Chapman. *Too Secret Too Long*. New York: St. Martin's Press, 1984.

Powers, Richard G. *Secrecy and Power*. New York: The Free Press, 1987.

Prange, Gordon W., with Donald M. Goldstein, and Katherine V. Dillon. *Target Tokyo: The Story of the Sorge Spy Ring*. New York: McGraw-Hill, 1984.

Raviv, Dan, and Yossi Melman. *Every Spy a Prince*. Boston: Houghton Mifflin, 1990.

Reader's Digest. *Great Cases of Scotland Yard*. Pleasantville, NY: The Reader's Digest Association, 1978.

Reeves, Thomas C. *A Question of Character*. New York: The Free Press, 1991.

Rexroth, Kenneth. *An Autobiographical Novel*. New York: Doubleday & Co., 1966.

Richelson, Jeffery. *American Espionage and the Soviet Target*. New York: William Morrow, 1987.

Robertson, Priscilla. *An Experience of Women: Patterns and Change in the Nineteenth Century*. Philadelphia: Temple University Press, 1982.

Rositzke, Harry. *The KGB: The Eyes of Russia*. New York: Doubleday, 1981.

Rowan, Richard Wilmer. *The Story of the Secret Service*. New York: The Literary Guild of America, 1937.

Rowan, Richard Wilmer, and Robert G. Deindorfer. *Secret Service: 33 Years of Espionage*. New York: Hawthorn Books, 1967.

Rowbotham, Sheila. *Hidden from History.* New York: Pantheon Books, 1973.

———. *Women, Resistance and Revolution.* New York: Vintage Books, 1972.

Sadat, Anwar. *Revolt on the Nile.* London: John Day Publishers.

Salisbury, Harrison E. *Black Night, White Snow: Russia's Revolutions 1905–1917.* New York: Doubleday, 1977.

Schellenberg, Walter. *The Labyrinth.* New York: Harper & Row, 1956.

Schmidt, Minna M. *Four Hundred Outstanding Women of the World.* Chicago: Minna Moscherosch Schmidt Publisher, 1933.

Schoenbrun, David. *Soldiers of the Night: The Story of the French Resistance.* New York: E. P. Dutton, 1980.

Seth, Ronald. *Encyclopedia of Espionage.* New York: Doubleday, 1972.

———. *Secret Servants.* New York: Farrar, Straus & Giroux, 1968.

Shiber, Etta. *Paris Underground.* New York: Charles Scribner's Sons, 1943.

Singer, Kurt. *Spy Stories from Asia.* New York: Wilfred Funk, 1955.

Smith, Page. *Daughters of the Promised Land.* Boston: Little, Brown & Co., 1970.

Sochen, June. *Movers and Shakers.* New York: The New York Times Book Company, 1973.

Spolansky, Jacob. *The Communist Trail in America.* New York: Macmillan, 1951.

Stein, Philip M. *The Oppenheimer Case.* New York: Harper & Row, 1969.

Stern, Philip Van Doren. *Secret Missions of the Civil War.* New York: Bonanza Books, 1959.

Tickell, Jerrard. *Odette: The Story of a British Agent.* London: Chapman & Hall, 1949.

Trepper, Leopold. *The Great Game.* New York: McGraw-Hill, 1977.

Tuck, Jan. *High Tech Espionage.* New York: St. Martin's Press, 1986.

United States Embassy, Paris. Telegram to the Secretary of State. 29 January 1957.

Volkman, Ernest, and Blaine Baggett. *Secret Intelligence: The Inside Story of America's Espionage Empire.* New York: Doubleday, 1989.

Weiser, Marjorie P. K., and Jean S. Arbeiter. *Womanlist.* New York: Atheneum, 1981.

Werner, Ruth. *Sonya's Report.* London: Chatto & Windus, 1991.

West, Rebecca. *The New Meaning of Treason.* New York: Viking, 1964.

Whitehead, Don. *The FBI Story.* New York: Random House, 1956.

Wighton, Charles, and Gunter Peis. *Hitler's Spies and Saboteurs.* New York: Holt, Rinehart & Winston, 1958.

Willoughby, Major General Charles A. *Shanghai Conspiracy.* New York: E. P. Dutton & Co., 1952.

Wise, David. *The Spy Who Got Away.* New York: Random House, 1988.

Wolfe, Bertram. *The Fabulous Life of Diego Rivera.* New York: Stein & Day, 1936.

———. "From the Other Shore." Reprint ca. 1948.

———. *Three Who Made a Revolution.* New York: Delta Books, 1948.

Wright, Peter. *Spycatcher.* New York: Viking Penguin, 1987.

Wyden, Peter. *Stella: One Woman's True Tale of Evil, Betrayal and Survival in Hitler's Germany.* New York: Simon & Schuster, 1992.

Yardley, Herbert O. *The American Black Chamber.* Indianapolis: Bobbs-Merrill, 1931.

———. *The Chinese Black Chamber.* Boston: Houghton Mifflin, 1983.

List of Acronyms and Abbreviations Used in This Book

ACGM   American Communist Group in Mexico.

ACLU   American Civil Liberties Union.

BCP   British Communist Party.

CIA   Central Intelligence Agency.

Comintern   Communist International.

CPUSA   Communist Party USA.

DF   *Distrito Federal,* Mexico's Federal District, or federal government enclave similar to the District of Columbia in the United States.

FBI   Federal Bureau of Investigation.

G-2   Second Section of the General Staff. This section deals with intelligence matters for the army.

GPU   See OGPU.

GRU   *Glavnoye Razvedyvatelnoye Upravlenie* (Chief Intelligence Directorate) of the former Soviet Union's military intelligence organization.

INS   Immigration and Naturalization Service.

IRB   Irish Republican Brotherhood.

KGB   *Komitet Gosudarstvennoy Bezopasnosti* (Committee for State Security), the civilian intelligence organization of the former Soviet Union.

MI-5   Britain's internal security organization.

MI-6   British foreign intelligence organization.

MBE   Member of the British Empire.

NATO   North Atlantic Treaty Organization.

NKVD   *Narodnyi Kommissariat Vnutrenniki Del* (Internal Affairs Commissariat), the Soviet state security and civilian intelligence organization; succeeded the OGPU and preceded the KGB.

OCI   Office of Current Intelligence, a section within Central Intelligence Agency that issues reports on the current status of world affairs.

OGPU   *Obyeddinenoye Gosudarstvennoye Politicheskoye Upravlenie* (United State Political Directorate), previously had been the GPU *(Gosudarstvennoye Politicheskoye Upravlenie.)* The GPU replaced the Cheka, the Bolshevik political police, in 1922, and OGPU replaced GPU in 1923 upon formation of the USSR. These were all Soviet civilian intelligence organizations and forerunners of the KGB.

OSS   Office of Strategic Services (USA).

PCM   Partido Comunista Mexicano (Communist Party of Mexico).

PLO   Palestine Liberation Organization.

PNG   *Persona non grata,* literally meaning "not a pleasing person." It is diplomatic language a host government will use when expelling a foreign diplomat for unacceptable behavior, which in most instances has been espionage against the host government. An unacceptable diplomat declared *persona non grata* can no longer be accredited to the host government and usually must leave the host country within forty-eight hours.

SOE   Special Operations Executive, the paramilitary arm of British Intelligence during World War II.

SS   *Schutz Staffel,* which literally meant "guard detachment," but it actually was the elite personal bodyguard of Adolf Hitler, the chancellor of Germany. Heinrich Himmler, Hitler's security chief, built the SS from a simple guard detachment into a major component of German security.

USO   The United Service Organization, which provided show business and community recreational support for servicemen and women during World War II and after.

Vcheka   *Vserossiiskaya Chrezvychinaya Komissiya po Borbes Kontrrevolyutsiei i Sabotazhem* (All Russian Extraordinary Commission for Combating Counterrevolution and Sabotage), which was originally formed by Felix Dzerzhinsky, the first chief of state security of the Bolsheviks. It was created largely to protect the leaders of the Bolshevik party. It was called Cheka originally but almost immediately changed to Vcheka (fore runner of the OGPU).

WAAF   Women's Auxiliary Air Force.

Index

Aaronsohn, Sarah, 3–4
Abbiate, Roland, 202
Abel, Rudolph Ivanovich, 45
Abrego de Reyes, Mercedes, 4
Acacius, Theodora, 4–5
Ageloff, Hilda, 6, 145
Ageloff, Ruth, 6, 145
Ageloff, Sylvia, 6–9, 145–146, 156
Aleman, Miguel, 31
Alexander I (czar of Russia), 219
Allende, Ignacio, 164
Allison, Gertrude, 7
American League Against War and Fascism, 21
Andre, Major, 212
Anti-Semitism, 65, 184, 192–193, 228. *See also* World War II
Armand, Inessa Elizabeth d'Herbenville, 9–11
Arnold, Benedict, 212
Arvad, Inga Marie, 11–13
Astor, Lord, 127, 178
Atlee, Clement, 99
Aubrac, Lucie, 13
Aubrac, Raymond, 13
Australia, 158–160
Ayer, Frederick, Jr., 12

Balabanoff, Angelica, 10
Banda, Gertrude, 15–16
Barbie, Klaus, 13
Barnett, John H., 87
Basedon, Yvonne, 16–17
Bassols, Narciso, 30
Bauer, Anne-Marie, 17–18
Beaumarchais, Caron de, 60
Beaurepos, Kitty, 18–19
Behn, Aphra, 19–20

Beker, Johanna Koenen, 20
Belgium
    World War I, 41–43, 60–61, 146–148
    World War II, 22, 31, 63–64, 114
Benario, Olga, 80
Bentley, Elizabeth Terrell, 20–21, 116, 182, 194–195
Bernier, Marie. *See* Basedon, Yvonne
Bervoets, Marguerite, 22
Betancourt, Ana, 22
Beurton, Leon Charles, 138, 139
Biblical times. *See* Israelites
Birckel, Marie, 22–23
Bird, Alice. *See* Smedley, Agnes
Black, Helen, 153
Black September, 175–176
Blackburn, Norman, 129–130
Blake, Arthur, 112
Blake, George, 94
Bleicher, Hugo, 40–41
Bloch, Emanuel H., 183
Bloor, "Mother" Reeves, 206
Bolivar, Simon, 4
Bolivia, 34–35
Bonnesen, Edith, 23–24
Borodin, Fanny, 152
Borodin, Mikhail, 152
Borue, Christine, 40
Bouchki, Ahmed, 175
Boudinot, Elias, 58
Bowser, Mary Elizabeth, 24, 217
Boyd, Belle, 24–27
Brazil, 80
Britain, 127–129
    and communism, 99–100, 127
    Egyptian espionage against, 180–181
    German interwar espionage against, 123–124
    and Irish independence, 69–70, 96–99
    and Napoleonic Wars, 68, 86–87
    and 1600s, 19–20, 65–67
    Soviet espionage against, 43–45, 46–47, 93–96, 139

Britain, continued
   and World War I, 3–4, 41–43, 224
   and World War II, 27–29, 162–163, 224–226
   See also World War I; World War II
Brooks, Gerald, 46
Brousse, Amy Elizabeth Thorpe, 27–29
Brousse, Charles, 29
Browder, Earl, 153
Brufau Civit, Carmen, 29–31, 156
Brusselmans, Anne, 31
Buchanan, Grace, 32
Budenz, Louis, 6–7, 88, 145
Bunke, Haidee Tamara, 32, 34–35
Byzantine Empire, 4–5

Calomiris, Angela, 37–39
Canada, 79–80, 129–130
Canaris, Wilhelm, 223
Cannon, James, 88, 89
Carré, Mathilde-Lucie Belard, 39–41
Cavell, Edith, 41–43, 62
Central Intelligence Agency (CIA), 16, 44
Chamberlain, Neville, 179
Chambers, Whittaker, 21
Chattopadhyaya, Virendranath, 197
China, 79, 80, 130–131
   Japanese espionage in, 126–127
   and nationalist espionage, 221–222, 229–230
   Soviet espionage in, 80, 137–138, 197–198
   and U.S. sympathizers, 115–116, 197–198
Chisholm, Janet Anne, 43–45
Chisholm, Roderick, 44, 45
Churchill, Peter Morland, 188
Churchill, Winston, 27, 148
Chu-teh, 198
CIA. *See* Central Intelligence Agency
Civil War (Spain), 27, 29, 45, 155, 158
Civil War (United States)
   Confederate espionage during, 24–27, 101–104, 168–169, 193–194
   Union espionage during, 24, 50–52, 76–77, 113, 215–218
Cohen, Lona Petka, 45–47, 94
Cohen, Morris, 45–47, 94
Cole, Angela. *See* Calomiris, Angela
Colombia, 4, 187
Communism
   Britain, 99–100, 127
   France, 155
   Germany, 137
   Indonesia, 16
   Korea, 130–131
   Mexico, 157–158
   Spain, 29–31
   See also U.S. communism; *specific Soviet headings*
Connolly, Jim, 98
Contreras, Carlos. *See* Vidali, Vittorio
Cooper, Merion C., 111, 112
Coplon, Judith, 47–50
Cortés, Hernán, 150
Cuba, 22, 32, 34, 35

Cuban Missile Crisis, 44
Cushman, Pauline, 50–52
Cynthia. *See* Brousse, Amy Elizabeth Thorpe
Czechoslovakia, 116–117

Dallin, David, 55
Dallin, Lilia Ginsburg, 53–55
d'Aquino, Iva Toguri, 55–57
Darragh, Lydia, 57–58
David, Zalmond, 88
Davis, Jefferson, 24, 104, 217
de Baissac, Lise, 58–59
de Beaumont, Charles Geneviere Louis Auguste Andre Timothee d'Eon. *See* D'Eon, Chevalier
de Bettignies, Louis, 60–63
de Cespedes, Carlos Manuel, 22
de Cissey, General, 65
de Jongh, Andree, 63–64
de Kaulla, Baroness, 64–65
de Keroualle, Louise, 65–67
de Mauduit, Countess Roberta, 67–68
de Preville, Nymph Roussel, 68
de Saint-Wexel, Edwige, 68–69
de Victorica, Maria Kretschmann, 69–71
Deldonck, Lucille, 147
Delilah, 71–72
Denmark, 23–24
D'Eon, Chevalier, 59–60
Dickinson, Velvalee Malvena Blucher, 72–74
Dierks, Hans, 78
Doña Maria. *See* La Malinche
Double agents, 32, 77–79, 92
Douglas, Chevalier, 59
Dreyfus, Alfred, 65
Druegge, Karl, 78, 79

Earhart, Amelia, 75–76
East Germany. *See* German Democratic Republic
Edmonds, Sarah Emma, 76–77
Egypt, 81–83, 87, 180–181
Eisler, Gerhardt, 151, 153, 185
Eitingon, Leonid, 30, 156
England. *See* Britain
Enigma, 27
Eppler, John, 81–82
Epstein, Schachno, 173
Erikson, Vera, 77–79
Erogov, Alexandra, 93
Erogov, Ivan Dmitrevich, 93
Ewert, Arthur, 79–80
Ewert, Elise Sabrowski, 79–80

Fathmy, Hekmath, 81–83
Fauquenot, Emile, 23
Fejos, Paul, 11
Female impersonators, 59–60
Fermi, Enrico, 116
Field, Herta, 153
Field, Noel, 153
Fiocca, Nancy Lake, 83–84
Flynn, Elizabeth Gurley, 84–85

Foote, Alexander, 138, 139
Ford, Gerald, 57
Forrestal, James V., 12
Fourcade, Marie Madeleine, 85–86
Foures, Bellitote, 86–87
Fourth International, 53–55
France, Joseph I., 112
France, 59–60, 65–67
    and communism, 155
    and Franco-Prussian War, 64–65
    and Napoleonic Wars, 68, 86–87
    Soviet interwar espionage in, 169–170, 213
    and World War I, 22–23, 61–63, 87–88, 177–178,
        235–237
    See also French resistance (World War II)
Francillard, Marguerite, 87–88
Franco-Prussian War, 64–65
Frankenberg, Marie-Louise, 133
Franklin, Irving. See David, Zalmond
Franklin, Sylvia Callen, 88–89
Fraunces, Phoebe, 89
French resistance (World War II), 39–41, 207–208
    and anti-Nazi propaganda, 13, 17
    and exfiltration, 18–19, 67–69, 83–84, 100–101, 227
    information for, 58–59, 187–189
    organization of, 85–86, 188
    and prisoner rescues, 17–18
    and radio operation, 16–17, 119–121
Fuchs, Klaus, 45, 182

Galkin, Alexi Ivanovich, 92
Garber, Joy Ann, 91–93
Garces, Santiago, 30
Gee, Ethel Elizabeth, 46, 93–96
German Democratic Republic, 32, 113–114, 136–137
German Federal Republic, 32, 113–114, 133–135,
    136–137
Germany
    and communism, 137
    and Franco-Prussian War, 64–65
    and interwar espionage, 123–124
    Nazi regime in, 11–12, 191–192
    Soviet espionage in, 107–109, 152–154
    U.S. interwar espionage in, 109, 111
    and World War I, 3–4, 22–23, 41–43, 69–71, 87–88,
        177–178, 189–191, 224, 235–237
    and World War II espionage, 77–79, 81–83, 178–180,
        222–223, 228
    See also French resistance (World War II); German
        Democratic Republic; German Federal Republic;
        World War I; World War II
Ghose, Salindranath, 195
Gil, Portes, 135
Ginsburg, Ralph, 54
Gitlow, Benjamin, 173, 206
Goebbels, Joseph, 11, 140
Goering, Hermann, 11, 179, 191
Gold, Harry, 116, 182, 183
Goldman, Emma, 163
Goldschlag, Stella, 96

Gollnow, Herbert, 107–108
Golos, Jacob, 21, 172, 194–195
Gonne, Maud, 96–99
Gordon, Betty, 99–100
Grant, Ulysses S., 217–218
Granville, Christine, 100–101
Granville, Lord, 104
Great Britain. See Britain
Green, William, 115
Greenglass, David, 182–183
Greenglass, Ruth, 183
Greenhow, Rose O'Neal, 101–104
Griffith, Aline, 104–105
Griffith, Arthur, 98
Grinke, Walter, 153
Gubitchev, Valentine, 49–50
Guevara, Ernesto "Che," 32, 34–35
Gumperz, Julian, 151–152

Haig, Earl, 148
Halifax, Lord, 179
Hamburger, Rudolf, 137
Harding, Mrs. Stan, 109, 111
Hardinge, James, 27
Harnack, Arvid, 107, 108
Harnack, Mildred Fish, 107–109
Harrison, Marguerite, 109–113
Hart, Nancy, 113
Heidel, Gudrun, 113–114
Heidel, Heinrich, 114
Henin, Marie-Louise, 114
Hernandez, Alonzo, 150
Hidalgo, Miguel, 164
Himmel, Hermann, 62, 63
Himmler, Heinrich, 121, 140
Hinton, Bertha, 116
Hinton, Carmelita, 114–115
Hinton, Jean, 115
Hinton, Joan Chase, 114–116
Hinton, William Howard, 115, 116
Hiss, Alger, 115, 151, 153
Hiss, Priscilla, 115
Hitler, Adolf, 11, 179, 180
Hoover, Herbert, 112
Hoover, J. Edgar, 12, 184
Horak, Bohuslav, 116
Horakova, Milada, 116–117
Houghton, Harry, 46, 93, 94–95
Hungary, 193

Inayat Kahn, Noor, 119–121
India, 195, 197
Indonesia, 15–16
Industrial Workers of the World (IWW), 84, 85
Ireland, 69–70, 96–99
Israel, 132–133, 170–172, 175–176, 180–181
Israelites, 71–72, 123, 176
Italy, 125–126
Ivanov, Eugene, 127, 129

Jackson, Stonewall, 26
Japan, 15–16, 55–57, 72–74, 75–76, 126–127, 140–142,
    167–168. *See also* World War II
Jezebel, 123
Jordan, Jesse, 123–124
Jordan, Thomas, 103
Justinian I, 4–5

Kamenev, Lev Borisovich, 10
Katona, Edita, 125–126
Kaufman, Irving, 183, 184
Kawashima, Yoshiko, 126–127
Keeler, Christine, 127–129
Keenan, Helen, 129–130
Kennedy, John F., 11, 12
Kennedy, Joseph, 12
Kennedy, Kathleen, 12
Kent, Frank, 109
Kent, Tyler Gatewood, 228
Kerbey, 26–27
Keyes, E. D., 103
KGB. *See* Communism; Soviet Union
Kim Suim, 130–131
Kiselnikova, Raya, 131–132
Kishak, Shula Arazi-Cohen, 132–133
Knuth, Maria, 133–135
Kollanti, Alexandra, 10, 135–136
Kolomyakov, Boris, 131, 205
Konig, Roberta, 136–137
Korea, 130–131
Kowerski, Andrew, 100
Kravchenko, Victor, 166, 167
Krivitsky, Alexander, 201, 202
Krock, Arthur, 11
Kuczynski, Ursula Ruth, 80, 137–139
Kuehn, Bernard Julius Otto, 140–142
Kuehn, Friedel, 140–142
Kuehn, Hans Joachim, 141
Kuehn, Ruth, 140–142
Kunze, Karl, 133
Kussonsky, Pavel A., 170
Kutyepov, Alexander, 170
Kuznetsov, Boris, 31

Labor movement, 84–85
L'Aloutte. *See* Richer, Marthe Betenfeld
Lamphere, Bob, 154
Laski, Neville, 139
Lattimore, Owen, 115
League for Industrial Democracy, 21
Lebanon, 132–133
Leclerc, Abbé, 68
Lee, Arthur, 60
Lee King-Kook, 130
Lenin, Krupskaya, 10–11
Lenin, Vladimir I., 6, 9, 10, 135
Leveugle, Elsie-Julie, 62
Lewis, John, 99
Liberation (France), 17
Lien, Jean-Paul, 86
Lincoln, Abraham, 26

Lonsdale, Gordon. *See* Molody, Konon Trofimovich
Lore, Ludwig, 172, 173
Lubeck, Peter, 7
Ludington, Sybil, 143

McBride, John, 98
McCoy, Tim, 13
Machado, Eduardo, 146
Machado, Gertrude, 145–146
MacKell, Lillie, 103
McKenna, Marthe Cnockaert, 146–148
Magrinat, Jose, 157
La Malinche, 148–151
Mao Tse-tung, 222
Markin, Valentine, 153
Martens, Ludwig C. A. K., 112
Martin, Jeanne, 54
Maslennikov, Pyotr Egorovich, 92
Massig, Hede Tune Eisler, 151–154, 239
Massig, Paul, 152, 239
Mata Hari, 15, 177, 233–237
Maximovich, Anna, 154–155
Mella, Julio Antonio, 157
Mercader, Eustacio Maria Caridad del Rio Hernandez,
    30, 155–157
Mercader, Ramon, 7–9, 30, 146, 156
Mexico, 135, 157–158
    revolution, 163–164, 218
    Soviet Cold War era espionage in, 30–31, 131–132
    and Spanish conquest, 148–151
    and Trotsky assassination, 6–9, 88–89, 145–146,
        156–157
Miller, Richard W., 161–162
Miller, Yevgeni Karlovich, 170
Millevoye, Lucien, 97, 98
Mink, George, 172–173
Minor, Robert, 111
Modotti, Asunta Adelaide Luigia, 157–158
Moghiliesky, Officer, 111, 112
Molody, Konon Trofimovich, 46, 94
Mora y Pena, Ignacio, 22
Morgan, John Hunt, 50
Morros, Boris, 88–89, 203
Mowbray, Margaret, 158–160
Muldowney, Dennis George, 101
Muth, Olga "Ollo," 138, 139

Napoleonic Wars, 68, 86–87
NATO. *See* North Atlantic Treaty Organization
Nearing, Scott, 21
Nechiporenko, Oleg, 131–132
Netherlands, 210–211
Nicolai, Walter, 62, 69, 189
North Atlantic Treaty Organization (NATO), 133, 134

Odette. *See* Basedon, Yvonne
O'Donnell, F. Hugh, 98
Ogordonik, Alexsandr Dmitrevich, 165
Ogorodnikova, Svetlana, 161–162
O'Grady, Dorothy Pamela, 162–163

O'Hare, Frank, 163
O'Hare, Kate Richards, 163
Okudo, Otojiro, 141
O'Leary, Jack, 97
Oppenheimer, J. Robert, 115
Orlov, Alexander, 30, 55, 156
Ortiz de Dominguez, Josefa, 163–164
Ovakimian, Gaik, 8

Pack, Arthur, 27, 29
Palestine. *See* Israel; Israelites
Palmer Raids, 206
Patterson, Cissy, 12
Peking Joan. *See* Hinton, Joan Chase
Penkovskiy, Oleg, 44–45
Petera, Eman, 125
Peterson, Martha, 165–166
Petit, Gabrielle, 63
Petrovna, Eliena, 166–167
Petter, Robert, 78, 79
Philistines, 71–72
Phillips, Claire, 167–168
Phoenicia, 123
Piggott, Emmeline, 168–169
Pinkerton, Allen E., 103, 217
Plaminkova, Frantiska, 116
Plevitzkaya, Nadezhda, 169–170
Poland, 209–210
Poliakova, Maria, 138
Pollard, Anne Henderson, 170–172
Pollard, Jonathan Jay, 171
Pontecorvo, Bruno, 184
Postman. *See* de Jongh, Andree
Poyntz, Juliet Stuart, 21, 172–174
Prestes, Luis Carlos, 80
Profumo, John, 127, 129
Pu Yi, Henry (emperor of China), 126
Py. *See* Abbiate, Roland

Rabinowitz, Gregory, 6, 88, 145
Rado, Alexander, 138
Rafael, Sylvia, 175–176
Rahab, 176
Reid, Betty, 99
Reihert, Mary. *See* Richter, Steffi
Reiss, Ignance, 152, 153, 201
Revere, Paul, 218
Rhee, Syngman, 131
Richer, Marthe Betenfeld, 176–178
Richter, Steffi, 178–180
Ritchie, Rhona Janet, 180–181
Rivera, Diego, 157
Rodiger, Carl, 70
Roeder, Manfred, 108
Roosevelt, Franklin D., 75–76, 153, 180
Rosenberg, Ethel Greenglass, 45, 181–184
Rosenberg, Julius, 45, 182–184
Rosmer, Alfred, 7
Rosmer, Marguerite, 7
Rossi, François. *See* Abbiate, Roland
Rothermere, Lord, 179

Rothstein, Brunhilda, 184–185
Roto Kapella, 20
Russia, 59–60, 219. *See also* Soviet Union

Sadat, Anwar, 81–83
Salameh, Ali Hassan, 175
Salavarrieta, Policarpa, 187
Samson, 71–72
Sansom, Odette Marie, 187–189
Schildbach, Gertrude, 202–203
Schmidt, Irmgard, 189
Schragmuller, Elsbeth, 71, 189–191
Schuessler, Otto, 8
Schulze-Boysen, Harro "Choro," 191–192
Schulze-Boysen, Libertas Haas-Heye, 191–192
Schwarz, Ute. *See* Heidel, Gudrun
Sedov, Lyova, 53–55
Senesh, Hannah, 192–193
Sharpe, George H., 215, 217
Shiber, Etta, 18–19
Shlyapnikov, Alexander, 135
Siddons, Belle, 193–194
Silvermaster, Helen Witte, 194–195
Silvermaster, Nathan Gregory, 115, 194
Siqueiros, David Alfaro, 6, 8, 156
Skoblin, Nikolai Vasilyevich, 169–170
Smedley, Agnes, 80, 137, 195–198
Soble, Jack, 54, 88, 203, 238
Soble, Robert, 54
Sokolov, Alexander, 91–93
Sorge, Richard, 137, 152, 195, 198
South Africa, 129–130
Soviet Cold War era espionage
    Bolivia, 34–35
    Britain, 43–45, 46–47, 93–96
    German Federal Republic, 133–135
    Mexico, 30–31, 131–132
    United States, 45, 47–50, 91–93, 161–162, 189, 199–200, 203–206
Soviet interwar espionage, 135–136, 166–167
    Canada, 79–80
    China, 80, 137–138, 197–198
    France, 169–170, 213
    Germany, 107, 152–154
    and Reiss assassination, 152, 201–203
    and Sedov assassination, 53–55
    Switzerland, 138–139
    and Trotsky assassination, 6–9, 88–89, 145–146, 156–157
    United States, 20–21, 80, 84–85, 137, 153–154, 172–174, 194–195, 200–201, 206–207, 238–239
Soviet Union, 9–11, 117
    and Penkovskiy case, 43–45
    U.S. espionage in, 111–112, 165–166, 226–227
    and World War II, 107–109, 138–139, 154–155, 184–185, 191–192, 213–214, 237–238
Spain
    and Civil War, 27, 29, 45, 155, 158
    colonies of, 4, 22, 148–151, 163–164, 187, 218
    and communism, 29–31
Spawr, Frances, 198–200

Spawr, Walter, 198–200
Stahl, Lydia Chkalov, 200–201
Stalin, Josef, 6, 10–11, 153, 156, 157, 173, 201, 213, 214
Stanton, Edwin M., 26, 27
Starr, John, 121
Steiner, Renata, 201–203
Stephenson, William, 27
Stern, Alfred Kaufman, 88, 203
Stern, Martha Dodd, 88, 203–206, 238
Stieber, Wilhelm, 65
Stilwell, Joseph, 197
Stimson, Henry L., 232
Stokes, Rose Pastor, 206–207
Storch, Despina, 70–71
Sukarno, Kusnasosro, 16
Suse, Ruth Kaethe. See Kuehn, Ruth
Swanson, John, 159–160
Switz, Marjorie, 200
Switz, Robert, 200
Switzerland, 138–139
Szabo, Violette Bushnell, 207–208

Tallmadge, Benjamin, 211, 212
Teitelbaum, Niuta, 209–210
Terwindt, Beatrix, 210–211
Three-Fifty-Five, 211–212
Tokyo Rose. See d'Aquino, Iva Toguri
Townsend, Robert, 211–212
Trachtenberg, Fanny, 54
Trepper, Leopold, 154, 155, 212–214
Trepper, Luba, 212–214
Tresca, Carlo, 173
Trotsky, Leon, 6, 7, 8–9, 55, 88–89, 145–146, 156–157.
    See also Fourth International
Tuomi, Kaarlo, 92
Turkey, 3–4

United States
    and Cold War era espionage, 104–105, 117, 165–166
    German espionage in, 32, 69–71, 222–223
    and interwar espionage, 75–76, 109–112, 226–227
    Israeli espionage in, 170–172
    Japanese espionage against, 55–57, 72–74, 140–142
    Soviet Cold War era espionage in, 45, 47–50, 91–93,
        161–162, 189, 199–200, 203–206
    Soviet interwar espionage in, 20–21, 80, 84–85, 137,
        153–154, 172–174, 194–195, 200–201, 206–207,
        238–239
    Soviet World War II espionage in, 184–185, 237–238
    and War of Independence, 57–58, 143, 211–212
    and World War I, 69–71, 163, 231–232
    and World War II espionage in Japan, 167–168
    See also Civil War (United States); U.S. communism;
        World War II
U.S. communism, 37–39, 114–116
    during interwar period, 84–85, 163, 172, 206
    and labor movement, 84–85, 172
    and Rosenberg case, 182–183

during World War I, 109, 111, 163
    See also specific Soviet headings

van Houtte, Marie Leonie, 62–63
Van Lew, Elizabeth, 24, 215–218
Vidali, Vittorio, 157, 158, 173
Viscario Roo, Leona, 218
Vogel, Wolfgang, 114
von Krudener, Barbara Juliana, 219
von Ribbentrop, Joachim, 11, 179

Wagner, Lorenz Harry, 20
Waldo, Richard, 21
Waldrop, Frank, 11, 12
Wanda. See Teitelbaum, Niuta
Wang Pa Mei, 221–222
Ward, Stephen, 127, 129
Ware, Harold, 153
Washington, George, 89
Washington Times-Herald, 11, 12
Webb, Helen, 222–223
Weill, Ruby, 6–7, 145–146
Wenner-Gren, Axel, 11
Werner, Ruth. See Kuczynski, Ursula Ruth
Wertheim, Lizzie, 224
Weston, Edward, 157
Wheeler, Barbara, 224–226
White, Harry Dexter, 115
Whitehead, Don, 47
Wiedemann, Fritz, 179–180
Wilkes, John, 60
Willoughby, General, 198
Wilson, Henry, 103
Wilson, May, 226–227
Witherington, Pearl, 227
Wolf, Hans, 223
Wolkoff, Anna, 228
Women's rights, 9, 22, 135
World War I
    Belgium, 41–43, 60–61, 146–148
    Britain, 3–4, 41–43, 224
    France, 22–23, 61–63, 87–88, 177–178, 235–237
    Germany, 3–4, 22–23, 41–43, 69–71, 87–88, 177–178,
        189–191, 224, 235–237
    Palestine, 3–4
    United States, 69–71, 163, 231–232
World War II, 27, 29
    Australia, 159–160
    Belgian resistance during, 22, 31, 63–64, 114
    Britain, 27–29, 162–163, 224–226
    China, 197
    Czech resistance during, 116–117
    Danish resistance during, 23–24
    double agents of, 32, 77–79
    Dutch resistance during, 210–211
    German espionage during, 77–79, 81–83, 178–180,
        222–223, 228
    Hungarian resistance during, 192–193
    Indonesia, 15–16
    Italy, 125–126
    Japan, 15–16, 55–57, 72–74, 75–76, 126–127, 167–168

Nazi collaborators in, 96
Polish resistance during, 209–210
Soviet Union, 107–109, 138–139, 154–155, 184–185,
	191–192, 213–214, 237–238
See also French resistance (World War II)
Wu, Eva, 229–230
Wu Chao, 228–229
Wynne, Greville, 46

Yakovlev, Anatoli, 182, 183
Yardley, Edna Ramsaier, 231–232

Yardley, Herbert O., 70, 231–232
Yeats, William Butler, 96, 97–99

Zborowski, Mark, 53–54
Zeifurt, Kurt, 30
Zelle, Margarete Gertrude, 15, 177, 233–237
Zimmermann, Alfred, 43
Zinoviev, Grigory, 10
Zlatovski, George, 205
Zlatovski, Jane Foster, 205, 237–238
Zubilin, Elizabeth, 153, 238–239
Zubilin, Vasilli, 153–154, 203, 238–239
Zukermanova, Anne Marie Edith. *See* Katona, Edita